DATE DUE

THE TENOR OF JUSTICE

THE TENOR OF JUSTICE

CRIMINAL COURTS
AND THE
GUILTY PLEA PROCESS

Peter F. Nardulli
James Eisenstein
Roy B. Flemming

University of Illinois Press
Urbana and Chicago

This book is printed on acid-free paper.

Library of Congress Cataloging-in-Publication Data

Nardulli, Peter F.
  The tenor of justice.

  Includes bibliographies and index.
  1. Pleas of guilty — United States.   2. Pleas (Criminal procedure) —
United States.   3. Criminal courts — United States.   4. Criminal jus-
tice, Administration of — United States.   I. Flemming, Roy B.
II. Eisenstein, James.   III. Title.
KF9654.N37   1988   345.73′05   87-10772
                         347.3055
ISBN 0-252-01463-4 (alk. paper)

To Marc and Beth

CONTENTS

V. Conclusions

PREFACE

Day after day courts throughout the United States make decisions that affect people's lives in profound ways. After an obscure beginning, the United States Supreme Court has developed into one of the most powerful political institutions in the world; little remains to be said about its role in American political life. One can say the same about kindred institutions such as federal appellate courts and state supreme courts. What many fail to appreciate, however, is the significance of the role played by lower courts, especially at the state level. These courts award custody of children in divorce cases, as well as divide property and determine payment schedules. They resolve myriad disputes between landlords and tenants, consumers and businesses, and among neighbors; these disputes can involve large amounts of money, as well as the peaceable enjoyment of one's immediate surroundings. In criminal cases these courts make decisions that affect individuals' personal liberties.

Perhaps because of the mundane nature of the problems with which they deal, lower courts lack the stature of appellate courts. While critics will often take exception to specific rulings of appellate courts, their legitimacy and competence is seldom questioned. Lower courts, on the other hand, often operate under a cloud. They are called upon to resolve some of society's most insoluble problems and to handle people with whom other social institutions have failed miserably. They seldom succeed. Unlike the situation in most appellate rulings, many outcomes at the lower level satisfy neither party; difficult situations are resolved frequently by splitting the difference.

Although important decisions of appellate courts are routinely reported in newspapers and in nightly news shows, most people take little note of what lower courts do, unless they do something egregious. This, of course, only serves to reinforce perceptions and to further undermine their credibility and legitimacy. In some ways it would do observers little good to look more attentively at lower court proceedings. They would see few instances of gifted oratory at the bar. Moreover, what is seen publicly is likely to be largely peripheral to the determination of the case; most important happenings in these courts take place in chambers, in corridors, and over the phone. The invisibility of these activities contributes further to the public's skepticism of these courts.

A good deal of research has been done recently on lower courts, especially criminal courts, which are the focus of this work. Much of this research, from the beginning, has shared the public skepticism of these institutions. Skepticism is often healthy in research endeavors; it can cause investigators to pierce through the superficial. However, to the extent that research amounts to little more than an attempt to document preconceptions, it can interfere with understanding and undermine objectivity.

In this research, we have tried to maintain a healthy skepticism without letting it interfere with our ultimate objectives, which are to obtain a better understanding of these vital institutions and an empirically based assessment of their performance. To move beyond our preconceptions, based upon both conventional wisdom and extensive prior research, we tried to develop a research strategy that differed from what we, and others, had used in the past. We studied a diverse set of medium-sized courts instead of troubled urban courts, and studied nine counties instead of just a couple. We blended soft data from observations and taped interviews with hard data from questionnaires, Q-sorts, case files, and official government documents.

We ended up with a mountain of data—hundreds of variables on thousands of cases, volumes of interview transcripts, and untold numbers of shorthand notes. It took years of data manipulations to sort out what we had and to make sense of it. We spent hundreds of hours on the phone and poring over draft manuscripts to sort out portraits of the various court communities. The scope of the task, and the variety of different ways to approach it, led us to the decision to present our thinking in three volumes. The companion volumes to *The Tenor of Justice* are *The Contours of Justice* and *The Craft of Justice*. The first author of each of these volumes was responsible primarily for the preparation of the manuscript, but the thinking and planning and analysis that went into each was the result of years of collaborative effort. From the perspective of the first author of this volume, these were years that we can never hope to duplicate, for both intellectual and personal reasons. The experience with my coauthors during the course of this project has been, and will remain, the most prized of my professional career. Whatever blemishes exist on the following pages would only have been worse without their prodding, wise counsel, and astuteness; most of those that remain were the result of my renowned stubborness.

With respect to the preparation of *The Tenor of Justice,* there were many false starts and fruitless detours down blind alleys. We shifted from highly qualitative emphases to periods when we believed that truth could be achieved best by the quantitative modeling of key decisions in the criminal process. Our commitment to the development of sophisticated statistical models was shaken when an anonymous, but insightful, reviewer commented that, although what we had done was indeed sophisticated, it told us no more about criminal courts than what might be available from a casual observer at the Greyhound Bus terminal.

This shocking revelation, needless to say, led us to reassess our approach. We ultimately shelved six chapters of quantitative analyses that were several years in the making and rethought the role of the quantitative data in our efforts to understand, and communicate, what makes criminal courts tick. We realized that the multivariate modeling of various decisions, while revealing, failed to capture the effect of a variety of forces that our observations and interviews led us to believe were real. We were getting fairly precise mappings of twigs while missing the contour of the forest.

What evolved from our deliberations was an iterative process that blended our qualitative and quantitative data into a much more finely meshed concoction. Our sense of how criminal courts operated and what was important to understand about them led us to pose a few simple but crucial questions. We then structured the data analyses to answer them. The initial answers led us to more refined questions and to reexaminations of earlier conclusions. This rather convoluted process led us to perspectives and judgments on criminal courts that none of us entertained as the ideas for this research germinated in our discussions at the American Political Science Association meetings in the fall of 1978. These views will not be the final word on criminal courts, nor should they be. Others will quibble and refine and revise, as they should. But for us, the findings, abstractions, and conclusions expressed here and in the companion volumes reflect our best judgments—formulated only after wrestling with a voluminous set of data, and one another, for almost a decade.

ACKNOWLEDGMENTS

The types of debts that accrue over the course of a project such as this—the idea was conceived in the fall of 1978 and we received our initial grant in the fall of 1979—are almost too innumerable to mention or remember. We must begin, however, by acknowledging the support of the National Institute of Justice (79-N1-AX-0062; 81-IJ-CX-0027) and the National Science Foundation (83-NSF-N0095).

A number of past and present people in the National Institute of Justice provided wise and useful guidance and encouragement, particularly Carolyn Burstein, Debbie Viets, Linda McKay, and Cheryl Martorana. We are also deeply indebted to Felice Levine at the National Science Foundation for her support at the later stages of this endeavor. Our advisory panel participated actively and productively in the early stages of the implementation of the research and made a number of excellent suggestions. The panel consisted of James Gibson, Thomas Church, Milton Heumann, George Gish, Magnus Seng, and Clifford Kirsch. The many comments and suggestions of anonymous reviewers were also extremely useful. Obviously, despite the important contributions from these various resources, we are responsible for the viewpoints and findings reported herein.

In addition to the outside financial support and advice we received, we are also indebted to our home institutions—the University of Illinois, Wayne State University, and Pennsylvania State University—for their support in the form of research assistants and release time. We are also indebted to a number of specific individuals who worked at our institutions and research sites.

In Illinois, David Chambers, Keith Emmons, Michael Bass, and John Carroll performed important tasks as graduate assistants. Arthur Jameson and Robert Illyes were invaluable as computer consultants. Karen Wilson,

Kathy Wilson, Carol Freund, Karla Kraus, Tammy Turner, and Darlene Riccuito were assistants who performed far beyond reasonable expectations. Ann Nardulli contributed untold hours to unsorting and organizing the Q-sort data. Students who very ably collected the case file data were Jan Powell, Frank Saibert, Ann Fohne, Laurie Edgar, Rick Morris, Scott Rubemeyer, Rich Hampton, Lisa Lindsay, David Bowers, and David West. Florence Edmison and Laurie Mitchell devoted many hours to the typing of interview transcripts. Shirley Burnette, Jean Baker, Lorena McClain, and Velma Sykes all contributed much to the typing of the final draft. Anna Merritt did her normal outstanding job in editing initial chapters, and Mary Giles of the University of Illinois Press put on the finishing touches. A special thanks is due the Director Emeritus of the Institute of Government and Public Affairs at the University of Illinois, Samuel K. Gove, for his support of this project and his tolerance of the disruptions it caused. Ellen Riggle performed superbly by completing the most thankless of tasks, the index.

The following people provided invaluable assistance in collecting the case data in Michigan: Jan Johnson, Janet Van Tiem, Peter Kalawert, Donna Larson, Elizabeth Lenihan, Michael Draving, Laura Skiragis, Rolf Heubel, Steven Rosenberg, Sharon Hansen, Stephen Roach, Scott Mahoney, and Robert Sydlow. Meg Falk, a graduate student at Wayne State, ably performed a variety of tasks relating to all phases of the field research. Evelyn Cloutier Lappan devoted many hours to preparing and sorting the Michigan Q-sort data, clipping newspaper articles, and a number of other important chores. Carol Wesson, Nancy Michaels Kaminski, and Linda Laird provided typing assistance.

Outstanding assistance was provided by many people in support of the research effort in Pennsylvania. Thanks go to: Mark Kessler for his outstanding participation in all phases of the project as the principal research assistant; Rich Feiock, Jeff Webster, Paula Carta, Tony Filippello, Terry Kline, and Mindy Morrison for a fine job collecting case file data in the field; Diane Colonna, Colleen Young, Chuck Kimmel, and Leslie Castaldi for performing a variety of chores during the early and middle phases of the research; Louise Foresman for her heroic labors in preparing, organizing, and sorting over 17,000 cards for the Q-sort; Martha Waldman for assistance during the later stages of the project; Chris Hopwood for doing just about everything; Bob Rutchick for computer assistance; Bonnie Grove, Mary Jane Johnson, Audrey Smith, Lee Carpenter, Elena DeLuca, and Jan Walther for a fine job typing data forms, reports, drafts, letters, etc., often on short notice; Lynne Kaltreider for quality editorial assistance on many of the chapters; Marva Hillard for an outstanding job in the difficult task of transcribing interviews; Greta O'Toole for competently handling all budget preparation and financial administration; and Irwin

Feller, Director of the Institute for Policy Research and Evaluation, for crucial support throughout.

All of the above-mentioned institutions and individuals contributed significantly in one way or another to the completion of this project. But, as anyone knows who has embarked upon such an effort, it was made possible only by the support and tolerance of our wives and families. For their role in this effort we will be eternally grateful.

I

INTRODUCTION

1

THINKING ABOUT CRIMINAL COURTS

Circuit court, recorder's court, court of common pleas, felony court, county court—although these courts go by a variety of names, virtually every county in the United States has one. Some major cities also have one. These criminal courts—as we shall refer to them in this volume—are responsible for processing defendants charged with serious crimes, *felonies* in legal parlance. They are ubiquitous, not because of the prevalence of serious crime, although it is prevalent, but because our court system is highly decentralized, and these courts are near the lower level of that pyramidal system. Such decentralization dates back to prerevolutionary times when colonists learned the power of the courts and the value of local control in the legal process. Although there are also other courts at this level (traffic, misdemeanor, domestic relations), we chose to study felony criminal courts because they deal with very serious problems and because the potential value of new insights seemed great.

Felony criminal courts have a common core of basic attributes. They perform comparable tasks, have similar sets of actors, corresponding legal safeguards, and equivalent proceedings. Despite these similarities, the decentralized and complex nature of American criminal justice has spawned a variety of court systems or communities, each with a distinct set of structures, norms, traditions, and personalities. Some of these differences are the result of adaptations to local pressures or influences; others are reflections of attempts by leaders in the court community to innovate or modernize. Still others are adaptations of ideas popularized by national figures in the legal or court reform community. Some of the differences in felony court systems are cosmetic and fleeting. But many are the result of long-term, deep-seated influences, and these make a real difference in how the courts process defendants.

This book describes and analyzes the basic attributes and processes of nine felony criminal court systems in three states. It is directed by twin goals. We want to say something about criminal courts that will be of enduring value to those concerned about the state of American politics and justice; at the same time, we want to develop and investigate a conceptual apparatus for the study of these courts that will facilitate the conduct of future research. It is important to say something of enduring value about the tenor of justice because felony courts affect, directly or indirectly, the lives of millions of people on a daily basis. They allocate a very fundamental political good, justice, in high-stakes cases. To better understand how these courts perform this task, and the multiple subtasks that performance entails, we must increase the stock of empirical knowledge concerning their nature and key processes. Only then will we be able to enhance these courts' ability to serve the communities they represent.

We have found it·challenging to reach for these twin objectives within a single volume. Our efforts to meet these challenges account for the basic structure of this book. Within this structure we initially introduce and develop a broad set of empirically based concepts that are essential for a refined understanding of how criminal courts function. However, this conceptual apparatus goes beyond the needs of the quantitative empirical analyses undertaken here, analyses that are restricted to the guilty plea process. This notwithstanding, the conceptual development undertaken here will facilitate our investigation of the plea process by placing it within the broader context of what we refer to as the "courthouse community." It will also stimulate thinking about other facets of the criminal process. The organization of this work will be described in more detail later in this chapter; here we are more concerned with a brief overview of the background and nature of our efforts.

Criminal courts have been the subject of empirical research since at least the 1920s, and research on trial courts has been conducted on an unprecedented level since the late 1960s. Many of these studies represented pioneering efforts, going far beyond the expectation of the early legal realists who spurred much of the interest in trial-level courts. However, like all pioneering efforts, they merely set the stage for more extended exploration; much more could not be expected. Most early efforts were restricted to a single criminal court—two or three at most—and used data from only a single level of analysis. We believe that continued progress in the study of criminal courts requires the use of multiple levels of analysis, as well as attempts to integrate data and observations from different theoretical approaches using a variety of analytical techniques. This work is a modest first step in the effort to map out an integrated approach to the study of criminal courts. We do not get much beyond the introduction and development of concepts that largely emerge from our fieldwork. Nonetheless, we hope other researchers will find our work useful in pushing back further the frontiers of knowledge in this area.

Efforts to develop a complex, multifaceted approach to understanding social phenomena too often devolve into largely methodological exercises that become drowned in the sea of data they generate. Important substantive questions and issues tend to become lost among methodological and statistical concerns that too often redirect the effort to more trivial questions. Determined not to fall into this bottomless, inane black hole of methodological preoccupation, we have limited the scope of our explorations. Although we want to make some very general comments about how criminal courts operate and how they differ, most of our detailed, integrative efforts will be focused on the guilty plea process. We want to make some observations about its fairness and about the level of manipulation and the nature of the inequities that may pervade it.

By biting off a smaller chunk of the entire dispositional process and focusing on key issues, the tension between our twin goals becomes more manageable. Trying to say something important in a systematic and sophisticated manner about areas as diverse as bail, guilty pleas, sentencing, and delay would be overwhelming and unwieldly. Focusing on the heart of the system—the guilty plea process—enables us to grapple effectively with an important set of issues and to develop an approach that can be extended—in other analyses and future research—to other areas of concern.[1]

The attainment of these multiple goals, especially the introduction, development, and investigation of a conceptual apparatus appropriate for studying courts, requires that we begin by dealing with some very general issues. Thus, we pause here to discuss why we think it is important to study lower courts (especially felony courts), our general views on criminal courts, and why we fashioned a particular approach for this study.

WHY STUDY LOWER COURTS?

For a long time, social scientists, especially political scientists interested in the judicial process, concentrated their research energies on the U.S. Supreme Court. This was true even after the "behavioral revolution" in political science, when researchers shifted their concern from structure and doctrine to decisions and outputs. Eventually, federal appeals courts and state supreme courts were included in these studies. This preoccupation with appellate courts was understandable. They are the most prestigious of our judicial institutions, and their decisions are not only extremely visible but they also are often of great symbolic as well as real significance. Indeed, some view the Supreme Court as the most prestigious of all American political institutions. Supreme Court vacancies and nominations, as well as decisions, undoubtedly receive more national media attention than what happens in all other courts combined.

A second reason for the preoccupation with appellate courts was the view that these courts were "where it's at" in the judicial process. That is, appellate courts decide important questions of law and legal policy. These decisions are then implemented by lower courts, which simply decide which facts are relevant to the application of the appropriate legal principles.[2]

In the late 1960s, the focus of sociolegal research began to shift to lower courts. By the 1980s, the transition was complete, and lower courts, especially felony criminal courts, had become the focus of most social science research on courts. Several factors led to this refocusing. First, despite the majesty, visibility, and symbolic importance of appellate courts, it is the lower courts (although not felony courts) that handle the bulk of the nation's judicial work. If ordinary citizens come into contact with the justice system at all, it is most likely to be in the context of a traffic, housing, juvenile, misdemeanor, felony, or civil court. These lower courts preside over divorce proceedings, decide child custody matters, revoke driver's licenses, decide personal injury matters, accept guilty pleas, and set sentences, among other things. They are more likely to have a direct impact on citizens' lives than appellate courts.

A second factor leading to a closer study of the lower courts is that, despite the "upper court myth," lower courts do not simply implement the decisions of appellate courts and legislatures. Vast discretion is vested in lower court actors. That this discretion is used to develop unique ways of handling routine problems, recalcitrant individuals, or disruptions in business as usual should surprise no student of bureaucracy or policy implementation. While the law acts as a constraint upon what these actors can do, it is only one of many constraints. Often it is not the most important, and there are often many ways in which legal dictates can be fulfilled, or at least not violated. Thus, if we are to understand how these courts perform the important tasks with which they are charged, there is no substitute for empirical analysis.

A third factor is that the lower courts, especially felony criminal courts, have been embroiled in some of the most heated social controversies facing American citizens today. We need a clearer picture of these courts if we are to understand their role in those larger controversies. Serious crime, and what to do about it, has been one of the most enduring domestic problems of post–World War II America. Commissions and scholars have studied it, agencies have been formed to combat it, and commentators have lamented it. Yet crime, and people's fear of it, continues and grows. Although most observers believe that criminal courts can do little to solve the crime problem, these courts are criticized for their present role in dealing with it. They are criticized, among other things, for handcuffing the police through their efforts to suppress illegally obtained evidence, granting pretrial release to defendants who allegedly constitute a threat to the community, engaging in excessive plea bargaining, levying sentences that are "too lenient," and taking too long to dispose of cases. Although each criticism may have some merit, too little appreciation is given to the constraints under which these courts operate (such as local jail capacities, or clear legal dictates) or to the fact that some demands may be contradictory, or at least mutually unattainable.

Until we know more about how courts operate, we will never be able to assess the validity of these criticisms or, more important, how, or if, the courts can respond to the concerns that underlie them. This lack of understanding, of course, has not prevented would-be reformers from proposing various changes in the way courts operate. Indeed, one of the ironies about the controversy over the role of courts in the "war against crime" is that many of the most vocal critics of the courts offer reform proposals in which the courts play a prominent role. More often than not, these proposals are conceived in the same blissful naiveté that generates much of the criticism. A great deal of energy is devoted to the debate of largely symbolic matters, such as preventive detention and limitations on the exclusionary rule. In reality, most courts already detain defendants they view to be dangerous. This de facto preventive detention is limited by local jail capacities and the costs of acquiring or leasing space. No preventive detention law that fails to address the capacity issue is likely to change what courts do. The value of limiting the exclusionary rule as it applies to unlawfully seized evidence is limited by its minor role in criminal dispositions, especially when the potential costs of the rule's abolition are considered (Nardulli, 1983; Davies, 1983).

Unless they are largely symbolic, popular reforms are often quixotic in nature or depend upon other, unstated, conditions to be effective. Efforts to abolish plea bargaining have been unsuccessful in limiting the level of guilty pleas because they have failed to address and grapple with the power and interest structure within the criminal court setting. They also ignore the fact that many pleas are not contingent upon charge reductions or firm sentencing commitments. These factors sustain the viability of negotiated pleas as a dispositional tool even in the face of concerted efforts to abolish them. Efforts to enhance the severity and consistency of sentencing—largely through the enactment of determinate sentencing laws— have failed to address the impact of these reforms on processing time or the penitentiary system. More people being sentenced to longer sentences are taking more of the court's time to be processed and filling the state's penitentiary system beyond reasonable limits. Human abuses and indignities, prison riots, early releases—often based upon dubious criteria—are frequently the results. These consequences are often followed by proposals to build expensive new penal facilities, the construction of which strains state resources even in the best of times. Moreover, little thought is given to what will happen if, as predicted, the crime-prone population drops markedly in the next decade (Blumstein, 1983).

A problem related to making criminal policy without a well-grounded understanding of criminal court operations is that many grass-roots efforts have been made to enhance court performance, especially in the areas of plea bargaining and delay reduction. These have been largely unnoticed and unevaluated, failing even to make the national agenda for reforms, which continues to be dominated by ideologically dictated proposals. Thus a solid, empirically based study of criminal courts may be as useful in generating methods of improving court performance as in evaluating the likelihood for success of the more popular reform measures. However, until we have this basic core of knowledge, we will neither know what role criminal courts can play in efforts to address the crime problem, nor how to structure them so they can perform their functions to the optimum.

There is one last compelling reason, albeit a more esoteric one, for studying lower courts, especially felony criminal courts. These courts present some unique opportunities for studying how the judicial process operates. One reason judicial scholars shifted their attention to lower courts in the late 1960s was that research on appellate courts had reached somewhat of an impasse. Judicial scholars were interested in the decision-making process in appellate courts, particularly the role of decision-maker attitudes and backgrounds. However, the inaccessibility of decision makers and the context of decision making impeded the development and testing of refined, empirically grounded models of the decision-making process.

No such barriers exist in most lower courts. Experience has shown that, when properly approached, many lower court participants are open to, even flattered by, inquiries. They will respond to interviews, questionnaires, and even more involved research procedures. They will permit outsiders to observe negotiations—the guts of much decision making—and they will open their case files for data collection procedures. Moreover, there is sufficient variation in court purpose, structure, and environment to permit rigorous comparative analysis on a number of levels. If researchers maximize the use of these opportunities, the potential for developing a refined, rigorous understanding of judicial processes is great. Moreover, the observations generated by rigorous studies of lower courts may be applicable beyond the judicial domain. They may yield insights into the nature of more general political or social processes, especially those involving continuing interactions among small groups of actors working together to produce a decision or some other type of output.

CRIMINAL COURTS: SOME INITIAL OBSERVATIONS

Before detailing our approach to this study of criminal courts, we should pause briefly and lay out our views on some very general questions about felony courts.

Criminal Courts as Case Processors

Our first question is, What do these courts do? At first glance, this may seem to be a simplistic question. However, it is one that can be answered at a number of different levels. If, for example, one contends that the work of a felony court is to deter or reduce crime, then we might expect the court to treat harshly those brought before it. Given this view, the courts might be urged to use pretrial detention extensively and be evaluated largely on the basis of conviction rates and the severity of sentences. Expectations might be quite different, however, if the work of these courts is defined as meeting the needs of individual defendants. Such a definition might, for example, place more emphasis on the availability of probation officers, work release facilities, and adult diversion programs. Dispositions would be evaluated in terms of their "appropriateness," not their severity.

Neither of these views of the work of criminal courts is wrong per se. A problem with both, however, is that they focus on how the courts *should* do what they do, not on what they *in fact* do. Such a focus is troublesome because it obscures the institutional uniqueness of criminal courts, thus inhibiting efforts to understand them.

Although identifying the largely unique attributes of institutions is frequently difficult, it is relatively easy in the case of the felony trial courts. These courts process defendants who have been apprehended by the police and formally charged with felony offenses. They decide the guilt or innocence of defendants and levy sentences on those found guilty. These tasks fall uniquely within the domain of felony trial courts because, although other social institutions may play a role in handling and resolving felony disputes, only a felony court of proper jurisdiction can officially label someone a felon, with all the attendant consequences. Police officers may "handle" some criminal disputes on the scene. They may also effectively sanction and achieve behavior modification through the use of curbstone justice. Much the same can be said of prison officers and certain personnel in the social welfare system. However, such activities do not formally overlap with the domain of criminal courts because they are not backed up with the authority of the state; their actions do not carry the weight of law.

Our answer, then, to the question, What do felony courts do? is that they process defendants charged with felony offenses. Beyond focusing on the rather unique characteristics of criminal courts, this definition has another attractive feature. It focuses our attention upon the fate of defendants, transforming the general question of, How can we better understand felony criminal courts? into a more specific and refined research question, How do felony courts process individual defendants charged with felonies? This permits us to concentrate on a set of tasks, stages, and outcomes common to the felony dispositional process across otherwise very different systems. It also provides us with a set of common criteria that can be used to assess the impact of different attributes, structures, procedures, and informal practices upon important decisions and actions, thus differentiating the important from the inconsequential.

Criminal Courts as Political Institutions

Equally important as our view of felony courts as case processors is our view of *how*, in abstract terms, these courts process cases. Our view is colored by the belief that criminal courts are an integral part of the political system. That is, like other political institutions, criminal courts allocate both tangible and intangible values in an authoritative manner. Within their domain, they affect who gets what in profound ways.

The primary recipients of these allocations can be categorized into three groups: the local community (including crime victims); the defendant and his or her family; and the local court community, including the court bureaucracy, affiliated sponsoring organizations, and members of the local criminal bar. Table 1.1 provides some examples of the values relevant to each group.

Obviously, court decisions on bail, guilt, and sentencing involving habitual personal or property offenders can have direct and indirect effects upon property rights as well as the personal safety of community members. The local court's policy on restitution (defendant reparations to the victim) can have a very direct impact upon the immediate victims of crime. In addition, pretrial detention and incarceration norms can affect the expenditure of public moneys because the maintenance and operation of jails consume considerable public resources. Incarceration can also result in reduced revenues and an increase in welfare expenditures. The intangible aspects of local criminal court actions can be as significant as the tangible

Table 1.1. **Illustrative Political Values Allocated by Criminal Courts, by Type of Recipient**

Type of Recipient	Type of Value	
	Tangible	Intangible
Local community	Personal safety, sanctity of private property, public moneys	Peace of mind, sense of representation
Defendants	Physical freedom, personal safety, employment prospects, bail requirements, restitution and fine payments, court costs	Psychological well-being, including family life
Court community	Public employment, indigent appointments, awarding of attorney fees, level of demand for private defense bar	Quality of work life

ones. A public sense that the courts are listening and responding to their demands and concerns can be as reassuring as the ramifications of the actions themselves.

The courts' activities have a much more direct effect upon an individual defendant. They can restrict the defendant's actions for varying lengths of time and harm his or her long-term employment prospects. The imposition and collection of fines, restitution, court costs, bail fees, and attorneys' fees transfer wealth. Many defendants undergo tremendous anxiety while they await formal charging, disposition, and sentencing. Incarceration disrupts family life and can produce fears of physical, sexual, or psychological abuse.

The courts also affect the life of the local court community: Many individuals, including judges, prosecutors, and other court personnel, are employed by courts. Detention and sentencing practices of courts affect the demand for governmental investment and employment in detention facilities and probation departments. Moreover, court appointments to represent indigents have bolstered many fledgling practices, and the prosecutor's pretrial screening and diversion practices affect the number of defendants hiring local defense attorneys. The atmosphere that prevails in the local court community—which is often the result of conscious decisions made at an earlier point—has much to do with the morale and stress levels associated with work in the criminal court system. Work in a quick-paced, combative atmosphere can be quite different from that in a more folksy, congenial setting.

Closely related to the courts' allocative role in the local political community is their regulative role. Although criminal courts are governmental entities with considerable power of their own, they are responsible for limiting the use of coercive power exercised by other governmental agencies. Although the public's growing concern with the crime problem over the past fifteen years has somewhat diminished the recognition of this function, it has in no way reduced its importance. Interest in controlling governmental power over individuals runs throughout our history, from prerevolutionary times to the present. Police power in particular attracts concern over the potential for abuse. This is reflected in the rhetoric of countless Supreme Court decisions. For example, Justice Douglas, writing in 1948 in a search and seizure case, observed "the right to privacy was deemed too precious to entrust to the discretion of those whose job is the detection of crime and the arrest of criminals. Power is a heady thing; and history shows that the police acting on their own cannot be trusted" (*McDonald v. U.S.*, 355 U.S. 451, 455, 948).

The importance of this regulatory role was perhaps expressed most eloquently by Thurmond Arnold in *Symbols of Government*:

> The center of ideals of every Western government is in its judicial system. Here are the symbols of all those great principles which give dignity to the individual, which give independence to the businessman, and which not only make of the state a great righteous protector but at the same time keep it in its place.... It is in this institution that we find concentrated to a greater extent than in any other, the symbols of moral and rational government.... For most persons, the criminal trial overshadows all other ceremonies as a dramatization of the values of our spiritual government, representing the dignity of the state as an enforcer of law, and at the same time the dignity of the individual when he is an avowed opponent of the state, a dissenter, a radical, or even a criminal. (1956, 123)

It should be stressed that we do not view criminal courts as political institutions merely because we believe that they perform functions similar to those of more overtly political entities. We also contend that the manner in which the courts perform these functions is generally similar to the way in which other political entities perform them. Although the concept of "law," modes of legal thought and reasoning, and formal procedural rules exert some influences on criminal court operations, so do the activity of interest groups and political constituencies, career ambitions, personal values and political beliefs, the dynamics of personal interactions, and pressures exerted by organizational hierarchies. The relevance of these influences makes it possible to select and utilize some general concepts and approaches used in the study of other political phenomena.

NOTES ON OUR APPROACH

In this study, we view felony trial courts from three distinct conceptual perspectives (the environmental, the contextual, and the individual), in the context of a comparative framework encompassing nine medium-sized jurisdictions. Our efforts to examine felony courts from a variety of perspectives reflect our belief that the primary theoretical problem confronting criminal court researchers today is the identification, development, and integration of key concepts at the various levels of analysis. The need for theoretical amplification and integration is clear to anyone familiar with the literature on criminal courts. Earlier works on courts tended to be fragmented and atheoretical. They focused on only one stage of the process or on only one participant, usually in a single urban jurisdiction.[3] Together they produced a body of research that exhibited the shortcomings typical of most early efforts to understand complex social processes.

Gradually, court researchers produced more refined studies. Increasingly sophisticated and rigorous empirical data bases have provided the foundation for a number of recent studies. Some gathered data from multiple jurisdictions, and more research designs have begun to view the process as an integrated system. However, to date these studies have not produced a generally accepted paradigm for the study of criminal courts, much less one with impressive empirical support. Rather, three distinct approaches have emerged in recent years.

At the individual level, scholars have examined the attitudes and role perceptions of the main courtroom actors, with particular emphasis on the judge.[4] Contextual approaches have focused upon such things as case and defendant characteristics, the norms of courtroom work groups (composed of the judge, prosecutor, and defense attorney), and the influence of sponsoring organizations on the composition and goals of those work groups. Generally, they have drawn upon organizational frameworks.[5] Environmental approaches have looked to the influence of factors outside the immediate courtroom setting and relied upon such concepts as local legal culture, political culture, the structure of institutions, the sociopolitical makeup of the community, statutes, precedents, and the like.[6]

Obvious problems plague all three approaches. Although those relying upon organization theory offer interesting insights and explanations, they have not rigorously addressed many of the conceptual and methodological issues raised by their research. Rather, they have relied upon impressionistic observations, unsystematic interviews, and untested assumptions. These problems are in large part due to the fact that researchers did not go into the field with a firm grasp of the contextual factors thought to be important in court operations. Such observations usually emerged after the fieldwork.

The attitude theorists' research suffers from equally serious problems. Although their operational measures of important concepts are more sophisticated than those used in contextual approaches, they are still lacking in important regards. Moreover, the links between attitudes and behavior are typically examined for only one aspect (usually sentencing) of one participant's behavior (the judge). Finally, this research fails to integrate insights found in the contextual approach (as contextual approaches ignore individual-level insights). For example, it ignores the context in which judges make decisions, telling us nothing about interactions with fellow judges, other courtroom personnel, or the political and social environment.

The environmental approach is the least well developed. The concept of "legal culture" has not been sufficiently well defined. The dimensions of variation in legal culture remain unexplored, and few operationalized measures exist. The factors that shape the content of local legal culture seldom receive any attention. In addition, environmental variables that go beyond local legal culture—such as political, social, and structural variables—are usually ignored. Finally, the links between environmental phenomena and the major participants in the felony process (police, judges, prosecutors) are either ignored or discussed unsystematically and impressionistically.

We sought to advance our understanding of criminal courts by addressing the shortcomings in each approach, simultaneously implementing them, and by beginning to integrate the observations garnered from each. Our approach to refining, extending, and fleshing out the skeletal structures provided by earlier researchers is explicitly empirical. While we were certainly aware of, indebted to, and guided by previous works on criminal courts and more general social science materials, we primarily talk about and develop phenomena that our fieldwork indicated was important. In these efforts, we seldom get beyond the level of conceptual development. The next iteration of work in this field will have to further refine these concepts, and integrate them into a cohesive theoretical framework, perhaps borrowing, in the process, from more general works in the political, sociological, and anthropological realms. We believe that some of the materials in the first two sections of this work will put future researchers on a firm footing to begin this task.

Our explicit primary reliance upon empirical sources for purposes of conceptual development and elucidation dictated the second key component of our design—its implementation in a comparative framework. Nothing less than a multicounty study could have been used here, because, although a limited application of an individual-level approach may have been possible in a very large jurisdiction, an understanding and assessment of many contextual influences, and most environmental ones, require a comparative setting. One obvious reason for this is the need to obtain sufficient variation on important factors at all levels of analysis. A less obvious benefit of field research in a variety of settings is that it sensitizes one to differences that would otherwise go unnoticed. Finally, no serious attempt to integrate concepts from different levels of analysis is possible without variation within each level. For example, the impact of individual-level influences (attitudes toward punishment) may vary in different counties because of contextual differences. A case study could not detect such differences, nor could it begin to address the nexus between individual and contextual factors.

In choosing sites to study, we decided to limit ourselves to medium-sized jurisdictions. First, we felt that large urban jurisdictions have been relatively overstudied and, moreover, were bound to be somewhat atypical. Almost all of our knowledge about felony courts comes from studies of a handful of large cities in which court dockets are often clogged with poor, black defendants. These jurisdictions have often been plagued by many of the problems that have alarmed court reformers since the early twentieth century. They have frequently been studied *because* of their severe problems. However valid these research efforts may have been, the biased selection process casts doubt upon the generalizability of whatever conclusions or impressions they have produced. Another problem with the concentration on large urban jurisdictions is that their size and complexity handicaps the research effort. Smaller, slower paced, and less complex systems are more revealing of basic processes and subtle personal interactions that may be both inherent characteristics of all court systems and important to understanding the dispositional process. Smaller court systems would also have yielded these insights but would not have had the variety of personnel and cases required to implement our research strategy fully.

Thus, our assessment of earlier criminal court studies, as well as the objectives of the study, dictated extensive empirical research at three distinct conceptual levels in a number of medium-sized jurisdictions. Despite the importance of maximizing variance across jurisdictions, budgetary constraints and other considerations limited us to our home states (Illinois, Michigan, and Pennsylvania). We decided to select nine counties with populations between two hundred thousand and one million, and where more than one trial judge heard criminal cases. To facilitate our comparative analysis, we tried to match the counties in each state with roughly comparable counties in the other states to create three different sets of triplets, one member of each set in each state.

The criteria for selecting the nine counties focused on several general characteristics. First, we decided to select one set of jurisdictions that suffered from the social ills of a declining industrial base, social cleavages, low-to-moderate average incomes, and county financial problems. We also wanted prosperous counties with fairly homogeneous populations and relatively high income levels. Beyond this, we sought a set of geographically isolated counties that—in terms of social, economic, and political characteristics—was near the midpoint between the first two sets. Finally, we wanted counties in which the level of political insulation of the courts differed.

Obvious problems were encountered in trying to maximize variation in the three sets of jurisdictions along these dimensions. This was handled by selecting one set of suburban "ring" counties—DuPage (Illinois), Oakland (Michigan), and Montgomery (Pennsylvania)—one set of "autonomous" counties—Peoria (Illinois), Kalamazoo (Michigan), and Dauphin (Pennsylvania)—and one set of "declining" counties—St. Clair (Illinois), Saginaw (Michigan), and Erie (Pennsylvania). Figure 1.1 shows the location of the research sites in each of the three states. Suburban ring counties, adjacent to each state's major metropolitan area (Chicago, Detroit, and Philadelphia), doubled as both the prosperous and politically insulated sites. The declining counties, of course, were the poorer sites, beset by the various social ills noted above. The autonomous counties were economically between these extremes but tended to have court systems that were less insulated politically than the ring counties. A more detailed description of the characteristics of the counties is presented in chapter 4.

PLAN OF THE BOOK

The bulk of the present volume elaborates upon and implements some of the general ideas introduced here. It is divided into five parts. The remainder of Section I will be concerned with describing the skeletal structure of our approach, introducing our research design and discussing some of the methodological problems we encountered and how we resolved them. Chapter 2 introduces, defines, and discusses some of the most important concepts at each level of analysis (environmental, contextual, and individual). Its purpose is simply to familiarize the reader with some basic concepts to be used throughout the analysis and to develop some of the implications that flow from their interaction. The discussion of research design, research strategies, sampling techniques, and measurement procedures will be presented in chapter 3. Much of this chapter is technical, and some sections are supplemented by technical appendixes. Because it specifies the operationalization of some of the concepts discussed in chapter 2, it is an important bridge between the introductory material and the core sections of the work.

Section II presents a more extensive discussion of each county in light of some of the concepts introduced in chapter 2. Chapter 4 describes

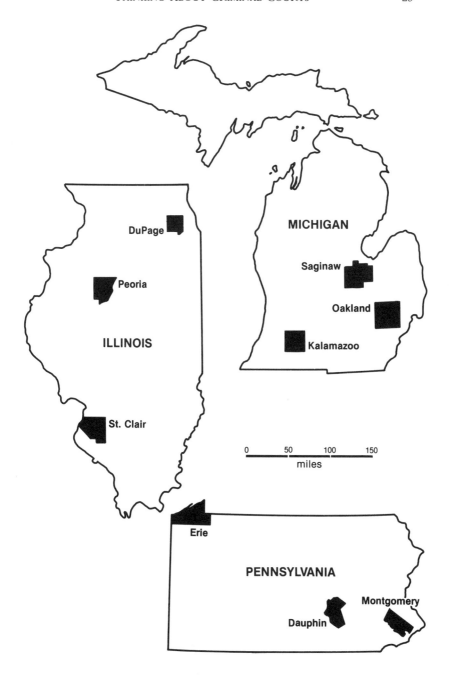

Figure 1.1. **Illinois, Michigan, and Pennsylvania Counties**

the sociopolitical setting of the counties, reports some data on crime rates and detention facilities, and describes some state-level differences in the environments of the nine counties. Chapters 5 and 6 discuss the context of local justice. Chapter 5 is concerned with developing the notion of the courthouse community and laying out some basic characteristics of these communities in each of the counties. Chapter 6 describes the infrastructures of the counties. Section II is built around the mounds of interview and observational data we collected in the fieldwork phase of this study. It is intended to convey, as best we can, the flavor of the different systems we examined and to provide a firm foundation for the remainder of the book. At this same time, however, it introduces a broader array of concepts than would be necessary to implement the quantitative analyses reported in Sections III and IV. The dividends from some of these discussions must await their application to other analyses.

Section III begins our assessment of the guilty plea process in the nine counties by discussing the theoretical and methodological problems involved in such an assessment as well as how we addressed those problems (chapter 7). Chapter 8 addresses the questions of manipulation and inequity in the guilty plea process by looking at the "big picture"—a pool of cases from all nine counties. Then we examine differences across counties and identify and examine four different types of plea systems based upon charge reduction patterns. Chapter 9 attempts to identify the contextual and environmental factors that contribute to these differences in charge reduction practices. Chapter 10 examines differences in the severity of sentencing norms in guilty plea cases as well as the factors accounting for those differences.

Section IV looks at the guilty plea process from a different perspective, that of the court community actors. Here we want to investigate the role of individuals in the formation of plea packages. Do actors with certain attributes either yield reductions more readily or secure them disproportionately? Does the structure of the court community affect the impact of individuals within the guilty plea process? We address the theoretical and analytical problems associated with these questions in chapter 11 and present the results of the qualitative analyses in chapter 12.

In Section V, we systematically lay out our concluding thoughts on the matters discussed here, as well as the issues and questions that they raise.

NOTES

1. For a review of some efforts based upon the data base used here, see Eisenstein, Flemming, and Nardulli (1988), Nardulli (1983), and Flemming, Nardulli, and Eisenstein (1987).

2. An important exception to this preoccupation with higher courts is the work of the crime survey researchers that began in the 1920s. The studies, however, were an outgrowth of the progressive movement's concern with crime and criminal courts, not sociolegal scholars' concern with the judicial process. For citations and a review of this body of literature, see Nardulli (1978, chapter 1).

3. For a review of these studies see Nardulli (1978, chapter 2).

4. See especially Hogarth (1971), Gibson (1978), Sarat (1977), Caldeira (1977), and Bass (1972).

5. For a thorough review of this literature, see Nardulli (1979).

6. See especially Levin (1972), Church (1978), Flemming (1978), and Kritzer (1979). Several studies conducted in Wisconsin, relying on previous work that classified the political cultures of four cities, sought to link the operation of the legal process to political culture; see Jacob (1969) and Milner (1971). Other research touching upon the links between local political and legal culture and behavior of decision makers in the legal process includes Peltason (1961), Eisenstein (1978), and Richardson and Vines (1978, especially chapter 3).

REFERENCES

Arnold, Thurmond. 1956. *Symbols of Government.* New Haven: Yale University Press.

Bass, Larry R. 1972. "Judicial Role Perceptions: Problems of Representativeness, The Identification of Types, and the Study of Role Behavior." Paper presented at Midwest Political Science Association meeting, Chicago.

Blumstein, Alfred. 1983. "Prisons: Population, Capacity, and Alternatives." In *Crime and Public Policy,* ed. James Q. Wilson. San Francisco: ICS Press.

Caldeira, Gregory. 1977. "The Incentives of Trial Judges and the Administration of Justice." *Justice System Journal* (Winter).

Church, Thomas et al. 1978. *Justice Delayed.* Washington: National Center for State Courts.

Davies, Thomas Y. 1983. "A Hard Look at What We Know (and Still Need to Learn) About the 'Costs' of the Exclusionary Rule: The NIJ Study and Other Studies of 'Lost' Arrests." *American Bar Foundation Research Journal* 3:611-90.

Eisenstein, James. 1978. *Counsel for the United States: U.S. Attorneys in the Political and Legal Systems.* Baltimore: Johns Hopkins University Press.

Eisenstein, James, Roy B. Flemming, and Peter F. Nardulli. 1988. *The Contours of Justice: Communities and Their Courts.* Boston: Little, Brown.

Flemming, Roy. 1978. "Pretrial Punishment: A Political-Organizational Perspective." Paper presented at American Political Science Association meeting, Washington, D.C.

Flemming, Roy B., Peter F. Nardulli, and James Eisenstein. 1987. "The Timing of Justice in Felony Trial Courts," *Law and Policy Quarterly.*

Gibson, James. 1978. "Judges' Role Orientations, Attitudes, and Decisions: An Interactive Model." *American Political Science Review* 72:911-24.

Hogarth, John. 1971. *Sentencing as a Human Process.* Toronto: University of Toronto Press.

Jacob, Herbert. 1969. *Debtors in Court.* New York: Rand McNally.

Kritzer, Herbert. 1979. "Political Culture, Trial Courts, and Criminal Cases." In *The Study of Criminal Courts: Political Perspectives,* ed. Peter F. Nardulli. Cambridge, Mass.: Ballinger Publishing.

Levin, Martin. 1972. "Urban Politics and Judicial Behavior." *The Journal of Legal Studies* 1:473.

Milner, Neal. 1971. *The Court and Local Law Enforcement: The Impact of Miranda.* Beverly Hills, Calif.: Sage Publishing.

Nardulli, Peter F. 1978. *The Courtroom Elite: An Organizational Perspective on Criminal Justice.* Cambridge, Mass.: Ballinger Publishing.

————. 1979. "Organizational Analyses of Criminal Courts: An Overview and Some Speculation." In *The Study of Criminal Courts: Political Perspectives.* Cambridge, Mass.: Ballinger Publishing.

————. 1983. "The Societal Cost of the Exclusionary Rule: An Empirical Assessment." *American Bar Foundation Research Journal* 3:585-609.

Peltason, Jack W. 1961. *Fifty-Eight Lonely Men.* New York: Harcourt, Brace, and World.

Richardson, Richard, and Kenneth Vines. 1978. *The Politics of Federal Courts.* Boston: Little, Brown.

Sarat, Austin. 1977. "Judging in Trial Courts: An Explanatory Study." *The Journal of Politics* 39:368-98.

2

CONCEPTUAL FOUNDATIONS OF AN INTEGRATED APPROACH

The need for a theoretically integrated approach to understanding criminal court operations is dictated by the inadequacies of existing approaches, all of which view criminal courts from only one theoretical perspective. A focus on individuals brings us closest to the action but ignores the joint nature of decision making and the impact of norms, traditions, and other contextual influences. Concentrating on work groups and their norms helps address the realities of criminal court operations but too frequently underplays the role of individuals, who, we suspect, can make a difference under certain conditions. Also, approaches that focus on courtroom settings have too often ignored the role of contextual influences in their immediate environs, such as the orientation of the prosecutor's office, the structure of the judge's work, the nature of the indigent defense system, and the availability of local jail space. These approaches also ignore more distant environmental influences, such as the court's social setting, the political makeup of the community, legal codes and principles, and the size and nature of state level correctional facilities. However, a concentration on these environmental factors alone would produce a far too abstract and sterile picture of these courts.

Instead of using such single-focus approaches, we must begin to look at individual decision makers in the context of a work group setting operating within a distinctive court community. Moreover, we must view this court community as it is molded and constrained by its social, political, and legal environment. In addition, we must recognized that the court's environment provides the raw materials for the local court system (cases, defendants), as well as the personnel who operate it. We must also be sensitive to the linkages, or ties, between these various levels of influences, because these linkages often reveal much about how different factors come to affect the process. Diagram 2.1 presents a very general picture of these factors, which will be discussed in more detail throughout this chapter.

The more inclusive approach embodied in Diagram 2.1 is not without pitfalls. The development of an integrated model requires a disciplined and discriminating effort to identify the most salient factors at each level of analysis. But, by reaching too far and viewing everything as relevant, one runs the risk of having a clear view of nothing. To avoid this pitfall, we carefully reviewed the pertinent literature, talked to hundreds of court officials, and reviewed, synthesized, and integrated thousands of pages of transcripts and interviews. This chapter shows some of the theoretical fruits (or seedlings, as the case may be) of these efforts. We begin by laying down the conceptual footings for the remainder of this work. We identify and discuss what we see as some of the most important concepts at each level of analysis—environmental, contextual, and individual. Within each category, we discuss the most relevant types of influences and the nature of their impact. As we move from environmental factors to individual actors, we will try to build upon and integrate various observations. The presentation of the building blocks at this point serves to illustrate the complexity of the dispositional process and the difficulty of the tasks ahead. It will also provide some guidance for later analyses.

Using Diagram 2.1 as a guide, we begin with a look at the environmental influences on the court system.

CRIMINAL COURTS AND THEIR ENVIRONMENT

Environmental factors are those influences that originate from sources outside the local criminal justice system. For our purposes these influences have a state and county dimension. Diagram 2.1 suggests that the relevant environmental influences comprise several aspects: the socioeconomic structure, the orientation and political makeup of the political system, and a structural-legal domain embodying relevant laws, codes, and rules, as well as facilities. Each aspect in turn has its own specific components, some of which (e.g., social heterogeneity and local political preferences) will vary from one county to another. Others (such as sentencing codes and procedural rules) will be similar for every county within a state.

Environmental influences are important for several reasons. They help us understand the flow of cases and personnel into a court system, the types of expectations to which the actors within the court community must respond, and the types of constraints with which the actors must contend. To understand how some environmental influences affect criminal

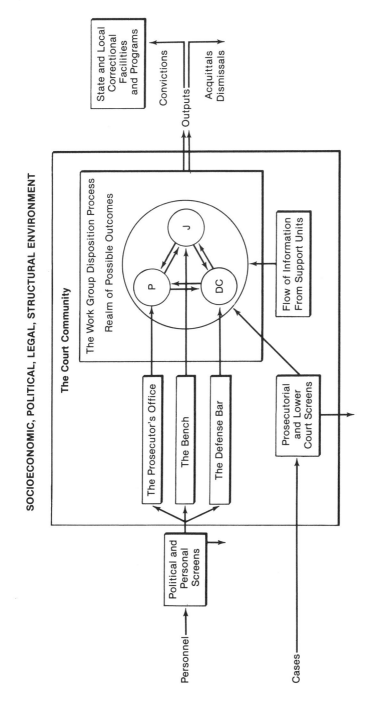

Diagram 2.1. General Integrated Model of Criminal Court Operations

court operations, we must also consider the political linkages between the court community and its environment.

Table 2.1 catalogs some of the most important factors under each of these three categories as well as some factors affecting political linkages. It also indicates the general source of each specific factor and whether it is a state or county level influence. More needs to be said about each general category.

Cases and Personnel

The first four factors listed under the general category of factors affecting the nature and flow of cases and personnel in Table 2.1 (social heterogeneity, affluence, economic composition and vitality, and size) are fairly straightforward, but each is complex in its own right. In addition, some interact with others to complicate matters further. Consider, for example, social heterogeneity and affluence. Various combinations of these factors could have different meanings for the court community. A very heterogeneous community that also spans the affluence spectrum could produce a varied caseload for the court system as well as political problems in staffing the court. A highly homogeneous community would present different problems, but the nature of the problems would probably vary with the level of affluence. A highly affluent, homogeneous community is likely to produce a caseload heavily weighted with drug and property offenses; a homogeneous, poor community would likely have more weapons offenses and violent crimes. The level of affluence is also likely to affect personnel recruitment. Less affluent counties will be likely to hire less competent attorneys, and personnel turnaround may be more rapid, depending upon office philosophy and the local market for private attorneys.

The size of the county is, all other things held constant, likely to increase the variety and seriousness of cases, thereby increasing the strain on court resources (despite likely differences in absolute resource levels). Size will also probably increase the availability and diversity of the personnel pool from which court community members are drawn. This— in conjunction with the wide variety of cases—may make it more difficult to attain high levels of consistency in the handling of cases. The nature of the area's economic system will, of course, affect its affluence and social heterogeneity, but it can also have more direct effects. The cyclical nature of some local economies can create problems for local courts. One-industry areas can suffer shutdowns, recessions, and strikes, which can produce a different set of logistical and political problems for affected court communities than would multi-industry areas. The way cases are handled that result from cyclical downturns may also affect the way in which these

Table 2.1. **Summary of Relevant Environmental Factors**

General Category	Variable	Type of Variable	Level of Variation
Factors affecting nature and flow of cases and personnel	Social heterogeneity	Socioeconomic	County
	Affluence	Socioeconomic	County
	Economic composition and vitality	Socioeconomic	County
	Size	Socioeconomic	County
	Dominance of one city	Socioeconomic	County
	Social and geographic features (especially of county seat)	Socioeconomic	County
	Orientation, structure, and competence of local police agencies	Sociopolitical	Subcounty
Factors that determine expectations of court community's work	Community's perception of the crime problem	Sociopolitical	County
	Political orientation of community	Political	County
	Local political culture	Political	County
Factors that act as constraints upon court community's work	Capacity of local jails	Structural	County
	Availability of local corrections programs and services	Structural	County
	Size and orientation of state penitentiary system	Structural	State
	Severity of state sentencing laws and norms	Sociolegal	State
	Rules governing judicial participation in plea bargaining	Legal	State/county
	Speedy trial laws	Legal	State
Factors affecting political linkages between the court community and its environment	Nature of crime problem	Socioeconomic/ Political	County
	Level of media coverage	Socioeconomic/ Political	County
	Level of political competition	Political	County
	Level of community involvement by court community members	Sociopolitical	County

courts handle "normal cases," thereby differentiating them from those serving areas with more stable or diverse economies.

Serving a county dominated by a major city can present both problems and opportunities for the local court community. A county with a major, magnet city can attract high quality legal professionals thus enhancing the caliber of the local bar and bench; other counties may have to depend solely on home-grown talent. The existence of a major city can also lead to a fairly concentrated defense bar. This, in turn, can create a fairly small and homogeneous court community, perhaps enhancing the consistency of case processing as well as the pace of justice. The presence of a dominant city increases the importance of police-prosecutor relations. Good police-prosecutor relations in such a setting can lead to smoother and more uniform handling of routine cases; bad relations can lead to nightmares.

The dominance of one city can lead to more politicized case processing. This is particularly true if, as is normally the case, crime and minority groups are concentrated in various pockets of the dominant city. It can lead to get-tough pressures for certain types of crimes or offenders. At the same time, it can lead to political problems with law enforcement officials in smaller towns, who may feel that their cases receive insufficient attention. These pressures can sometimes lead to differences in the handling of routine cases, depending upon their city of origin.

The importance of the competence, capacity, and orientation of local police agencies for the flow of cases into the court system is too obvious to require much elaboration. These factors will also be discussed further in the next section.

Expectations

Local expectations about what the court community does may be affected by three factors; two (the community's perception of the crime problem and its political orientation) have fairly direct effects, and one (the local political culture) has a more amorphous effect. The first two factors can interact and have strong implications for the type of political pressures on the court community. For example, in a politically conservative county where there is widespread concern with crime, there will be strong pressures to charge harshly, incarcerate offenders awaiting trial, dispose of cases quickly, and sentence severely. These pressures do not, however, always translate into actions. There may be considerable constraints (structural or legal) upon the ability of criminal court actors to respond to such pressures. Also, the court community may be politically insulated from these pressures.

The impact of political culture upon criminal court actors is more diffuse. It can affect how decision makers perceive various aspects of a case and how they integrate them into a decision. This factor can help explain how decision makers react to political pressures from various segments of the community, as well as the value they place upon issues such as administrative efficiency, the professional development of court community members, within system autonomy, and procedural niceties. Equally important, it can have direct or indirect effects upon the tenor of the dispositional process. High levels of charge manipulation and sentencing disparities may be less acceptable, and less feasible, to practitioners who operate within the confines of a reformist, public-regarding political environment. This may be especially true where the political linkages between the court community and its environment are tight. Conversely, it may be more difficult for a prosecutor in an unreformed, private-regarding culture to effect the changes necessary to reform the guilty plea process.

Constraints

The first four factors listed as constraints upon the court community's work in Table 2.1 apply primarily to sentencing, although some also have implications for pretrial detention practices. The limits on punishment, which these factors create, is quite clear. It is difficult, in the long run, to continue to fill jails or prisons substantially beyond capacity. Increases in capacity can lead to, indeed may be a condition for, corresponding increases in severity. But regardless of capacity, it is legally impossible to sentence a defendant to a prison term beyond the statutory maximum. Less obvious is the symbolic impact of these factors. They can serve as a signal to local decision makers as to the appropriateness of current sentencing practices. Increasing penal capacity or enhancing the statutory penalties for certain crimes can act as an effective constraint upon lenient sentences. Enhancing local rehabilitative services may send the opposite message. Finally, statewide, or even regional, sentencing norms may act as a constraint or signal to local decision makers (witness the wide differences in incarceration rates between southern and eastern states).

The two other factors listed in Table 2.1 (procedural rules on plea bargaining and speedy trial laws) relate to plea bargaining and delay, respectively. Their actual impact depends upon their content as well as their enforcement mechanism. State supreme court rules barring judges from plea negotiations until an agreement is reached by the state and defense can minimize the judge's role in sentencing and can lead to charge and/or count bargaining. This can enhance the state's hand, because the prosecutor controls charging. The impact of speedy trial laws will vary with their "teeth." If excessive delays lead to mandatory dismissals, they can have a real impact; otherwise, they may be largely symbolic. This symbolic impact may not always be desirable. The designation of 120 or 160 days as a "speedy trial" may send a message (much like sentencing levels) to local decision makers, who may adjust their behavior accordingly, perhaps extending delay.

Political Linkages

The notion of political linkage relates to the ties between the court community and its environment. The looser the linkage, the less likely that certain environmental influences will affect various criminal court activities. Table 2.1 lists four linkage variables that can influence such activities. In reality they are indicators of two separate aspects of political linkages and merit some additional comment.

With the exception of a few highly publicized cases, most decisions made by criminal court practitioners (and even office heads) are of low visibility. The public's vision is obscured even further by the judicial shroud that covers much courtroom activity. Only the cumulative impact of these routine decisions is noticed by the general public, if even then. Political elites, however, such as county board members, local mayors, and civic activists, may be more aware of what the courts are doing, and they may be important sources of input into the court system.

Even with these elites, however, most court communities work within a comfortable zone of indifference. Routine decisions within that zone are not likely to result in negative publicity or have any lasting repercussion that might adversely affect business as usual—a vital concern to court community regulars. This relatively high degree of political insulation notwithstanding, the political linkages between the court community and its local environment must be considered. They can affect the practitioners' perceptions of their latitude as well as the costs attached to venturing beyond this zone of indifference.

Although perceptions of latitudes and costs are, in important respects, individual-level phenomena (i.e., they vary by practitioner), they have "global" aspects as well. These global aspects are important because they can lead to institutionalized procedures or norms, which make boundary violations more or less likely (i.e., procedures related to the exercise of discretion by individuals, plea bargaining practices, etc.).

With respect to perceptions of *latitude* (the breadth of the zone of indifference), two global factors come to mind in the criminal court context: the nature of the crime problem (violent crime in particular) and the extent of media coverage in the county. These two factors can be expected to have an interactive effect upon the practitioners' perceptions of their latitude. Where violent crime is a rare occurrence, crime is unlikely to be a salient local political issue. Although exceptional occurrences are likely to generate much publicity, court practitioners can do largely what they wish with mundane cases. In all likelihood, no one is watching. This is especially true in a community where there is little media coverage. Moreover, court community members can point to minimal crime rates and argue that their procedures are working. However, where violent crime rates are high, and where an area is saturated with media (i.e., daily newspapers and local television stations), the members of the court community may feel that their latitude is restricted significantly.

Independent of latitude are the *costs* that practitioners associate with violating community expectations. Two general types of global factors are considered important here—one determined externally, the other determined internally. The first is the overall level of political competition in the county. This is important because it affects the perceived costs of negative publicity. Where political competition is very low—everyone always wins big—the cost of "incidents" is less dear. High levels of electoral competition can lead individuals to proceed more cautiously because a small change in public sentiment could lead to uncertainty and possible disruptions in business as usual, such as personnel and policy changes.

The second factor is the level of local involvement by court community members. Some court communities are staffed with what might be called "imports"—young lawyers without roots in a community who are attracted by a variety of professional, personal, and economic considerations. Others are dominated by locals who have grown up in the community and have strong ties to it. The level of community involvement in the latter is expected to be greater than in the former, and this has important implications for the nature of the political linkages between the court community and its environment. Locals are expected to be much more familiar with the community's sentiments and much more concerned with its welfare than imports. This can lead to procedures as well as a general atmosphere that place a high premium on avoiding decisions that might be interpreted as betrayals of the public's trust.

CONTEXTUAL INFLUENCES

We define contextual influences as those that emanate from the setting in which criminal court actions and decisions occur. Although there are a variety of such influences, we will deal with only three: the court community, the court's infrastructure, and a set of support agencies. They are summarized in Table 2.2. Each has its own degree of abstraction and is important to consider for a different reason.

The concept of the *court community* is the most diffuse and abstract

Table 2.2. **Sources and Examples of Contextual Influences**

The Courthouse Community	The Court Community's Infrastructure	Support Service Agencies
Social dimension	The bench	Local police forces
Communication flows: the grapevine	Integration of lower courts	Pretrial release programs
Cultural-historical dimension	The administrative structure	Court administrator's office
The power structure	Organization of docket	Probation/work release office
	Calendaring system	
	The prosecutor's office	
	Screening mechanism	
	Personnel assignment	
	Centralization of plea bargaining	
	The defense bar	
	Level of concentration	
	Public-private mix	
	Type of indigent defense system	

of the three. It includes not only those actors who regularly interact with one another in the disposition of criminal cases, but also the structure of communication patterns among the actors (the "grapevine"), a cultural dimension, and the power and authority relations among actors. All of these work to give the local court community a distinctive flavor. The infrastructure of the local court system is more concrete than the notion of the court community. As indicated in Table 2.2, this refers to the organization of the bench, the prosecutor's office, and the defense bar. Together these components determine the way the actors interact and the amount of discretion they have. In many ways they define the terrain with which the actors must deal in mapping out dispositional strategies. Support agencies, such as police departments, probation services, and work release programs, could be seen as part of a more inclusive infrastructure within the court system. We separate them here for analytic purposes because the organization of the bench, prosecutor's office, and defense bar have a more direct impact upon a court community than does the structure of these support agencies. Nonetheless, they perform a function similar to the other units. The nature and availability of support functions influence the types of information available to the participants and in some ways define their options, thereby shaping the terrain that the local actors must operate within.

In the sections that follow we will introduce the notion of court community in a very preliminary way and then outline the important dimensions of the court system's infrastructure. Then we briefly touch upon the nature and role of support functions.

The Courthouse Community

After spending an enormous number of hours in various county courts, we became convinced that the concept of a courthouse community can be an immensely useful tool in trying to understand them. Despite its importance, it is an elusive concept. In fact, it may never submit to concrete specification or rigid operationalization. Its value lies in its utility as a unifying metaphor that can be used to organize and integrate a wide array of disparate concepts. Here we only begin to develop its general outlines; more in-depth analyses will be provided in chapters 5 and 6.

One of the first things we did in every county was to determine the regular actors in felony cases. The ease with which sets of names could be gathered in each county suggested that a definite social dimension does in fact exist, at least in the minds of those involved. Perhaps this should not have been so surprising given the fact that these individuals share a common work terrain on a continuing basis. Whatever the case, the sense of association with a larger group, one that spanned formal organizational lines, is what initially led us to the notion of the courthouse community. Despite the fact that the outlines of a community could be detected in nearly every county, they varied considerably in terms of their cohesiveness. Some counties had very strong communities held together by a complex web of social ties, whereas others were much more diffuse.

Another important aspect of the court communities we studied, one that is closely tied to the level of cohesiveness, is the grapevine. The existence and pervasiveness of grapevines made practitioners in these relatively smaller systems less isolated than their counterparts in larger court systems. The primary function of grapevines is the collection and dispersion of information. This is fairly easy in a prosecutor's office or a centralized public defender's office, simply because such offices have an internal cohesiveness. Attorneys can return to their offices with the latest news about a judge or another attorney and soon the whole office will know about it. The coffee lounge, nearby restaurants, and clubs are also vital parts of the grapevine in some communities. Court community members frequent these places to swap news and update "books" on attorneys or judges. Personal experience, bolstered by such information, becomes part of the actors' working knowledge about how the court system "really" operates.

Although the relatively small size of our court communities may help diffuse information and gossip, size does not determine the shape of the grapevine or the corresponding communication patterns. In addition to divisions paralleling the formal organization of the courthouse, the communities we looked at had crisscrossed webs of informal relationships. In some counties, parts of these webs were spun years earlier when the participants were growing up in the same neighborhoods or through early political interaction. In other counties, attorneys knew each other in law school, or in their clerkship days. Other webs were derived from residential, religious, athletic, or social ties. As a result, even in jurisdictions that had diffuse court communities, members were not normally strangers to one another.

The cultural dimension encompasses the various norms, values, and expectations of the court community, as well as the processes by which these are transmitted to newcomers. What is a particular case worth in a plea bargain? What types of cases should go to trial? What should happen in the case of "unnecessary" trials? How should frivolous motion practices by defense attorneys be handled? What prosecutorial practices constitute overreaching? Veteran members play an important role here. They act as repositories of collected experiences, observed relationships, and court lore. They pass this information on to new recruits during various formal and informal encounters. This repository function is important, because it provides stability and continuity to the court's activities. Although leaders and assistants come and go, the court community's traditions and norms change very slowly. The nature of these traditions and norms are important aspects of a court community's personality and distinctiveness.

A final aspect of court communities that gives them a distinctive character is the identity and distribution of prime movers or authority figures. By virtue of personality, professional skills (or reputation), political power, longevity, or some other attribute, one or more individuals (usually not more than a few) seem to play a dominant role within a court community at a given time. It may be the head prosecutor, the chief felony prosecutor, or a particular criminal court judge; it is rarely a head public defender or defense attorney. Those who occupy this position tend to dominate the court community through a variety of techniques. Some attract and monopolize media attention. Others dominate by becoming involved in various activities on various levels; their actions and/or contacts keep others on the defensive, constantly reacting to their initiatives. Still others dominate by virtue of their position and/or charismatic qualities that engender loyalty, respect, and deference from their fellow court community members.

Who these individuals are and how they dominate can have important implications for the tenor of the court community. Moreover, while the impact of some individuals will fade upon their retirement, if not earlier, others can have a lasting effect on the norms and structure of the court community. For example, a newly elected, aggressive prosecutor with considerable political resources may be able to revamp plea-bargaining procedures and upset going rates, at least for a while. The changes, however, may well lead to organized opposition on the part of the defense bar, perhaps with the implicit support of the judges. This opposition may be in the form of more trials, increased delays, or adverse rulings. The same changes introduced by a widely respected prosecutor or judge with long tenure in the system may have a more lasting impact, especially because protégés of these individuals may carry out their policies long after they have left the system.

The Court System's Infrastructure

Court systems throughout the country vary considerably in how they organize their work. These structural variants are important to note because they have an important impact upon the terrain in a court community. Also, while the structure of work in a county court system is affected by a complex mix of influences, how a court system organizes its tasks can sometimes yield insights into the orientation of the court community, a topic to which we will return in chapter 6.

The Criminal Bench

Next to the private defense bar, the judges who hear criminal cases are often the most loosely organized segment of the court community. Most judges are subject to very few bureaucratic controls in their conduct of day-to-day affairs. Nonetheless, recognizable variants occur in the organization of criminal benches. Some of the most important for our purposes are to be found in their relationship to lower courts, the administrative structures, and their assignment policies.

A critical aspect of the court's organization is the relationship between the county's felony trial courts and the lower courts. Lower courts can be major disposition points within a system, or they can routinely pass cases on to the trial courts. By using rigorous preliminary examinations and extensive plea bargaining, lower courts can filter out cases with weak evidentiary foundations and those with less serious charges; at the same time, they can forward stronger, graver cases to the circuit courts. This has important implications for the workload of trial court personnel, who can establish, enhance, and/or monitor the lower court's screening function only if they have some control over the selection of lower court actors and/or the operation of these courts. This is likely in unified court systems. It is less likely where lower courts are located in various cities throughout the county, especially if the magistrates are locally elected officials. Such officials are more likely to be responsive to the wishes of their local constituents than to the desires of trial court personnel in the county seat.

Less important than the relationship between the trial courts and the lower courts is the bench's administrative apparatus. Most local court systems are headed by a chief judge, but their power, method of selection, and tenure vary considerably. Also, some of them have a court administrator at their disposal, and this can have an important impact upon the flow of cases within the court community. But court administrators vary tremendously in their background, credentials, abilities, and powers. The type of court administrator employed in a court community can say almost as much about the work orientation of the community as whether or not one is employed.

The manner in which judges are assigned to different facets of the county court's work, and the way in which cases are assigned to judges, are two of the most important structural features of a local court system. They are of great interest to the courthouse community and have a marked impact upon the composition and activities of courtroom work groups. Frequently they are also quite involved and complex. The court's work, such as civil cases, criminal cases, and probate cases, can be organized in various ways, and a trial court's time can also be divided in various ways (continuous dockets or periodic dockets). Moreover, once these matters have been set, courts must decide upon a calendaring method (master or individual) as well as how cases are to be assigned to judges (randomly, sequentially, or personally). The many permutations and the implications of each are beyond the present discussion. They will be addressed in chapter 6.

The Prosecutor's Office

The most bureaucratized segment of the court system is the prosecutor's office. Each office we observed had a hierarchy, formal channels of communication, and specialization of labor. Many offices also attempted to establish formal policies in a variety of areas and to centralize important functions. The orientation of a particular office depends largely upon the style of the chief prosecutor. We found that some chief prosecutors tended to be strong policymakers, whereas others saw themselves as "first among equals." The former type attempted to restrict the amount of discretion given to assistants, adopted formalized procedures wherever possible, and appeared to be more outward looking and less concerned with internal court community relations. They also tended to experiment with innovative procedures more frequently, including computerized information systems. The latter type of chief prosecutor tended to view assistants as private attorneys simply appended to the public prosecutor's office. This more relaxed style left much discretion to assistants.

A measure of the impact of the chief prosecutor's style can be seen in how the charging and screening functions were handled. Strong policymakers can be expected to implement some centralized screening mechanism (depending upon state law, past county procedures, and police resistance), perhaps even with some written charging guidelines or policies. Our observations suggested that the most visible and important impact of prosecutorial style is in the area of plea offers. Several of our counties used a variety of mechanisms to centralize plea offers and to restrict the discretion of assistants.

The recruitment and deployment of personnel is another important structural variant. Some offices hired largely on a political basis often requiring some form of recommendation, whereas others were more merit oriented. With respect to deployment, some offices used continuous (vertical) prosecution; in other words, an assistant was assigned to handle a case at the preliminary level and kept the case until its completion. Other offices separated the performance of preliminary hearings from felony trial work, with different staffs handling each (horizontal prosecution). The latter method requires a procedure for deciding how to assign assistants at the trial level. They are usually assigned either to judges or to cases. The type of assignment mechanism used has important implications for the efficient use of resources, the professional development of assistants, and work-group formation. These issues will be discussed in more detail in chapter 6.

The Defense Bar

The local defense bar is the most amorphous subcomponent of the court system. Perhaps the most salient aspects of these criminal defense bars are their level of concentration, their private-public mix, and the nature of the indigent defense system.

The extent to which felony criminal work is concentrated in the hands of a small group of attorneys can affect the composition of work groups, the level of consistency and efficiency in handling cases, and perhaps even the system's adversariness. The level of concentration, as well as the defense bar's private-public mix, is affected by both public policies and private markets. Clearly, defendants who are relatively more affluent are more likely to hire private defense attorneys. This leads to a more diffuse defense bar. However, even in counties with large proportions of indigent defendants (those defended by publically paid attorneys), a highly concentrated defense bar is not insured. This depends upon the structure of the indigent defense system.

Each indigent defense system is somewhat distinctive. Perhaps the most important structural distinction is its location on a private-public continuum. At the private end are systems in which members of the local bar are chosen or appointed on a case-by-case basis and paid to represent poor defendants. At the other end are public defender offices with full-time staffs working under a more or less centralized administration. Between these poles are "quasi-public" models in which a law firm or group of attorneys, often on a part-time basis, handle indigent defendant cases on a contractual basis with the court or county. Obviously, bureaucratic and quasi-public systems lead to a more concentrated defense bar, especially when the public sector handles a large portion of the felony defense work.

Support Service Agencies

This study did not focus much attention on the support services available to various components of the courthouse community; to do so would have required a very different research strategy and would have diluted available resources to unacceptable levels. Nonetheless, support service agencies can have an important effect and deserve some comment. Depending upon their availability and structure, they present criminal court actors with an array of problems, options, and opportunities. Their primary significance for criminal court decision making is that they can affect the realm of possible outcomes for individual cases and can restrict the discretion of the primary actors. Although several of these agencies (local police departments and local correctional services, for instance) could be categorized as environmental factors, their proximity to the day-to-day affairs of various actors leads us to view them as contextual in nature.

Local police units can affect criminal court operations in a number of ways. The training and screening functions of a prosecutor's office can be greatly simplified if a county has only a handful of highly professionalized police departments. The task can be monumental, however, if there are numerous departments of varying quality serving very different types of communities. A single large department that dominates the county can present prosecutors with a different set of problems. The establishment of uniform practices may be easier, but the department may feel that it should have a say in what those policies are, thereby infringing upon what most prosecutors would view as their turf.

The existence of well-staffed pretrial release programs, court administrator offices, and local correctional programs increases the capability of court actors to analyze and integrate information. They can also increase their options and enhance their ability to pursue rational courses of action. But they can also restrict the discretion of different actors. Consider pretrial release units, which can gather much more information on defendants than most prosecutors and defense attorneys. A judge who releases a defendant on the basis of the recommendation of such a screening unit can diffuse responsibility in case there are adverse consequences. However, in performing these functions, the pretrial release unit may well uncover information that a defense attorney, or prosecutor, may not wish to bring to the judge's attention. And the unit's recommendations may not always please the judge, who may feel bound by them nonetheless.

Court administrator offices may be useful to criminal court actors because they facilitate many of the mundane tasks that the disposition of a large number of cases entails. A court administrator may develop more rational procedures than could be expected of an individual judge. These same procedures, however, may reduce the ability of prosecutors and defense attorneys to wheel and deal in plea negotiations. It may be more difficult, or even impossible, to route cases to accommodating judges if the court administrator controls scheduling and case assignment procedures.

Similar problems may be encountered with well-staffed probation departments, which operate a variety of local correctional programs. They provide actors with more information and more options, but their expertise can bring to light information that one party or another deems undesirable. At the same time, their recommendations can act to limit the discretion or maneuverability of different actors.

INDIVIDUAL-LEVEL INFLUENCES

Individual decision makers are the crucial link between a court's environment, the structural aspects of the court community, and case outcomes such as mode of disposition, sentence, and delay. Of these decision makers, the judge, prosecutor, and defense attorney are the most important. No one else parallels their power to affect the disposition of most cases. Environmental and contextual factors may limit, constrain, or channel the actions of these decision makers, but they usually do not determine their actions—except under highly unusual circumstances. For the most part, individuals, or groups of individuals, have wide discretion in making criminal court decisions. Given a set of similar constraints, different individuals may respond differently. Thus, individuals constitute a potentially independent source of influence upon the dispositional process.

Nonetheless, the role of court community members in the handling of felony cases is anything but clear. Human beings are a complex amalgam of values, orientations, attitudes, skills, backgrounds, and personalities. What aspects of an individual's repertoire of attributes are most important? Does their relevance vary across different tasks, or in different settings? To what extent does the political process preselect individuals whose attributes mesh well with the orientation of the community they serve? What role do long-established court community norms, legal dictates, structural controls over discretion, and resource constraints play in limiting the impact of individuals? How do individuals come together to handle a case?

In this section, we lay out our thoughts on some of these matters. First, we discuss those decision-maker characteristics most likely to enhance our understanding of the individual's role in the dispositional process. Then, as a way of illustrating the linkages across levels of analysis, we present some very general thoughts about how individuals mesh with environmental and contextual factors in the criminal court setting.

Attribute Repertoires

The most important decision-maker attributes are work-specific attitudes, operating styles, and bargaining skills and resources. Diagram 2.2 depicts these attributes and their interrelationships. The backgrounds of actors are not included here because they are considered to be less immediate determinants of behavior than these other attributes. Background and career data are nonetheless useful in providing an overview of who the courtroom actors are and how well they reflect the community they represent. Moreover, they help us to understand differences in work-specific attitudes. These attitudes, in conjunction with certain aspects of operating style, may clarify the predispositions of various actors toward various decisions or actions. Bargaining skills and resources, the last category of attributes, show how effectively an individual can realize attitudinal predispositions.

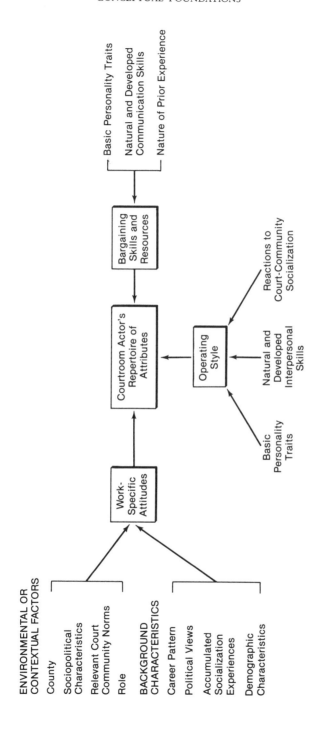

Diagram 2.2. **Components of Courtroom Actor's Repertoire of Attributes**

Table 2.3 **Available Measures of Principal Decision-Maker Attributes**

Work-Specific Attitudes	Operating Style	Bargaining Skills and Resources
Belief in punishment	Responsiveness involvement*	Machiavellianism
Regard for due process	Docket concern*	Trial competence**
Concern with efficiency		

* Judges only
** Attorneys only

Along with operating style, these skills and resources can provide insights into how individuals interact within the work group setting.

Table 2.3 reports the available measures we have of the three principal sets of attributes. Their derivation will be reported in chapter 3. These measures are not perfect, nor do they necessarily tap every relevant dimension of the actor's repertoire of attributes. But they do stress the point that courtroom actors bring with them a complex bundle of attributes that only a multidimensional approach can hope to tap. Not every aspect of this repertoire will have implications for every stage of the dispositional process, or for every task that needs to be accomplished. Some will be relevant for bail setting, some for plea discussions, and others for sentencing. Moreover, some attributes may depend on others to have an impact. For example, the impact of a defense attorney's views on punishment upon negotiated sentences may depend upon the level of his or her trial skills or personality. The impact of a judge's views may depend upon his or her level of involvement in the plea negotiations.

Diagram 2.2 also shows that we have a more concrete understanding of the determinants of work-specific attitudes than of the other components. In part, this is because attitudes have been a part of the reigning paradigm in judicial research for a long time. But it is also because of the fact that attitudes can be influenced. It is not at all uncommon for a new recruit's work-specific attitudes to change once he or she either becomes more familiar with the work or changes roles or settings. Such things as responsiveness, trial skills, and basic personality traits, however, are likely to be more deep-seated in a person's psyche and less amenable to change. Some people will simply never be outstanding trial attorneys — or accommodating or trustworthy — regardless of their position or surroundings.

An appreciation of the role of individuals in the dispositional process only begins with an understanding of attribute repertoires and their possible determinants. Diagram 2.3 puts the role of courtroom actors into a broader perspective by integrating them with environmental and contextual factors. A review of the diagram helps illustrate the role of individual-level influences in this setting.

The Environment and Individuals

At the far left of Diagram 2.3 is the pool of available personnel in a given county. In most counties, this pool is composed entirely of lawyers, but some systems permit nonlawyers to perform certain roles (magistrates, for example). The small circles represent the attribute repertoires of actors. The L indicates that the actor is a local, the I indicates an import, a derisive term used by some locals to refer to attorneys who move to a community solely because it is a desirable place to live and practice law. It is important to distinguish between these two sets of attorneys. A highly local court community can mean a high level of understanding of, and concern for, community sentiment. Locals are more apt to be familiar with issues and incidents that shaped certain policies or practices. Outsiders, however, may bring a fresh perspective on things.

The placement of the line that separates the private bar from the public practitioners will vary from county to county as will the sharpness of the dividing line. Much depends upon the structure of the indigent defense system in the county. In counties that use an assigned counsel system, large numbers of private attorneys will be involved in many of the court's cases, thus blurring the public-private distinction. In a system that requires a large number of public defenders, the distinctions will be sharper and the role of the private bar more limited. Each variation will produce a different public-private mix and will determine to a very great extent the composition of the court community itself. Some will be dominated by regulars, others by a mix of semiregulars and nonregulars.

Independent of the type of indigent defense system in a county, the distribution of regulars, semiregulars, and nonregulars in a county will be affected by the socioeconomic characteristics of a county. Large sprawling counties speckled with medium-size towns and villages will lead to a decentralized private bar, and the caseload will be handled by a large number of nonregulars. A dominant central city will breed a small ring of specialists. The socioeconomic factors will also affect the number of imports, as well as various aspects of the actors' attribute repertoires. Imports will be more numerous in larger communities—because they are likely to be banking, industrial, or commercial centers—especially if these communities also have other social attractions such as a good climate,

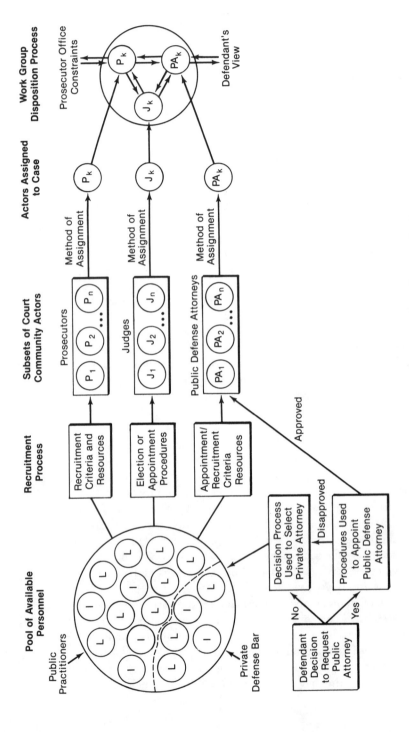

Diagram 2.3. **Individuals in the Criminal Court Setting**

cultural attractions, or an appealing landscape. A law school, or even a university, in or near the county seat will also attract outsiders.

A pool of available personnel with a high level of locals may mirror the community, at least roughly. For instance, in a largely working-class community, the lawyers may be first generation college graduates who attended local law schools. In middle-class or professional communities, the pool of available attorneys may have a higher proportion of individuals who graduated from more prestigious institutions. This could have important implications for the mix of actors from which work group members are selected. More divisive climates could emerge in court communities with members who have marked differences in attitudes, skills, self-perceptions, and approaches, especially if these are not softened by long personal ties.

An important point must be stressed here: Wide differences within the pool of available personnel do not necessarily translate into a heterogeneous court community. The recruitment process — which is directly or indirectly affected by political considerations — screens individuals who seek a public role within the court community. On the private side, self-selection works in such a way that lawyers who have no aptitude, interest, or taste for criminal work seldom venture into the criminal arena, at least not on a regular basis. The exact nature of the screening process for public members varies by role and by county. Judges are usually elected, but in some areas they are appointed. Provisions for judicial retention also vary. Moreover, although the head prosecutor is normally elected, the criteria used for the selection and retention of assistants vary. The controls over the public defense attorneys vary by type of indigent defense system. Personnel screening can be done by judges or head public defenders, or a private attorney can receive an appointment simply by placing his or her name on a list. Judges or county board members can sometimes indirectly affect the screening and retention process.

Theoretically, these screening mechanisms will provide the court community with public members who meet the needs and interests of the populace, or at least the political leaders of the community (including leaders in the court community). Clearly no mirror image of the community is expected. Nonetheless, we would not expect to find the local court system staffed by liberal Democrats in a highly conservative, Republican county. Nor would we expect it to be dominated by cosmopolitan imports educated at Ivy League law schools in an economically depressed, blue-collar, smoke-stack county.

The actual makeup of the court community will be influenced by the local political culture as well as the political linkages between the court community and this environment. Where these factors lead to politicized appointments, the public actors within the court system are more likely to mirror the community; where merit appointments are stressed, the correspondence becomes more problematic. Even under the most politicized conditions, however, it is unlikely that any more than a rough correspondence will exist between public actors in the court community and the sociopolitical characteristics or orientation of the county. Several constraints are operative here. First, as is the case in many recruitment situations, it is often difficult to know what one is getting. This is particularly true with young attorneys fresh out of law school. Their potential may remain unfulfilled, or they may simply change as they mature. They may attempt to disguise, or simply not draw attention to, undesirable attributes such as views on punishment, voting record, or experience. This may be less true with judges who normally have a lengthy record and are more thoroughly screened. Even maverick judges who somehow circumvent normal screens must stand before the electorate at some point.

A second important constraint is that individuals come as a package. Although some aspects of one's attribute repertoire may be highly desirable, others may not be. The prosecutor's office in a working-class, conservative county with a sizable Irish Catholic community may heavily recruit the sons and daughters of Irish Catholic families who "made good." In the process of making good, however, these individuals may have developed more liberal outlooks on important matters. A reformist prosecutor's office in a middle-class suburban county may be looking for experienced, skilled trial attorneys. Here again, those available may not be as Republican or as conservative as the county. Another potential constraint could arise if an office did not have the resources to recruit an individual who would meet its needs. Competing offers from the private sector may force the public offices to accept the leftovers. This may involve trade-offs, thereby making it difficult for them to get Mr. or Ms. Right.

To say that no more than a rough correspondence between the attribute repertoires of actors and the desires of the county they serve exists is not to say that the actions of these actors are necessarily inconsistent with the expectations of the local community. Various mechanisms operate to bring about satisficing dispositions. Newcomers who may be out of step philosophically are socialized to respect office or court community norms. Formalized controls on individual discretion may also operate in some offices in some counties. Finally, various forces can be brought to bear on individuals who simply refuse to fulfill expectations or conform to conventions. Reassignments, curtailments in indigent assignments, failures to make reasonable concessions, and outright dismissals are prominent among these mechanisms.

Contextual Factors: Matching Actors and Cases

A useful way to illustrate the nexus between individual and contextual factors in the dispositional process is to discuss the manner in which actors are matched with cases. Little can be said about the case of private attorneys. Defendants who can afford private attorneys may retain one in a variety of ways, such as prior contact, personal referrals, reputation, advertising, or local bar association referral services. Most defendants do not know how to go about making such a selection, and they probably have very little idea of whether their selection fits their needs (i.e., it may be a largely random process).

Public actors present a far different situation. How they are assigned to cases is an important aspect of the court community's infrastructure. Conscious decisions must be made about how individuals are assigned to handle cases. The decision affects not only the individuals within the disposition process, but also the flow of cases through it. In some systems, the method of matching cases and actors results in random groupings of personnel, with uncertain results. In other systems, an attempt is made to match individuals with cases or other individuals. Where actors are matched with cases, the potential for maximizing the impact of individual influences is great. Where actors are matched with others in a semipermanent grouping, group influences probably displace individual influences, at least to a degree.

Most systems rely heavily on the judge and the judge's case assignment process. Counties can use a personalized, random, or sequential assignment process. A personalized system permits the case assigner to match the case with the judge. In this way, important cases can be handled by the "right" judge. Personalized assignment of judges in situations where the prosecutor and/or defense attorney is known can also be useful in achieving compatible work groups, which can be important in routine cases. The type of calendaring system used by the judges can also affect individual influences. Master calendars can permit plea routing, whereas individual calendars do not. Where plea routing is available, skillful and knowledgeable defense attorneys can use the differences among judges to their advantage. Plea routing may also change the nature and timing of plea decisions. Negotiations may be held up until the judge is known, and in some situations defense concessions may have to be made in order to get a case into or out of a particular judge's courtroom.

For prosecutor offices and bureaucratically organized public defender offices, the basic choice at the trial level is whether to assign attorneys to cases or to judges; there are important tradeoffs with each. By assigning attorneys to judges, an office can influence two-thirds of the work group. If the judge and attorney are nicely matched, a common understanding can emerge, thereby facilitating the expeditious processing of cases. This arrangement also has administrative advantages because it minimizes time conflicts. A drawback to this system is that it can result in an occasional mismatch between a case and the abilities of the attorney. It can also stifle an attorney's professional development, because each attorney works only with a single judge rather than a wide range of judges. Assigning public attorneys to cases permits a matching of individuals with cases as well as with opposing attorneys. Although this arrangement has administrative drawbacks and can lead to extended delays because of time conflicts, it enhances the professional development of the attorneys. Moreover, if used wisely and under certain conditions, it can permit an office to maximize the advantages of staff with diverse qualities, skills, and beliefs.

If all prosecutor and public defense attorneys are assigned to a judge with an individual calendar who receives cases blindly, many avenues for individual influences are cut off. Cases cannot be routed to favorite judges, and attorneys cannot be targeted to specific offenses. Moreover, pressures exist to reach a group consensus on the handling of cases, especially routine ones. While this group consensus undoubtedly reflects the configuration of attributes in the work group, the impact of individual attributes is muted. In contrast to individual calendar systems, master calendar systems provide a greater opportunity for individuals to make a difference. They can do so because of several factors, each of which is complicated and all of which depend on the stage at which they occur. We can discuss them only generally here; more specific discussions will follow in the analyses of individual decisions and tasks.

A general understanding of their role can be understood best by referring to the last component of Diagram 2.3. It depicts the members of the court community who are ultimately assigned to handle a case. After assimilating the factors and circumstances surrounding a case, these actors construct a set of initial expectations concerning how the case should be disposed. These expectations will vary with the attribute repertoires of the actors, but they are bounded by, among other things, the realm of possible outcomes and constraints emanating from the prosecutor's office, and the defendant's views. The realm of possible outcomes includes the range of dispositions that are reasonable for the type of case under consideration. This realm is defined principally by legal factors, court community norms, and resource limitations. The impact that an individual can have varies with the size of this realm; it is larger in more serious cases and smaller in routine ones where clearer norms are more likely to prevail. The constraints emanating from the prosecutor's office vary with office policy, the type of case, and the experience of the prosecutor. Where operative, office controls over plea discussions can limit the discretion of the prosecutor handling a case and limit the impact of his or her views.

The defendant can also cause constraints by vetoing a defense action and limiting the flexibility of the defense attorney. Realistically, however, the defendant's impact depends upon his or her bargaining resources and the stage of the proceeding.

We can only allude here to the complexities introduced into the dispositional process by such factors as resource contraints, environmental expectation and political screening, office policies, structural arrangements, the group context of criminal court decision making, and court community norms. However, it should be clear that in routine cases they can minimize the role and impact of the maverick actor or even the manipulative powers of accepted regulars. The burden of precedent, the limitations of resources, the pulls of office policies all militate against an individual tampering with accepted court community norms in routine cases too extensively or too frequently. The result is a system characterized by bureaucratic justice, as opposed to individualized justice, a theme to which we will return in our discussion of the guilty plea process.

First, however, we must turn to a discussion of the research design and procedures used to develop and explore empirically some of the general ideas discussed here.

3

RESEARCH DESIGN, IMPLEMENTATION, AND OPERATIONALIZATION

As important to an appreciation of this research as its conceptual foundations is an understanding of the manner in which we organized and implemented our empirical work. First, we will discuss how well our sites fit our site selection criteria. Then we provide an overview of our research methods and the data we collected. Here we also discuss the quantitative data on decision-maker and case attributes. In addition, sampling techniques are presented, and the types of information collected are described. Finally, we lay out the procedures used to integrate these large amounts of data into a handful of case-level and individual-level measures that we used in the empirical analyses reported in Sections III and IV. Examination of the environmental and contextual factors generally required less involved derivation and are reported in chapters 4, 5, and 6.

SITE SELECTION AND CHARACTERISTICS

Our assessment of earlier criminal court studies, as well as our research objectives, dictated extensive empirical research in a number of jurisdictions. The constraints noted in chapter 1 led us to select one ring, one autonomous, and one declining county in each of our three home states (Illinois, Michigan, and Pennsylvania). Our selections were further restricted by the fact that only a limited number of counties in each state (9 in Illinois, 16 in Michigan, 27 in Pennsylvania) had at least two criminal judges and a population between two hundred thousand and one million.

Table 3.1. **Selected Counties**

	Illinois	Michigan	Pennsylvania
Ring	DuPage (outside of Chicago)	Oakland (outside of Detroit)	Montgomery (outside of Philadelphia)
Autonomous	Peoria	Kalamazoo	Dauphin
Declining	St. Clair	Saginaw	Erie

These minimal qualifications ensured that a county was sufficiently large and diverse to produce interesting variance on important matters, but not so large as to overwhelm our research efforts and budgets.

After collecting extensive amounts of demographic, geographic, and political data on fifty-two potential counties, we selected the nine that best fit our criteria. These are listed in Table 3.1.

The suburban ring counties, adjacent to each state's major metropolitan area, doubled as both the prosperous and the autonomous or politically insulated counties. The data reported in Tables 3.2 and 3.3 generally support these designations; they also reveal other attributes of the counties. Table 3.2 shows that DuPage, Oakland, and Montgomery are large and, with the exception of Montgomery, growing rather quickly. Each has the highest per capita income for all counties in their respective states and are overwhelmingly white (95 percent to 98 percent). Each is composed of a large commuter population that works in the adjacent major metropolitan area— Chicago, Detroit, or Philadelphia—and lives in one of a number of small to medium-sized towns, none of which dominate the county. The small size of these towns and the presence of big city media create the potential for a relative void in the reporting of local public affairs. No television stations focus their attention solely on any of the ring counties, and only rather small community newspapers report on local affairs. Each of the counties is either overwhelmingly or predominantly Republican (Table 3.3).

The three declining counties—St. Clair, Saginaw, and Erie—differ markedly from the ring counties in most regards. Their populations are considerably smaller and are either losing population or not growing very quickly. One exception is Erie County, which is actually growing. Despite the county's growth, however, the city of Erie had lost 8 percent of its population between 1970 and 1980. The 1970 per capita income of the declining counties was markedly lower than that of the ring counties; they also had far more people below the poverty level in that year. Again with the exception of Erie, the declining counties have a far higher proportion of blacks than the ring counties. Moreover, the largest city

Table 3.2. **Selected Demographic Characteristics of Research Sites**

	Illinois			Michigan			Pennsylvania		
	DuPage (Ring)	Peoria (Autonomous)	St. Clair (Declining)	Oakland (Ring)	Kalamazoo (Autonomous)	Saginaw (Declining)	Montgomery (Ring)	Dauphin (Autonomous)	Erie (Declining)
1980 population	658,177	200,466	265,469	1,011,793	212,378	228,059	643,621	232,317	279,780
Percent change in population since 1970	35.0	2.6	−6.3	11.4	5.4	3.8	3.1	3.9	6.2
Median household income, 1970	$14,457	$10,633	$ 9,540	$ 13,826	$11,033	$10,875	$12,747	$ 9,710	$ 9,363
Percent under poverty level, 1970	2.3	6.5	12.4	3.8	5.9	7.7	3.3	7.7	6.8
Percent of county which is black, 1970	1.2	10.7	27.7	4.7	7.5	15.7	4.9	13.5	4.4
Percent of county population residing in largest city, 1970	6.5	61.9	20.8	7.6	37.5	34.0	9.6	22.9	42.6
Percent of county's black population residing in the largest city, 1970	13.7	96.2	71.7	59.5	78.5	76.9	8.7	74.2	93.2

Table 3.3. **Selected Information on Nature of Linkages Between Court System and Its Environment**

	Illinois			Michigan			Pennsylvania		
	DuPage (Ring)	Peoria (Autonomous)	St. Clair (Declining)	Oakland (Ring)	Kalamazoo (Autonomous)	Saginaw (Declining)	Montgomery (Ring)	Dauphin (Autonomous)	Erie (Declining)
Number of commercial television stations in county	0	3	0	2*	1	1	0	3	3
Number of countywide papers	0**	1	1	0**	1	1	0**	1 (morning and afternoon editions)	1 (morning and afternoon editions)
Percent voting Republican in 1980 (Reagan)	72.5	60.1	52.2	60.0	58.5	52.1	65.1	61.4	51.5
Percent voting Republican in 1978 governor's race	69.9	57.7	38.4	67.7	64.9	53.3	65.8	66.5	53.7

* While the broadcast facilities of two stations are located in Oakland, the county is not the primary focus of local news coverage.
** Several community papers exist, but the market is dominated by major metropolitan papers (Chicago, Detroit, or Philadelphia).

within each of the declining counties, which accounted for a fairly large proportion of the total county population, also has the highest concentration and largest number of blacks in the three counties. The declining counties also differ somewhat from the ring counties with respect to the linkage between the court system and its environment. Each has at least one countywide newspaper, and Erie and Saginaw have television stations located in the county seat. St. Clair has no independent stations because it borders St. Louis, which makes it a ring county of sorts. Finally, with the exception of St. Clair, which votes strongly Democratic, the other two declining counties had competitive party systems.

The most distinctive characteristic of the autonomous counties — Peoria, Kalamazoo, and Dauphin — is that they are "free-standing" counties dominated by one central city accounting for a fairly large proportion of the county's population. This dominant city accommodates at least one countywide newspaper and at least one commercial television station (Dauphin and Peoria have three). The home base of the county court system is also located in this central city. Socially and economically these autonomous counties tend to lie somewhere between the ring and declining counties. The main exception is Dauphin, which has an income level comparable to Erie, has more people below the poverty level, and actually grew more slowly than Erie. Moreover, the city of Erie comprises a larger proportion of Erie County than Harrisburg does of Dauphin County. Politically, the autonomous counties more closely resemble the ring counties — they are strongly Republican.

Our efforts at selecting sites in accordance with the prescribed criteria were not totally successful. The real world often plays havoc with the best of research designs. The triplets are not identical. Some counties in some categories share certain attributes with counties listed in another category. Most counties fit reasonably well, however. Erie, which appears to be the most deviant on the basis of the data contained in Table 3.2, fits the declining mold much better than the statistics suggest, largely because of the nature of the city of Erie. Fieldwork and qualitative assessments indicate that it has much more in common with Saginaw and St. Clair than it does with Dauphin, or any of the other autonomous counties. Dauphin is the state capital and has a stable white-collar and service work force. Erie relies primarily on a declining industrial-manufacturing base.

DATA COLLECTION PROCEDURES

To achieve the objectives outlined in chapter 1 and to operationalize some of the concepts discussed in chapter 2, we had to collect comparable data on a variety of phenomena in each of the nine counties. Some data required a somewhat different research technique and/or strategy than others. We used open-ended interviews, questionnaires, a personality test, a Q-sort procedure to obtain personnel evaluations, and a case file data form to record case-specific information. Much of this information is summarized in Table 3.4. Table 3.5 reports, by county, the number of interviews successfully obtained as well as the number of defendants sampled.

Although some information on environmental and contextual factors was derived from organization charts, census and voting data, scholarly works on the counties, and local media, most of it came from personal interviews. More than three hundred interviews were conducted over several months; they ranged in length from twenty minutes to three hours, with an hour being the norm. Virtually all were tape recorded; more than ten thousand pages of transcripts were produced. Most of the interviews were conducted by the three principal investigators, although a few line personnel were interviewed by experienced graduate assistants. Whenever possible, some interviewing in each county was done by two or all three principals. This enabled us to obtain firsthand impressions of one another's home jurisdictions. In addition, it provided us with the opportunity to meet at the end of the day to exchange observations from our day's experiences as well as to draw comparisons with other counties.

The aim of the interviews was to obtain as much relevant information as possible on each court system's environment and component units, as well as on organizational and personal interrelationships. Toward this end, we first interviewed all organization leaders—the head prosecutor, the chief judge, and, where applicable, the head of the public defender's office. We then scheduled interviews with line personnel—judges, prosecutors, public defenders, and those private attorneys who played a regular role in their county's felony court system. Only a handful of these individuals— all defense attorneys or public defenders—declined to be interviewed, and virtually everyone agreed to be taped. Most were refreshingly candid, and informal follow-up contacts were made with many. Finally, in some counties, formal, taped interviews were held with people outside the court system. These individuals included sheriffs, police chiefs, newspaper reporters, county board members, and members of local criminal justice commissions.

All of these interviews were semistructured. For each role, we developed a checklist of items about such things as case flows, assignment procedures, hiring or selection procedures, office or system structures and policies, and various aspects of the court's environment. Most of these items became routine midway through the interview schedule in each county. In later interviews, we tried to develop insights gained from earlier

Table 3.4. **Summary of Data, Sources, and Research Techniques Used in Study**

	Environmental Influences	Environmental Linkages	Contextual Influences	Contextual Linkages	Decision-Maker Influences	Individual Linkages	Case Attributes and Outcomes
Nature of data	Qualitative/ quantitative	Qualitative/ quantitative	Qualitative/ quantitative	Qualitative	Quantitative	Quantitative	Quantitative
Source of data	Personal interviews, census data, voting data, local newspapers, available scholarly works on characteristics of research sites	Personal interviews, voting data, local newspapers	Personal interviews, organization charts, manpower reports, "Local Legal Culture Questionnaire"	Personal interviews	"Attitudes and Views on Criminal Justice Questionnaire," "Background and Career Questionnaire," Personnel evaluations	Machiavellian scale, personnel evaluations, prosecutor and clerk files	Prosecutor and clerk files

Table 3.4 (continued)

	Environmental Influences	Environmental Linkages	Contextual Influences	Contextual Linkages	Decision-Maker Influences	Individual Linkages	Case Attributes and Outcomes
Research techniques or strategies	Development of open-ended interview check sheets, selection of personnel to be interviewed, scheduling and conduct of interviews, transcription of recorded interviews, identification of relevant works and data, subscription to and limited content analysis of local newspapers	Same as for Environmental Influences	Scheduling and conduct of interviews, identification and collection of relevant "in-house" documents	Same as for Contextual Influences	Selection of personnel to be questioned and/or evaluated; development, pretesting, and administration of questionaires and Q-sort evaluation procedure	Same as for Individual Influences	Sampling of cases, transcription of relevant data onto common data collection instrument

Table 3.5. **Summary of Data Gathered, by County**

County	Open-Ended Interviews			Attitude, Background, and Legal Culture Questionnaires			Q-Sorts of Personnel Evaluations			Defendant Case Files
	Judge	Prosecution	Defense	Judge	Prosecution	Defense	Judge	Prosecution	Defense	
DuPage	7	16	23	6	16	23	6	16	22	908
Peoria	3	7	13	2	7	13	2	7	12	1,042
St. Clair	4	7	19	4	7	17	3	7	17	1,162
Oakland	8	18	19	6	18	19	6	7	19	915
Kalamazoo	4	13	12	3	12	10	3	10	10	719
Saginaw	4	12	13	4	12	13	4	8	12	682
Montgomery	7	12	24	7	11	20	8	12	21	687
Dauphin	6	9	16	4	7	16	5	8	13	766
Erie	5	9	16	5	10	19	5	10	18	594
Total	48	103	155	41	100	150	42	85	144	7,475

discussions. Many individuals used the interview to vent their anger or frustration about various aspects of the system; this produced a number of ideas that were pursued later. We also used the interviews to challenge certain explanations of events and to offer our own interpretations, thereby generating other topics for discussion. Thus, although a common format was planned, much of what transpired in individual interviews was unique to the county, the interviewer, and the respondent. The information generated by these open-ended interviews has been examined, analyzed, and organized into nine detailed case studies published in an earlier work (Eisenstein, Nardulli, and Flemming, 1982). The information in these case studies provided us with many of the theoretical insights discussed here, and the chapters in Section II will attempt to synthesize them in a manner consistent with the format laid out in chapter 2.

More important for present purposes is an overview of the quantitative data collected on line personnel and individual cases, as well as the procedures used to collect them. Collection and utilization of these data required rigorous research strategies. A meaningful overview of the research cannot be presented without addressing the issues and problems encountered here, along with the manner in which we resolved them.

DECISION-MAKER DATA

To assess the impact of individual-level influences upon the handling of criminal cases, we collected information on the backgrounds, careers, and attitudes of criminal court practitioners. In addition, we attempted to tap dimensions of their personality, or work style, which might tell us something about how their views, beliefs, and interests translate into case outcomes in the work group dispositional process. To obtain these various pieces of information, we used several questionnaires for personal information and a Q-sort procedure for information on co-workers.

The two basic questionnaires—a "Background and Career Questionnaire" and an "Attitudes and Views on Criminal Justice Questionnaire"—were normally administered immediately after the conclusion of the open-ended interview. In some instances, these documents were completed in the presence of the interviewer; in other cases, they were completed later and either picked up by or mailed to the interviewer. Virtually everyone who was asked to complete the questionnaires complied, although some respondents did not answer all questions or failed to fill out the form correctly. The Q-sort procedure in which the practitioners were asked to evaluate one another was administered in a second, follow-up interview. At this time respondents were also asked to complete a third questionnaire,

"Attitudes and Views on the Local Criminal Court System," which provided some limited information on local court community norms.

All judges, prosecutors, and public defenders who had handled felony cases regularly during the period in which cases were selected were included in these interviews. If, for example, we had case file data on all cases disposed of during 1979 and 1980, an attempt was made to identify and interview all public practitioners who had played a regular role in the felony process during that time frame. This information was readily available from various office heads or their aides. Greater difficulties were encountered with respect to private defense attorneys and appointed counsel. In some counties, hundreds of attorneys represented at least one defendant during the sampling frame. As it was neither budgetarily possible nor practically worthwhile to interview each of these, a decision was made to interview only the most "regular" private practitioners. Where possible, we used court records and/or disposition lists to determine the identity of these attorneys. In other instances, we obtained their names from the judges and prosecutors. Subsequent checks with the case data confirmed that virtually all those private attorneys who represented a large number of defendants had been interviewed.

Backgrounds and Attitudes

The purpose of the Background and Career Questionnaire was to inventory respondents' social and political characteristics, as well as to ascertain their professional backgrounds. Questions dealt with such things as basic demographic traits, political activities, and career patterns and characteristics. This information will be useful in providing an overview of the social and political makeup of the various components of the criminal court system in each county as well as how this makeup varies across counties. The types of variables available for these inquiries are reported in Table 3.6.

The function of the first part of the Attitudes and Views on Criminal Justice Questionnaire was to elicit information on the respondents' views toward important facets of, or issues in, the criminal justice process. More specifically, we wanted to tap their views regarding such matters as due process, bail, efficiency, plea bargaining, and punishment in the criminal court setting. Toward this end, a set of attitudinal items was developed for each of the categories mentioned. These are reported in Table 3.7. Some of these questions (particularly those regarding punishment) were selected from prior studies, Hogarth (1971) in particular. However, because so little prior work existed that met the needs of this project, most questions had to be developed. A pretest was conducted in one county in each state,

Table 3.6. **Summary of Background and Career Characteristics**

Background Characteristics	Political Characteristics	Career Information			
		General	Judges	Public Attorneys	Private Attorneys
Age	Strength of partisan affiliation	Law school	Length of time on bench	Length of time with office	Length of time in local private practice
Sex	Number of times elected to public office (excluding present office)	Date of graduation	Manner of initial selection (elected or appointed)	Type of position (full or part-time)	Number of lawyers in firm
Race	Number of times appointed to public office	Number and types of bar memberships	Nature and length of prior professional experiences	Was this first job after law school?	Percent of practice devoted to local felony cases
Percent of life in county	Ever held an office in local political party?			Nature and prior professional experiences, if any	Ever a prosecutor?
Organizational memberships				Contemplates a legal career in local public sector?	Ever a public defender?

Table 3.7. **Items Employed to Tap Various Dimensions of Processual Attitudes**

Sentencing Items

Most people charged with serious crimes should be punished whether or not the punishment benefits the criminal. (P)

It is important to sentence each offender on the basis of his individual needs and not on the basis of the crime he has committed. (P)

The frequent use of probation is wrong because it has the effect of minimizing the gravity of the offense committed. (P)

Prisons should be places of punishment. (P)

The failure to punish crime amounts to giving a license to commit it. (P)

Most people are deterred from crime by the threat of heavy penalities.

Most criminal behavior is the result of forces largely beyond the control of the offender.

Our present treatment of criminals is too harsh. (P)

The most important single consideration in determining the sentence to impose should be the nature and gravity of the offense.

Plea-Bargaining Items

In practice, plea bargains produce more just outcomes than jury trials.

Defendants who save the state the expense of a trial by pleading guilty should get a break.

Jury trials more accurately determine guilt and innocence than plea bargaining.

Plea bargaining subverts the rights of defendants.

Bail Items

Most people charged with serious crimes should be kept in jail until their trial, even if they have strong ties to the community. (P)

Even with a prior record, most people with strong community ties should not be detained prior to trial. (P)

Bail should not be used to give defendants a "taste of jail."

Due Process Items

Existing Supreme Court decisions protecting the rights of defendants which jeopardize the safety of the community should be curtailed. (DP)

It is better to let 10 guilty persons go free than to convict one innocent person. (DP)

The Supreme Court's decisions of the past 20 years expanding the rights of the defendants are basically sound. (DP)

Administrative Efficiency Items

Programs designed to speed up the pace of criminal litigation inevitably produce unjust and improperly hurried resolutions of criminal cases. (E)

Most criminal court practices which interfere with the expeditious processing of criminal cases should be modified. (E)

Handling the administrative challenges involved in my criminal court work is as satisfying as handling the legal challenges.

The criminal court should be run like a business. (E)

In the handling of criminal cases efficiency is important as an end in itself. (E)

Key: P denotes item used in Belief in Punishment scale;
　　DP denotes item used in Regard for Due Process scale; and
　　E denotes item used in Concern for Efficiency scale.

and necessary revisions were made before the formulation of the final document.

The collected data were then factor analyzed to see if the various items hung together as groups in the intended manner. Three composite measures were produced. These were labeled *Belief in Punishment, Regard for Due Process,* and *Concern for Efficiency.* The items in Table 3.7 that loaded on these various factors are marked (P), (DP), and (E), respectively. A more detailed derivation is presented in Appendix I. The analysis was considered only partially successful because none of the bail or plea bargaining items hung together in the intended manner, although two of the bail items were very highly correlated with the punishment factor. It is not clear whether this failure was because of conceptual ambiguities, clumsily constructed questions, or inadequate variance in views on these subjects.

Part of the Attitudes and Views on Criminal Justice Questionnaire contained two miniversions of a Machiavellian scale.[1] This scale is generally recognized as a means of tapping a respondent's feelings about whether other people can be manipulated. "High Machs" are thought to be more apt to manipulate others to obtain desired objectives than "low Machs." These questions were included because we felt it was important to obtain a measure of the practitioners' tendencies to assert or act on their beliefs forcefully when encountering those with different beliefs or goals. This was considered crucial given the context within which most criminal court decisions are made.

The Machiavellian scale was chosen to tap these tendencies because it is relatively well established in the psychological literature, conceptually close to our needs, is not role-specific, could be reduced to a manageable format, and could be easily administered and scored. It is expected to have a number of applications in various phases of this research, especially in the examination of sentencing. For example, high Machs with distinctive views on punishment may be more cunning negotiators, and their views may be reflected in the sentence more than those of low Machs. More about this will be discussed in Section IV.

Operating Styles and the Q-Sort Procedure

In a social setting characterized by long-term interactions among a relatively small set of actors and collegial, negotiated decision making, we must know more about actors than their personal views. We must also know how each individual relates to others, as well as how they approach their role-specific tasks. Collectively we refer to these traits as the actor's operating, or work, style.

The measurement of operating styles required a very different meth-

Table 3.8. **Evaluation Questions Asked About Judges**

Question	Descriptive Qualities
1. Please indicate how familiar you are with the local judge's style and behavior in handling a criminal case.	Familiarity
2. Is it easy or difficult to talk to this judge informally with opposing counsel present about the disposition of cases?	Informality (*I*, *R*)
3. How active a role does this judge play in seeking to affect whether a case will be tried, dismissed, or pleaded?	Active (*I*)
4. Without direct information from him, how well can you predict what this judge's sentence will be in a case, merely from the offense, evidence, and defendant's characteristics?	Predictability
5. Does this judge dislike, and try to avoid, trials in every case, or does he seem to enjoy them?	Trial Preference (*I*)
6. What is your opinion of this judge's willingness to be accommodating, and to help you deal with problems and pressures you face?	Accommodativeness (*R*)
7. To what degree can this judge be pursuaded to change a decision or to accept an argument initially rejected?	Reasonableness (*R*)
8. If I were a judge, I would handle cases much the way this individual does.	Overall Assessment
9. Does this judge seem to worry about whether his docket is current, or does he seem unconcerned?	Docket Concern (*D*)

Key: *R* denotes item used in Judge's Responsiveness scale;
    I denotes item used in Judge's Involvement scale; and
    D denotes item used in Judge's Docket Concern scale.

odology. The reliability of self-reports would be questionable, at best. We therefore decided to ask co-workers about each other. After much deliberation and pretesting, we decided that a Q-sort procedure was the most feasible method.[2] A set of questions was developed that asked occupants of each role (judge, prosecutor, defense attorney) in a given county to evaluate the occupants of the other roles. Different sets of questions were asked depending upon whether the person being evaluated was a judge or an attorney (prosecutor or defense attorney). Questions asked about judges are reported in Table 3.8; questions asked about attorneys are reported in Table 3.9.[3] Most questions deal with how a person performs a specific task or relates to others in the work setting.

The Q-sort procedure produced a wealth of data, as well as a host of methodological problems. Many of these problems derived from the fact that, in its raw form, the Q-sort data comprise a large set of individual

Table 3.9. **Evaluation Questions Asked About Attorneys**

Question	Descriptive Qualities
1. For this set of attorneys, please indicate how familiar you are with their style and behavior in handling a criminal case.	Familiarity
2. What is your opinion of each individual's ability to try a case before a jury?	Trial Competence (T)
3. What is your opinion of the reliability of information about cases each gives you, and their record in keeping verbal commitments?	Trustworthiness (R)
4. What is your opinion of their willingness to be accommodating, and to. help you deal with problems and pressures you face?	Accommodativeness (R)
5. How well can you predict what each will do in handling a case?	Predictability (R)
6. How comfortable are you in discussing cases fully and frankly with an eye to a plea or other nontrial disposition with this attorney?	Informality (R)
7. My job would be much more difficult if I developed very bad personal relations with this attorney.	Importance
8. If I were an attorney (defense attorney, prosecutor) I would handle my cases and clients pretty much like this attorney does.	Overall Assessment

Key: R denotes item used in Attorney's Responsiveness scale;
    T denotes item used in Attorney's Trial Competence Scale.

evaluations on a number of different dimensions. We resolved many of the problems by producing aggregated (mean) scores for each evaluatee on each question reported in Tables 3.8 and 3.9. We produced a general mean evaluation score for each individual along with two role-specific means. For each role-specific mean, a judge, for example, would get one mean score based only on prosecutor evaluations and one based only on defense attorney evaluations. Prosecutors would get a judge-specific and a defense-attorney specific mean, etc.

The next step was to see if the set of mean evaluation scores for each of the specific questions reported in Tables 3.8 and 3.9 could be reduced to a smaller, more manageable number of measures. We first used factor analysis in conjunction with the general mean evaluation scores. This reduced the nine questions asked about judges to three variables. Two are composite variables and have been labeled *Judge's Responsiveness* and *Judge's Involvement*. A third, labeled *Judge's Docket Concern*, derives from the Docket Concern question reported in Table 3.8. The factor analysis showed it to be largely independent of the other variables; its substantive importance requires that it be used despite the fact that it is not a composite.

The Judge's Responsiveness measure derives from the questions about Informality, Accommodativeness, and Reasonableness reported in Table 3.8. The factor analysis showed that these qualities hang together quite tightly. Judges who ranked high (or low) on one, tend to rank high (or low) on the others. Judges exhibiting the three traits can reasonably be regarded as responsive to the courthouse community; they are viewed by others as flexible and reasonable in their day-to-day transactions. Moreover, more responsive judges can probably be relied upon to help dispose of cases in a manner satisfactory to all members of the courtroom work group, thus reducing uncertainty and the unnecessary expenditure of personal and system resources.

The Judge's Involvement scale evolved from the Active, Informality, and Trial Preference questions. It taps a judge's inclination to deviate from the textbook description of the judge as a passive, neutral arbiter. The most significant component of the Involvement composite is the Active variable. Judges who are evaluated as very active in affecting, or attempting to affect, the disposition of a case will score very high on this scale. Informality plays a part here too, because a judge could not maintain highly formal relations with other participants and still become integrally involved in shaping the outcome of cases. A more formal judge would either simply react to proposed pleas or dispositions, or prefer to supervise the conduct of trials. The role of the *Trial Preference* variable in the composite is not as clear-cut. It may be that judges who dislike trials believe they can have a greater impact, or at least a more meaningful impact, upon a case in a more informal setting. However, the causal relationship may in fact be the other way around; some judges may dislike trials so much that they have come to rely on the informal setting. Whichever is the case, it cannot be definitively resolved with the available data. Suffice it to say that more "involved" judges prefer to work in an informal setting.

Factor analyses performed on the attorney data revealed two independent dimensions: *Attorney Responsiveness,* a composite variable, and *Trial Competence,* which is based upon the single question concerning the trial skills of the attorney. Responsiveness measures how well attorneys relate to the social needs of co-workers. This is considered quite important for the conduct of business in an informal setting. Trial Competence indicates how others assess an attorney's formal skills, which are important for the conduct of more formal tasks. Although these two dimensions may not exhaust the concept of operating styles, they provide a good beginning by covering both formal and informal aspects of courtroom behavior.

The Attorney's Responsiveness scale comes from the Informality, Accommodativeness, Trustworthiness, and Predictability questions. The Informality and Accommodativeness questions are important because they also appeared in the construction of the Judge's Responsiveness scale. This, of course, reinforces the interpretation of responsive participants as those who structure their behavior to meet or accommodate the social and personal needs of co-workers. Trustworthiness and Predictability are simply other facets of being a responsive co-worker. Trustworthiness, or keeping one's word, is an integral part of this general trait because participants must frequently go out on a limb to get a particular plea approved, to set a particular bail, or to persuade a client to plead guilty. If a participant cannot rely upon the veracity of a co-worker, many problems, some potential embarrassment, and much additional work is created. Predictability, although it is less important than the other traits, is relevant because it reduces the need to worry about the antics or strategems of co-workers. Predictable participants will operate in a consistent manner, and co-workers can depend upon their actions.

A more detailed description of the derivation of these measures is contained in Appendix II. It also reports the results of the role-specific factor analyses, which produced a corresponding set of measures.

CASE-BASED DATA

To obtain information on case and defendant characteristics, as well as on case dispositions, we collected an extensive amount of information from the files of the prosecutors' and clerks' offices. To ensure that we obtained comparable data and to facilitate the analysis of these data, a common data collection sheet was developed. The types of data collected are presented in Table 3.10. Most of the information is fairly standard, although some of the evidence data and the information on legal motions have not been routinely employed, even in very recent studies. The real promise of these case data lies not in their uniqueness, but in the fact that they are available from a number of very different jurisdictions. Moreover, they exist in conjunction with other data on the characteristics of those responsible for the case's disposition.

A problem that was as difficult as deciding what data to collect was the question of how it should be collected. We wanted to collect data on comparable samples in each jurisdiction. In addition, for each county, we wanted to sample a large number of cases during a time frame in which the practitioners we interviewed handled a large number of cases. These requirements presented a number of problems. Illinois, for example, has a unified court system with information readily available on lower court and trial court proceedings. Michigan and Pennsylvania have separate systems with separate record-keeping systems. Moreover, in some counties recent elections led to large-scale personnel turnover in the prosecutor's

Table 3.10. **Examples of Data Collected from Case Files**

Case Characteristics	Defendant Characteristics	Intermediate Process Characteristics	Case Outcome Variables
Charge Common code for each stage of proceedings	Social Age, race, sex, marital status,* occupation,* education,* employment status*	Delay Total and intermediate delays	Bail outcomes Type, amount, size and direction of any bail change, pretrial release status
Seriousness Type and use of weapon, nature of injury, amount of stolen/damaged property, amount of drugs involved	Criminal history Number of prior arrests, convictions, jail or penitentiary commitments; present probation or parole status; number of other pending indictments	Legal motions Number, type, outcome Prosecutor's initial plea offer* Type of plea, sentence offered	Type of disposition Dismissal, trial, guilty plea, etc.
Evidence Availability of statement, proceeds, polygraph results, weapon, etc.		Identity of judge, prosecutor, defense attorney At bail, lower court disposition,* trial court disposition, sentence	Sentence Type, length, amount of costs, etc.
Victim characteristics Type of victim, age,* sex,* race,* existence of prior relationship with defendant*			

* Indicates that this information was not available in every jurisdiction.

offices. This required us to pursue a different sampling frame than we would have used if the offices had been more stable. It also reduced the number of available cases that met our needs.

Table 3.11 summarizes some of the characteristics of the case samples in each county. Systemwide samples were available only in the Illinois counties. In the other states, all of the sample cases were disposed of by the trial courts; those disposed of at the lower court level were not included. This will require some adjustment when certain statistical comparisons are made; we simply exclude the Illinois cases disposed of at the preliminary hearing. As the selection criteria presented in Table 3.11 show, the universe of cases disposed of during a designated period of time was the sampling frame in most counties. In Oakland County, the universe of cases disposed of by one division of the circuit judges was selected, while in Montgomery County, every other case for a nine-month period was selected. In Kalamazoo, no diversion cases could be accessed, but we obtained an estimate of the number of diverted cases for the five-year period preceding the study. It revealed that approximately 21 percent of the defendants that made it through the prosecutor's initial screen were admitted to a diversion program. This figure was fairly stable and will be used to adjust Kalamazoo sentencing data where needed. In Dauphin County, every third accelerated rehabilitative disposition (ARD) case was selected, which meant that a weighting scheme had to be used to obtain the proper representation of these diversion cases. Missing ARD cases in Erie were less of a problem, but they were random, and no weights could be calculated to adjust for them. In every county but Saginaw the only cases selected were those that were already completed. In Saginaw, all cases bound over by the lower court were selected, which meant that some cases remained open at the completion of our fieldwork.

In Michigan and Pennsylvania, the determination of which cases met the selection criteria was made on the basis of a list produced by the clerk or prosecutor's office. In Peoria and St. Clair, completed cases were sequentially filed in separate files for each year. Coders simply worked backward through the files for the designated time period. In DuPage, workers had to use a list of all cases introduced into the system at the preliminary hearing level. The files of many of the cases on that list could not be found, indicating that the cases were still in the system or that the files were lost. A similar problem was encountered in Kalamazoo. The impact of these missing cases upon the representativeness of the sample is not known, but the types of offenses involved suggest that it was a fairly random occurrence.

The last row in Table 3.11 refers to the procedure used to determine whether a defendant had any other pending indictments—resulting from independent arrest encounters—at the time the sampled case was com-

Table 3.11. **Overview of Sampling Procedures Used in Selected Counties**

	DuPage	Peoria	St. Clair	Oakland	Kalamazoo	Saginaw	Montgomery	Dauphin	Erie
Sample type	Felony system sample (includes felonies disposed of at both preliminary hearing and trial court level)	Felony system sample (includes felonies disposed of at both preliminary hearing and trial court level)	Felony system sample (includes felonies disposed of at both preliminary hearing and trial court level)	Felony trial court sample	Felony trial court sample	Felony trial court sample	Felony trial court sample	Felony trial court sample	Felony trial court sample
Selection criteria	All felony cases disposed of between Jan. 1978 and May 1980	The last 1,042 cases disposed of before May 1980	The last 1,162 cases disposed of before May 1980	All trial court cases disposed of by one of 7 judges, in "Division I," between July 1979 and June 1980	All trial court cases disposed of between July 1979 and June 1980	All trial court cases arraigned and bound over in District Court between July 1979 and June 1980	All trial court cases disposed of between Jan. 1980 and Oct. 1980; every other case selected	All trial court cases disposed of between Jan. 1980 and Oct. 1980, except ARD cases; every third ARD case selected	All trial court cases disposed of between Jan. 1980 and Oct. 1980

Table 3.11 (continued)

	DuPage	Peoria	St. Clair	Oakland	Kalamazoo	Saginaw	Montgomery	Dauphin	Erie
Status of case when sampled	Closed	Closed	Closed	Closed	Closed	Open	Closed	Closed	Closed
Source of information used to identify eligible cases	Clerk's listing of all cases were initiated between Jan. 1978 and May 1980	Prosecutor files of completed cases were sequentially ordered	Prosecutor files of completed cases were sequentially ordered	Printout of closed quarterly reports of assigned defense attorneys	PRO-MIS* list of closed cases	District Court preliminary hearing schedule, prosecutor	Prosecutor's office's list of completed cases	Trial list, miscellaneous court list (guilty plea cases) ARD list	Trial list, arraignment list

* Prosecutor's Management Information System

pleted. To determine systematically the existence of other pending indictments, coders in each jurisdiction checked the defendant's name in an
alphabetical file used to record the local criminal history of all defendants
recently processed within the county. DuPage County had no such file,
but this information was contained in a memo prepared for each case by
the prosecutor.

A final point should be stressed regarding the sampling procedure.
Defendants were sampled, not cases. If defendants were indicted separately
on a string of charges arising from the same occurrence, these were simply
treated as additional charges, not additional cases. This was done to maintain
comparability across jurisdictions, because charging practices vary considerably across prosecutors. Also, this procedure is necessary to obtain a
realistic measure of what happened to a defendant. Dismissals of "string
indictments" are not very meaningful if the defendants also plead guilty
to a charge.

MEASURES OF CASE AND DEFENDANT ATTRIBUTES

Most of the measures of case and/or defendant attributes did not
require computations. Such things as age, race, sex, prior relationship with
victim, type of injury, existence of a statement, and availability of physical
evidence were coded directly from the file data. Data on offenses were
coded directly from the case files. However, before a common offense
code for the three state codes could be constructed, a good deal of analysis
of certain offenses was required. Some state codes break down offenses
such as aggravated assault, battery, theft, forgery, and drug violation, into
a variety of separate offenses. Not all of these categories are meaningfully
different to local decision makers. For these troublesome offenses we used
such things as statutory descriptions and average sentences to create as
simple a set of offense categories as possible. The result was approximately
forty discrete categories, with only a handful of cases coded "miscellaneous." Not all counties or states had cases in each category.

One defendant attribute that required extensive analysis was the
severity of the defendant's criminal record. We had independent measures
of prior arrests, convictions, jail commitments, and penitentiary commitments. However, these were highly intercorrelated. A factor analysis revealed that various measures could be reduced to one composite measure.[4]
Although this is a more abstract measure of prior record, it summarizes
a good deal of information and facilitates complex, multivariate analyses.
Thus, the composite measure as well as a trichotomized version of it will
normally be used in the empirical analyses to be reported in Sections III
and IV.[5]

One final case-level measure that required a good deal of analysis and calculation was the derivation of offense seriousness, which is always challenging because statutorily defined measures are usually too crude. Moreover, they seldom correspond to the county-specific norms that actually prevail in most county court systems. These problems are compounded here by the existence of three different criminal codes, nine different sets of norms, and the need for a single measure of offense seriousness across all offenses and counties. Our solution was to construct a set of dummy offense variables for each offense that was represented in an appreciable number of cases. The dummy variables for the most serious offense at the sentencing stage were then entered into a regression equation for each county (using all sentenced defendants in that county) with minimum jail time (probation coded as 0) as the dependent variable. The results of these nine equations ($A + B1 * DUMMY1 + B2 * DUMMY2 +.....+ Bn * DUMMYn$) were then used in conjunction with the case's county to assign an offense seriousness score for each case. The score assigned to each offense is equivalent to the mean score accorded defendants convicted on that offense in a given county.

A second version of the offense seriousness measure was computed by using all sentenced cases in the nine counties—as opposed to individual county samples—to derive the offense weights. These pooled or grand scores do not show county-specific norms, but they do permit us to control for offense seriousness when we want to determine the impact of county characteristics upon the sentencing process.[6]

The sites, data, and procedures just outlined comprise the raw material from which we will mold our analyses of the guilty plea process. Before we present them, however, it will be fruitful to use some of these data to explore in more detail the environmental and contextual characteristics of our counties. This will set the stage for the empirical analyses. More important, it will add flesh to the skeletal theoretical structure we introduced in chapter 2 and enhance our understanding of how criminal courts operate. It is to be hoped that later researchers will use and develop the insights from this chapter—as well as those in Section II—not only to guide their data gathering and concept formation, but also to help in site selection. This will facilitate the development of more enlightened comparative studies, thereby enriching even further our understanding of how these courts operate.

NOTES

1. See Christie and Geiss (1970). Of the several versions of the Machiavellian scale available, two were used here. First, eight items from the full Mach IV

scale were chosen on the basis of their patterns of correlation in prior studies. In addition, six sets of questions were chosen from the Mach V version of the scale. It is different in format from the Mach IV since respondents face a triadic choice among socially undesirable alternatives. It is hoped that this will mitigate the bias toward socially desirable alternatives. It has been termed a "Machiavellian" Mach scale.

2. In a Q-sort procedure a respondent is given a set of cards or objects and is asked to sort or categorize them according to certain criteria or rules.

3. The actual procedure used here was as follows: Each of the questions reported in Tables 3.8 and 3.9 was printed on a colored sheet of paper. The sheet of paper also had a scale from 1 to 5 on it, with directions concerning which characteristics were to be given high and low scores. Each sheet of paper was presented to each evaluator, one at a time. The evaluator was also given a set of color-coded index cards, which matched the color of the paper on which the question was printed. Each index card had the name of an evaluatee. The evaluator was then asked to rank each individual on the dimension in question by dropping the color-coded index card with the individual's name on it into a slotted "ballot box." The slots were marked from 1 to 5; in addition there was one "Don't Know" slot. The evaluator was given a separate set of colored index cards for each question. The responses were then coded with the evaluator as the unit of analysis. The variables for each respondent corresponded to that evaluator's assessment of each evaluatee on each of 8 or 9 questions.

4. The results of the factor analysis used to compute the "Criminal Record" variable are reported below. They show a strong, simple factor solution which yields a straightforward interpretation. The factor score for a given case is computed by summing its scores on the weighted standardized variables (weights = factor loadings) used in the factor analysis.

Table 3.12. **Results of Factor Analyses for Criminal Record Variable**

Variable	Factor Loading
Prior arrests	.68
Prior penitentiary commitments	.64
Prior convictions	.93
Prior jail commitments	.76
Eigenvalue	2.3

5. An analysis of the composite criminal record variable revealed that about half of all defendants were first offenders, and these defendants were given a score of 1 on the trichotomized version of the scale. The other defendants were evenly split into a less and more serious offender category.

6. A few comments should be made regarding these procedures. First, while some may view the use of a variable containing mean sentences for a given offense (especially in an analysis of sentencing) as "circular," the results are

identical (by definition) to using a dummy offense variable approach—which is considered entirely legitimate and "noncircular." And, like the traditional dummy variable approach, it allows us to control for the effect of offense so that the effects of other, more theoretically interesting variables can be confidently examined. It differs from the dummy variable approach in one important respect: it is more economical and flexible. It permits us to control for offense seriousness with one variable that can then be employed in an interactive statistical model. This is essential for our analysis. It also provides us with information needed to assign seriousness scores to each charge in a case. In this instance we had seriousness scores for as many as three charges at four stages (arrest, preliminary hearing, indictment, and sentencing). The approach used here is extremely conservative in controlling for offense seriousness, especially for a sentencing analysis. It permits offense to explain as much variance as possible before other types of variables are permitted to enter into the equation.

REFERENCES

Christie, Richard and F. L. Geis. 1970. *Studies in Machiavellianism.* New York: Academic Press.

Eisenstein, James, Peter F. Nardulli, and Roy B. Flemming. April 1982. "Explaining and Assessing Criminal Case Disposition: A Comparative Study of Nine Counties." Final report submitted to the National Institute of Justice (Grant 79-N1-AX-0062).

Hogarth, John. 1971. *Sentencing as a Human Process.* Toronto: University of Toronto Press.

II

THE SETTING

4

THE ECOLOGY OF CRIMINAL COURTS: AN OVERVIEW OF ENVIRONMENTAL SETTINGS

Progress toward an integrated perspective on criminal courts requires that we delve more deeply into the various types of influences (environmental, contextual, individual) affecting their operations. Chapter 1 identified the research sites we studied as well as the reasons for their selection, while chapter 2 sketched a skeletal outline of relevant environmental factors. Neither discussion, however, provides us with the scope and richness of information necessary to enhance our understanding of how environmental influences shape criminal court processes and outcomes. This information is essential in trying to make sense of the patterns of results to be presented in the next section and weave them into an overall picture of how courts operate. Thus, we stop here to lay out in more detail the environmental landscapes that surrounded our nine court communities. Chapters 5 and 6 provide an overview of important contextual features, while a discussion of individual-level factors is postponed until Section IV.[1]

The discussion here will blend insights culled from hundreds of hours of taped interviews and extensive observations with a variety of hard data on important aspects of the court system's operating environment. We will first examine briefly the socioeconomic and political characteristics of the nine communities. Next, we will review crime trends, detention facilities, and, finally, provide an overview of statewide sentencing codes and practices.

Most of these features can be thought of as relevant to our under-standing of how courts operate. But it should be stressed at the outset that environmental factors are, in many ways, the most difficult to deal with in the study of criminal courts. This is in part due to the amorphous and indirect nature of environmental influences. Assessing the impact upon criminal court operations of a diversified economy, heterogeneous community, and a multidimensional political culture presents different analytic problems than analyzing such factors as docket type, a defendant's race, or the attitudes of the judge. Environmental factors tend to be more difficult to identify, measure, and chart. Moreover, their impact is often on aspects of court systems (personnel selection and physical facilities) that researchers have not studied very much.

The assessment of environmental influences also presents formidable problems in the area of research design and implementation. Examining their impact requires data on a large number of sites, which is costly in both monetary and human terms. Because prior research has not told us very much about these factors, it is even difficult to determine what characteristics to vary in selecting the courts we should study. As a consequence of these various problems, the role of environmental influences is largely uncharted. Researchers have either ignored the possible effect of externalities or, almost as an afterthought, they have attributed what they cannot explain to broad, largely undefined, and unmeasured environmental influences (e.g., political culture and local sentiment).

In attempting to deal with environmental factors in this context, we chose a pragmatic approach. We simply selected three sets of counties that differed on some very basic dimensions. We believed that the basic differences in these counties would lead to variance in other important areas, even though it was not initially clear to us what those other areas would be. As our interviewing and preliminary quantitative analyses progressed, the other areas became clearer. It also became clear that, although our site-selection strategy did produce important differences in some areas, it produced less variance in others. Moreover, the differences do not always fit as neatly into the ring-autonomous-declining categorizations as one might expect, as the following discussions will show.

SOCIOECONOMIC AND POLITICAL CHARACTERISTICS

We start our discussion by focusing on the ring counties. Of these, it is helpful to begin with DuPage and Montgomery. They are the best match (from an environmental perspective) among the three ring counties, and typify the type of sprawling suburban setting we were trying to capture in the selection of the ring counties. This can be seen in different ways by examining Tables 4.1 and 4.2, and comparing the data on DuPage

Table 4.1. **Demographic Data**

	DuPage (Ring)	Peoria (Autonomous)	St. Clair (Declining)	Oakland (Ring)	Kalamazoo (Autonomous)	Saginaw (Declining)	Montgomery (Ring)	Dauphin (Autonomous)	Erie (Declining)
Population (1980)	658,835	200,177	267,531	1,011,793	212,378	228,059	643,621	232,317	279,780
Percent population changes									
1960–70	56.5	3.32	8.80	31.53	18.76	15.20	20.80	1.60	5.17
1970–80	35.02	2.64	−6.32	11.45	5.37	3.78	3.13	3.85	6.12
Percent black in 1980	1.17	10.73	27.53	4.74	7.46	15.7	4.80	13.46	4.44

Source: U. S. Bureau of the Census, Table 2 (1977); Table B (1983).

Table 4.2. Characteristics of the Major Cities in Each County

	DuPage (Ring)	Peoria (Autonomous)	St. Clair (Declining)	Oakland (Ring)	Kalamazoo (Autonomous)	Saginaw (Declining)	Montgomery (Ring)	Dauphin (Autonomous)	Erie (Declining)
Total number of incorporated localities	39	15	32	44	10	8	41	22	14
Incorporated localities over 5,000 in population	33	9	5	21	2	1	7	3	3
Major city	Wheaton	Peoria	East St. Louis	Pontiac	Kalamazoo	Saginaw	Norristown	Harrisburg	Erie
Population of major city, 1980	42,772	123,591	54,966	76,270	79,568	77,384	32,891	53,113	118,964
Percent of county's population residing in major city	6.5	62	21	7.6	37.5	34	5	23	42.6
Percent of county's black population residing in major city	13.7	96	72	59.5	78.5	77	25	74.2	93.2

Source: U. S. Bureau of the Census, Table D (1983).

and Montgomery with the others. They are among the largest counties, surpassed only by Oakland, and both have very small, stable black populations. If we look at Table 4.2 we can see even more clearly the diffuse, suburban structure of these counties. Both are characterized by a large number of municipalities (39 in DuPage, 41 in Montgomery). Even though DuPage's cities tend to be generally somewhat larger than Montgomery's, neither has a major, dominating city. Wheaton, the largest city in DuPage, has only 6.5 percent of the county population; Norristown constitutes only 5 percent of Montgomery's population.

This lack of a major central focus in the county inhibited the emergence of a major newspaper with countywide clout, or indeed any type of a paper with a countywide circulation. As Table 4.3 makes clear, neither DuPage nor Montgomery has any major newspaper or any local television station that has a locally oriented news bureau. This media vacuum is accentuated by the dominance of Chicago and Philadelphia, which overshadow the counties in important ways. Most coverage of local events in the metropolitan area focuses on the central city, even though suburban coverage is on the increase compared with a decade ago. No one interviewed in these counties felt that local media were an important source of influence. Moreover, the absence of any dominant law enforcement agency compounds the political insularity of the court community and strengthens the hand of the court community in setting criminal justice policy.

The relatively invisibility of county government, including the court community, is due to the ring status of these counties. This status, however, led to a different type of pressure, one that is internally generated. With a remarkable similarity in language, court actors in both DuPage and Montgomery evidenced a desire to be "not like Chicago" or Philadelphia. They also strongly asserted that they *were* not like their neighboring megalopolis. They stressed their commitment to good, clean government that operated on nonpartisan, businesslike principles. This was an important, defining characteristic of the two court communities that led them to be very careful about appearances and led them to stress the differences between them and their urban neighbors.

Table 4.4 reports some data on economic measures that underscore the relative affluence of DuPage and Montgomery. They ranked second and third in terms of average per capita money income and had the lowest level of AFDC recipients (per one hundred thousand population) of all nine counties. This latter figure indicates the lack of any discernible underclass in these counties. In conjunction with the data on racial composition these economic data support the thesis that these counties were relatively homogeneous.

Finally, we turn to some data on the political environment in these

Table 4.3. **Levels of Media Concentration**

	DuPage (Ring)	Peoria (Autonomous)	St. Clair (Declining)	Oakland (Ring)	Kalamazoo (Autonomous)	Saginaw (Declining)	Montgomery (Ring)	Dauphin (Autonomous)	Erie (Declining)
Number of commercial television stations in county	0	3	0	2*	1	1	0	3	3
Number of newspapers with countywide circulation	0**	1	2	0**	1	1	0**	1	1

* Although the broadcast facilities of two stations are located in Oakland, the county is not the focus of local news coverage.

** Several community papers exist, but the market is dominated by major metropolitan papers (Chicago, Detroit, or Philadelphia).

Table 4.4. **Selected Measures of Economic Well-Being**

	DuPage (Ring)	Peoria (Autonomous)	St. Clair (Declining)	Oakland (Ring)	Kalamazoo (Autonomous)	Saginaw (Declining)	Montgomery (Ring)	Dauphin (Autonomous)	Erie (Declining)
Per capita income, 1979	$10,495	$8,388	$6,550	$10,675	$7,776	$7,263	$9,764	$7,581	$6,680
Public assistance recipients (per 100,000 population), Feb. 1980	713	4,689	12,409	3,202	5,838	9,778	1,569	5,165	5,361

Source: U. S. Bureau of the Census, Table B (1983).

counties. As one might guess from their socioeconomic makeup, citizens in DuPage and Montgomery are very Republican in terms of their political affiliation, as Table 4.5 makes quite clear. Because of the difficulties in accurately gauging partisan affiliation, we report several very different indicators of affiliation (percent of elected county, state, and federal officials for selected positions who were Republicans). DuPage and Montgomery score high on every measure and are the most consistently Republican of the nine counties. As one might guess from these figures, both DuPage and Montgomery had very powerful and active local Republican organizations. What is not evident is that although DuPage's was highly decentralized, Montgomery's was very centralized—a difference that, as we will see, had important implications for their respective court communities.

The effect of these strong parties can be seen in their level of political competition. Political competition, like media concentration, affects the insularity of county government. As there is again no single, widely acceptable measure of political competitiveness, we use data on the margin of victory in the three most recent elections (for the period ending in 1980) for a variety of state and county offices. These are reported in Table 4.6, along with the average margin of victory across all elections. As these data make clear, DuPage, and to a lesser extent Montgomery, have very low levels of political competition in general elections. For example, the average margins (row 7) range from 11 percent to 32 percent, with DuPage evidencing the least competitive elections. Montgomery was tied with Dauphin and Kalamazoo for the next least competitive, with an average margin of victory of 24 percent. This again underscores both the lack of electoral pressure in these counties and the relative homogeneity of their population.

One final political measure we examine is the general political views or ideology of the county's populace. Even though Republicans are generally more conservative than Democrats, we must be careful in not reading too much about ideology into high levels of political affiliation with one party or another, especially at the local level. A very strong Democratic county may well have elected leaders who are fairly conservative on many matters. A county's Republican leaders may be well entrenched simply because of their moderate views. The most direct approach to gauging general political views would be a specially designed survey of county citizens. Because such a survey was beyond available resources, we resorted to two more indirect approaches.

The first takes the liberal and conservative rankings of the voting records of each county's U.S. representative in Congress, for the sessions between 1971 and 1980 (the 92nd through the 96th Congress). Using a procedure outlined in Appendix III, two ideological rankings (ACA, ADA)

Table 4.5. **Party Affiliation Measures by County**

	DuPage (Ring)	Peoria (Autono-mous)	St. Clair (Declin-ing)	Oakland (Ring)	Kalamazoo (Autono-mous)	Saginaw (Declin-ing)	Mont-gomery (Ring)	Dauphin (Autono-mous)	Erie (Declin-ing)
Percent of elected county executive officers who were Republican, 1977*	100	66	22	83	100	50	86	86	44
Percent of time that county voters cast a majority of votes for the Republican candidate in state representative elections (last 3 elections)*	97	66	64	75	100	75	85	83	46
Percent of time county voters cast a majority of votes for the Republican candidate in federal elections (1972–80)**	100	91	18	75	64	64	100	82	64
Overall categorization	Strong Repub-lican	Repub-lican	Demo-cratic	Repub-lican	Repub-lican	Repub-lican	Strong Repub-lican	Strong Repub-lican	Weak Demo-cratic

* Data derived from official reports of vote results in the various states.

Table 4.6. **Political Competitiveness Measures for Selected Elections**

	DuPage (Ring)	Peoria (Autono-mous)	St. Clair (Declin-ing)	Oakland (Ring)	Kalamazoo (Autono-mous)	Saginaw (Declin-ing)	Mont-gomery (Ring)	Dauphin (Autono-mous)	Erie (Declin-ing)
Average margin of victory (per-cent) in last three elections for:									
Statewide candi-dates									
Governor	49	22	9	21	24	6	12	16	10
Senator	25	15	23	11	11	11	28	28	11
Legislative district candidates									
Representative	29	1	16	9	25	2	23.8	22	11
Senator	32	10	30	11*	36*	48*	31	23**	8*
Countywide crim-inal justice offices									
Sheriff	20	37	3	10	22	22	25	21	3
Prosecutor	35	18	20	25	25	12	25	32**	22
Overall average margin	32	17	17	15	24	17	24	24	11

* Indicates results of only one election reported.

** Indicates results of only two elections reported.

Source: Scammon and McGillivray (1973, 1975, 1979, 1981); telephone and mail surveys to various county offices.

were used to compute a conservativism measure for each county, one that is weighted by the percent of the vote given to the representative in the county, since a low level of support would indicate less ideological agreement than a high level. The second measure was the average support given to conservative candidates in ideological elections (Goldwater in 1964; Nixon and Wallace in 1968; Nixon in 1972; Reagan in 1980). Table 4.7 shows data on the average support given conservative presidential candidates in ideological elections and the more involved weighted conservatism scores. The voting totals and the conservativism scores were fairly similar, as indicated by the rank orderings for each measure; they were used to produce an overall categorization. Here again, DuPage and Montgomery are both similarly ranked at one end of the continuum. Along with Peoria, they are the most conservative counties.

The strong geographical, demographic, and political similarities between DuPage and Montgomery should not be allowed to obscure some important differences that exist and have important implications for the court system. The most important of these for present purposes is the marked differences in the growth rate of the two counties, as can be seen in Table 4.1. While DuPage has grown dramatically over the past two decades (growth rates of 56 percent and 35 percent), Montgomery has remained fairly stable, especially for the decade that directly proceeded our study. Although this has many social and economic implications, the most relevant one for present purposes is political. The influx of outsiders in DuPage did not challenge the supremacy of the local Republican party, but it did cause strains within it. These differences permeated the court system and had important consequences for the atmosphere of the court community. DuPage's growth had turned it into the dominant Republican stronghold within the state. Stakes were quite high for the local Republican leaders, and this led to fierce intra-party struggles for political control. Thus, while the party was centralized and relatively homogeneous in Montgomery, DuPage was decentralized and factionalized.

Oakland County was, by far, the largest of the counties we studied, totaling about one million people in 1980 (Table 4.1). While it was one of our three ring counties, being adjacent to Detroit, it did not fit the mold quite as well as the other two. The media vacuum that existed in Oakland is the most important shared characteristic with the other suburban counties. It was covered by Detroit television and had no countywide dailies (Table 4.3). However, Oakland was much more diverse than DuPage and Montgomery. This is, in some respects, epitomized by the fact that Oakland County spanned two congressional districts, one represented by a liberal Democrat and the other by a fairly conservative Republican. Oakland has swank suburbs such as Bloomfield Hills, but it also includes Pontiac, an industrial city of more than 75,000. Although, like DuPage

Table 4.7. **Political Conservatism Scores by County**

	DuPage (Ring)	Peoria (Autonomous)	St. Clair (Declining)	Oakland (Ring)	Kalamazoo (Autonomous)	Saginaw (Declining)	Montgomery (Ring)	Dauphin (Autonomous)	Erie (Declining)
Weighted conservatism score (weighted by proportion of vote received in county in election following the session for which voting was ranked)*	38.7 (3)	47 (2)	−31 (9)	13.6 (5)	10.3 (6)	−2.6 (7)	47.6 (1)	18.3 (4)	−16.5 (8)
Averaged vote percent for conservative presidential candidate(s) in "ideological" elections (1980, 1972, 1968, 1964)*	68 (1)	55 (4)	43 (9)	53 (5 tie)	53 (5 tie)	51 (7)	56 (3)	60 (2)	46 (8)
Overall categorization	Conservative	Conservative	Moderately liberal	Moderate	Moderate	Moderate	Conservative	Moderate	Moderately liberal

* Rank orderings are in parentheses below the data entry.

and Montgomery, Oakland had a large number of municipalities (44), 21 percent of its population lived in Pontiac, which contained almost 60 percent of Oakland's minority population (Table 4.2). Many of the municipalities in Oakland were blue-collar towns that cropped up during the early to mid part of this century to provide Detroit's industrial workers with adequate but modest housing. These various data suggest that in many respects Oakland lies somewhere between the ring counties and some of the autonomous counties. This is reinforced by the economic data reported in Table 4.4. While Oakland had the highest median per capita income in 1979, it also had a considerably higher rate of public assistance recipients than DuPage and Montgomery, a rate that placed it between them and the three autonomous counties.

Oakland also differed from the other two ring counties politically. Its overall political views were more moderate, but this is largely due to the existence of two very different political communities within the county, as reflected in the different postures of the two congressmen representing Oakland (Table 4.7). Elections were also more competitive in Oakland (Table 4.6) than the other two ring counties. Even though it was largely a Republican county (Table 4.5), the party was not nearly as dominant an influence in county affairs as it was in DuPage and Montgomery. The county board was composed of sixteen Republicans and eleven Democrats, and the county had, in recent history, elected a Democratic sheriff and prosecutor. Another important contrast between Oakland and the other two ring counties is that in Oakland the court community members were not as preoccupied with Detroit as their counterparts were with their respective central cities. Part of the reason for this is that Oakland did not appear to be threatened by Detroit and Wayne County. Indeed, for a variety of reasons, not the least of which were migration patterns and economic and social problems in Detroit, many members of the court community in Oakland felt it was only a matter of time before it eclipsed Wayne County as the premiere county in Michigan.

A number of stark contrasts in the court community's environment can be seen between the ring counties and the autonomous counties. In Peoria, which was not even a third as populous as DuPage and Montgomery (Table 4.1), the court community operated in a fishbowl as three television stations, a number of radio stations, and a very powerful, conservative, countywide daily focused on it (Table 4.3). These media were, of course, centered in the city of Peoria, which contained 62 percent of the county population and almost all its black population (Table 4.2). The city of Peoria also provided the court system with more than 80 percent of its cases, making the Peoria chief of police a major figure within the county criminal justice system, one who could gather considerable media attention and whose policies could drastically affect the operation of the court community.

While Peoria seems every bit as ideologically conservative as DuPage and Montgomery, and more so than Oakland (Table 4.7), it is not quite as Republican in its voting patterns (Table 4.5). This competitiveness is reflected in the relatively low average margin of victory in selected elections — 17 percent as contrasted with 32 percent in DuPage and 24 percent in Montgomery (Table 4.6). Moreover, this 17 percent figure probably understates the level of political competitiveness at the county level. There was no single dominant local party, as existed in DuPage and Montgomery. This can be seen clearly within the court community as one of the two criminal court judges was a Democrat, the other a Republican. The head prosecutor was a Republican but was replaced in the year after our fieldwork by a Democrat; the circuit clerk was a Democrat but was replaced by a Republican.

This level of political competition, along with the media concentration in Peoria, strengthened the linkages between the court community and its environment, making that linkage quite different from that which existed in the ring counties, especially DuPage and Montgomery. The close linkage between government and its political environment is a defining characteristic of Peoria. An equally important, but more nebulous, characteristic is a deeply felt sense of civic pride that many Peorians evince, one that borders on civic boosterism. The city of Peoria underwent a significant government reform movement during the early fifties, one that transformed its corrupt and inefficient government tradition and won it acclaim as a model city. This tradition had been perpetuated by its elite and is an important influence upon city and county government, including the criminal court system.

The civic pride so strongly felt by Peorians is a result of its relative cosmopolitanism, a stable industrial base, and tradition of producing political leaders. Bradley University and a medical campus of the University of Illinois are located in Peoria, as is the world headquarters of the Caterpillar Corporation. It is also a medical, legal, and financial center for the area. These attractions have brought diverse sets of individuals into Peoria, including a large contingent of middle-management personnel and professionals.

The caliber of Peoria's political and bureaucratic leadership is evident outside as well as within the court system. The mayor of Peoria is a past president of the U.S. Conference of Mayors as well as a respected Republican leader in the state. In 1980, he ran for the Republican nomination for U.S. Senator. Peoria's congressional representative is the Republican minority leader in the House, and Everett McKinley Dirksen was from nearby Pekin. The chief judge is a former chairman of the ABA research committee, a former U.S. attorney under President Johnson, and a member of the Illinois Law Enforcement Commission's advisory panel. The state's attorney has a statewide reputation in law enforcement circles, has sat on a number of statewide commissions, and enjoys the genuine respect and admiration of local officials. The chief of police in Peoria is one of the most respected in the state. He is the former director of the Illinois Law Enforcement Commission, a member of a U.N. panel on crime and criminal justice, and is very active in national police organizations.

Kalamazoo County is similar to Peoria in several respects but differs in others. They are about the same size, around two hundred thousand, and have about the same size minority population, almost 8 percent compared to Peoria's 11 percent (Table 4.1). Despite this, Kalamazoo has only one local television station compared to Peoria's three. The city of Kalamazoo is only about two-thirds as large as the city of Peoria and constitutes somewhat less than 40 percent of the county population. Nonetheless, it is still the social, political, and cultural center of the county and dominates it almost as much as Peoria dominates Peoria County. Like Peoria, Kalamazoo is a largely Republican county, especially at the county level (Table 4.5). The level of political competition is greater in Peoria than Kalamazoo, which is actually quite similar to Montgomery (Table 4.6). Despite this, no strong local Republican party existed in Kalamazoo. Kalamazoo is more moderate on our ideological ranking than Peoria (Table 4.7).

This mixed statistical picture notwithstanding, a visitor to Kalamazoo would find many general similarities to Peoria, especially between the two major cities. The city of Kalamazoo is a progressive community with a diversified economy composed of various sectors, including a large paper and chemical complex. It also has a state university and a reputable liberal arts college. These attractions coupled with a pleasant geographical setting, a performing arts center, an art museum, and a relatively new enclosed shopping mall make Kalamazoo a magnet community attracting a large number of professionals, scientists, and business people. Many move into Kalamazoo's older sections, gentrifying neighborhoods that otherwise might have deteriorated. All of this has led to an inordinate amount of civic pride and what has been termed a public-regarding ethos. Within this ethos, government and politics are viewed as appropriate vehicles to serve community purposes; the pursuance of individualized, personal ends and interests are not viewed as acceptable. This, of course, leads to pressure on government to operate on sound, rational, businesslike principles. Graft, chicanery, and politics should play no role in government operations, including the judiciary.

The *Kalamazoo Gazette,* the county's principal newspaper, is a principal booster of the community. It views itself as a responsible newspaper that eschews sensationalism and is less ideologically strident than the *Peoria Journal Star*. In some ways it views itself as an ally of government in maintaining Kalamazoo's image and tradition rather than its adversary. In one incident, it turned over information on a police scandal to the police department to have the corrupt officers removed rather than sensation-alizing the event. Its editorials also helped achieve the peaceful desegre-gation of Kalamazoo's schools, while nearby Pontiac experienced a great deal of turmoil. These policies extend into the *Gazette*'s coverage of courts and crime. It covers these topics at about the same level as the other papers in the autonomous and declining counties but does not sensationalize them. Its court reporter was more of a member of the court community than an outsider; he showed little interest in unnecessarily rocking the boat. In this sense, the Kalamazoo court community was probably more insulated than Peoria's, especially with respect to day-to-day activities.

Although Dauphin County is about the same size as Peoria and Kalamazoo (Table 4.1), is dominated by its largest city, Harrisburg (Table 4.2), and is saturated with media (three television stations and one coun-tywide newspaper, Table 4.3), it differs from the other two autonomous counties in important regards. It is far more heterogeneous on a social level and, most important, does not share the political orientation that so characterized Peoria and Kalamazoo. In many ways the city of Harrisburg is similar to the cities that dominate the declining counties, especially Saginaw and Erie. It stands apart from the suburban and rural communities that surround it. It is a center for vice and crime, has a sizable underclass, deteriorating neighborhoods, and declining industries. In the words of one private defense attorney, "People used to think, 'Oh, this used to be a nice city.' And it just died. It's not a nice city now. Maybe it was in the past. To me it's a toilet. I have as little to do with Harrisburg as I can."

At the same time, however, Harrisburg is the state capital of Penn-sylvania, a fact that lends the city a cosmopolitan tone and attracts many outsiders to the community, such as other features bring newcomers to Kalamazoo and Peoria. Even though our electoral data indicate that Dau-phin is strongly Republican and not very competitive, several observers noted that the influx of Democrats brought in by various governors during the mid-sixties and early seventies changed the political landscape con-siderably. Nonetheless, most county officeholders were Republicans who were elected with fairly comfortable margins (Table 4.5 and 4.6). Unlike Peoria and Kalamazoo it has an active, dominant local Republican party. Dauphin, like Kalamazoo, ranks toward the middle of our ideology meas-ures (Table 4.7).

As we move to the economically declining counties, we encounter a socioeconomic and political environment that stands in stark contrast to the affluence of a DuPage or a Montgomery and to the political culture of a Peoria or a Kalamazoo. St. Clair County is perhaps the prime example of the type of county we were trying to select in choosing the socially heterogeneous, economically declining counties, and it stands apart when contrasted with the other counties. This can be seen quite clearly on a statistical level. St. Clair is the only county of the nine that actually lost population between 1970 and 1980, and it had a black population in 1980 (27 percent) almost twice as high as the county (Saginaw) with the next highest proportion (Table 4.1), and four or five times as great as several others. Moreover, most of the blacks (72 percent) in St. Clair live in East St. Louis (Table 4.2), a city whose social, economic, and political problems are legendary. St. Clair also had, by far, the highest number of public assistance recipients per 100,000, a level (12,409) that was 17 times as high as DuPage and more than double any other county's except Saginaw (Table 4.4). Also, the median per capita income in St. Clair was the lowest of the nine counties, around two-thirds the level found in the ring counties.

The picture portrayed by these hard data is reinforced and expanded upon by a life-long resident of St. Clair, who was also a prominent member of the court community.

> It's the United States in microcosm. It is! In a very short period of space, geographically, you have socially everything that is in this whole country in St. Clair County. You have Scott Air Force Base, a large military installation, so we have military personnel. You have rich farmlands. You have rich coal mines out on the east end, and you have a small rural community with a small rural police department, low crime rates. We have major commercial complexes out in Fairview Heights. You know the most rapidly expanding commercial area may be here for the whole country as far as expansion goes. It's just exploding out there. Yes, I'm talking about Sears, Venture, Famous-Barr, Ford, all the major chains are putting developments out there. Yet, you have Belleville which is a stagnant Dutch community of about 40,000 very conservative, largely white. And then, in East St. Louis, you have the worst ghettos in the world. You have some major industry in Monsanto.

The present character of St. Clair County can be better understood with a brief historical overview. The county, and especially East St. Louis, has had a history of absentee ownership in its major industries, which were attracted by tax breaks given by corrupt local officials and by cheap immigrant labor— European as well as blacks migrating from the South. In 1917, East St. Louis had one of the nation's earliest urban race riots. Labor problems and technological innovations led the absentee owners to depart, leaving East St. Louis in a state of permanent economic decline and giving rise to a host of social problems (crime, poverty, urban decay). Most of the white immigrants left East St. Louis, notably the large Irish population, for Belleville and other surrounding communities, thus enhancing the social divisions in the county. Today East St. Louis is almost totally black.

The large black and immigrant (especially the Irish) population in the county led to the development of a strong Democratic party; it votes more heavily Democratic than any of the other nine counties (Table 4.5). However, the average margin of victory for the Democrats is not relatively large (17 percent, Table 4.6), undoubtedly reflecting the high degree of social heterogeneity within the county. Much the same can be said about the general ideological orientation. While it was the most liberal on both of our measures (Table 4.7), it was categorized as only moderately liberal because neither score is exceptionally low (both were in the second quadrant). This ranking does not reflect moderation in St. Clair as much as the effects of a heterogeneous community, much as was the case in Oakland.

While the powerful local Democratic party in St. Clair was built around the Irish, German, and black working class, an unhealthy alliance between corrupt local officials and absentee owners further enhanced the party's strength. This alliance also removed the business community as a primary impetus for political reform. While historically the county has been dominated by an East St. Louis paper and a Belleville paper (the East St. Louis paper stopped publication a few years before our study), they, like the business community, have had little effect upon the political situation. There is no television station in the county. The Belleville *News Democrat* is a very aggressive newspaper in terms of its coverage of local events, including the courthouse. Its court reporter, unlike the one in Kalamazoo, was not considered an integral part of the court community. Court officials routinely accused it of engaging in sensationalism and of being a "rag sheet" that did not always get its facts straight.

This reputation may have undermined the credibility of the newspaper in attempting to spearhead changes, and undoubtedly it contributed to an apparent stagnance in St. Clair politics. Another contributing factor is that there may simply be no broad-based public support for change. Whatever the cause, St. Clair County has never undergone successful, far-reaching political reform. It is the epitome of a private-regarding ethos. The immigrants who dominated local Democratic politics, especially the Irish, introduced a kinship system in which politics meant power and personal gain. As one courthouse official proudly put it, "Real Illinois Democrats do their undergraduate work in Cook County and come to St. Clair for their advanced graduate training." Prostitution, gambling, voting fraud, official bribery and corruption, patronage, and organized crime flourished under this system. The proximity of St. Louis, which was not so wide open, also enhanced the profitability of the vice industry, which was largely located in East. St. Louis.

Saginaw County is similar to St. Clair County in a number of regards, although it is not nearly as distinctively deviant a case. It is more socially heterogeneous than most of the other counties. Although it does not have as large a minority population as St. Clair, it ranked second (Table 4.1). It has one of the lower growth rates for the 1970s but, unlike St. Clair, it did not lose population (Table 4.1). The city of Saginaw was somewhat larger than East St. Louis, and it housed a larger proportion of the county's population, as well as more than three-fourths of the black population. While the median per capita income in Saginaw was not as low as St. Clair, it had an extremely high level of public assistance recipients per one hundred thousand population (Table 4.4). This level was lower than St. Clair's, but almost twice as high as in Erie.

If we look more closely at Saginaw, we can see other rough parallels with St. Clair. The city of Saginaw is a racially and economically diverse, declining industrial center with a history of being a wide-open town, rife with gambling, prostitution, and drugs. It is surrounded by an agriculturally rich hinterland dominated by German Lutherans and was influenced in part by the reformist ethic that pervades much of Michigan. This diversity prevented the emergence of any clear, unified vision of what was expected of the local court system, in contrast with counties such as DuPage, Peoria, and Kalamazoo.

Not being encumbered by such expectations, the court community in Saginaw had much more latitude. The dominant newspaper, the *Saginaw News,* was aggressive, but it was not a shrill, muckraking institution. Moreover, it had little competition. There was only one other major media outlet, a local television station, located in the county. This latitude was enhanced by a lack of electoral competition. Despite the lack of a powerful local political organization, Saginaw was a solidly Republican county (Table 4.5) that ranks toward the middle of our ideological rankings (Table 4.7), perhaps for the same reasons St. Clair and Oakland were ranked moderately. While the average margins of victory reported in Table 4.6 were not relatively large in Saginaw (17 percent, on average), the court community was more insulated than those numbers would suggest. With the exception of Johnson landslide in 1964, the state's attorney's office had been dominated by the Republicans for as long as most could remember. No judge had faced an electoral opponent since 1948! Indeed, the five Saginaw judges had been in office so long that the courts were almost their personal fiefdoms. The three "old-timers" had been judges for between twenty-four and thirty-five years, while another had been on the bench for thirteen years.

Even if the court community in Saginaw, and to some extent St. Clair, appeared somewhat insulated from their environment, another type of linkage to the community becomes evident in the declining communities—long-standing personal ties. Because these counties are not large, rapidly changing communities and are dominated by a major city, close personal ties between court community actors and other segments of the community were evident to an extent that did not exist in the other counties. These ties can be clearly seen within the Saginaw court community. For example, two of the judges were brothers and two others had social and professional ties dating to 1956. These close judicial ties were reflective of the bar as a whole. Because Saginaw is not a magnet community, the lawyers had often grown up with one another, or watched as later generations grew up. The high incidence of family firms and constant references to long ties among lawyers led to an examination of a lawyer's list maintained by the county clerk. It revealed that at least 20 percent of the attorneys were related by blood ties.

Economically and socially, Erie is as close to Saginaw as DuPage is to Montgomery. It is an old, economically declining county that is racially homogeneous to a large extent. Its politics and social life are dominated more by religion and ethnicity than political allegiances. Although the county traditionally votes Democratic, the regions outside the city of Erie are largely Republican, and there is no single dominant party. The county as a whole went for Reagan in 1980.

Personal and family ties were much more important in Erie than the political ties that bound court community actors together (or alienated them) in DuPage and Montgomery. This is partly a function of size—the bars in DuPage and Montgomery number well over one thousand, while there were only a few hundred attorneys in Erie. Equally as important, however, were the stable population trends in Erie. Many professionals with long-standing family ties returned to practice in Erie, and it attracted few outsiders. It paralleled Saginaw in that close personal ties linked the court community to its environment in ways not uncovered in the other counties. One lawyer described Erie as follows: "Erie's an interesting community in that there are a lot of people in this community who are related to one another. I mean with strings, and cousins, and distant cousins—there's that problem. A lot of the marriages—I can think of several older Republican families, and their families have married, and their offspring have married. There are a lot of small 100 to 200 small industrial firms that have been run by older Erie families. It's in the school board, it's in the government, it's just everywhere."

CRIME RATES

It is important to consider the nature of the crime problem in each of the counties, not because of its implications for the court system's workload but rather because of its political import. Whatever the deficiencies of the FBI's Uniform Crime Index for measuring the magnitude of "real" crime in a given locale, it is virtually the only crime data that is widely disseminated. Community responses to these data form the basis for political pressures upon various members of the court community. An understanding of the differences in these crime rates may shed light on externally, and internally, generated demands to "do something."

An examination of crime data for the one or two years surrounding the conduct of this study is inadequate, because crime rates for such small locales are volatile; moreover, they fail to reveal long-term trends and pressures. Graphs 4.1 and 4.2 report the rate and trend of violent personal crime and property crime for each county over a ten-year period (1971–80).[2] In many ways the personal crime figures are the most important because they include the types of crimes that make headlines and generate the most fear among the citizenry. Clear categories emerge here (Table 4.8). Peoria and St. Clair have the highest rates; Kalamazoo and Dauphin are poor seconds. Two Michigan counties (Oakland and Saginaw) have fairly low personal offense rates, whereas two of the ring counties (DuPage and Montgomery) and Erie have the lowest. Property crimes are affected by different factors (e.g., affluence, extent of commercialization) and can generate different types of pressures. The rankings are somewhat different here. While Kalamazoo and Peoria are still fairly high, St. Clair drops two categories; Oakland moves up one. Dauphin and Erie both drop one, while DuPage, Erie, and Montgomery remain in the lowest category.

One last component of the crime problem concerns city-county differences. It was noted earlier that a major city dominated some counties, and that city-county cleavages often exist in those locales. One way to gauge the extent to which the crime problem in a county is a city problem is to compare rates in the major city with those in the county outside the city. These data are reported in Table 4.9. For violent personal crime, the "problem" is focused in the major city for all but the ring counties, where the major city is not a large component of the total county population. Of the non-ring counties, personal crimes are most heavily concentrated in the cities of Peoria, East St. Louis, and Kalamazoo; Saginaw has the lowest concentration. The city of Erie, however, has the lowest personal crime rate of the non-ring counties, and the second lowest overall. A very different picture emerges with respect to property crime. In the non-ring counties, except Peoria, the proportion of property crimes committed in the major city is not as extreme as the proportion of personal offenses.

DETENTION FACILITIES

Crime rates, political attitudes, media attention, electoral competition, and other sociopolitical influences emanating from a court's environment

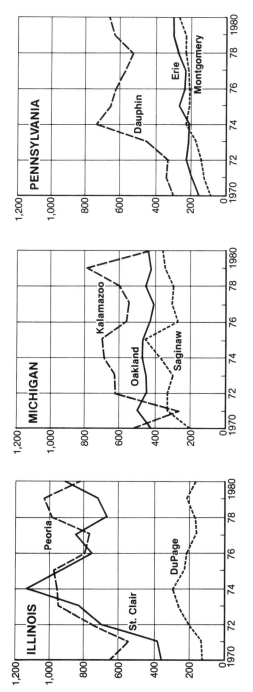

Graph 4.1. Trend of Violent Personal Crime by County: 1971-80 (Rate per 100,000)

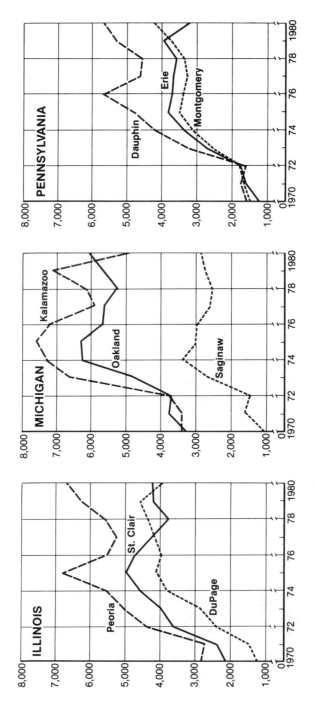

Graph 4.2. Trend of Property Crime by County: 1971-80 (Rate per 100,000)

Table 4.8. **Categorizations of Crime Levels**

	Higher	Medium High	Medium Low	Lower
Personal crime	Peoria (860) St. Clair (792)	Kalamazoo (582) Dauphin (520)	Oakland (442) Saginaw (333)	Erie (243) DuPage (205) Montgomery (201)
Property crime	Kalamazoo (5,960)	Peoria (5,392) Oakland (5,291)	Dauphin (4,142) St. Clair (4,029)	DuPage (3,222) Erie (3,132) Montgomery (3,061) Saginaw (2,568)

Note: Figures in parentheses are the ten-year average crime rate (per 100,000 population).

are significant because they push local court communities toward one set of policies or another. From a practical perspective, however, it is impossible to separate the impact of these factors from the issue of detention facilities, especially for certain aspects of court operations. These facilities act as an important constraint upon what court community actors can do. They make certain actions possible while ruling out others. Because similar actors in politically similar counties may operate under different resource constraints, consideration of detention facilities may help explain otherwise perplexing differences in outcomes and practices.

Consider, for a moment, county jail facilities. The quality and capacity of a county's jail can affect decisions concerning pretrial incarceration as well as sentencing. A decrepit jail may give a judge second thoughts about bail decisions, especially in cases involving youthful offenders; a low capacity may virtually eliminate pretrial incarceration for all but the most serious cases. Judges operating under fewer constraints may adopt a more punitive pretrial detention policy. The lack of a local jail option may also lead some judges to give marginal defendants probation or a fine as opposed to a short term in the local jail; other judges, however, may be more inclined to send these defendants to the penitentiary. A relative abundance of local space may alleviate the need for other judges to make this hard choice.

Table 4.10 reports some data on the local jails in each of our counties. All of the Michigan jails were built during the 1970s; only the jails in St. Clair in Illinois and Erie in Pennsylvania were built during that decade.

Table 4.9. **Comparison of Crime Rates between County and Major City, 1980**

	DuPage (Ring)	Peoria (Autonomous)	St. Clair (Declining)	Oakland (Ring)	Kalamazoo (Autonomous)	Saginaw (Declining)	Montgomery (Ring)	Dauphin (Autonomous)	Erie (Declining)
Violent Personal Crimes									
Rate per 100,000 in major city	67.8	1,162	3,322	2,216	1,539	1,586	1,380	2,011	494
Rate per 100,000 in county outside of major city	166.86	245	256	293	272	415	208	257	150
Percent of all county crimes committed in the major city	2.8	88	77	38	77	66	26	69.8	70.8
Property Crimes									
Rate per 100,000 in major city	2,551	8,627	6,819	9,238	9,660	9,536	7,200	10,830	3,592
Rate per 100,000 in county outside of major city	3,897	3,433	3,417	5,752	4,962	5,006	3,945	4,067	2,762
Percent of all county crimes committed in the major city	4.4	80	34	11.5	54	50	9	44	49

Table 4.10. Characteristics of the Local County Jail

	DuPage (Ring)	Peoria (Autonomous)	St. Clair (Declining)	Oakland (Ring)	Kalamazoo (Autonomous)	Saginaw (Declining)	Montgomery (Ring)	Dauphin (Autonomous)	Erie (Declining)
Date built	1958	1915	1970	1971	1971	1972	1859	1952	1975
Detention capacity, 1980	125	150	248	450	264	220	186	222	208
Are prisoners normally housed outside the county?	No	Yes	No	Yes	No	No	Yes	No	No
Have there been any court orders limiting capacity?	No	Yes	No	Yes	No	No	No	No	No
Capacity per 100,000 population	19.0	74.8	93.4	44.5	124.3	96.46	28.43	95.55	74.3
Capacity per arrest for violent personal crimes plus burglary, 1980	.15	.14	.28	.18	.29	.24	.10	.16	.24

Table 4.11. **Counties Categorized by Local Jail Capacities**

	Larger Capacities	Medium Capacities	Smaller Capacities
Categorized on the basis of population rates	Kalamazoo St. Clair Saginaw Dauphin	Peoria Erie	Montgomery DuPage Oakland
Categorized on the basis of arrests	Kalamazoo St. Clair Saginaw Erie	Peoria Dauphin Oakland DuPage	Montgomery

The DuPage and Dauphin jails were built during the 1950s. Peoria's jail is more than 65 years old, while Montgomery's is more than 120 years old. Not surprisingly, both Peoria and Montgomery, along with Oakland, regularly housed prisoners outside the county, at a considerable cost. Peoria and Oakland were operating under limits imposed by court order; Montgomery was not. While not affecting capacity directly, the Saginaw jail also was under a court order.

Both measures of capacity rates (per capita, per arrest) show significant variation, but they are not always consistent.[3] For example, if capacity per 100,000 population is examined, Kalamazoo has, by far, the most capacity (124 beds per 100,000 population). St. Clair, Saginaw, and Dauphin rank next highest with about 95 beds per 100,000 population, followed by Peoria and Erie with about 75. The three ring counties have the lowest rates, with DuPage and Montgomery below 30—less than one-fourth of Kalamazoo's rate. A look at capacity per arrest for serious crimes changes some of our views on capacity (Table 4.11). In this case two of the ring counties (DuPage and Oakland) with higher populations but less crime, move from the "Smaller" to the "Medium" category. Dauphin also drops from the "Larger" to the "Medium," while Erie does the opposite. Montgomery stands alone in having exceptionally low jail capacity.

We now turn to the structure and capacity of the state penal system. Here again we are concerned with more than just capacity. The quality and orientation (centralized, decentralized) of the state system, as well as the number of spaces available, can affect the sentencing practices of judges. Table 4.12 reports selected indicators of the nature and quality of the three state penal systems. A number of observations can be made on the basis of these data. First, the structure and orientation of Michigan's penal system seem to be quite different from the systems in Illinois and Pennsylvania. Michigan has the largest number of facilities (row 1), and they are decentralized throughout the state (rows 2, 3). While Illinois and

Table 4.12. **Selected Quality Indicators of State-Level Correctional Facilities**

	Illinois	Michigan	Pennsylvania
Total number of facilities	10	23	8
Percent with a capacity under 500	40 (4)	73.9 (17)	25 (2)
Percent with a capacity over 1,000	40 (4)	8.6 (2)	37.5 (3)
Percent that are maximum security	50 (5)	26 (6)	25 (2)
Percent that are minimum security	10 (1)	56.5 (13)	25 (2)
Percent built before 1925	30 (3)	8.6 (2)	50 (4)
Percent built after 1950	30 (3)	73.9 (17)	25 (2)
Percent built after 1970	20 (2)	26 (6)	0 (0)
Percent of state budget devoted to corrections (1979)	1.53	1.53	1.12
Dollars spent per prisoner (1979)	$14,084	$14,177	$14,306
Ratio of inmates to full-time staff	3.3	2.5	2.7
Percent of cells greater than or equal to 70 sq. ft.	15	59	51

Source: *Sourcebook of Criminal Justice Statistics—1981.*

Pennsylvania have largely maximum and medium security institutions (90 and 75 percent, respectively), the majority of Michigan's institutions are minimum security (row 5). Michigan's institutions also tend to be newer (rows 6–8), as almost three-quarters were built after 1950 and one-quarter during the 1970s. Four of Pennsylvania's eight institutions were built before 1925, as were three of the ten in Illinois.

Other aspects of Michigan's penal system are somewhat less distinctive. The state does not, for example, devote a higher proportion of its budget to corrections than Illinois; Pennsylvania has the lowest proportion. However, Pennsylvania's per prisoner expenditures are fairly comparable to those of the other states (row 10). Pennsylvania's inmate/staff ratio is comparable to Michigan's, and both have significantly lower ratios than

Table 4.13. **Capacity Measures of State-Level Adult Correctional Facilities**
(1979)

	Illinois	Michigan	Pennsylvania
Confinement capacity (number of prisoners who can be accommodated)	11,320	11,627	8,093
Capacity per 1,000,000	100.66	127.39	68.67
Capacity per adult arrest for serious UCR crimes (violent personal crime plus burglary), 1979	.43	.62	.34
Proportion of capacity utilized (Dec. 31, 1979)	.99	1.15	.91

Source: *Sourcebook of Criminal Justice Statistics—1981*. Excludes community-based facilities. This information was supplemented by inquiries to state correctional departments to ensure comparability.

Illinois. Pennsylvania and Michigan also have a higher proportion of larger cells than Illinois (row 12). In sum, although Pennsylvania does not have the capital investment in correctional facilities that Michigan has, it is fairly comparable to Michigan in terms of expenditures per inmate, the level of supervision, and cell size. Both rank above Illinois on all three dimensions.

Another important dimension to state penal systems is their capacity. The criteria a judge uses for determining whether a defendant merits "state time" may include—consciously or subconsciously—the relative capacity of state institutions as well as the extent of their utilization at a given time. If this is true, then the flow of prisoners to the state penal system may rise to fill the available spaces and may slow once capacity is reached. Table 4.13 shows that Michigan has significantly greater capacity than either Illinois or Pennsylvania. This is true regardless of what measure is used. Michigan has more absolute capacity, more capacity per one hundred thousand population, and more capacity per 1979 arrest for serious crimes, as defined in the Uniform Crime Reports. Illinois ranks consistently behind Michigan, and Pennsylvania ranks even lower. The data on utilization reveal that Pennsylvania has both the lowest capacity as well as the lowest utilization; Michigan, on the other hand, has the highest capacity and the highest utilization. This overutilization led to a court ruling that held that Michigan's entire adult penal system violated constitutional standards. Similarly, selected prisons in Illinois have been placed under court order. Pennsylvania was one of only thirteen states that did not have any type of pending litigation concerning its penal system in 1982.

SEVERITY OF THE STATE SENTENCING CODE

Another state level influence is the severity of sentencing codes. Although such codes normally provide criminal court decision makers with a wide range of sentences and a good deal of discretion, some measure of statutory severity must be considered. The sentencing code sets the parameters within which plea bargaining takes place and helps shape its form and content. County-specific going rates for individual offenses are apt to be affected, although certainly not determined, by the statewide code. In addition, the severity of the code is important for symbolic reasons. Most convicted defendants do not receive the maximum penalty for their offense. But the participants' perceptions of a given offense are likely to be influenced by the state code, especially if it has recently been revised. The code's treatment of a given offense can be viewed roughly as a statement by the political community of its concern about a type of proscribed behavior. The statement—and the will of the community— will vary depending on the crime and the times. Code provisions dealing with peripheral, victimless crimes (those involving marijuana, blue laws, and gambling) are not apt to be accurate reflections of societal concerns at a given moment. Those that deal with the staples of the criminal justice system (rape, armed robbery, burglary, and theft) are more likely to reflect such concerns, especially if there have been recent revisions.

A number of problems are encountered in attempting to gauge the relative severity of state sentencing codes. Minimums and maximums are often specified for large numbers of offenses. For some types of offenses (drug violations, some property and personal offenses), penalties vary with some objective measure of severity not readily comparable across codes, such as the amount and/or type of drugs involved, the recency of a criminal conviction, and the existence of a prior record. Moreover, the definition of some crimes varies across states; this is especially true of forgery, fraud, and different types of assault and battery cases.

Some of these problems (differing definitions and enhancement provisions) have no resolution and, therefore, weaken the validity of any attempt to scale sentencing codes. Nonetheless, by using the following procedure we feel it was possible to construct an adequate severity scale. First, the scope of the effort was limited to a handful of selected crimes. These are reported in Table 4.14 along with the statutory minimums and maximums in each state. These offenses were chosen because they are relatively comparable across states and, together, constitute the bulk of all

Table 4.14. Statutory Minimums and Maximums for Selected Offenses, by State (in Months of Potential Incarceration)

Offense	Illinois			Michigan			Pennsylvania		
	Minimum	Maximum	Rank of Maximum	Minimum	Maximum	Rank of Maximum	Minimum	Maximum	Rank of Maximum
Voluntary manslaughter	0	84	3	0	180	1	0	120	2
Rape	36	360	2	0	life (480)	1	0	240	3
Armed robbery	36	360	2	0	life (480)	1	0	240	3
Robbery	0	84	2 (tie)	0	180	1	0	84	2 (tie)
Burglary	0	84	3	0	180	2	0	240	1
Aggravated	0	84	2	0	120	1 (tie)	0	120	1 (tie)
Battery	0	60	1 (tie)	0	60	1 (tie)	0	60	1 (tie)
Theft	0	60	2 (tie)	0	72	1	0	60	2 (tie)
Unauthorized use of weapons	0	36	2	0	60	1 (tie)	0	60	1 (tie)
Driving while under the influence of alcohol	0	12	1 (tie)	0	3	2	0	12	1 (tie)
Possession of heroin	0	60	1	0	48	2	0	36	3

Table 4.15. **Summary Measures of the Severity of Sentencing Codes**

	Illinois	Michigan	Pennsylvania
Average standardized offense-specific score	−.10	.13	−.03
Average ranking	1.91	1.27	1.81

sentenced cases in the counties. For example, in the Illinois counties, these offenses account for 67 percent of sentenced cases. The comparable figures for Michigan and Pennsylvania are 54 and 71 percent, respectively. As Table 4.14 indicates, the minimum for all offenses in each state is probation (0 months in confinement), except for rape and armed robbery in Illinois. This lack of variance eliminates the use of minimum sentences in the ranking scheme. In contrast, a good deal of variation can be seen among the maximums. Moreover, a cursory examination of the rank ordering across the three states indicates that the Michigan maximums are the highest (or are tied) in over two-thirds of the eleven offenses and second highest in the others. The relative ranking of Illinois and Pennsylvania, however, is less clear.

To refine and clarify these rankings the following procedure was used. A "standardized" score was assigned to each offense for each state based upon its distance from the mean of the maximums for all three states.[4] The eleven resulting standardized offense scores were then averaged to derive a general severity score. These scores, along with the average rank ordering (derived from columns 3, 6, and 9 of Table 4.14) are reported in Table 4.15. The Michigan sentencing code clearly ranks as the most severe on both measures. Pennsylvania ranks second, but the difference between it and Illinois is not great. Given the coarseness of the measures, it is doubtful that Pennsylvania and Illinois differ significantly.

STATEWIDE SENTENCING NORMS

It has often been argued that constant interactions among judges and other participants in the same county give rise to a going rate for common offenses. A similar, more general effect may exist at the state level. Clearly, the interaction among judges at a statewide level is not nearly so great as in a county, but they do meet formally at regular intervals. Moreover, although judges from different counties are almost certainly subject to different local influences that may affect their sentencing practices, there are also a number of centripetal forces that draw them together. For example, they are all subject to the same sentencing code and probably read the same or similar continuing education review manuals on sentencing and other relevant matters. And all of them face the same state penal system even though local conditions (such as jail capacity) may differ sharply.

These centripetal forces may combine with other aspects of the state political and legal culture to form the basis for statewide sentencing norms. To suggest that such norms exist does not imply that counties, or indeed individuals, do not have different sentencing norms and practices. Rather, it simply suggests that punitive or lenient counties or judges in different states deviate from different statewide norms. A lenient county in a punitive state may have a norm of four years in the state penitentiary for an armed robbery—the statewide norm may be six years. This may, however, be above the norm for a punitive county in a lenient state.

Hypothesizing about these state norms and measuring them are two entirely different matters. Good, comparable sentencing data on a statewide basis are difficult to obtain, especially over a long period of time. The time dimension is important in the discussion of norms, because the notion of norm implies a certain stability. One relevant set of comparable data that does exist for a long period of time is data on incarcerated prisoners in state institutions, gathered by the Census Bureau since 1926. These data (prisoners per one hundred thousand population) are reported in Graph 4.3.[5]

As one might expect on the basis of the data on sentencing codes and penitentiary systems, Michigan incarcerates more individuals per hundred thousand residents than either Illinois or Pennsylvania—and has done so for more than forty years. The differences are fairly large and stable from about 1945 to around 1960. The rate of all three—as with the nation as a whole—drops during the 1960s. Michigan's drop is not as sustained as that of Illinois or Pennsylvania. Moreover, Michigan apparently responded much more eagerly to the law and order movement of the late sixties and seventies than did Illinois. In relative terms, Pennsylvania responded hardly at all. Part of the explanation for these different responses, of course, has to do with penitentiary capacity. Michigan opened six new penal facilities during the 1970s, while Illinois opened two, and Pennsylvania added none. Thus, Pennsylvania judges were not as able to respond as those in the other states.[6]

One last set of data yields a partial look at differences in sentencing norms and is presented in Table 4.16. It reports data on the average time actually spent in confinement for the seven UCR offenses. Its value is limited for our purposes, because release time is not always highly correlated with the judge's sentence. More important, these data ignore defendants who received no time in the penitentiary. Despite these deficiencies, Michigan still appears to be the most punitive state. Pennsylvania

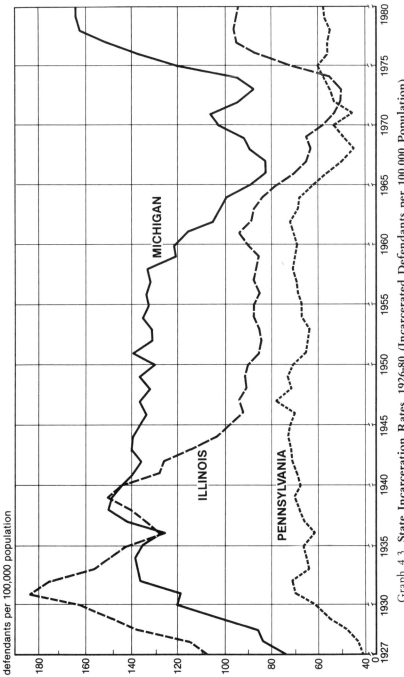

Graph 4.3. **State Incarceration Rates, 1926-80** (Incarcerated Defendants per 100,000 Population)

Table 4.16. **Average Time Served for UCR Offenses, 1976-77**

	Illinois	Michigan	Pennsylvania
Homicide	40	99	46
Rape	46	NA	32
Robbery	21	33	27
Assault	20	28	22
Burglary	15	22	22
Theft	13	15	18
Car theft	13	16	21

Source: Winer (1981).

may be more punitive than it appears to be in Graph 4.3 simply because, although Pennsylvania judges do not send as many defendants to the penitentiary as do those in the other states, their sentences are just as high for those defendants they do send.

SUMMARY

It might prove useful to pause here and try to briefly summarize the similarities and differences across counties and states on some of the dimensions just reviewed. If we think first just in terms of broad social and demographic patterns, we can see some parallels between several pairs of counties. DuPage and Montgomery seem to fit well together as rather typical, white, relatively affluent suburban counties. Peoria and Kalamazoo also seem to share many parallels as free-standing communities with very positive self-images and relatively homogeneous populations, even if they are not as homogeneous as DuPage and Montgomery. Saginaw and Erie, as somewhat stagnant but close-knit and fairly homogeneous communities, also seem to fit together well. Oakland, given the existence of Pontiac, does not fit the suburban pattern nearly as well as DuPage and Montgomery. Dauphin seems to have more in common with Erie and Saginaw than Peoria and Kalamazoo, but not enough to link it with them. Finally, St. Clair is simply too deviant a case on too many dimensions to fit well with any of the other counties in either social or demographic terms.

With the exception of St. Clair and Erie, all of the counties were fairly solidly Republican. However, a strong local party existed in only DuPage, St. Clair, Montgomery, and Erie. There seems to be three ideologically conservative counties (DuPage, Peoria, and Montgomery), four moderate ones (the Michigan counties and Dauphin), and two that were moderately liberal (St. Clair and Erie). Peoria, Dauphin, and Erie had the greatest concentration of media followed by Kalamazoo, Saginaw, and then St. Clair. The ring counties were subject to very little media scrutiny that had countywide clout.

The analysis of ten-year crime levels revealed some surprises in that the declining counties did not have markedly higher crime rates than the other counties. Although St. Clair had one of the highest overall rates of personal crime, Peoria had the highest. Kalamazoo was next behind St. Clair but, with respect to property crime, Kalamazoo was the highest followed by Peoria. This is surprising given the social and political ambiance of those counties. It is less surprising when it is recognized that, as revealed in Tables 4.2 and 4.9, the cities of Peoria and Kalamazoo are among the largest cities in our counties and the vast majority of all crime occurred within their boundaries. The relatively low crime rates of Saginaw and Erie, both declining counties, is less surprising when their close-knit nature is recalled. The earlier comments about the similar suburban nature of DuPage and Montgomery are underscored by their consistently low crime levels. Likewise, the middling levels of crime in Oakland and Dauphin reinforce our judgment that they were somewhat different than their counterparts in the other states.

If we look at county jails, we see some significant differences but few patterns. Montgomery's county jail was built in 1859 and was simply decrepit; the next oldest was Peoria's, built in 1915. Every other jail was built during the 1970s except for DuPage's and Dauphin's, which were built in the 1950s. Several counties (Peoria, Oakland, Montgomery) regularly had to house prisoners out of the county. Based upon our two adjusted measures of detention capacity Kalamazoo, St. Clair, and Saginaw each had relatively high levels of capacity, while Montgomery clearly had the lowest.

If we look at the various pieces of state-level data collected here (penitentiaries, sentencing codes, sentencing norms), we see that Michigan appears quite distinctive. It has a more decentralized penitentiary system, more prison capacity, and more severe sentencing provisions than either Illinois or Michigan, and has routinely sentenced more people to the penitentiary than the other two states for more than forty years. Although Illinois has a greater penitentiary capacity than Pennsylvania and sends a greater proportion of its populace to the penitentiary, it is less distinctive on other grounds.

NOTES

1. Even the more detailed discussions to be presented here and in chapters 5 and 6 do not do justice to the intricacies and the realities of the phenomena

being addressed. They are synopses of even more detailed discussions presented earlier. For these more in-depth presentations, see Eisenstein, Nardulli, and Flemming (1982). A more succinct presentation can be found in Eisenstein, Flemming, and Nardulli (1988).

2. The crime rate data for Illinois and Pennsylvania come from statewide reports on crime broken down by county (*Crime in Illinois; Crime in Pennsylvania*). Michigan's financial situation made these data inaccessible for that state. Therefore, we compiled totals by using data from the FBI's *Crime in America*. Although this provided reliable data for Saginaw and fairly reliable data for Kalamazoo, we had to piece together data on Oakland from city breakdowns (Oakland is in the Detroit Standard Metropolitan Statistical Area). This made the data less reliable, especially for the earlier years when not all units reported. We had good data on Kalamazoo and Oakland for 1975 and 1980, and these were compared with our calculations from *Crime in America*. The comparisons indicated that our Oakland figures were underreported by 20 percent and those for Kalamazoo by 5 percent. The figures reported in Graphs 4.1 and 4.2 are adjusted to compensate for these underestimates.

3. Because of state cutbacks, information on the total arrests for 1980 in the Michigan counties was unavailable. Data on 1977 arrests were available, however. In comparing the non-Michigan counties with good 1977 and 1980 arrest data (DuPage, Montgomery, Dauphin, Erie), it was determined that 1980 arrests for the five categories reported in Table 4.4 were, on average, 5 percent greater than 1977 arrests. Thus, the Michigan arrest figures were adjusted (using the 5 percent figure) to estimate 1980 arrests. Although the unavailability of good 1980 data is unfortunate, the figures in row 6 are fairly inelastic (i.e., changes in raw arrest figures would have to undergo large changes before the capacity rates change much). Thus, we feel that the Michigan figures are fairly reliable.

4. The exact procedure used was as follows:

$$\text{Standardized Offense Score} = \frac{\text{State maximum} - \text{Mean of the three state maximums}}{\text{Mean of the three state maximums}}$$

5. While category titles changed and some other minor modifications occurred, these data are consistent over time. However, their source has changed over the years. The data from 1926 to 1946 can be found in the Department of Commerce's *Prisoners in State and Federal Prisons and Reformatories*. By 1950 the reporting of prison statistics had shifted to the U.S. Department of Justice; data from 1950 to 1970 can be found in *Prisoners in State and Federal Institutions*. In 1970, responsibility for these statistics was again transferred, this time within DOJ. From 1971 to 1977, the Law Enforcement Assistance Administration in conjunction with the National Justice Information and Statistics Service published prison statistics in a national prisoner statistics bulletin entitled *Prisoners in State and Federal Institutions on December 31*. After 1977, while the source remains the same,

publishing responsibilities were again shifted. DOJ established a Bureau of Justice Statistics with responsibility for all department-sponsored statistical reporting including (but not limited to) national prisoner statistics.

6. Whatever the causes behind the changes evident in Graph 4.3, the long-term differences in incarceration rates may not be the sole result of differences in state-level sentencing norms. Differences could exist if sentencing norms were identical but crime and/or arrest rates were different (i.e., Michigan has high incarceration rates because it has more crime, and its law enforcement officials catch more criminals). It is extremely doubtful, however, that differences in crime and arrest rates across the three states account for the large differences revealed in Graph 4.3; Michigan's average incarceration rate (per one hundred thousand citizens) since 1940 is 40 percent greater than it is in Illinois, and the Illinois rate is 34 percent greater than Pennsylvania's.

A complete examination of this possibility cannot be made because comparable, meaningful data on crimes and arrests do not exist for the years 1926-80. Data on UCR crime are useful only for the post-1958 period, and these do not cover all crimes subject to penitentiary commitment. Moreover, most states did not begin publishing statewide arrest figures until the 1970s. Despite these problems, two partial examinations of the crime-arrest thesis were conducted. First, employing multiple regression to conduct an analysis of covariance, we examined the impact of state dummy variables while controlling for the level of personal violent crime (murder, rape, robbery, assault) in each year since 1958. Personal violent crimes were used because they were considered the most likely of available crimes to receive a penitentiary sentence. After controlling for the personal violent crime rate, the differences between the states survived. Michigan's adjusted rate is 58 percent greater than that of Illinois, which is 19 percent greater than Pennsylvania's. Each of those differences is statistically significant beyond the .01 level.

REFERENCES

Eisenstein, James, Roy B. Flemming, and Peter F. Nardulli. 1988. *The Contours of Justice: Communities and Their Courts.* Boston: Little, Brown.

——. April 1982. "Explaining and Assessing Criminal Case Disposition: A Comparative Study of Nine Counties," vols. 1-5. Final report submitted to the National Institute of Justice (Grant 79 N1-AX-0062).

Federal Bureau of Investigation. 1971-80. *Crime in America.* Washington: Government Printing Office.

Illinois Department of Law Enforcement, Division of Support Services. 1971-80. *Crime in Illinois.* Springfield: State of Illinois.

Law Enforcement Assistance Administration. 1971-77. *Prisoners in State and Federal Institutions on December 31.* Washington: Government Printing Office.

Pennsylvania State Police, Bureau of Research and Development. 1971-80. *Crime in Pennsylvania*. Harrisburg: State of Pennsylvania.

Scammon, Richard M., and Alice V. McGillivray, comp. and ed. 1973, 1975, 1979, 1981. *America Votes*, vols. 10-14. Washington: Congressional Quarterly Press.

Sourcebook of Criminal Justice Statistics—1981. Washington: Government Printing Office.

U.S. Bureau of the Census. 1977. *County and City Data Book, 1977*. Washington: Government Printing Office. Table 2, "Counties," 126, 138, 234, 390, 402.

————. 1983. *County and City Data Book, 1983*. Washington: Government Printing Office. Table B, "Counties: Population and Households," Table D, "Places: Area, Population, Income, and Housing," 130, 144, 270, 466, 834-39, 854-61, 895-908.

————. 1926-46. *Prisoners in State and Federal Prisons and Reformatories*. Washington: Government Printing Office.

Winer, Jonathan M. 1981. "High Disparities in Jail Time." *The National Law Journal*, February 23:1.

5

THE CONTEXT OF JUSTICE, I: COURTHOUSE COMMUNITIES

The rather abstract, distant nature of the ecological influences just reviewed emphasizes the importance of contextual factors in our efforts to understand the workings of criminal courts. This is especially true of the concept of the courthouse community. It serves as a key conceptual link between the environment and case outcomes which, in many respects, are the bottom line in most analyses of criminal courts. At the same time, the notion of courthouse community provides us with a broader theoretical focus than mere case outcomes. This focus helps us think about the milieu in which various actors with different attitudes and abilities interact, and the impact of that milieu upon the dispositional process.

Despite the utility and apparent centrality of the notion of a courthouse community, little has been said here to develop it conceptually. Why is it a useful concept? What affects the cohesiveness of a courthouse community? What sustains them? How do court communities differ, and why do they differ? Are they good? By addressing these questions, we both enhance our understanding of this concept and lay the groundwork for a discussion of the situations we found in our nine counties.

THE CONCEPT OF A COURTHOUSE COMMUNITY: SOME PRELIMINARY THOUGHTS

The notion of a courthouse community is a useful conceptual device in the study of criminal courts because it captures some very fundamental aspects of their social milieu: Criminal courts are operated by a group of actors who are tied together by a variety of interdependencies and who share a common workplace. (For a parallel discussion of the notion of courthouse community and how it fits within the sociological literature of community, see Eisenstein, Flemming, and Nardulli [1988, chapter 2].) The interdependencies that bind together the various actors are hard to deny. They routinely meet on different sides of the same case, each performing different formal roles. How each performs role-specific tasks has a marked impact on the others. Establishing and fulfilling certain common expectations and behavior patterns can simplify the work lives of all and can lead to shared outlooks on important aspects of work life. The fact that actors interact within a common workplace over an extended period of time facilitates the development of these expectations and outlooks.

The realization among members of specific court communities that, to a large degree, they share common destinies frequently leads to a sense of identification with a larger, more encompassing group, one that transcends formal organizational boundaries. The strength of this sense of identification within a court community, its cohesiveness, can vary significantly across counties. It is affected by the level of personal interactions in work-group settings; by long-standing professional, social, or even familial relationships; by overlapping memberships in local political, civic, or religious organizations; or by some combination of each. Normally, the more extensive the network of interpersonal ties, the more cohesive the community (i.e., the stronger the sense of identification). These ties serve as constant reminders that the actors' work lives and activities are not an isolated part of their existence, that there are real costs involved in narrowly and rigidly defining their roles—even when such definitions are justified, even dictated, by their formal roles. Consequently, when individuals are intertwined in a tightly woven web of personal ties, they begin to define their functions and roles more broadly, normally in a manner more consistent with others in their network. They search for common ground to share in their everyday work life. These ties also stress the interdependencies of life and the rewards that accrue to those who sail with the wind, to those who don't rock the boat. Those who are deeply involved in these networks understand well the meaning of the old adage "what goes around, comes around."

The larger sense of identification associated with the notion of a courthouse community is nurtured and maintained by information flows facilitated by the grapevine. The very existence of this grapevine, with shoots that extend wherever nourishment is provided, reinforces ties to the larger community and emphasizes the arbitrariness of formal organizational boundaries, as well as the futility of organizational attempts to isolate themselves. The notion of the grapevine is so central to the concept of the courthouse community that it can almost be used as a barometer of the health and cohesiveness of a community. Where gossip does not flow freely across organizational boundaries, it is doubtful that individuals feel a sense of belonging to a larger entity. The grapevine is also a key component because it is the vehicle that transmits the local court community culture.

A bit more should be said about the local courthouse culture because it contributes to the distinctiveness of individual court communities. The core of the local court community's culture outlines general values and details specific norms and expectations—many of which override and conflict with those associated with formal organizational dictates. While distinctive values or orientations were manifested in a number of areas in the different counties, some of the most important include the appropriate role of partisan political considerations, the importance attributed to conflict maintenance, and views concerning the approach to be used in structuring the work of the court community. Although these are treated as independent dimensions, it is not unlikely that future research will uncover relationships among them as a more refined understanding of local court culture emerges.

In terms of the legitimate role of partisan political considerations, it was very clear from our interviews and observations that in some counties the omnipresence of politics with respect to such matters as hiring, promotion, and the structure of some systemic operations (the provision of public defense, in particular) was simply assumed. Appointments of assistant prosecutors or public defenders had to be cleared with, or approved by, the county board, or were reserved for prominent party members, party regulars, or their designees. Long-term county residence and letters from political sponsors were often required. Nominations for office heads or circuit judgeships were tinged heavily with political consideration, as were indigent defense appointments. In other counties, however, partisan considerations were met with open disdain. Office heads prided themselves in not knowing the partisan affiliation of their attorneys or having to clear appointments with anyone. Judgeships and administrative appointments were rewards for diligent service.

The importance attached to conflict avoidance and conflict maintenance is another important component of the court community's court culture. In some communities, a good deal of emphasis was placed upon going along and getting along, upon not rocking the boat. To do so would have important, and perhaps lasting, consequences on both a personal and a professional level. There was much talk of an idyllic "family" atmosphere in these counties. Tensions existed in them, but it was considered unseemly and unbecoming to hang out the dirty linen in public, and problems were worked out privately. In other communities, individuals were not preoccupied with congeniality. They viewed conflict as a normal part of communal life and an inevitable consequence of their professional roles. It was not important to go to extremes to avoid conflict or to assure that it was properly punished. Congeniality at any cost was simply not considered that important, nor was it attainable, anyway. Other objectives were sometimes more important, and that was understood by everyone. The crucial point was that these conflicts did not always rupture long-term relations or have long-term repercussions. After a cooling-off period, everyone expected things to return to normal. Thus, in terms of courthouse communities, cohesiveness and congeniality were neither synonymous nor inevitable. We observed different blends of both in different counties.

Our court communities also differed with respect to their approach to the work of the court community. Every court system has a core set of functions it must perform, and there are a variety of ways in which each of the integral tasks may be structured. How a court community chooses to structure them can sometimes say something important about the views and orientations of the court community's elite and may reveal important insights into the court community. We discerned three loosely integrated but distinctive sets of rationalizing principles that were used to explain why particular tasks or functions were structured in the way they were. We term these *work orientations*.

The first, and most difficult to summarize succinctly, is a structural or formalistic work orientation. It reflects a strong desire to project an image as a first-rate, highly professionalized operation, one that will be held up as a role model to peer counties. This orientation is concerned with the professionalism of its personnel and places a high value on compliance with professional norms concerning the value of limited discretion, the autonomy of distinct functions (judging, prosecuting, defending), and the importance of evenhandedness. The appearance of professionalism and compliance with professional norms is attained by the careful design of the court system's formal structure. Much importance is placed upon careful, thoughtful planning of ways to attain these objectives by organizational design. Tinkering and innovation with the design are a way of life. In contrast, an efficiency work orientation reveals a strong emphasis upon maximizing the utilization of systemic resources. A high value is placed upon making all the parts of the system work in harmony. Marginal changes are made in an incremental manner as problems emerge and solutions become clear. The contrast between formalistic and efficiency-oriented approaches is not always clear but can be seen most clearly in instances where the dictates of professionalism interfere with the efficiency of the process (i.e., where limiting discretion, or the appearance of evenhandedness, interfere with the smooth flow of cases through the system).

In efficiency-oriented offices, the concern with the expeditious processing of cases will normally prevail.

A pragmatic orientation is characterized by a more haphazard approach to the work of the court community. Tasks were structured in a commonsensical manner, one that satisfied the relevant array of interests at the time. When problems cropped up, the system was "fixed until it worked" using the same no-frills approach. The system tended to stay fixed in the same way until it broke again.

The local courthouse community's culture also specifies norms and expectations that deal with the more mundane, concrete aspects of the member's work life. Although there are a variety of these norms and expectations and they may be categorized in a number of different ways, we were most aware of three: cordiality norms and expectations, processual norms, and expectations concerning the use of legal prerogatives. Cordiality norms deal with such things as the level of informal disclosure expected of all participants, the importance of keeping one's word and maintaining one's reputation, and the inviolability of private confidences. They also define the courtesies extended to private defense attorneys and their ensuing obligations. Finally, these norms include the appropriate responses to those who violate norms. Are their clients to suffer? Do the attorneys simply get the cold shoulder and get cut out of normal communication flows? Are efforts made to fire them or curtail court appointments?

Processual norms largely concern the informal rules governing the guilty plea process. What level of involvement is expected of judges? What are the rules governing blind pleas (i.e., pleas with no agreed sentence)? When does "creative charging" become overreaching and coercive? What are acceptable ranges of sentences for normal defendants (those with unexceptional criminal histories) charged with normal offenses (those not accompanied by particularly vicious circumstances)? What obligations are owed novice prosecutors or defense attorneys unfamiliar with these norms?

Norms dealing with the use of legal prerogatives could include the charging norms mentioned earlier as well as norms concerning hearings, proceedings, and motions. When is it appropriate to conduct preliminary hearings? When are they expected to be waived? Under what conditions is it appropriate to indict someone while a preliminary hearing is pending? At what point, and under what conditions, does the extensive use of legal motions (to substitute judges, challenge jurors, change venue, suppress evidence, etc.) go beyond the duty owed to a client (i.e., become "over-motioning")?

The specific values shared by court community members and the structure and content of its norms evolve over long periods of time. The degree of support for these values and norms ebbs and flows, but in the short run, they are normally quite resistant to change. The evolution of the local court culture is shaped, where relevant, by such things as legal codes and resource constraints. But for the most part, these factors have little to do with most aspects of a court community's culture. More important are such things as various sociopolitical factors (state and/or local political culture, the nature of the ties between the court community and its environment, whether it is a stagnant or growing community, etc.), the views of powerful individuals who dominate the court community for long periods of time (prominent judges, head prosecutors, bar leaders, etc.), and the needs and interests of the practitioners. The latter set of factors may be fairly constant across most American jurisdictions, but their interplay with the first two factors is what introduces diversity into court communities.

The fact that these values and norms are so firmly imbedded in the fabric of these communities and their environments is what makes them so resistant to change. Transient interlopers ensconced in powerful positions for short periods of time may disrupt norms, realign loyalties, and interrupt normal communication flows, but they are normally little more than blips in a court community's history. Most scandals are weathered quite well by cohesive court communities. Prolonged and highly visible scandals that unearth truly unacceptable practices could well lead to the reform of normal operating procedures but, over time, adjustments are frequently made to changes that conflict with the interests and desires of practitioners. Factors that have perhaps the most disruptive impact upon the fabric of court communities are those that emanate from broadly based changes in its environment. Included here would be such things as political, ethnic, or racial cleavages resulting from population changes due to economic growth or deterioration. By reducing the consequences of independent action or enhancing the benefits to be gained by it, they erode the very foundations upon which the community is based. Depending upon the nature of these changes, new values and norms may emerge or the community itself may simply deteriorate.

While we might lament the demise of a court community, or the failure of one to emerge, we must be careful to disassociate the concept from its emotive overtones. The concept of a community conjures up thoughts of a warm, close, "good" setting in which human relationships evolve and take shape. Yet in the legal context with which we are presently concerned, a moment's reflection indicates that, in some respects, the notion of a highly cohesive community is antithetical to our adversarial system of justice. The attorneys are supposed to be advocates, not collaborators. Legal rights and procedures are supposed to ensure procedural justice, not to be used as the medium in an elaborate system of exchange and accommodation. At the same time, we can recognize that the permeability of the formal system of justice with the values and norms of the local community, through the participation of its members in the legal process, is both an integral part of our political machinery and an inevitable consequence of democratic rule. Also, the norms and expectations that are such an integral part of the courthouse community may well further such values that are quite compatible with our formal system of justice: efficiency, consistency, and fairness.

The answer to this apparent paradox is, of course, wrapped up in ideological and empirical questions that we can only begin to unravel here. What should be clear is that the existence of a highly cohesive courthouse community is not necessarily something that is good or to be nurtured. Much, of course, depends upon the structure and orientation of the court community, the values it maintains and the practices it encourages. To further illustrate this, as well as to provide a description of the court communities we studied, we now turn to a brief description of each. In doing so, we should stress that the notion of a courthouse community was not part of the conceptual apparatus we took into the field. It emerged from our field observations. Consequently, we were not able to gather comparable data systematically in the various counties.

Despite this, we can use bits and pieces of observational and interview data to draw portraits of the different court communities we studied. We are well aware of the pitfalls in such an approach. We can only guess at the values and norms embodied in the various court communities by assessing what they say and seeing what they do. Certain values and norms are quite evident within certain sectors in some counties but less so in other sectors. But does this mean they are not shared? What degree of support is necessary before we can say something is an integral part of the court community's culture? What if articulated values and norms are inconsistent with observed practices, practices that are determined by more direct, intervening factors?

These and a host of methodological problems involved in systematically mapping the contours of local court communities will have to await future research, research that will be aided by our efforts to utilize the rich body of observational and interview data we have gathered to enhance our understanding of these communities. Here we want to use these data to provide a more qualitative, subjective sense of the flavor and color of the different court communities. We want to illustrate some broad differences in the atmospheres that pervaded these communities, but we also want to discuss specifically their cohesiveness as well as the reach and vibrancy of their grapevines. Although we have little useful and comparable data on norms, we will be able to deal with views on the role of partisan political considerations and the level of conflict within court communities. Much of our discussion of work orientations will be deferred until the discussion of the court's infrastructure in chapter 6.

We find it most convenient to proceed by type of county in drawing these portraits.

THE RING COUNTIES

In some ways the notion of a courthouse community is the most difficult to develop with respect to these counties. They are relatively populous, sprawling counties with mobile populations and large private bars and court bureaucracies. There are other centrifugal forces at work in these types of counties that mitigate against the development of a strong sense of community. The operation of these forces, and their effect, is quite clear in the case of DuPage. The tremendous growth that DuPage experienced in the two decades preceding this study led to an influx of attorneys who located in the towns and cities that had developed only after World War II. These attorneys had few roots in the communities and even fewer ties to one another. This growth also led to considerable strains within the local Republican party as new people with different ideas, ambitions, and loyalties challenged long-time party activists. These fissures surfaced within the local court system during the 1970s. In addition, the rapid growth of this affluent and overwhelming Republican county made it the largest and most powerful Republican organization in the state. Republican success in close statewide races often depended upon the turnout and margin in DuPage County, along with the Cook County suburbs and some of the other ring counties surrounding Cook. Its size, centrality, and abundance of talent made DuPage Republicans powerful statewide figures. This, of course, increased the stakes of local political struggles, exacerbating the tensions that emerged from these other factors.

The effect of the strains in the local Republican organization can be seen in the bench, which was split between judges who had loyalties to different party factions. The nature of judicial operations, however, is such that these stresses manifested themselves only infrequently, such as in the slating of judges, the appointment of associate judges, and the selection of a chief judge. The infusion of DuPage's political environment into the court community, and the consequences thereof, can be seen more clearly in the public defender's office. It was largely a patronage operation. The head public defender was an active precinct committeeperson—an important position in DuPage County politics—who was appointed by the judges. He had been in office for eleven years at the time of this study and spent much of his time trying to satisfy divergent interests within the party. The result was an office with relatively abundant resources and politically protected attorneys who were permitted to engage in private practice on a part-time basis, making the office a very desirable entry-level position and patronage resource. An unforeseen consequence of this, however, was that assistant public defenders tended to stay in the office for much longer periods of time (five to seven years, in some cases) and developed a professional lethargy or malaise that severely eroded their position within the court community, if not their effectiveness as public defenders. While most became much more interested in their private practice, they did not want to give up the security of their public positions.

No other public defender office enjoyed the type of facilities DuPage offered. The salary ranges of the part-time assistants were higher than those paid to full-time assistants in other counties. In addition to manageable caseloads (assistants were assigned to a particular judge who had a full civil docket in addition to a criminal docket), the office had eight secretaries, a number of full-time investigators, several video telephones that assistants could use to talk to incarcerated clients, a law library, and computer facilities. As one assistant said: "We are adequately funded, we have an adequate investigation staff, we have good secretaries. We have law clerks to do our running around, to do our researching, except that sometimes they aren't around to do our research. About half the time I do my own research. I think we have five or six full-time investigators, mainly former police officers. They do all of our interviews, all of the individual interviews. There is no other public defender's office that has a staff, an investigative staff like we do."

The office was also top-heavy with administrative personnel. In addition to a full-time head, they had a first assistant and a head of the felony division, positions unheard of in other similar-sized offices. The extent to which these were patronage jobs was clear when it was suggested that the functions of these supervisors were unclear. One person was very explicit concerning the head of the felony division: "We have a head of felonies and that's ———. ——— has no function whatsoever. I'm not kidding, you can ask any of the other attorneys. ——— is not assigned to a judge, although ——— does take preliminary hearings a couple of days a month."

This was almost corroborated by the person in question, who said, "Most of the judges I am sure don't even know that I am head of the criminal division even though I have been for three years. They don't even know that. I keep a low profile. There's no reason to let them know."

The effects of patronage were also clear in the lower echelons of the public defender bureaucracy, and they had a significant deleterious impact upon the atmosphere in the office. For example, one assistant public defender was assigned to a judge who subsequently became the chief judge. After being elected chief judge, he refused to take any new criminal cases.

Even though most of his old ones were disposed of, no effort was made to assign new duties to the assistant. He spent most of his time at his private office. A somewhat similar situation concerned a misdemeanor assistant who was so incompetent that none of the judges wanted her in their courtroom. According to one of her colleagues:

> We were just talking about that this morning; they reward those that are not very competent. They keep them and they move them into the background. They move them out of the courtroom into the office, and they do no work, and then they get paid whether or not they do work. We were just talking about it today. It's sort of funny because there's another person in misdemeanors who various judges don't even, well they say the same thing about ———, they don't even want them in their courtroom. So they take ———, and put ——— in the office. Now ——— doesn't go to juvenile court, ——— doesn't come here. ——— works about one day a week, you know, and that's how it goes. The worse you are, the better off you are.

Another assistant stressed the political overtones by noting that many assistants were elected precinct committeepersons and others had a specific sponsor or political connection; the head cleared all personnel appointments with the county board. Another noted, "You know, we've got the governor's nephew, the judge's son, the judge's girlfriend, and all other kinds of people with contacts."

We dwell on the role of politics in the public defender's office because it says something important about the role, legitimacy, and acceptability of partisan political considerations within the DuPage court community, especially the bench and public defender's office. But this situation also illustrates the effect that ecological factors can have upon the cohesiveness of the courthouse community. The effect of the highly partisan atmosphere in DuPage was to atomize relationships and perspectives. The situation in the public defender's office worked against a sense of common purpose or destiny and caused petty resentments because everyone knew that the assistants had a "good deal"—including the assistants. At the same time, many of them thought the others were receiving differential treatment. This caused a great deal of animosity, worked against an office espirit de corps, and aggravated the professional malaise brought about by the rel- atively long tenures. Many simply wanted to put in their time and have as little to do with the office and the court community as possible, devoting time and energies to the development of private practices and leaving a void in the court community.

The impact upon the cohesiveness of the court community of the highly partisan, factionalized, high-stakes political situation in DuPage— due in large part to the tremendous growth it experienced over the last several decades—was not limited to the public defender's office. Indeed, its most direct and visible effect was through the prosecutor's office, a much more powerful post than the public defender's, and one traditionally used as a vehicle for higher political positions. The attractiveness of the office led to a primary challenge to the DuPage Republican organization's candidate in 1976. The challenger was a well-to-do, accomplished attorney who, although he had relatively broad legal experience, was not a local insider. He spent a large sum of his own money, ran a well-organized and relatively sophisticated campaign, and defeated the regular party candidate.

The new state's attorney cleaned house, appointed other outsiders to top administrative positions, revamped office policies, and refused to hire applicants sent to him by the party. He eagerly filled the void created by the problems in the public defender's office. No attempt was ever made to mend fences with party regulars, and he alienated the defense bar by destroying its previously cozy relationship with the prosecutor's office. This previous relationship was based upon generous warrant and charge reduction policies, which created many "junk" cases that were easily, and profitably, handled by the private bar. The new prosecutor even removed the public defender's office from some space in State's Attorney's annex, which was proximate to the courthouse, to an old bank building a considerable distance from the courthouse.

In response to the prosecutor's heavy-handedness, a group of defense attorneys formed the DuPage County Criminal Defense Bar Association to oppose his policies. They charged that the prosecutor's office suffered from insecure, paranoid leadership that was inhumane, vindictive, and politically motivated. In addition, they felt the leadership was cultivating a crusader's mentality and a deep mistrust in the new assistants toward defense attorneys, one that challenged their legitimacy and integrity. Some felt that the newcomers were not being taught to be "respectful." This was very difficult for the defense attorneys to accept, because many were former prosecutors and/or had been around the system a long time. Many had fond memories of days before hostility and adversary relations had displaced close-knit, cooperative relationships.

Feelings of hostility ran deep among defense attorneys, especially private ones, and this worked against any sense of common identity or shared purposes. These sentiments tended to reinforce formal roles. Speaking of the prosecutor's office, one private attorney, a former official in the state's attorney's office, said:

> They cannot make the distinction, in my opinion, between innocence and not guilty, and there is a distinction. An innocent man never committed the crime, a guilty one cannot be proved without a reasonable

doubt. They say he's either innocent or he's guilty, there's no middle ground, there's no not guilty. There really is a difference. Laymen always ask me, how can you defend guilty people? I say well, they're not guilty until proved guilty in the Constitution, which I am sworn to abide by and I believe in. It says the state has the burden and that's all I am doing is making the state meet the burden. Well they don't realize that if they can't meet that burden they lose. I've never seen anything like this. It makes me feel good to be a defense attorney. Up until they came in here, I think I was just kind of doing my job and making a few bucks here and there. I knew what had to be done. *I really believe that a prosecutor's office like this helps me to realize what a defense attorney's role in society is.* (emphasis added)

This situation fractured the DuPage court community. The private defense bar and the head prosecutor were at loggerheads, while the public defender's office was immobilized by internal problems. The judges had divided loyalties and mixed sentiments. The grapevine was fractured, with only a few shoots bridging the gaps that divided the court community. Process and cordiality norms were largely ignored as the prosecutor revolution-alized the plea process by drastically reducing the discretion of his assistants, and mutual distrust among prosecutors and defenders spread. The many courtesies that defense attorneys had learned to expect were no longer forthcoming, while adversarial postures and "unexpected" developments were becoming more common. This, of course, led to a further withering of the grapevine.

Much of the stress within DuPage derived from the fact that the head prosecutor placed little value on minimizing conflict, both because of his personality and the fact that conflict had gotten him where he was. Moreover, it was the only way he saw of getting where he wanted to be. He wanted to change things quickly, and the only way to accomplish this was by confrontation, which was, in any event, hardly unknown in the fractionalized politics of contemporary DuPage County. He also chose confrontation because he believed he had the will and resources to win.

The once vibrant state of the courthouse community in DuPage indicates that a highly cohesive court community is not unattainable in a large sprawling county. Moreover, the insurgent prosecutor was finally ousted by the Republican party in 1984, after eight rancorous years. Many predicted a return to the "good old days." But we do not have to refer to history or predict the future to support the point that cohesiveness can be attained in larger jurisdictions. We can merely look to Montgomery County to see a very different level of cohesiveness in a setting similar to DuPage's. In talking to members of the court system in Montgomery, constant references were made to the notion of family. Indeed, several used the phrase "we are one family." There was a considerable amount of rapport among the defense attorneys and prosecutors, and there was a preoccupation with not rocking the boat, with maintaining a congenial atmosphere. The comments of many interviewed were well summarized by a public defender: "I'd say that generally the lawyers in the county are trustworthy. And there's a good relationship usually between the prosecutors and lawyers. There's no question of shenanigans. There's no judges that can be bought. So the system has a certain amount of integrity to it which I think helps it operate."

Many attorneys were exceptionally concerned with their reputation for cooperation and fair dealing, which had a significant impact upon their conduct. Both prosecutors and defense attorneys tried to avoid violating well-understood norms and would go to what many would consider extreme lengths to maintain their reputation and avoid conflict. For example, defense attorneys emphasized nonadversarial postures and stressed that they did not attempt to take advantage of the inexperienced prosecutors that regularly rotated through the system. As one commented, "There have been many cases where a D.A. has made a deal with me and I look at him and I say, 'Hey, that's not enough. You're too low on the case.' The guy says he wants a $250 fine. I say, 'No, make him pay $500.' Because it's fair."

The same attorney commented on his efforts not to avoid certain judges, and said that if he was assigned to a particularly harsh one, "Fine. That's where I go. I don't get sick. I don't have a conflict. But do you understand, if you play the game that way, at least I think it's proper, you have credibility with the court, you have credibility with the D.A.s. And after a while when you get up and say something, they believe you. And I am not disbelieved."

The preoccupation with reputation and not making waves is because of the widespread belief in Montgomery that deviance from accepted norms had consequences. One interviewee who failed to win endorsement of the area leaders for the GOP nomination for a county office explained why he did not seek to overturn their decision at the county convention: "I decided that I maybe should not do that because around here when you put up a stink, they generally hold it against you when it's over." This was possible because the local Republican party was both powerful and, unlike in DuPage, highly centralized. One legal aid attorney who had repeatedly agitated the establishment with legal tactics was asked if he could practice in the county once he left his present position. He responded, "Well, I don't know if the opportunity would avail itself, because it's such a closed club up here of private attorneys that are all tied with the Republican party and the judiciary, which is Republican.

It's like the good old boys, and they all know each other and it's a lot of inbreeding...."

The homogeneity and cohesiveness of the court community was confirmed by many, including a judge who noted that despite the size of the Montgomery bar (about 1,200), "Here, more lawyers know at least half the other lawyers of the bar.... I guess I know most of the members of our bar, more than half. Everybody knows everybody."

The highly accommodative, family-like atmosphere in Montgomery was reinforced by a very effective grapevine. One attorney's comments describe its nature and operation:

> Anytime someone has been chastized, the letter is typed by a secretary and mailed by a secretary. And you'd better believe that grapevine is faster than any grapevine you would want to know. If you could tap into that grapevine, you've got it made. The word gets around, maybe without any names being mentioned. "So and so is in trouble because he did so and so."... You know, you have to be here for a few years to realize how the grapevine works. All right, one of our secretaries is now a secretary to a judge and somebody else in this office is now a crier to a judge, and he's friendly to the secretary. The secretary comes up here to drink coffee with these secretaries and they have lunch together everyday. So it spreads back. It just goes back and forth.

This type of setting was conducive to the development and enforcement of norms within the court community. What these rules were was quite clear to some members of the bar. One attorney contended that the formula for success in the Montgomery bar was to register Republican, attend all bar association affairs, and refrain from associating with Jewish members of the bar. Other attorneys explained how they made sure to spread the word when an opponent lied or generally acted unacceptably. A public defender noted that a local attorney had placed an ad offering 10 percent discount coupons for senior citizens, and he felt the bar's legal ethics committee was going to "get" the attorney.

The comments of a judge aptly describe the role that sanctions play in reinforcing the norms against nonconformity, in shoring up the strength of the court community, and in managing conflict in a county such as Montgomery. They are worth quoting at length.

> [Even] in a county such as this, where we have a much closer relationship between bench and bar, and where you have the overwhelming majority of members of the bar who think alike, you end up with black sheep... who would go off on these tangents. And I think they'd be subject to a tremendous amount of peer pressure both from lawyers and judges. And I use peer pressure because of the close relationship

between judge and lawyer in this county. This is more of a homogeneous bench/bar relationship here, a legal relationship.

And I think the judges are in a position to talk to and influence lawyers. And the overwhelming majority of the bar would not stand for those shenanigans without pressures being brought. . . .

Outside of a courtroom, if I see attorneys who are bringing a lot of nonsensical pleadings and filing objections or 64 pages of interrogatories that are absolutely unreasonable beyond any point of rationality, then I would talk to that attorney directly one-on-one and try to smarten him up. . . . Lawyers who don't get the message find that a lot of courtesies and niceties which we enjoy affording them disappear, and that they lose the benefits that a close rapport with the judge can bring. . . . There are many subtle ways in which a lawyer can be given the message. If a guy really wants to be difficult, a rat to his colleagues, I suppose he can do it and go along for a long, long period of time. His clients will probably pay a terrible price in that other attorneys will react in-kind, the court will act in-kind, the administrative officers will react in-kind, and I guess eventually it catches up with them.

. . . and if some fellow gives you a very obnoxious and calculatedly difficult time, without an appropriate basis, he'll pay for it some day, because he's gonna have to come back to you.

The strength of the highly centralized Republican organization in Montgomery—and the court community's concern with, and effectiveness in eliminating, deviance, deviants, and conflict—worked against the emergence of a dominant, activist leader within the criminal justice system. No one similar to the DuPage prosecutor existed in Montgomery, and it would have been difficult for such a figure to emerge and survive, or to have such a disruptive impact upon community norms. Thus, confrontation was less acceptable in Montgomery, even though there was a certain amount of back-biting, gossiping, and petty squabbles.

Another important difference between Montgomery and DuPage concerns the role of partisan considerations in court affairs. Partisan considerations were wholly acceptable in both counties, especially with respect to personnel matters. But, although most hirings in Montgomery were patronage jobs that had to be cleared with the party, they were not patronage plums. Simply put, Montgomery County had a well-deserved reputation for being cheap. There were no divergent factions that had to be accommodated with larger shares of an expanding pie. Entrance-level salaries for assistant prosecutors and public defenders were extremely low (around $12,000 in 1980), especially considering the relative wealth of the county. In some cases, comparable positions in Montgomery were paid $20,000 less than those in DuPage. Consequently, positions in the prosecutor and public defender offices turned over very quickly. Despite this, or perhaps because of it, the attorneys developed a sense of comraderie. They did not identify strongly with their positions, because they knew they were but a brief stopping place in their careers, a type of apprenticeship they shared on the way to something better.

If Montgomery had a relatively homogeneous, cohesive court community that was held together by a variety of external and informal factors, and DuPage's once close-knit community had been fractured by a different mix of similar forces, Oakland presented an entirely different situation. Unlike in Montgomery, there was little sense of identification with a larger group in Oakland; unlike in DuPage, there were no deep organizational cleavages that were accompanied by overt hostilities and distrust. Extremely diffuse is the best way to depict the character of the court community in Oakland.

One could point to Oakland's size as the reason that a cohesive community did not emerge. It was almost twice as large as DuPage and Montgomery. Its bar association, which totalled 2,100 lawyers, was also almost twice as large as those in the other ring counties. This explanation, however, is far too simplistic, and it ignores a variety of centrifugal forces at work in Oakland that worked against a high level of cohesiveness. One set of factors that interacted with size in Oakland can be labeled geophysical. The Oakland county courthouse is located on a campus of other government buildings. Every other courthouse is located in a central commercial district surrounded by law offices, restaurants, watering holes, and other features that nurture and reinforce a sense of cohesiveness and community. It was inconvenient to hang around the Oakland courthouse area after handling a case, and few did so on a routine basis.

Structural factors also worked against a cohesive community in Oakland. Despite its size, it was not large enough to develop a significant regular's bar specializing in criminal work. There were simply not enough cases to support such a specialization, as in places like New York, Chicago, Detroit, and other metropolitan areas. This, of course, led to the involvement of far more private attorneys in criminal work. Compounding this was the fact that Oakland had no public defender's office and that Oakland judges controlled appointments for indigent clients. Thus, instead of six or seven public defenders handling 50-60 percent of the cases, Oakland had hundreds of attorneys involved in the handling of a few cases each. The sheer numbers involved impeded the development of a sense of collegiality. But, perhaps more important, many of the attorneys involved had little stake in the development of lasting interpersonal ties and shared understandings. Such things require time, and their time is best invested developing other facets of their private practice. Personal ties and shared understandings also depend upon continuing interaction to establish and reinforce the sense of mutual dependencies. These continuing interactions were less common in Oakland because of its size and the structure of its indigent defense system. Just as important, however, is the fact that the Oakland judges regularly switched from a criminal to a civil docket at six-week intervals, making interactions even more sporadic.

Finally, several political factors were also instrumental in creating the diffuseness that characterized the Oakland court community. One obvious point here is that because Oakland was not dominated by a centralized party, the local organization could not act as a strong centripetal force as it was in Montgomery. Less obvious is that a weak party structure creates opportunities, power vacuums perhaps, that attract, or create, strong leaders. Persons seeking office where party structures are weak must maintain a high profile in order to gain visibility and supporters. This, of course, makes them independent of the local party, which is less able to broker problems among different offices, leading people to go their own way. The impact of the weak party structure was enhanced in Oakland because of its statewide prominence. As in DuPage, many Oakland leaders were statewide figures. This led them to be more outward-looking than inward-looking, less concerned with the needs of maintaining a cohesive work setting. This, again, reinforced the other centrifugal forces.

This can be seen in the case of both the prosecutor and the judges. The Oakland head prosecutor was politically very visible in the state and ambitious. He had run unsuccessfully for the Republican nomination for the U.S. Senate and for governor since being elected prosecutor. He also spearheaded statewide campaigns to abolish "good time" in the prison system, create preventive detention, and reinstate the death penalty. He was elected head prosecutor after he challenged the incumbent, who had earlier fired him in a dispute over plea bargaining policies. Thus, like the head prosecutor in DuPage, the Oakland prosecutor was a quasi-outsider, a rebel, and the dominant figure in the local court system, one whom the judges did not care to challenge. Upon taking office, the Oakland prosecutor instituted massive changes in office operations and policies after clearing out the former employees. He bureaucratized the very large office (55 attorneys, 120 total employees), which was quite amorphous under his predecessor. Separate units were created, section chiefs appointed, and office manuals drafted. Many functions, including plea bargaining, were centralized. He also eschewed political hiring by recruiting directly from law schools; the prior practice was to hire attorneys who had prior dealings with the county, especially the judges. One of the avowed purposes of these changes was to realign assistant prosecutors' loyalties. Traditionally, they were very close to, and dominated by, the judges. Assistant prosecutors often owed their jobs to a judicial contact and were assigned to individual courtrooms on a semipermanent basis. Thus the work group ties were strong.

Although the relations between individual prosecutors and judges were generally quite good, the efforts by the prosecutor to reassert control over what he considered his domain led to institutional tensions, although not nearly as acrimonious as those in DuPage. These were exacerbated by several other encounters between the bench and the prosecutor's office. In one instance, the judges tried to preemptorarily annex part of the prosecutor's office so they could accommodate three new judges. As one prosecutor related the incident, "One day they issued an Administrative Order telling us to get out. We just told them where to get off. When we took that hard line position they finally sat down and started talking. The judges, they're unique animals. I don't know how to best describe the relationship but they, they serve higher ends than the rest of us and they wear different colored costumes. They take themselves too seriously sometimes."

Another conflict grew out of a grand jury investigation conducted by a circuit judge into a welter of accusations involving improper activities on the part of the prosecutor's office and the Pontiac police department, which traded charges of impropriety. The situation arose from a series of gambling raids made by the prosecutor's organized crime task force. The judge's active role rankled the prosecutor's office, which felt that its efforts and activity to combat crime were being compromised by the judiciary. It was also embarrassed by the continuing publicity given the incident.

These tensions and the prosecutor's efforts to realign the loyalties of his assistants reinforced formal organizational identities, working against a broader sense of allegiance. Several attributes of the Oakland bench further atomized perceptions and relationships. First, like the head prosecutor, many of the judges were professionally ambitious, in contrast to most judges in other counties who viewed a judgeship as the capstone of their career. These aspirations led the judges to distinguish themselves as individuals. While the bench was fairly collegial, individual prerogatives were guarded carefully. There was also a healthy sense of competition among the judges, one that led them to experiment, innovate, and "be different." This was almost a natural outgrowth of their higher aspirations, but it was encouraged by certain norms and practices, the most important of which was the chief judge's practice of ranking the judges monthly in terms of their docket. As one observer noted, "They have a good competition among themselves. . . . A monthly report that they get shows where they stand in line with the others and what their caseload is and how old it is. And one judge calls the others to let them know that he has finally worked his way up to third place."

This competition and independence was evident in a number of areas.

The judges had individual dockets, and a variety of approaches to docket management were used. As one attorney noted, "It's kind of mind-boggling. Not only do you have fourteen different ways [of managing dockets], you have fourteen different ones every week. They change because the judges are so aggressive and they are so statistically minded that they're constantly striving. They're never satisfied."

This diversity of approach also surfaced with respect to the appointment of counsel for indigents. Some judges made appointments to a handful of attorneys, while some appointed attorneys at random; others used a mixed approach. Finally, while none of the judges would regularly commit themselves to a sentence in plea discussions, judges varied in the extent to which they would even "ballpark" sentences. The closest thing to a common policy was a sentencing panel established to help minimize disparity across the fourteen judges.

Other benches had professionaly ambitious judges and were competitive, yet cohesive court communities existed. One reason that these considerations assume such importance in Oakland County is that they acted in concert with the factors mentioned earlier: size, geophysical factors, political factors, and prosecutorial orientation. Also, one got the feeling that the judges felt more was at stake in Oakland County. They viewed it as inevitable that Wayne County would be bypassed by Oakland as the preeminent county in Michigan— culturally, socially, economically, and politically. With it they saw the chance to become the preeminent bench. They wanted to be "not like Detroit," but they also wanted to be better then everyone else.

In their view the court, like the county, was still evolving as an institution and gaining prominence as it grew. Accordingly, there were opportunities to impress on it a stamp of innovativeness and a tradition of efficiency. The judges pointed to their accomplishments in computerizing the court's records and procedures, displayed the computer terminals in their chambers as electronic totems of their faith in modern court technology, and instituted a mediation program to expedite civil cases. One judge experimented with telephone conference calls as a substitute for appearances in civil cases. The court also used mail arraignments in criminal cases to save time on what some felt were routine chores. In all of these endeavors, they were constantly looking outward, anxious about how they were viewed by others and willing to innovate even further to impress. This increased the competitive and individualistic forces already in operation. While they were looking outward, they were also looking over their shoulder. Wholly internal considerations were simply not as important in Oakland, because the judges were hunting bigger game.

The diffuseness of the Oakland court community makes it difficult to discuss the structure of shared values and perspectives. However, in the principal areas with which we are concerned— views on the appropriate role of politics and the value placed upon conflict avoidance—a number of things are apparent. First, the role of partisan political considerations did not appear to be nearly as universally acceptable in Oakland as in DuPage and Montgomery. This is partly because of the fact that partisanship was simply not as relevant in Oakland. Judges were not selected through partisan elections, and neither party was dominant enough to bring pressure on individual offices. Moreover, there was no Oakland public defender's office, the office most amenable to partisan pressures, and the head prosecutor was a powerful, highly visible, and ambitious figure who strove to build a reputation as a reform-minded innovator. He could not afford to, nor did he have to, succumb to localistic, partisan pressures. Many of the judges were reputed to show favoritism in their indigent defense appointments, but not of the partisan kind. Many of the judges used a random, or at least unbiased, appointment procedure.

In Oakland, there was neither the concern with conflict avoidance nor the mechanisms for controlling conflict found in Montgomery. At the same time, there was not the level of overt hostilities as existed in DuPage, despite the fact that the stakes were at least as high in Oakland. One got the sense that the manifestation of petty hostilities and animosities was considered to be inconsistent with the image that Oakland actors sought to project. There were confrontations to be sure, but they were conducted more on an institutional level than a personal one. Pent-up feelings seemed to be channeled into more productive activities and seemed to surface in the form of healthy competition, one-upsmanship across individuals and institutions.

The state of the grapevine reflected, as is so often the case, the nature of the court community in Oakland. It cannot be said that a unified grapevine existed in Oakland. Rather, the situation was more similar to a vineyard, with plants rooted in individual courtrooms. If a unified grapevine existed in an earlier era, the atomization of the Oakland court community caused the unnourished branches to wither and die. What remained was simply a network centered on individual courtrooms. There was neither need nor sufficient nutrients for a more extensive flow of information. In the large, diffuse Oakland setting, indigent assignment was controlled by individual judges, and assistant prosecutors were assigned to courtrooms. Happenings were so courtroom-specific that a broad base of information was not of prime importance. It was also difficult to obtain. Aside from a cafeteria in the courthouse, there was no common gathering place or watering hole. Moreover, trial prosecutors were housed separate from the chief prosecutor's office, further hampering the collection and wide dissemination of information. The absence of a public defender's office compounded the problem, with the result being the emergence of several more limited grapevines.

THE AUTONOMOUS COUNTIES

The very distinctive political ethos and other attributes shared by Peoria and Kalamazoo counties contributed to the formation of court communities that were similar in many regards, but by no means identical. They were much smaller court communities than those in the ring counties and were more cohesive, with some exceptions. The views and practices of defense attorneys were not highly adversarial or formalistic, especially when contrasted with some of the private attorneys in DuPage. The largely cooperative stances of the defense bar in these counties eliminated a major source of tension within the court community. There was also an unstated assumption that overt hostilities were both unseemly and counterproductive. Thus, despite the fact that we observed no inordinate concern with not rocking the boat, and virtually no one talked about the consequences of nonconformity, there was clearly a high value placed upon harmony and the avoidance of avert conflict in Peoria and Kalamazoo. This was a partial consequence of the reformed political culture shared by these counties. Another concomitant of this reformed orientation is the illegitimacy of partisan political considerations in the conduct of the court community's business in both Peoria and Kalamazoo.

Size is one of the most notable differences between the court communities in the ring counties and Peoria and Kalamazoo. In Peoria, two judges and five felony prosecutors heard virtually all of the felony caseload. The judges heard only felony cases for several years at a stint. There were eight public defenders who accounted for more than 60 percent of the felony caseload (see Table 6.5 in chapter 6). In Kalamazoo, there were four judges (each also heard civil cases) and ten felony prosecutors. Ten attorneys handled the indigent defense cases, which totalled more than 80 percent of all felony cases, the largest percent in the nine counties (see Table 6.5). Moreover, the local bars were much smaller in Peoria and Kalamazoo, a few hundred compared to slightly more than a thousand in DuPage and Montgomery and more than two thousand in Oakland. Of equal significance is the fact that the bar in Peoria and Kalamazoo, unlike in the ring counties, is concentrated in the downtown area of the county seat (the cities of Peoria and Kalamazoo) instead of being dispersed throughout the county. The courthouses are surrounded by eating and drinking establishments, and most private offices are within walking distance of the courthouse. These factors combined to give Peoria and Kalamazoo the two most concentrated criminal bars of the nine counties, a relatively small handful of attorneys accounting for more than 82 percent and 90 percent of the felony cases, respectively (Table 6.5). It also facilitated the development of a healthy, active grapevine in each.

Constant interactions between such a small group of individuals does not guarantee a harmonious and cohesive court community and, indeed, petty squabbles between the Peoria head prosecutor and head public defender, and among the Kalamazoo judges, were well documented. These were largely based upon stylistic and personality differences, however, and were insignificant compared to the rancorous bickering in DuPage. The higher degree of mutual interdependence in these smaller communities may have helped minimize interpersonal problems, especially because many of the attorneys in these communities did not have long-standing personal ties. Unlike in the declining counties, many attorneys in Peoria and Kalamazoo were imports who moved there for professional reasons. Another important factor in producing cohesiveness and harmony is that the civic pride and boosterism so evident in the community at large seemed to have an impact upon the court community. Indeed, the comments of several participants suggested the existence of a mutual admiration society.

This was very evident in Peoria, as a police official noted. "We have an extraordinary local relationship. We have a really good set of judges now; we have a nonpolitical prosecutor and a very professional group of people. They're all working hard, and they work rather well together trying to solve problems. I would guess we probably have the best local criminal justice system in the state, or maybe in the Midwest. . . . The caliber of the people and the way they're working and functioning together . . . is far higher than you'd expect to find elsewhere."

In stark contrast to DuPage, a private attorney assessed the Peoria prosecutors as follows: "In general they are pretty easy to deal with. In other words, they're looking for a negotiation too, except on a given case where both sides know, 'Hey, we're not talking about anything but a trial on this. Let's make it as simple as possible for both of us.' Complete disclosure is discovery. By that I mean even beyond what the discovery rules call for. No games as well."

Another attorney said of the judges, "I think we are very fortunate with the caliber of judges we have. I for one don't have tremendous respect for the office. I, unfortunately, feel to a large degree, we have the office of circuit judge filled with incompetents, not only in the state of Illinois, but nationwide, as far as I'm concerned—people who couldn't make it in practice, or were lazy, or were strictly politicians, one of the three, but sometimes the combination of all of them. However, frankly in Peoria, I think that we are lucky and blessed with judges."

The level of harmony was widespread and genuine in Peoria, characterized by widely shared perceptions on fundamental issues. Part of this harmony must be attributed to the exceptionally conservative defense bar in Peoria, an orientation that often obscured the distinction between prosecuting and defense attorneys. Indeed, as a group the defense bar in Peoria scored higher on the Belief in Punishment scale described in chapter 3 than did St. Clair's prosecutors! Disarmingly antidefendant attitudes were displayed in several interviews with defense attorneys, public and private. One expressed his feelings as follows:

> I don't really identify with my clients. You always like to be able to, you know, identify with the type of people you're working for and I just don't. You know I'm not from that level of society.... Some public defenders develop a very good rapport with their clients, at least that's the appearance that you get. They cater to them and they give them a shoulder to cry on. "Too bad you're getting raked over the coals." But you know, I don't do it anymore. I just don't have the capacity to really get upset with these guys' plights.... A lot of them feel I'm sure that I'm not too sympathetic with them, just because I don't say, "Gee, you're a victim of circumstances."...
>
> Sometimes I feel awkward because I subscribe to the ideas that [the prosecutors] do. You know I live here, I don't want any bums on the street.

Practitioners in Kalamazoo were not as overtly effusive in their praise for one another as those in Peoria. This is largely because of a number of strains that existed across several corridors within the court community, in particular within the bench. Much of the strain emanated from attorneys' relations with the bench, which were in part a reflection of problems within the judiciary. The problems were based upon personality and style and led to much disharmony within the bench. The judges were relatively old, averaging more than sixty, yet inexperienced. All but one were serving their first term on the bench. Each had had a previous career in private practice and was unaccustomed to the demands of public service. They were unable to agree on uniform docketing procedures, with the result being the emergence of different practices and a severe backlog problem. The judges were also harshly critical of one another's plea practices.

The backlog and problems resulting from the failure of the judges to organize their work effectively came to a head when the judges dismissed more than a dozen felony cases for the failure of the prosecution to bring them to trial within Michigan's 180-day time limit. The prosecutors countered that they had been "knocking on the courthouse door" trying to schedule the cases. Tensions were enhanced when, before the 1980 election, a highly publicized set of cases created a good deal of animosity between the defense bar and the judges, one in particular. The cases involved more than forty men accused of homosexual conduct in a public restroom.

The judges had to rule on the issue of whether videotapes could be accepted as evidence. Because of the random assignment procedure used in Kalamazoo's individual calendaring system, each of the four judges had to decide the question. The judges ultimately issued separate opinions, with two rulings on one side and two on the other. One judge in particular drew the ire of attorneys, who formed a Trial Lawyers Association to denounce the quality of his decision openly, along with the fact that he waited several months before announcing it. In addition, this judge antagonized attorneys in the courtroom. In large part because of this incident, the judge in question was rated "not qualified" by more than 60 percent of the Kalamazoo bar. He was defeated for reelection, a first in Kalamazoo. Indeed, it was the first time a sitting Kalamazoo judge had even been challenged in thirty years.

The dissatisfaction with the prosecutor's office stemmed from their effort to centralize control over the dispositional process. The central operational figure in these efforts was the trial chief. As one former prosecutor noted, "For a while I had that position. It bothered me, but I continued to do it. Now ———— has it. He's the lightening rod. There's no question about it. The defense bar dislikes him. The judges dislike him. Cops dislike him because many times on warrant screening he handled it."

Just as important as the existence of these tensions in Kalamazoo, which suggest that size does not eliminate stresses, is that they did not paralyze or unduly preoccupy the court community. The contrast with DuPage is very clear: In Kalamazoo, one did not hang the dirty linen out in public. Problems existed, to be sure, but, with the exception of the bench, they were not to be dwelled upon or allowed to interfere with the day-to-day operation of the courts. It was an attitude similar to one attributed to the local newspaper and is traceable to the civic pride shared by so many in Kalamazoo. As a prominent member of the court community said:

> Kalamazoo really has this positive self-image and it has a lot of good reasons for it. The newspaper, to a certain extent I think, has helped foster that feeling in the community and is very proud of it. They are perhaps more reluctant because of that to rock the boat, even when it knows there's a problem.
>
> A number of years back, for example, there was a problem in the police force there with corruption. If my facts are correct, it was very close to something like this. Several policemen were essentially stealing contraband that was seized in raids. They were even taking it home with them. The newspaper found out about it, they talked to

the police chief and he got rid of the guys. The newspaper never really wrote anything about it. . . .

The editor in Kalamazoo has lived in Kalamazoo his whole life. He's been editor for 21 years. The most well-known person in town. He's done many good things with the newspaper too. For example, they supported the school desegregation plan which was immensely unpopular, and it helped desegregate Kalamazoo without any violence. Pontiac and Kalamazoo desegregated the same day. CBS crews were in Kalamazoo and Pontiac in the morning. By afternoon they were all in Pontiac, and no one ever paid any more attention to Kalamazoo. A lot of that was, of course, the way the newspaper had worked on that subject, educated the people about it, urged calm and all that. So I'm not saying that they don't do things that are important. But their instinct is not to make a big deal out of things because it will give the town a bad name, a chamber of commerce kind of thing.

Another reason that the strains Kalamazoo experienced did not affect its court system to the extent those in DuPage did was that the defense bar was much better integrated, as in Peoria. However, unlike in Peoria, the reasons for this integration in Kalamazoo were institutional and require a bit of court history to understand. In 1974, Kalamazoo instituted a contract system to replace its old practice of appointing counsel for indigents from a roster of private attorneys. However, practitioners cited a number of problems with the attorneys who won the first contracts in 1974 and 1975. They apparently provided a vigorous, careful, deliberate, and aggressive form of representation. One of the judges contended that the original group was "going beyond what I felt a defense attorney owes his client. . . . They were hard-working, aggressive, but they were turning over rocks, filing every possible legal motion that could be filed in every case, and to some extent contributed to our backlog." Others also attributed the backlog of cases that plagued Kalamazoo to the first group's style of practice. Another judge, for example, complained, "The first group we had, it took a day and a half to draw a jury, and we never recovered from it." Others felt that these original contract attorneys were reluctant to plea bargain.

One of the organizers of the group of attorneys who held the indigent defense contract at the time of this study described what happened to the previous group. He claimed their propensity to file motions led to conflicts with the prosecutor's office. This caused the D.A.s to stiffen on plea bargains, further contributing to the backlog. He noted that, "The judges, of course, were sick and tired of listening to those flakey, crappy motions—a lot of paper, a lot of time. Nothing ever got done—a terrible backlog." The judges let it be known to county officials that they were displeased and would prefer another group to seek the contract.

This led several local practitioners to initiate a consortium of attorneys to bid for the indigent defense contract. Each of the ten attorneys had been around the local court system for a while, seven were former prosecutors. The new group clearly understood the financial implications of the earlier group's time-consuming strategies and were well aware of the judges' concern for expediting the flow of cases and the avoidance of "unnecessary" formalities. They gave assurances of less obstructionist stances and negotiated a highly favorable contract, one that cost the county nearly twice as much as the prior contract. Their prior institutional ties with the prosecutor's office, plus the financial incentives built into the fixed-cost-per-case contract, mitigated the operational impact of whatever institutional stresses existed between the defense bar and the prosecutor's office. There was no payoff for sustained conflict.

The relatively distinctive structure of the indigent defense system in Kalamazoo was reflective of the reformist, management orientation to public affairs so characteristic of the political ethos that prevailed in Kalamazoo. The overriding consideration was: How could this service be structured so that it facilitated the flow of cases? A traditional, bureaucratic public defender's office, with its ample opportunities for patronage and political reward, was not considered seriously in Kalamazoo, even though most of the similarly sized counties in our study had one. Interestingly, the only other county with a indigent defense system similar to Kalamazoo's was Peoria. Rather than contracting with private attorneys on what amounted to a per-case basis, Peoria County had a part-time head who contracted with eight attorneys on a fixed-sum basis. The result was the same: There was no public bureaucracy, which was so distasteful in a political culture such as Peoria. It gave the impression of an efficient, privately operated public service. Neither partisan nor political considerations were relevant, but then neither was there much concern for an adversarial defense of the defendant.

The management orientation that characterized the court community in these two counties can also be seen in the prosecutor's office, especially in Kalamazoo. It was headed by a very forceful, hard-working leader who considered himself an outsider. He was a former Wayne County deputy sheriff, who after law school worked his way up to chief deputy prosecutor. He succeeded the office head, who did not choose to run for reelection. Despite his inside credentials, he considered himself the people's advocate within the system and was an extremely popular figure within the county. He championed Kalamazoo's good government orientation within the court system and prided himself in running an innovative, management-oriented office. And it was by most standards. He maintained and updated an office policy and procedure manual that first appeared in 1969. The office had a well-organized and effective screening mechanism, as well as a centralized plea system with sophisticated checks on the discretion of assistants. Office hiring was on a truly nonpartisan basis. In addition, the Kalamazoo prosecutor's office maintained a career criminal unit (even after federal funds expired), its own diversion program, a victim-witness assistance program, a consumer and commercial fraud unit, and a mail-in warrant process for minor offenses to cut down on police overtime and the drain on prosecutorial resources. It had an up-to-date Prosecutor's Management Information System (PROMIS) program, and prided itself in having adapted word-processing technology to handle routine prosecutorial paperwork efficiently. Finally, it broke tradition and hired a management specialist who was not a lawyer as office manager.

Peoria had a more traditional efficiency orientation. For example, the prosecutor's office was not as innovative as that in Kalamazoo. It experimented with standard forms, but it had not yet advanced to the computer age. Some new federally funded programs were used, but they had a short existence. Nonetheless, the Peoria prosecutor, who like his Kalamazoo counterpart was an extremely popular local leader, was very management oriented, especially when compared with most other counties of its size. He regularized the screening process and centralized plea offers to some extent. Partisan hiring was largely eliminated from the office. When the Republican state's attorney announced his intention not to seek reelection, five of his assistants filed for his job—three in the Republican primary and two in the Democratic.

Another point to emphasize about Peoria in this regard is that the judges were far more efficiency-oriented than the Kalamazoo judges, who were more concerned with the maintenance of judicial prerogatives. There were two full-time felony judges who took personal pride in keeping all other actors on their toes. They overscheduled cases, cajoled attorneys to be prepared, and frequently worked well into the evening to complete trials. One also got the sense that the entire court community in Peoria worked together more effectively, as some of the earlier quotations suggested. Within Peoria's local political culture, such cooperation simply seemed to be the thing to do.

Perhaps more so than even Oakland, Dauphin county's court community defies succinct characterization. In part, this is because, although it lacks any truly distinctive attributes, it does not really fit the mold of any of the other counties. It was a cohesive court community. Ties were especially strong among judges and public defenders. However there was not as strong a sense of identification with a larger group such as in Peoria and Montgomery. Many of the attorneys had only shallow roots in Dauphin, and others actually lived outside the county. Despite this, the structure and the relatively small size of the Dauphin court community (it was about the size of Kalamazoo) made a viable grapevine easy to maintain. One link among many of the Dauphin practitioners was their affiliation with the local Republican party. This set it off from Peoria and Kalamazoo, which did not have dominant local parties. But despite the existence of these party ties and the lack of a reformist, political tradition in Dauphin, partisan political considerations were not as important as in DuPage and Montgomery. At the same time, there was not the management orientation we observed in Peoria and Kalamazoo; inertia was a far more influential force. Finally, there was a high value placed upon cordial relations and the avoidance of open conflict. Even when conflicts surfaced, they did not have the far-reaching effects as they did in a county like DuPage.

The makeup of the Dauphin bench illustrates some of these general points. Five judges, four of whom were Republicans, heard felony cases. Most (four) had been on the bench quite some time (ten to fifteen years). These four were older and were close friends; two drove to work together daily, and two were former law partners. The judges met and dined together monthly. One summarized the relationships among the judges as follows: "The thing about our court is that we're all pretty good friends. Actually, most of us are of the same vintage. We were practicing lawyers together, and we were post–World War II veterans who came back about the same time and we've known each other for twenty-five to thirty years on a very close basis.... And we respect each other, I would say, and we feel perfectly free to go to someone if we have something that we want to talk to them about."

At the same time, however, another stressed that, "we are autonomous, independent. In the . . . years that I have been on the bench [we have been] respectful of our colleagues, motivated by our sense of self-respect and professional integrity, but very autonomous." Despite this, one could only describe the Dauphin bench as cohesive and compatible, especially when compared with the judges in places like Kalamazoo. This situation was facilitated by the president judge who, while the only Democrat, was a widely admired diplomat who was a master at diffusing conflict, whether it was among the judges, with the county board, or with the public defender's office.

Relations were cordial within the prosecutor's office, but it did not appear to be quite as cohesive as the bench. There was no bickering among the prosecutors, and no one dwelled upon any problems with the judges. However, there was a good deal of grumbling over inadequate resources, especially support staff and salary levels (the starting salary was $14,000, and most made between $15,000–16,000, while a seven-year veteran made $20,000). The office did not even have a dictaphone, much less a computer or word-processing equipment, a stark contrast to places like DuPage,

Oakland, and Kalamazoo. These resource problems accounted for the rapid turnover in personnel and, perhaps, for the lack of partisan considerations in hiring. The situation was even worse in the public defender's office. Although the public defenders had salary parity with the prosecutor, that was no great accomplishment. Their overall budget was less than half the prosecutor's. The office, which was located in part of a dilapidated old building away from the courthouse, did not even have a copying machine.

There was obviously not much enthusiasm for funding public defense in a conservative Republican county like Dauphin. The head public defender, who was appointed, understood his precarious position, as did most of the assistants. Consequently, the office evidenced a style of practice that can be described as pragmatic and cooperative. This obviously contributed to the largely cordial atmosphere in Dauphin. For example, the public defender's office did not require a physician at every mental health hearing; it readily stipulated to evidence. One experienced attorney expressed the dominant view in the office, "I feel we are under somewhat of a duty to—not to try to deliberately disrupt the court even though we could do it and then justify it because it's a legal right...I don't think that the attorneys in the office do that."

Despite this feeling, the office tolerated several attorneys who prided themselves as being dissidents or advocates, and few people thought the public defenders would not rigorously represent a defendant whom they thought was innocent. Moreover, from time to time, they took actions that irritated the judges and prosecutors. One public defender publicly asked a judge to remove himself from a case because of bias toward the defendant. Later, however, the assistant was forced to issue a written apology to the judge. Commenting upon the situation, an assistant prosecutor noted, "When you rock the boat in Dauphin County, boy, you've got a tough row to hoe."

Boat-rocking did not occur very often in Dauphin, because the actors generally seemed to know how far they could go. As one public defender said, "However, if we were to be disruptive in every standpoint, maybe some of the political things that we don't see, or maybe some of the political pressures...never felt in this office, such as being able to hire the people that we want to and things like that, maybe we would feel them if we were to go to that point. To say that we don't feel that or don't sense that would be wrong, because we do sense it...."

An equally important point to note about Dauphin is that, as in Kalamazoo, when waves are made, they seldom end up capsizing the boat. Conflicts are handled and are not allowed to cause deep, long-lasting rifes. For example, a potentially disruptive situation arose when the extremely popular head prosecutor, who had held office for fourteen years, decided not to seek reelection as head prosecutor. The Republican party slated the head public defender (the son of a long-time Republican warhorse) to succeed him. This candidate was challenged by the two chief aides to the former prosecutor. One of the aides eventually dropped out of the race, but the other, with the help of the retiring head and some fortunate occurrences during the campaign, soundly defeated the party's slated candidate. An analogous situation led to eight years of strife in DuPage. In Dauphin, there were some tensions between the two offices for a while, but they declined when a former law school colleague of the new prosecutor was named as head public defender. The victorious challenger ran with the rest of the county slate, and the fences with the local party were mended easily.

THE DECLINING COUNTIES

Despite the fact that St. Clair was the most heterogeneous of our counties—and perhaps because it was—its court community was one of the most homogeneous and close-knit. It was a small court community, along the lines of Peoria and Kalamazoo, but because St. Clair is not a magnet community, it did not attract as many outsiders as did Peoria and Kalamazoo. Consequently, most of the felony practitioners had long-standing social and personal ties and deep roots within the community. All three criminal court judges were local Irish Catholics. One, when asked where he was born and raised, pointed out his third-story window to the house of his birth and to his parochial school. The state's attorney was a former Belleville football star who attended Notre Dame, as was one of the judges. One of the younger judges played baseball with a group from the state's attorney's office and was said to drink and socialize frequently with them and other bar members. The public defender was a boyhood friend of the son of one of the judges; an assistant public defender was the brother of a former judge. Several neighborhood bars in the courthouse vicinity were useful in cementing these relationships as well as serving as important conduits in St. Clair's thriving grapevine.

A local reporter summarized the relationship within the court community, "You have a very clubbish atmosphere. Judges are former political figures who are elected. They have ties to the political system, so do the state's attorneys. The police chiefs in this are highly political. I think there's a clubbishness there, you know. They're all a bunch of good old boys. Their roots are all within the same system. This is pretty much a one-party county, a one-party area. Their roots are all together. They have connections, nobody wants to rock the boat."

A private defense counsel put it somewhat differently: "This is a great county to practice law in. You have access to the state's attorney, which in many counties you don't. They'll talk to you at any time. You can go over and talk to any prosecutor at any time, go over and sit in his office and talk to him about your case. It's an open book policy, they'll show you anything they've got. You can see anything. . . . This is as I said a very homogeneous bar. We're all just sleeping together. I mean we're all close to one another."

Despite the long-standing personal relationships and close-knit community that existed in St. Clair, a high value was not placed upon conflict avoidance. The felony practitioners in St. Clair bickered constantly, gossiped about one another openly, and enjoyed it all immensely. The public defenders and defense bar in particular were feisty, in marked contrast to places like Kalamazoo and Peoria and some of the public defenders in Dauphin. The St. Clair public defenders boycotted one of the three felony court judges for a period because they felt he was violating well-understood plea-bargaining norms concerning open pleas. The head public defender once issued a formal complaint against this judge for making racial slurs in reference to a client. The same judge made a habit of intimidating, correcting, and scolding attorneys who practiced in his courtroom. The judges got along well but openly complained about the uneven distribution of the interesting, highly publicized cases (assignments were controlled by the senior criminal court judge).

Conflict was an accepted part of everyday life in St. Clair, but it seemed to have little long-lasting effects. The type of bitter animosities that prevailed in DuPage were unknown in St. Clair; memories were short, and hard feelings dissipated quickly, often over a drink. The bickering that took place did not have any discernible, lasting impact upon the process as was the case with the Kalamazoo judges. This may have been because court community members viewed themselves as a family living in a hostile neighborhood, which quickly put things into perspective. It may have also been because stakes were so low in St. Clair. No one had ambitions that extended beyond the local community, and local success was highly dependent upon good cooperative relations with co-workers. In short, there was no future in lasting bitterness.

Another defining characteristic of St. Clair is the extent to which political considerations played a role in the day-to-day activities within the court community. In this respect it was the polar opposite of the autonomous counties. Not only were partisan political considerations expected to play a major role, but they were also viewed by most as wholly legitimate. But the role and nature of politics (in the tainted sense of the word) in St. Clair was quite different from that in a county like DuPage, where it involved partisan hirings, padded payrolls, and people concerned with higher political office.

Court lore in St. Clair is replete with incidents of patronage, corruption, abuses of power, and power plays for personal gains—sometimes very petty gains. Because the government is a major employer in this economically depressed area, patronage is very important, far more important than in the ring counties. People talked very freely about the "lugging system" whereby patronage employees—some of whom earned $6,000-$7,000 per year—were required to contribute 2.5 percent to the St. Clair Democratic party. Professional employees were asked to purchase tickets to Democratic party affairs. Partisanship and personal contacts also play a role in recruitment, especially among judges. One criminal court judge was an old Republican warhorse but he was also the personal attorney of two of the most important Democratic officials. When he decided to run, they agreed not to slate anyone to run against him. Another judge's father was a prominent party official. The son became an associate judge within months of completing the bar and was appointed a full circuit judge when a vacancy occurred shortly thereafter. A third judge had been a prominent assistant state's attorney for years, a past president of the local bar, and a highly respected attorney. He, however, was only an associate judge. Although he handled the same caseload as the circuit judges and was highly respected by the bar, he never had enough clout to become a full circuit judge and gain the office's considerably greater salary and prestige.

Personnel politics are not the only aspects of the local criminal justice system affected by St. Clair's corrupt heritage and distinctly unreformed orientation. Ticket-fixing by local police chiefs seemed to be widespread and was a major issue at the time of this study. A former police official in East St. Louis was indicted on federal civil rights charges when he allegedly turned his dog on a suspect accused of burglarizing his sister's home. A series of drug cases had to be dropped when it was discovered that a sergeant in the East St. Louis Police Department had sold the drugs held for evidence. Defense attorneys tell numerous stories of defendants being brutalized by members of various local police departments. Even prosecutors say that the police hold some defendants three to four days before the attorneys are aware of it. A former head of the state's attorney's office was indicted on federal racketeering charges, and a judge was also implicated in the investigation. Neither was convicted. Yet another judge was indicted when, after his son committed suicide, the police found several boxes of guns in the judge's home. They had been evidence in prior cases and were marked "To Be Destroyed."

This unreformed political orientation was also manifested in some of the case processing policies within the court system. Many evidenced pragmatic and what might be termed "unenlightened" approaches. One member of the state's attorney's staff who was discussing the handling of misdemeanor batteries commented, "I'd say there's some redeeming value in letting the police go out into neighborhood fights, write a battery ticket for trespassing or something, then wash it through the system. [We would] make a few bucks if the ticket's any good, if the case is any good. I just think that's where we're at."

And along the same lines, a defense attorney noted that it is a tradition in St. Clair to arrest and charge people even when there is only a slim likelihood of conviction. The idea is that the defendant will at least be punished by the payment of legal fees; a collateral occurrence, of course, is that the private defense bar is commensurately enriched. This used to be supplemented by what was termed the "fall roundup." According to one defense attorney: "In the old days, when ———— was state's attorney, they used to have what they called the fall roundup. On drug cases, they would go out and issue a couple of hundred drug cases at one time, and all the private bar would get rich for a couple of months. They'd wind up dismissing half of them." The same thing was done with prostitutes: "They'd arrest them all and then they'd charge them $25 or $50 in costs and the justice of the peace would get his cut and the cop would get his cut and then let them go back on the street again."

The types of innovations and reforms so prominent in some of the ring and autonomous counties were largely absent in St. Clair. The head prosecutor attempted to institute a rather modest reform, the screening of felony cases before filing. It was met with so much resistance that he ultimately decided against running for reelection and loosened screening criteria considerably toward the end of his tenure. There was virtually no support for ideas or procedures based upon solely professional considerations, nor was there an inclination to innovate. The primary consideration seemed to be, "What makes things easiest for all involved?"

The following passage—while admittedly an extreme expression of views to which many in St. Clair would disagree vehemently—captures the flavor of the pragmatic, unenlightened outlook better than any summary.

> Adult felony cases? I've always had a philosophy that they're starting at the wrong end. They pump money into these areas, to get jobs for teenagers, and so forth, and I think they are starting too late. I think they have to start when the child is born, especially down in the black neighborhoods, teach them respect for the law then. It's too late by the time they're sixteen. You can waste all the money you have, it won't make a damn bit of difference. . . . They don't understand probation. I've heard them, outside here, "Hey, I knew what I was gonna git, my feets is still on the street." They figured it out, and it's [taught to them] in the juvenile system. You'll see a fellow arrested forty-five times as a juvenile. Lectured, warned, and released. Now that's crap. . . .

I just think they have to establish some measure of respect among the so-called ghetto type. Now I came from a very poor family. We lived up in the Stockyards District, and there were mostly Irish up there, Irish and Poles. Now those two races, they work. They don't ask anybody to give them anything. In fact, they resent somebody trying to give them something. That isn't the situation we have anymore. Half of your criminals that come out of this felony court here, that are over twenty-one, are on relief. Now that is for the birds. And as far as rehabilitation, some of them have never been habilitated to start with. You can't rehabilitate them. And it's a change thing to me. It has been this permissive generation among the whites. Your professional class, the doctor who is so busy making himself a multimillionaire that he does not have time to discipline his boy. So his boy goes next door and vandalizes the entire house, rips up everything. And daddy runs out saying, don't worry about it, I'll pay for it. That's not the answer, daddy paying for it. That's what the kid figured on. The kid wants daddy to come in and knock his teeth out....

By the time they get here it's too late. I take a look into, I put a lot of stress on their school attendance. Attendance first, grades second. And I've discovered that you don't have to pass. They have what they call social promotions now. When the teachers aren't in the picket line, they're busy passing people who have failed. And, as I have said repeatedly, that the criminals down there are the teachers.

Now, among your blacks, you'll find it's a matriarchal society. The father, all he has is a stiff penis. And when you find one who lives with his family and works, he's a convicter. You say, "What do you do?" "I work for American steel." "How long have you been with them?" "Twenty-nine years." "Do you have any children?" "I have four." "Where are they?" "One of them's up in Purdue, the other one's here." You've got a convicter right there. He owns his own property, he wants law and order. But you take the next character, "When did you work last?" "Oh, 1965, I worked a couple of days that year." "What have you been doing since?" "I've been on relief." He's not worth a shit. I think it's a sense of responsibility. In our hurry, in our big rush to apologize for making them slaves, we've gone overboard the other way....

I don't know what the answer is. I know one thing, the answer is not the way we're going about it now. And the answer is not to have some misguided white broad go down to the black neighborhood and say, "Well I understand...." The next thing you know she is going to be on her back and then she'll come and say, "I was violated." So what? I mean, violated, you son-of-a-bitch, if you had any brains, you wouldn't have been down there. But, blacks are good people if they're treated right. But they have to be treated firm.

The long-standing personal ties among many Saginaw court actors and the ample opportunity for informal interaction defused most situations that could potentially produce serious conflict. Conflict simply did not play the role it did in some other counties, but this did not appear to be because of the fear of repercussions, as in Montgomery and Dauphin. The norm in Saginaw was to work it out. The preference for a conflict-free work environment seemed stronger in Saginaw than St. Clair but, as in St. Clair, conflict did not appear to have long-lasting effects in Saginaw.

Despite the fact that Saginaw County had neither a public defender's office nor a strong local political party, one had the sense that the county had a close-knit, cohesive court community. There were only five judges and about eight prosecutors involved in handling of felony cases. However, the fact that Saginaw used an Office of Assigned Counsel to distribute indigent defense cases to interested private attorneys meant that far more defense attorneys were involved in the disposition of felony cases. At the same time, Saginaw had a relatively small bar, about 325. Reviews of the docket indicated that only about one hundred attorneys accepted felony cases. More important, the fact that Saginaw was not a dynamic, growing community meant that many of the practitioners in the local court system had deep roots within the community and enjoyed a complex web of personal relations. Indeed, a survey involving 295 Saginaw attorneys done in 1979 revealed that 20 percent had blood ties.

Other factors also contributed to and reinforced a strong sense of comraderie within the court community. Perhaps more so than any other county, Saginaw had a well-developed and structured informal network. It was facilitated by the criminal court building's location in the heart of one of Saginaw's main commercial districts. Most lawyers' offices were within a ten-minute stroll of the courthouse. Moreover, despite the fact that Michigan did not have an integrated court system, all of the organizationally separate district court judges were housed in Saginaw's strikingly modern courthouse. This was not true in any of the other non-Illinois counties; they had district courts sprinkled throughout the county. This setting, of course, greatly facilitated the operation of Saginaw's grapevine. Just as important, however, were a set of restaurants, bars, and a private club across the street from the courthouse. One group of private attorneys met for breakfast at irregular intervals in one particular restaurant, but a regular noon meeting at another restaurant was the real nerve center of the Saginaw court community. A set of tables accommodating fourteen attorneys was put together and regularly reserved for courthouse regulars. A group of five circuit and district court judges lunched there regularly as well. One judge guessed that within a week about 60 percent of the local bar would meet at this restaurant to be informed of courthouse happenings.

Certain rules had evolved to govern who could attend the lunches and what could be discussed at the table. It was expected, for example, that only attorneys who already had earned their spurs in the courtroom would be permitted to sit at the table. Both ethics and etiquette influenced what could be talked about, and it was understood that confidences would be kept with the circle of the group. One attorney pointed out that "you'll notice sometimes that if there is an attorney with a big mouth there that everyone will leave early or they'll bury their faces in their hands and not talk very much to each other." These sessions were an opportunity not only to gossip, but also to talk about and trade solutions to problems with attorneys who had some experience and who were trusted. The attorney just quoted even suggested that judges found the discussions helpful, and he talked about an instance when a judge who had had an unusual case for the first time chatted about it with the lawyers.

The structure of the circuit court bench in Saginaw was, in many respects, a microcosm of its court community. It was a cohesive, homogeneous group that had associated together for some time. Indeed, of the five judges, two were brothers, and two had a social and professional relationship that dated to 1958. Three of the judges had spent between twenty-four and thirty-five years on the bench. Their place on the bench was secure; until 1980, no sitting judge has been challenged since 1948. While there was the expected level of quibbling about who was shouldering their caseload burden, the judges were a fairly collegial group. They were not as competitive as those in Oakland or acrimonious as those in Kalamazoo or DuPage. Although like most judges they preferred decentralized operation and guarded their personal prerogatives, they were not averse to cooperating when a situation required consistency or strong unified action. Observers pointed to a series of such collective actions. One of the most recent was a decision to toughen up on cases involving the sale of heroin. The judges began imposing a set of extremely severe sentences (ten to twenty years) on those convicted of such offenses, actions that led a local attorney to challenge the so-called "Saginaw policy" in the appellate court.

The cohesiveness of the Saginaw court community and its strong informal structure undercut whatever tendencies existed to reinforce formal role dictates or to stress role prerogatives. A Saginaw policy could not have emerged in DuPage, Oakland, or Kalamazoo. In a manner similar to St. Clair, Saginaw had a very pragmatic orientation. They were neither driven by a desire to be, or appear, inordinately efficient or professional. The leaders of the court community in Saginaw were not driven by any broad conception of how a court system should operate. Rather, they tended to adopt whatever procedures appeared to satisfy the most interests at a given point in time. One of the reasons for this pragmatic orientation was that the nature and mix of social forces within the county impeded the development of any consensus on reform. The lack of electoral pressure on both the bench and the prosecutor, as well as the long tenure of the judges, worked against the forces of change. Prosecutors and judges could be pushed to change, but they seldom initiated it. The prosecutor's office, for example, was not characterized by any of the innovations depicted in DuPage, Oakland, or Kalamazoo.

Like the other declining counties, Erie had a relatively small court community. The bar itself was just over three hundred, but the felony caseload was dominated by a much smaller group. There were only five judges and nine prosecutors. Fourteen public defenders and five private attorneys handled about 70 percent of the cases (see Table 6.5). As in St. Clair and Saginaw, many of the court community members in Erie had long-standing personal ties. The description of an experienced defense attorney's ties to people in the district attorney's office illustrates the nature of these relationships. "One is a personal friend of mine. He's over at my house; I'm over at his. A lot of those guys are personal friends. I have a corporation with another prosecutor. That's the thing that's unique about this county. Most of the lawyers—there's a couple of cliques—where everybody knows everybody else. After trial we go out and have dinner.... That's just the way we are."

A prosecutor, asked what one needed to know about Erie's court community, summed the situation up nicely as follows: "My experience here has been that it's—I don't want to say that it's a family operation necessarily—but it's a fairly close interpersonal sort of operation with some notable exceptions like the Public Defender's office.... in terms of the relationships, most of them are based on individual relationships with each other. Like given lawyers in this office and given probation officers on the third floor, or even given lawyers and judges."

Given the relatively small cohesive court community in Erie, and its location in downtown Erie, it is not surprising that it had a healthy, far-reaching grapevine. Indeed, in no other county were people so preoccupied with it and its centrality within the court community. A public defender commented: "I don't know how it is in other counties, but in this county the courthouse is just the fastest grapevine I've ever seen. If I fire a secretary at 9:00, the whole courthouse knows about it by 9:30."

A prosecutor in Erie reported that judges' disagreements that arose at their meetings seemed to always leak out. "It's part of the grapevine. When the judges have a meeting, usually someone is there—either the court administrator, top staff, or somebody. And word comes out. It's that way. It's that type of place."

Another attorney, when asked if there were any secrets in the court community, said, "I'll tell you. Probably not very many. Because if you get around and know the people, you'll find out."

It is not surprising that criticism and conflict gave way to moderation and cooperation under such circumstances. As one attorney explained, "Sometimes you have to be very careful who you criticize in this town just because you never know who you're talking to." Mutual accommodation and working things out provided the principal formula for dealing with each other, as in Saginaw. One prosecutor expressed the belief that he shared a common goal with public defenders, that if their client needed a break, they should "come see me." The ability to "talk about it" extended to judges. "I don't really have a problem walking in and seeing them at just about any time subject to their schedule," observed a prosecutor. At least some attorneys expect to receive a sympathetic ear during these encounters. As one public defender put it, "Everybody, by virtue of being a good guy, has so many chips a year that you can cash in. You go into a judge and you say, 'Look, Judge. I'm busting my buns every day in this dang court, and I need a break on this case. It has nothing to do with justice, nothing to do with law. I need a break!' Okay! You get so many chips a year that you can cash in."

The preceding quote illustrates what was evident in our other interviews in Erie: The same type of pragmatic orientation toward the operation of the criminal process that characterized St. Clair also applied to Erie, to a degree. The unreformed political culture that surrounded the Erie court community, in conjuction with the general lack of internal or external pressures, permitted them to operate independent of a wholistic view of how the criminal process should operate, or with a genuine commitment to efficiency or professionalism. Even when the tranquility of the community was shaken up, as, for example, when an insurgent successfully challenged the Democratic party's nominee for county prosecutor, far-reaching changes were not introduced into the system. The new prosecutor was reform-oriented and got tough, as promised, but he did not introduce the type of innovations that we saw in other counties.

One last distinctive point about Erie concerns its judiciary. It had a long tradition of having a powerful president judge, and the present one was no exception. In many ways he was the most influential figure in the local court community, which was relatively unique in our nine counties. Only the chief judge of the criminal division in St. Clair approached the Erie president judge's power in the court communities we studied. Perhaps because of the local tradition, the Erie judges did not mind the centralizing influence of such a figure, but most judges we studied jealously guarded their discretion, even judges in places like Dauphin and Saginaw. In contrast, the Erie judges had coffee each morning and talked openly about sentencing and dispositional practices. As one might guess, personal relationships in Erie went back many years. The three judges had heard criminal cases together for seven years, and two had been on the bench fifteen years. Indeed, at one point in their career the three judges who heard the felony cases had all been elected county prosecutor.

SUMMARY

In trying to develop the notion of the courthouse community, we outlined some of its key characteristics and components. We then tried to add flesh to the skeleton by discussing various attributes of the court communities in our nine counties.

A broader sense of identification was more evident in some than others. The smaller court systems located in the more stagnant communities were perhaps the most cohesive, although Montgomery actors also shared a strong sense of community. DuPage was illustrative of a court community in the throes of change. It was rocked by disturbances that emanated from outside, and its future course depended upon how those forces played themselves out. Oakland was an example of an extremely diffuse court community. It was neither highly acrimonious nor tightly knit. One of the benefits of having a diverse set of counties was that the crucial role of contextual and ecological factors (size, geophysical, political, demographic, etc.) in the formation of court communities was illustrated clearly, if only in a casual way.

Our observations concerning the health and vibrance of the grapevines in these communities parallel the observations concerning cohesiveness. The grapevines were both extensive and lively in the smaller, more stagnant communities, but were very effective as well in Montgomery, Peoria, and Kalamazoo. Oakland was characterized by a series of grapevines rooted in individual courtrooms and sponsoring organizations. DuPage had grapevines that operated within the various cleavages, although some vines bridged the various breaches where personal or social ties nourished them.

If we examine views on the role of political considerations—either partisan or personal—some distinct patterns emerge. Although the nature of politics differed substantially across counties, it is clear that there was a more general acceptance of political considerations in DuPage, Montgomery, Dauphin, St. Clair, and to a lesser extent, Erie. Oakland, Peoria, and Kalamazoo prided themselves in being avowedly nonpolitical. Saginaw represented a mixed situation, but it was closer to being nonpolitical.

Finally, we saw a variety of views on conflict and conflict management. DuPage represents a situation in which, for a variety of reasons, conflict maintenance mechanisms broke down completely. There was conflict at both the institutional and personal level to an extent that was unknown in the other counties. It continued almost unabated for an eight-year period, and it seriously fractured the court community. Conflict and confrontation were accepted ways of interacting in St. Clair. They were not constant phenomena, but, when kept within recognized limits, had few lasting consequences. Norms against conflict appeared to be strongest in Montgomery and Dauphin, where it was feared that dire consequences would follow. In counties such as Peoria and Kalamazoo, conflict was not a serious problem, the notable exception being relations among the judges in Kalamazoo. The homogeneous nature of the court communities and their commitment to efficiency led to generally congenial relations. Much the same can be said about Oakland; conflict was simply not consistent with the image they sought to portray. The long-standing personal and social ties that prevailed in Saginaw and Erie led to a fairly congenial environment.

We now turn to a more systematic analysis of these court communities' infrastructures and how the notion of work orientations can help us understand them.

REFERENCE

Eisenstein, James, Roy B. Flemming, and Peter F. Nardulli. 1988. *The Contours of Justice: Communities and Their Courts.* Boston: Little, Brown.

6

THE CONTEXT OF JUSTICE, II:
THE INFRASTRUCTURE

By the term *infrastructure,* we mean the structural arrangements of the court system's basic subcomponents: the bench, the prosecutor's office, and the defense bar. A broader definition would include the organization of the more tangential subcomponents, such as the probation office, the circuit clerk's operation, and social services, but they are really beyond the scope of this effort. The infrastructures of the primary units are a core concern here because they can affect the tenor of justice provided by a local court community. They shape the local terrain that affects the strategy used by actors in performing role-specific tasks. In some counties, the terrain is so significant that options that actors have to choose from are reduced drastically. In others, the terrain is such that a wide variety of tactics are possible, perhaps permitting the views and operating styles of individuals — or other idiosyncratic factors — to play a greater role in the determination of strategies and outcomes.

The infrastructure in a particular court community is a very complex entity, one that is in continuing flux. A snapshot of the infrastructure, or one of its component parts, can often be perplexing to one attempting to understand how it fits together and why. In the long run, we think that the notion of work orientations will be of immense help in our efforts to understand the meaning and implication of differences in infrastructures. This conceptual device will provide us with a means of understanding what different mixes of structures and practices mean at a more abstract level. It can also provide us with insights into the cultural dimension of court communities.

Because of the long-range benefits of developing the notion of work orientation, we stop here to develop the three styles more fully. We also use these devices to walk through and describe the nine infrastructures we encountered in this study. But, for a variety of reasons, we cannot use these work styles in conjunction with our field observations to say much about the local court communities' cultural orientations. One reason concerns the evaluation of the work orientations concept in our thinking. It is not as deeply anchored in our empirical observations and inquiries as some of the other concepts employed here. We did not go into the field with this notion. Indeed, it emerged years after the fieldwork was completed, as we filtered through various explanations of how and why things were done in a particular community. This means that our development of the notion of work orientation is in an embryonic stage. We were not able to press interviewees on points and ideas that were not yet clear in our own minds.

What further confounded our efforts to say much about the cultural orientations of the various court communities by examining their infrastructures is the fact that work orientations are only one of many sources of influence upon the formation of a county's infrastructure. The most influential local actors in the formation of most facets of a county's infrastructure are the office heads (chief judge, prosecutor, and head public defender). But it would be ludicrous to assume that the prevailing infrastructure reflected their current views or that their views were representative of the court community. Many prevailing practices are simply holdovers from an earlier era; inertia is as strong a force within court systems as it is in other complex social entities. Thus, the present structure may say little about the present views even of these powerful figures. If it did accurately reflect those views, the prevailing structure may send mixed or confusing signals. Not all may hold similar views nor may they hold them with equal fervor. Also, they operated under different constraints and with different incentives.

The relationship between work orientations and infrastructures is neither simple nor direct, making the leap from latter to the former all the more problematic. For example, some important practices or procedures may have little to do with work orientations. Where a particular work orientation does have direct implications for how a task should be structured, other factors may intervene to obscure the relationship between orientation and practices. One such factor is state law. It may mandate, or in some cases forbid, a particular procedure, structure, or practice. State law may limit the options available to office heads and may lead to a level of uniformity across jurisdictions in a state one would not expect because of local cultural differences. Closely related to this are the effects of the statewide political or legal culture. The diffusion of innovations, structures, and practices brought about by statewide meetings, publications, and grapevines may lead to structures that one may not otherwise expect to find. Size can also have an effect. Differences in size can lead some jurisdictions that are similar otherwise to adopt different structures or practices. The need for a court administrator or more bureaucratic procedures, for example, may be dictated by the magnitude of workloads. Finally, a set of more random occurrences such as scandals, bad experiences with previous practices, competition with neighboring counties, and other such things may account for a seemingly anomalous situation.

A well-developed concept succinctly laying out different work orientations and their implications could be an immensely valuable tool in the observational stage of a study such as this. Much prodding, probing, and digging could well uncover the prevailing work orientation(s) within a court community and their relationship with the prevailing infrastructure. But clearly what is needed to unravel this relationship fully is a picture album, if not a movie camera with a wide lens that also had a zoom capacity. All that is available to us is an old, somewhat unfocused snapshot. To work backward from this snapshot to say something about the values and views of the court community is simply not feasible, for the reasons just reviewed. The most we can do here is develop these work orientations as fully as possible and then use them to guide us through the maze of structures and practices within our counties. This will help us to appreciate the implications of adopting one practice over another and to illustrate the differences between the various options. While we will attempt to categorize concrete structures according to our definition of work orientations, we will avoid making extrapolations to prevailing court community views and values.

WORK ORIENTATIONS AND THE COURT COMMUNITY'S INFRASTRUCTURE

We discerned three distinct work orientations in our interviews and observations in the various court communities, a formal/structural, an efficiency, and a pragmatic orientation. As noted in chapter 5, these work orientations may be best understood as rationalizing principles used to explain and/or justify a particular structure or practice. As we reviewed interviews with individuals about why certain aspects of their system were structured as they were, we began to observe patterns in the explanation they offered. These patterns form the basis for the different work orientations. A careful scrutiny of them suggests that three different dimensions can be used to illustrate the differences among them. One difference concerns views toward personnel matters, including concern for professional development, career employees, and office perks. Another is the attitude toward the exercise of discretion by line personnel. The third is the commitment to the development and implementation of innovative procedures and the use of available technology to help structure, control, and monitor different aspects of the criminal process.

While each of these points is useful in differentiating generally among the various orientations to the structure of work, they are not equally useful across subcomponents. For example, recruitment and an emphasis upon career personnel has little relevance to the bench. Neither do views on the exercise of discretion; most would agree it is an integral part of judging. Less obvious is the fact that the control of discretion is not as significant an issue in indigent defense systems as in prosecutors' offices. The work of public defense attorneys is more reactive, whereas prosecutors tend to be more proactive, giving more immediacy to questions over the control of discretion. For similar reasons, the commitment to innovative procedures and practices is not as useful in differentiating among orientations within indigent defense systems as prosecutor offices. The former are simply not as policy oriented as the latter. They do not have to deal systematically with issues such as screening, charging, and plea recommendations. They are largely on the defensive, reacting to situations and cases with which they are confronted.

Persons or systems committed to a formal/structural work orientation evince, in the area of personnel matters, a great concern for the career development and professional enhancement of the people working within the system. This necessitates structuring case assignments such that judges are exposed to a wide variety of cases and public attorneys are exposed to a wide variety of judges. That the procedures used to attain these goals may interfere with the efficient use of systemic resources is unfortunate but not of paramount importance. This concern with professionalism in personnel matters includes nonpartisan, merit-based hiring, promotion, and assignment procedures, as well as practices designed to minimize personnel turnovers among public attorneys. Formalistically oriented systems are more likely to send practitioners to training and continuing education programs as well as to provide them with the trappings of professionalism (such as an accessible law library, attractive offices, adequate secretarial assistance, and modern business equipment). Obviously this makes plentiful resources a necessary condition for the implementation of a formalistic orientation, even though it is not a sufficient condition.

Another key attribute of the formal/structural work orientation is a certain unease with the existence of unbridled discretion in the hands of line personnel. Related to this is a distaste for procedures that permit knowledgeable insiders to manipulate the process and a concern for the formal autonomy of the various subcomponents, especially the indigent defense system. These concerns are grounded in the belief that it is unbecoming of a system to have a process that is rife with unfettered discretion, or is subject to manipulation or coercion. Thus, among other things, cases should be assigned blindly and, once assigned, should not be susceptible to manipulation. The police should not have inordinate control over the initiation and charging of cases, nor should assistant prosecutors have unfettered discretion in plea negotiation. Appropriate measures should be taken to insure the integrity and autonomy of publicly paid indigent defense attorneys. While these various concerns may help insure that due process is accorded defendants, we should be slow to attribute any civil libertarian bent to proponents of a formalistic work orientation. Such an orientation is as consistent with get-tough policies as due process policies. It would be more appropriate to view these concerns as being rooted in political-legal values concerning the desirability of limited discretion, the appearance of autonomy, and the importance of evenhandedness.

One final attribute of a formal/structural work orientation is a commitment to the development and deployment of innovative procedures and the use of available technology to structure, control, and monitor the dispositional process. This may involve the hiring of a court administrator, the purchase of high tech-office machines, including computer systems, the establishment of a well-defined office hierarchies and operating manuals, and the development of formal, often centralized, procedures to control such things as screening, charging, indigent assignment, plea offers, and sentencing.

An efficiency work orientation is similar to a formal/structural one in some ways, but there are also important differences. First, while there is much emphasis placed upon merit recruitment and promotion, there is not the concern for career development and professional enhancement, especially where the achievement of such goals interferes with the efficient use of systemic resources or entails significant monetary commitments. There is less concern for professional enhancement because it is not always cost effective. An efficiency-oriented prosecutor, for example, may not believe that it is crucial to keep a staff of six-year veterans when most cases are routine pleas; a couple of veterans in key spots is usually a more cost-effective strategy. Thus, there is little expectation that employees will pursue a public career as a prosecutor or defender, and little is normally spent on costly perks or on maintaining high salary scales to keep a highly experienced staff. All that is normally expected of new recruits is that they perform in an acceptable manner while in the public employ.

In efficiency-oriented systems there is not the level of concern with political-legal values concerning limited discretion, evenhandedness, and autonomy. More importance is placed upon all of the parts of the systems moving together smoothly, and this sometimes requires discretion, flexibility, and cooperation. This is not to say that persons engineering efficiency-oriented structures are unconcerned with these values. They may well be. What separates them from the more formalistically oriented is their lower level of tolerance for time- and resource-consuming procedures and practices that have less than a direct relationship to desirable objectives. There is simply not the skepticism over discretion and cooperation among those who are efficiency oriented; nor is there the driving need to structure the behavior of line personnel. In their view, a little discretion, flexibility, and cooperation can facilitate the flow of cases without threatening the integrity and fairness of the system. In some instances, cooperation and the wise exercise of discretion can enhance the equitable treatment of all parties concerned. Cumbersome procedures can interfere with appropriate resolution of cases, in this view, as well as consume valuable resources. However, where wide discretion is counterproductive, efficiency-oriented managers can be expected to develop procedures to control it. The point is that they do not have the concern with unfettered discretion evidenced by those with formalistic orientations; their concern is with the consequences of wide discretion.

Another important point to note about discretion in efficiency-oriented systems is that strong norms usually exist against using it to grant favors or repay prior obligations. Such practices are considered unseemly and have the potential to jeopardize the smooth functioning of the system. The grapevine usually disseminates such information rapidly, generating more demands for special consideration. Thus, real distinctions are made between flexibility and manipulation, on the one hand, and cooperation and coercion on the other. Discretion is tolerated only to the extent it is used to eliminate problems and bottlenecks within the system.

Those who are efficiency oriented, like their formalistic counterparts, are likely to look favorably upon the development of programs and the use of technology to enhance the working of the criminal process. Efficiency adherents, however, are apt to be far more skeptical of innovations and more likely to proceed incrementally with changes. This is especially true with respect to more expensive technological innovations. They take more of a "show me" attitude. It would not do to simply have an expensive but unusable computer system for the sake of appearances, to look sophisticated or modern. Efficiency proponents embrace businesslike principles, but would be less likely to overbureaucratize their office structure than formalistic adherents. Moreover, the innovative procedures they develop are more likely to be concerned with enhancing the smooth operations of the system than with managing discretion.

It is more difficult to characterize a pragmatic orientation to structuring the work of the court because it is not dedicated to a relatively specific objective such as the furtherance of certain legal values or the attainment of efficiency in systemic operations. Rather, the structure of work is largely the result of a brokering of competing interests, often short-term ones. The results of such brokering are usually perpetuated by a healthy dose of inertia. Nevertheless, several general contrasts can be made with the other two approaches. First, very little emphasis is put on career enhancement and professional development. This is especially true of public attorneys. What is important for them to learn is the informal norms and mores of *this* system and how to operate with *it*. Broad exposure and continuing education are simply not that relevant. Another important contrast here is that there is not always much emphasis placed upon merit. No one expects to attract high-caliber individuals and it is often useful, convenient, and acceptable to hire and promote someone with political or personal connections.

Perhaps the major contrast between the pragmatic approach and the other two is its perspective on discretion, especially as it concerns public attorneys. Within the pragmatist approach discretion is viewed as an intrinsic component of their role, almost as an inalienable right; systemic flexibility and cooperation are viewed as essential to the exercise of that right. It is very unlikely that pragmatists, on their own initiative, would attempt to control or channel the discretion of line personnel. It is viewed as an essential, if not the most essential, tool of their trade, as important to lawyering as it is to judging. It reflects the belief that the best way to achieve justice in a case is for the various parties to discuss the case openly and resolve it in an informal and unencumbered context. Good lawyers know how to use discretion in a positive way. Abuse of it should be met with reprimands and firings, not large-scale restructuring of the process that the management of discretion entails.

The lack of concern over appearing professional, maximizing efficiency, and structuring the behavior of line personnel also means that the development and use of innovative programs and technology does not consume much time or energy. There are normally few resources to expend on such activities, nor is there much incentive to do so. Things are the way they are for a reason and are likely to stay that way until a major crisis forces the court community to institute some type of reform. Because of the premium placed upon discretion and the lack of emphasis upon innovation, there is little need for a highly differentiated hierarchy or elaborate bureaucracy. Supervisory personnel often spend much of their time doing what line personnel do—handling cases.

The distinctions among these different orientations will become clearer as we apply them to the various components of the court community.

THE JUDICIAL INFRASTRUCTURE

In addressing the infrastructure of the bench, we must be concerned with certain aspects of lower courts as well as the trial courts. The most important aspect of lower courts' organization for our purposes is the degree to which they are integrated with, and subject to the control of, the trial courts. In unified, or highly integrated, systems, the lower court is a component of the trial court. The trial judges appoint, remove, and determine the work assignments of the lower court judges, often called district or associate judges, or magistrates. Decentralized or unintegrated systems have magistrates elected from geographical subdivisions of the trial court's territory. They are normally only responsible for cases arising in their district; they are subject to removal only by the electorate or a judicial conduct board. A variety of other arrangements exist that can produce systems falling between these two extremes.

One important consequence flowing from the degree of integration is the extent to which trial judges can impose consistent constraints upon the discretion of lower court judges. This is an important point from a formalistic work orientation. In integrated systems, responsibility for bail setting and the conduct of preliminary hearings can be assigned to one or two magistrates. If bail decisions or screening of cases at the preliminary hearing strays from the trial judges' guidelines or wishes, they can reassign and, sometimes even fire, the lower court judge. Control can be enhanced even further by physically locating the magistrates in the county court-house. In decentralized systems, bail decisions, and preliminary hearings take place throughout the county. Trial judges infrequently encounter lower judges face-to-face, and they can do little to change the decisions made on bail or in preliminary hearings. Localistic concerns can play a greater role in their decisions.

The degree of integration between lower and trial judges also affects significantly the work of both prosecutors and defense attorneys. In de-centralized arrangements, the logistics of providing representation at pre-liminary hearings increase the time and staff required. Representing in-digent defendants appearing in any of twenty-nine separate lower courts obviously presents far more difficulties than staffing one or two courtrooms in the courthouse. There are often insufficient prosecutorial resources to conduct preliminary hearings regularly in decentralized systems. Conse-quently, arresting officers often handle preliminary hearings in decen-tralized systems. This, of course, makes it exceedingly difficult for the prosecutor to control discretion by implementing consistent policies on bail and the early screening of cases.

We would obviously expect those with formalistic or efficiency work orientations to attempt to better integrate the lower courts. This enhances their control over the early stages of the process and permits them to husband scarce resources. All other things being equal, those with a pragmatic orientation to the court's work would be less likely to tamper with the decentralized structure of lower courts, which evolved in the

American states through the nineteenth and early twentieth century. They would perhaps be more sensitive to Jacksonian conceptions of the judiciary and feel that local communities ought to have more input into the criminal process. In any event they would be less inclined to seek out ways to control the behavior of the magistrates.

A glance at Table 6.1 reminds us that the relation between these courts and the trial courts is largely controlled by state law and hence is invariant within states. Thus, these data can yield few insights into the orientations of these nine court communities. In Illinois, state law permits circuit judges to appoint associate judges for a fixed term, and they have countywide jurisdiction. The circuit judges have a considerable amount of corresponding control over the associate judge's work. This is especially true in our three Illinois counties, where one judge was designated to handle all preliminary hearings. In the other two states, the magistrates were elected locally and were likely to be more sensitive to the concerns of their constituents than the circuit judges, whom they seldom encountered. The only differences between Michigan and Pennsylvania were that Michigan elected their district judges on a nonpartisan basis, whereas Pennsylvania magistrates ran in partisan elections, and Pennsylvania did not require magistrates to be attorneys. The large number of judges handling preliminary hearings in these counties underscores the problem of control and management encountered at the county level. Significant differences in the quality and types of cases reaching the trial level from the local districts can be expected. Many cases that should have been pruned earlier were undoubtedly sent to the trial level. These problems were somewhat mitigated in Saginaw, where all the district judges were housed in the county courthouse.

If we turn our sights to the trial courts, we can see that one of their most visible characteristics is their administrative organization. Most county courts in the United States are headed by a chief or presiding judge. The power of these administrative officials varies considerably, depending upon such factors as the formal authority granted to them in statutes or statewide court rules, mode of selection, nature and length of tenure, force of personality, countywide political influence, the resources available to the office, and local tradition. A chief judge who is elected for a long tenure in a county that provides ample resources to the court and has a full-time, professional court administrator and staff will be much more powerful than one who serves at the pleasure of his colleagues in a resource poor system. Despite the actual amount of control wielded by the chief judge, it should be stressed that this control is largely in administrative areas and external relations. Most trial judges jealously guard their prerogatives on substantive matters.

Table 6.2 reports information on various aspects of each court's

Table 6.1. **Structure of Lower Court Systems**

	DuPage (Ring)	Peoria (Autonomous)	St. Clair (Declining)	Oakland (Ring)	Kalamazoo (Autonomous)	Saginaw (Declining)	Montgomery (Ring)	Dauphin (Autonomous)	Erie (Declining)
Selection procedure	Selected by circuit judges	Selected by circuit judges	Selected by circuit judges	Nonpartisan elections district-wide	Nonpartisan elections district-wide	Nonpartisan elections district-wide	Partisan elections district-wide	Partisan elections district-wide	Partisan elections district-wide
Must judge be lawyer?	Yes	Yes	Yes	Yes	Yes	Yes	No	No	No
Nature of geographic jurisdiction	County-wide	County-wide	County-wide	Districts within county	Districts within county	Districts* within county	Districts within county	Districts within county	Districts within county
Extent of trial court supervisory power over judges	Great	Great	Great	Minimal	Minimal	Minimal	Minimal	Minimal	Minimal
Number of lower court judges	23	6	10	30	7	6	29	12	17
Number of judges normally conducting preliminary hearings	1	1	1	All	All	All	All	All	All

* District judges were all centrally located in county courthouse.

Table 6.2. **Characteristics of Trial Court's Administrative System**

	DuPage (Ring)	Peoria (Autonomous)	St. Clair (Declining)	Oakland (Ring)	Kalamazoo (Autonomous)	Saginaw (Declining)	Montgomery (Ring)	Dauphin (Autonomous)	Erie (Declining)
Method of judge's selection	Election by circuit judges	Election by circuit judges	Election by circuit judges	Election by county judges	Election by county judges	Election by county judges	Election by county judges	Judge with most seniority, under 70	Judge with most seniority, under 70
Tenure of chief judge	At pleasure of circuit judges	At pleasure of circuit judges	At pleasure of circuit judges	2 years (annual rotation is norm)	2 years	2 years (one judge has been reelected several times)	5 years	Until mandatory retirement	Until mandatory retirement
Type of court administrator	Professional administrator	Professional administrator (civil cases only)	Case coordinator	Professional administrator	Professional administrator	Professional administrator	Professional administrator	Case coordinator (civil cases only)	Case coordinator

administrative structure. Except for Dauphin and Erie, where the judge under seventy years of age and who has seniority is automatically the president judge until retirement, the chief judge in each county is elected by the trial court judges. Among the counties with elective systems, the chief judge's tenure varies considerably. In the Illinois counties, they serve at the pleasure of their peers, whereas in Montgomery County they have a five-year term. In Michigan counties, these judges have two-year terms, by Supreme Court rule. However, local practices have nullified this rule in some instances. In Oakland, the chief judges step down annually, whereas in Saginaw, one judge has filled the chief judge's slot for years. Distinctions among the various elective systems are difficult to make, but set terms of office are clearly more conducive to strong administrative leadership and the initiation of change than tenure at the pleasure of peers. However, we cannot say much about the orientation of the various court communities on the basis of Table 6.2 because their procedures are all mandated by statewide rules, even though two of the Michigan counties deviated from these rules somewhat. An even more important limitation is in inferring too much from these differences that the key indicator of work orientations in elective systems is the type of judge elected in a particular county. In this regard it must be noted that, with the exception of Erie County, all of the presiding or chief judges in our counties did very little to interfere with the trial judges' discretion. This is true even in Montgomery, where the president judge had a five-year term. Evidently norms on judicial discretion are too well established to enable presiding judges to intervene except in rare situations.

One last point concerning the administrative hierarchy of trial courts relates to the use of some type of administrator to facilitate the flow and handling of cases. More formalistic or efficiency-oriented systems would be expected to maintain professional court administrators, that is, persons with professional training and/or advanced degrees. Pragmatically oriented systems would be more likely to have none, or merely case coordinators, elevated clerks who are assigned to help schedule cases. As we can see in Table 6.2, DuPage, Peoria, all of the Michigan counties, and Montgomery have professional administrators. The others have case coordinators; Dauphin was the only county with no one working in such a role. In Dauphin, the case coordinator handled only civil cases; the prosecutor's office assigned criminal cases to courtrooms.

Far more important for our concerns than the structure of the circuit court's administrative hierarchy is how the bench organizes its work. The court must make a variety of decisions about how to allocate and distribute a set of relatively fixed and scarce resources to meet the myriad demands made upon it. One of the initial decisions it must make concerns the matching of judges with the various types of cases they must handle.

Besides criminal cases, courts are besieged with civil cases in areas such as domestic relations, tort, juvenile, probate, and contract. The basic choice encountered in covering these diverse demands is whether to assign judges to specialized or to mixed dockets. In the former, each judge is responsible only for either civil or criminal cases; in the latter, each judge handles a mix of civil and criminal cases. The type of docket chosen affects the organization of assistant prosecutors and public defenders, as deployment patterns and work schedules of these individuals will vary depending upon whether the judges handling criminal cases must set court time aside for civil cases. The efficient deployment of public attorneys would dictate the use of specialized dockets. Most would agree that specialized dockets are the most efficient use of judicial resources as well. The argument for mixed dockets, however, is that the diversity of cases enhances the professional development of the judges by exposing them to a wide variety of cases and legal issues.

Closely related to the issue of specialization is the type of trial term employed in a jurisdiction. Some jurisdictions have continuous trial dockets, whereas others have only periodic trial terms. In systems with continuous trial terms, judges preside over trials, accept guilty pleas, hear pretrial motions, and conduct other miscellaneous business without interruption. In systems with periodic trial terms, trials can be conducted only during specified time periods. These trial terms are normally determined at the beginning of each year. Thus, everyone will know that the first three weeks of every other month in the following year will be set aside for trials. Some systems have separate trial terms for civil and criminal cases. One consequence of this is that in systems with mixed dockets and separate (civil and criminal) periodic trial terms, judges really have rotating dockets. That is, when they are in criminal terms, they handle only criminal and vice versa. This is quite different from systems that have mixed dockets and continuous trial terms and must integrate civil and criminal cases on a continuing basis.

At first glance, periodic trial terms give the appearance of a cumbersome, archaic method of organizing the court's work, one that is intended to perplex the layman or outsider. Why do we have to wait until the Thursday after the second Tuesday of every other month to set a case for trial? It leads people to question what the various court-related bureaucracies do during the off-term periods and to wonder if undue pressures do not operate as the end of the trial term approaches. The cumbersome nature of this approach seems all the more apparent when compared with the evident benefits of the continuous trial term. It permits the efficient organization of systemic resources and appears to avoid bottlenecks while permitting the orderly, unhurried processing of cases.

In many instances the images evoked by these different systems are significant, and the choice of trial terms can say something important about the court community's orientation to its work. Discontinuous trial terms are frequently the result of a pragmatic brokering of interests, as the system frequently yields extended periods of down time for court community members, even if it also leads to periods of high pressure. The unnatural splintering of time periods with its concomitant diseconomies is not at all appealing to those concerned with efficiency or dedicated to implementing an orderly conception of the criminal process. However, there may be compelling factors that lead a court community to choose periodic trial terms. The most important of these is size of the community. In a small county, one with only a few judges, the choice may be either specialized, continuous dockets with just one or two judges handling criminal cases (a sometimes highly undesirable situation), or choosing to adopt a mixed docket with periodic trial terms so that a broader array of judges can become involved in criminal cases.

Yet another issue in the organization of the court's work is case assignment; it has two major dimensions. The first concerns the permanency of assignment and depends upon the type of calendar system used—individual or master. In individual calendar systems, cases are normally assigned to individual judges who see them through to final disposition. In master calendar systems, all cases are part of one pool. Judges receive cases from that pool but cannot point to any set of cases that are exclusively theirs. In some systems, judges draw cases one at a time from the larger pool; in others, they receive a group of cases for a given term. But even in the latter systems, a case assigned to one judge during a particular term may be assigned to a different judge during the next term.

The second aspect of the case assignment problem is the method of assignment. There are three main variants: personalized, blind, and sequential. In personalized assignment systems, someone has formal discretion to assign cases to individual judges, often with few explicit constraints. This someone is usually the chief judge, the court administrator or case coordinator, or a member of the hierarchy in the prosecutor's office. In the blind assignment system, cases are assigned to individual judges in some predetermined, unbiased manner. In the third variant, sequential assignment, cases are normally given a certain priority or ranking. When the case reaches the top of the active trial list, it will be assigned to the next available judge. For example, in a master calendar system using periodic trial terms, fifty cases may be designated for trial during the criminal session. Judges are each initially assigned a case for trial. When a judge completes a trial, the judge is simply assigned the case with the highest priority or ranking on the list.

Individuals with different work orientations react differently to the various methods of case assignment. For example, the use of individual calendars with some type of unbiased assignment would have the most appeal to those with a formal/structural orientation. Those who are efficiency oriented would also place a high value on unbiased assignment but, at least under certain circumstances, may prefer a master calendar. If properly administered, many feel that a master calendar system can most efficiently utilize judicial resources in that cases can be quickly routed to available courtrooms as they become available. In more pragmatically oriented systems, we would be more likely to find a master calendar system, but for other reasons. A master calendar enhances the flexibility of the system and enables individuals to route pleas to individual judges. It simplifies the work of individuals by enabling them to present the fruits of their efforts to a judge who will be receptive. Some sort of personalized or "pliable" sequential assignment would be expected in pragmatically oriented systems, especially if they operate under a individual calendar.

Table 6.3 reports information on the structure of the judge's work in our nine counties. From these data it is clear that DuPage has all the earmarks of a formalistically oriented bench. It has a mixed docket with a continuous trial term, which means that judges were continually switching from one type of case to another. Most were very candid in saying that the reason for this arrangement is that the judges liked the challenge and diversity of different cases and would be bored by just criminal cases. The system prevailed even though it played havoc with the efficient use of prosecutorial and public defender resources, as well as case scheduling. DuPage also had individual calendars and blind assignments, which minimized manipulation. It was not possible to route plea cases to individual judges.

Peoria was similar to DuPage in all regards but two. However, they are crucial differences and clearly reveal a marked efficiency orientation. First, Peoria had specialized dockets even though it meant that only two judges heard criminal cases. The thought of having truly mixed dockets in Peoria was never seriously considered because of the scheduling problems it would entail, even though, because of the smaller number of judges, they were far less serious than the ones with which DuPage had to deal. Second, Peoria had personalized assignments. This was not done to facilitate manipulation, but was done to enhance the smooth operation of the system. The judges deferred to the prosecutor by simply hearing the cases he assigned to assistants who were assigned to their courtroom. No one in the defense bar suggested that the head prosecutor abused his discretion by routing specific cases to particular judges, who tended not to differ much in any event.

St. Clair presents yet another situation, one that is clearly more pragmatic in structure. The dockets were specialized, but they used discontinuous trial terms. There was no talk of boredom among the judges,

Table 6.3. Calendaring and Scheduling Practices of Trial Courts for Judges Hearing Criminal Cases

	DuPage (Ring)	Peoria (Autonomous)	St. Clair (Declining)	Oakland (Ring)	Kalamazoo (Autonomous)	Saginaw (Declining)	Montgomery (Ring)	Dauphin (Autonomous)	Erie (Declining)
Type of docket	Mixed	Specialized	Specialized	Mixed (rotating)	Mixed (rotating)	Mixed (rotating)	Specialized	Mixed (rotating)	Quasi mixed (rotating)
Number of judges	12	7	7	14	4	5	14	6	5
Number of judges hearing criminal cases	7	2	3	All	All	All	5	5	All
Type of trial term	Continuous	Continuous	Periodic	Periodic	Periodic	Periodic	Continuous	Periodic	Periodic
Type of calendar	Individual	Individual	Master	Individual	Individual	Individual	Master	Master	Master
Method of case assignment	Blind assignment	Personalized (assignment controlled by prosecutor)	Personalized (assignment controlled by case coordinator)	Random draw	Random draw	Random draw	Sequential	Personalized (assignment controlled by prosecutor)	Personalized (assignment controlled by case coordinator)
Availability of plea routing	No	No	Yes, in off trial term periods	No	No	No	Yes	Yes	Yes

who seemed very content to hear just criminal cases. They had trial terms every two weeks. This served two purposes. First, it permitted all members of the court community to have a regular period of slack time. Second, it enabled attorneys to route cases to a particular judge in the off-trial term periods. A master calendar system was used, and the case coordinator, a former clerk employee, could switch cases from one judge to another in the off-term period. Pleas could also be taken directly to a judge during this off-term period.

If we examine the structure of the judge's work in the Michigan counties revealed in Table 6.3, we see much more consistency than in Illinois. Indeed, structurally the counties vary only in the organization of trial terms. This uniformity is the result of statewide rules that mandate, with some exceptions, the use of individual calendars and random case assignments. The Michigan counties also have mixed dockets. One could contend that in counties that have benches the size of Kalamazoo and Saginaw, four and five trial judges respectively, a mixed docket is almost assured as there would hardly be enough judges to maintain specialized dockets. However, two judges were assigned to criminal court in Peoria and three in St. Clair, one of whom was an associate judge certified to hear felony cases. Thus, even though the Saginaw and Kalamazoo benches were somewhat smaller than those in Peoria and St. Clair, specialized dockets were not out of the question if there had been strong sentiments against the structural implications of the statewide rules. Instead, they felt comfortable with the mixed dockets. Unlike in DuPage, however, the Michigan counties did not have true mixed dockets; they rotated between civil and criminal terms at predetermined times throughout the year. To complicate matters further, they also had a tradition of periodic trial terms.

The structure of the judges' work in the three Michigan counties must be categorized as formalistic in tone. The random assignment of cases to individual judges eliminated the possibilities of judge-shopping or plea-routing. There was simply very little opportunity to manipulate the system in this regard. That notwithstanding, it should also be stressed that the formalistic overtones evidenced in the structure of the Michigan benches were, in large part, the result of statewide mandates and do not, by themselves, tell us much about the work orientation of these judges.

In the Pennsylvania counties, we also observed a good deal of consistency, but of a different kind. The structure of the judge's work in all three had distinctively pragmatic overtones. None had any type of blind or random case assignment procedure evidenced in most of the other counties. Even though Montgomery had sequential assignments, it operated such that plea cases could be routed to specific judges. Indeed, the identity of the judge was an integral part of plea discussions in each county. Master calendars were used in all three Pennsylvania counties. Although this undoubtedly enhanced the utilization of systemic resources, it also led to a situation in which output levels differed considerably across judges, especially in Montgomery. Also, the flexibility of calendaring and assignment systems in these counties led to informal role specialization among judges. Some received more trials than others, whereas others got certain types of plea cases. In Dauphin, a "junk court" was set up to take plea cases, and much of what went there depended upon who was assigned to it. Erie had a motions court over which three judges took turns presiding. If the proper judge was presiding during a particular week, pleas could be taken at that juncture.

Of the three Pennsylvania counties, only Montgomery had a specialized docket, although assignments shifted at regular six-month intervals so that most judges were exposed to a fairly broad array of cases. Their relatively large size afforded them that luxury. They combined this specialized docket with a continuous trial term. However, while it had all of the trappings of a streamlined, efficient system (specialized dockets, continuous terms, and master calendar), its actual operation was another matter. The root of the problem lies in the well-entrenched Montgomery tradition — one that was shared by the other two Pennsylvania counties — of using judge assignments as an integral part of the plea process. The sequential assignment was anything but blind, and it was quite an involved system, but one that met the interests of the participants involved. Indeed, the system was so intricate that many felt it would collapse if the case coordinator would leave. Thus the system's overall operation placed it nicely within the pragmatic mold.

Dauphin had a rotating, mixed docket in that the judges shifted from civil to criminal trial terms. Erie had a quasi-mixed docket in that three judges heard criminal cases regularly; the two other judges joined them in conducting criminal trials during the periodic trial terms. These arrangements played havoc with the attempts of others, especially the prosecutors, to allocate resources effectively. It led to periods of great, intense effort, including a good deal of pressure to plead cases at the end of trial terms. However, the judges, especially those in Erie, placed a high premium on the serenity of the off-term periods. Inertia played an important role in the failure to reform and rationalize the case-processing structure in these counties.

THE ORGANIZATION OF PROSECUTORIAL
TASKS AND POLICIES

Every prosecutor's office must perform certain functions, and the organization of these functions can have important consequences for the flow of cases through the system. Moreover, in some instances the approach adopted fits well within one of our work orientation categories. Case screening is one such task. Screening is the initial review of arrests at some point before the formal initiation of felony charges. At that point there are several options, including the decision to terminate all formal proceedings, to divert the case to a special pretrial program, or to handle it as a misdemeanor. Not all prosecutor offices regularly screen cases, and those that do organize screening in different ways; an office's position on screening cases can reveal something about its views on the exercise of discretion. To not review cases at this point means that the police define the initial stages of the proceedings, independent of legal controls. It also means that they control the workload, and often the official conviction rate of the prosecutor's office. Much unnecessary work can be created for the prosecutor's office by the initiation of unsubstantiated charges, trivial offenses, or cases involving disinterested victims—even though the police officer clears the case with an arrest. Formalistic and efficiency-oriented offices would be inclined to establish some sort of screening. Pragmatic offices would be less inclined simply because, in many locales, it is extremely difficult to establish a screening procedure. The police are normally opposed to such reviews and often vocally oppose their establishment. Moreover, the prosecutor normally has few allies in these efforts, with the exception of the public defender (if one exists). The private criminal defense bar, if it does not oppose screening, will not support it, as it eliminates much of their easy profit. The first cases to be eliminated under such reviews are marginal cases that the defense bar can win and can turn over quite easily. A centralized review of cases also causes controversy in heterogeneous counties where smaller towns may feel that their cases are not treated as seriously as those emanating from a larger city.

If a screening mechanism is established, the question of its structure must be addressed. Two basic models exist. One is a rotating model in which the prosecutors, usually experienced trial assistants, take turns reviewing cases as they arise. A second model is a centralized one in which one or more individuals do nothing but screen cases. These positions can be used for entry-level personnel or can be filled by an experienced trial attorney. There can also be some specialization in centralized operations where certain attorneys are responsible for drug cases, sex offenses, violent offenses, etc. Formalistically oriented offices would be expected to opt for the rotating model because it utilizes experienced attorneys to perform this very sensitive function, even though it may unduly burden them and interfere with the smooth operation of the system. Efficiency-oriented offices would be expected to adopt the centralized model, perhaps with experienced personnel. If a pragmatic office engages in any type of screening, it may simply use entry-level personnel in a centralized arrangement.

It is doubtful that such offices would use experienced trial attorneys for such a task.

Table 6.4 reports data on screening mechanisms in the nine counties. All of the counties outside Pennsylvania regularly screened felony cases; none in Pennsylvania did. The existence of screening in the Michigan counties is less meaningful than in Illinois because state law vests the power to initiate charges in the county prosecutor. It in a sense mandates screening. In Illinois, the legal situation is similar to Pennsylvania, but all three Illinois counties adopted some form of screening.

If we look more closely at St. Clair, we see that the screening function was handled by one entry-level prosecutor. It was the only county that relied solely upon inexperienced personnel. The screening mechanism in St. Clair was set up because the prosecutor's attempts to secure additional assistants were continually frustrated; the screening reform was viewed largely as a method to control their workload. Nonetheless, it took a tremendous effort by the prosecutor to create the screening mechanism, as the police strongly and vocally opposed it. The private defense bar aired its discontent in more subtle ways. Similar problems were encountered in DuPage, but the use of a rotating system handled by experienced felony trial attorneys calmed the fears of local police departments. In the other counties except Kalamazoo, a centralized mechanism with experienced personnel was used.

Among the counties that screen cases, another important dimension to the screening mechanism is the substance of the charging policies pursued; these are extremely important policies and merit some discussion. Some counties used quite stringent criteria in both initiating cases and determining charges, whereas others used less stringent criteria. The reasons for these variations differed considerably, however. Kalamazoo and St. Clair, oddly enough, used the most stringent criteria for filing and charging cases, a "reasonable likelihood of conviction" criteria. According to available data, Kalamazoo eliminated about 36 percent of the cases brought to them in 1980 by the police, many of which went to a diversion program. Also, row 3 of Table 6.4, which reports the incidence of multicount indictments — a rough measure of overcharging — shows that Kalamazoo had the lowest incidence. Multiple counts occurred in only 16 percent of Kalamazoo cases at arrest. St. Clair's criteria may have been more stringent than Kalamazoo's, even though their multicount indictment rate was slightly higher (21 percent). Indeed, private defense attorneys complained that the office was too timid and initiated charges only when it had confessions or on-the-scene arrests — a far cry from the complaints registered by defense attorneys in most counties. No official statistics were available, but the office head estimated that about 20-25 percent of the arrests were not issued as felony complaints. However, he also noted that

Table 6.4. **Prosecutorial Screening Mechanisms**

	DuPage (Ring)	Peoria (Autonomous)	St. Clair (Declining)	Oakland (Ring)	Kalamazoo (Autonomous)	Saginaw (Declining)	Montgomery (Ring)	Dauphin (Autonomous)	Erie (Declining)
Pretrial court screening:									
Does prosecutor screen cases?	Yes	Yes	Yes	Yes	Yes	Yes	No	No	No
Type of screening mechanism	Rotating (all felony prosecutors)	Centralized (1 experienced trial prosecutor, 1 less experienced)	Centralized (1 entry level prosecutor)	Centralized	Rotating (all felony prosecutors)	Centralized (2 experienced prosecutors)	NA	NA	NA
Percent of cases involving multicount indictments (n of cases)	65 (877)	38 (885)	21 (1,070)	35 (891)	16 (699)	34 (1,013)	70 (680)	27 (1,031)	48 (572)

the office used the grand jury as a screen because the judges refused to eliminate weak cases at the preliminary hearing. Our data show that 15 percent of the St. Clair cases were eliminated in the grand jury; most of the other counties hovered around 1 percent. Thus, all together, St. Clair probably prunes more cases than Kalamazoo.

Despite the similarity in screening and charging criteria in these two very different counties, their reasons for adopting them differed considerably. In St. Clair, it was a response to managing a heavy caseload with limited resources. They wanted to eliminate the less serious cases, and they wanted to enhance their credibility among the judges and defense bar on the cases they did pursue. Kalamazoo's use of stringent criteria emanated from the head prosecutor's concern with the image of justice in the county. As a former Wayne County deputy sheriff, he disliked the bargaining image projected by so many local court systems and set out to change it. His charging policy was an important part of these efforts. He felt that loose practices led to inflated charges and unsubstantiated cases that led to dismissals and negotiated charge reductions. His plan was to nip these tendencies in the bud.

DuPage, Oakland, and Saginaw evidenced less stringent screening and charging practices, using what might be termed a probable cause criteria. The philosophy underlying this criteria was well articulated by some Oakland prosecutors, "Our office policy basically is. . . . You will issue the warrant if there are sufficient facts, probable cause, that you can get through the preliminary examination. You as an assistant prosecutor in the warrants division shall not make the decision as to issuing a warrant on whether you are going to win the case or not."

Another put it less formally, "We can either look at the hole in the doughnut and never write a warrant in this office or we can look at the doughnut itself. . . . We're not going to be judges in these offices. We're not going to decide the case. If it's there and it's triable, let the judge make the decision, let the jury."

In Oakland, they are much more hesitant to refuse a prosecution than in Kalamazoo or St. Clair. Office records showed that they refused warrants in about 22 percent of all cases brought to them by the police, considerably lower than in both Kalamazoo and St. Clair. The use of multicount indictments in Oakland, 35 percent, is also substantially higher than in Kalamazoo and St. Clair. Oakland prosecutors were determined to concede very little at the outset.

DuPage's policies were similar to Oakland's but even more aggressive. DuPage prosecutors did very little initial pruning of cases, probably less than 10 percent, although hard data are not available. They also used multicount indictments very extensively; they occurred in 45 percent of all DuPage cases. This was all part of the head prosecutor's policy to charge "whatever is there," charging practices that were part of his efforts to assert control over the guilty plea process using whatever legal tools were available to him. His charging policies infuriated much of the defense bar; in no other county were so many horror stories so emotionally related.

In contrast, Saginaw's screening and charging practices were less structured, more by happenstance than prosecutorial design. While the warrant process was formally centralized and specialized (certain prosecutors handling certain types of crimes), scheduling problems and other exigencies caused the system to devolve into a highly decentralized process. For a good part of the period covered by this study, the police in Saginaw County could, and did, seek out the prosecutor whom they thought would be most sympathetic to their case. The possibility of prosecutor-shopping led to both inappropriate charging and count multiplication. The multi-count indictment level was similar to Oakland's. The warrant process in Saginaw became so inflated at one point that it became a point of contention with both the judges and the county board, which was concerned with the expense of processing so many warrants.

Peoria county differs somewhat from these various patterns. Like the less stringent counties, they seldom prune cases at an early stage. Indeed, the veteran that headed the screening office did not view pruning as his job, even though he admitted denying warrants in 5-7 percent of the cases. At the same time, no one asserted that Peoria's charging practices were inflated or aimed at facilitating the acquisition of pleas, even though they issued multiple counts in 38 percent of the cases initiated. Most felt that the charging practices were very realistic, perhaps reflecting a reasonable probability of conviction standard.

The method by which assistant prosecutors are deployed is another important aspect to the organization of prosecution; it has two dimensions. One concerns the continuity of assignments (continuous or discontinuous), the other is method of assignment (to cases or to judges). All other things being equal, continuous deployment would be the preferred method of assignment because the same attorney would be in charge of the case from the outset and would be better able to understand and deal with it. However, because preliminary hearings are almost always held in a different court, sometimes in a different town, it is very difficult to maintain continuous representation. It is much more efficient to have a separate unit handle earlier proceedings. This provides entry-level personnel with valuable experience and saves experienced attorneys for trial work.

Assigning prosecutors to cases rather than judges is considered beneficial for their professional development because they are exposed to a broader range of judges. This practice, like continuous representation, can be an ineffective use of prosecutorial resources—depending upon the type of calendaring system the judges employ. When judges have individual

Figure 6.1. **Deployment Practices of Prosecutor Offices**

Assignment Policies

	Judges	Cases
Representation Policy		
Continuous		Saginaw
Discontinuous	Peoria St. Clair (changed to cases, May 1980) Oakland	Kalamazoo Montgomery Dauphin Erie

calendars, it is very difficult to assign prosecutors to cases because of potential scheduling conflicts, especially in counties with more than two or three judges. When a master calendar is used, however, prosecutors are almost always assigned to cases. The judge's identity in master calendar systems may not be known until it is ready for trial or disposition, at which point there would be insufficient time for the prosecutor to become familiar with the case.

Figure 6.1 reports data on prosecutor deployments. No county but Saginaw used continuous representation. This underscores the difficulties in using continuous representation, especially in Michigan and Pennsylvania, where preliminary hearings are held throughout the county. Saginaw had centralized all of the preliminary hearings in the county court building, and this facilitated the practice of continuous representation. But in the Illinois counties, all preliminary hearings were also conducted in the county court building, and yet none used continuous representation. In light of earlier patterns, it is not unexpected that both Peoria and Oakland have adopted discontinuous representation, especially Oakland, with its large number of district courts. In the cases of Kalamazoo and DuPage, discontinuous representation was more surprising but, as will be seen, the county prosecutors used other devices to insure the quality and continuity of representation. Continuity of representation was largely a moot point for the Pennsylvania prosecutors because they normally did not conduct preliminary hearings, leaving that task to the police.

The method of case assignment is also reflected in Figure 6.1. Prosecutors were assigned to judges in Peoria, St. Clair, and Oakland. This is clearly consistent with the other efficiency-oriented structures operating in Peoria and is not inconsistent with the blend of formalistic and efficiency-oriented practices evidenced in Oakland. When it is considered that fourteen judges heard criminal cases in Oakland, case-based assignments would have been very difficult to manage. St. Clair was able to use judge-based assignments even though St. Clair had a quasi-master calendar system. Cases only shifted from a judge's calendar in the period between trial terms, and there was usually a sufficient amount of stability across terms to allow the platoon-type deployment of prosecutors. Midway through our study, however, St. Clair shifted to case-based assignments in order to better match the judge's master calendar system.

Saginaw had to use case assignments because they maintained continuity in appointments, and the Pennsylvania counties adopted it to match the judge's master calendar system. DuPage, however, employed a case-based assignment method with an individual calendaring system. With seven judges and fourteen trial prosecutors, the scheduling permutations became a nightmare at times. The county stuck with its assignment system, however, because of the conviction that it developed better attorneys.

One of the most important characteristics of prosecutor organizations, perhaps the most important for our purposes, is their approach to the formation and control of guilty plea offers. This area is important because it can have a direct impact upon the guilty plea process, case outcomes, and the office's relations with other components of the court community. In addition, it tells us something about the organization's orientation to the most central prosecutorial task: the procurement of guilty pleas. What differentiates offices in their approach to this task is the level of discretion that assistants enjoy in the plea process.

The different approaches roughly form a continuum. Some offices adopt a laissez-faire approach, which is very consistent with a pragmatic orientation. In this approach, individual assistants are viewed as lawyers who are hired and trained to exercise their judgment. They know their cases better than any supervisor and are, therefore, given almost total discretion. They do not need prior approval of plea offers, and the review of their decisions is minimal. In many ways assistants are viewed as private practitioners simply appended to the prosecutor's office. In the view of its proponents, this approach enhances the system's flexibility and ability to respond to new and different types of information. Among the office hierarchy, it reveals a high degree of comfort with the exercise of discretion. It also increases the likelihood that a host of idiosyncratic factors may be introduced into the deliberations.

At the other extreme is the bureaucratic approach. Here assistants are viewed as agents of the head of the office. They are essentially trial specialists who ply their trade within the policies set by the elected prosecutor. Their discretion is very limited, in a manner appealing to those adhering to a formalistic work orientation. Plea offers in individual cases are set by the head prosecutor, the chief of the felony division, or a central committee. No deviations from the official offer can be made without prior approval, a constraint that often interferes with the smooth flow of cases. Case dispositions are scrutinized closely for their consistency with approved offers. Accountability is clearly vested in the office head.

A variety of mixed approaches is possible between these extremes. Most are designed to impose some constraints upon discretion without interfering with the efficient functioning of the system in the way a more bureaucratic approach does. For example, a near laissez-faire approach binds assistants to very general plea policies. Examples of these policies include: "don't reduce armed robberies," "never agree to probation," and "always get two years for residential burglaries." Offices in which assistants are allowed to formulate their own offers, but are required to clear them with a supervisor before officially communicating them to the defense attorney, are closer to the bureaucratic approach. A less bureaucratic approach would involve post hoc reviews of plea bargains to insure general compliance with office policies.

DuPage and Kalamazoo both had in place elaborate, bureaucratic mechanisms to formulate and monitor plea offers. The process in DuPage was initiated by the assistant prosecutor's submission of a prosecutor's memo to the "indictment committee" (composed of the hierarchy of the prosecutor's office). The indictment committee, in conjunction with the trial assistant, then set the bottom line—a plea offer specifying charge and sentence. The assistant could not accept a plea to a lesser charge or sentence without the committee's approval. A formal compliance procedure was instituted to make sure that deviations did not occur—all dispositions were checked systematically against the bottom line. The highly centralized approach was very effective because Illinois Supreme Court rules held that judges could not become involved in plea negotiations but could be presented with an agreement to give their views on it. Thus, until an agreement was reached between the defense attorney and prosecutor, no contact with the judge was possible.

A different but equally effective approach was used in Kalamazoo. The prosecutor issuing the warrant—a regular trial assistant—engaged in an assessment of its worth and set, in writing, a bottom-line sentence similar to DuPage's. It was "good" until after the trial court arraignment; if it was not accepted at that point, the offer could be reassessed. Assistants handling the case could not agree to an offer below the bottom line, and the trial chief reviewed and had to approve all pleas. The assistant could argue for a deviation at that point, but his or her discretion was constrained by another procedure. At various stages in a case's life prosecutors were required to fill out a case form. The case form contained, among other things, a ten-point scale that ranked the strength of the case. This was an important management tool because an assistant's discretion to grant concessions on the day of trial is reduced when two or three other assistants ranked the case as very strong. In addition to these checks, the office head had established a very strong policy against primary charge reductions (knock-downs of the most serious offense), further restricting what assistants could do with a case.

In Oakland, the head prosecutor imposed a number of constraints upon his assistants, but the mechanism was far less structured than in DuPage or Kalamazoo. Constraints tended to be more carte blanche, less oriented to specific situations. For example, sentencing agreements of any type by assistant prosecutors in Oakland were prohibited. Primary charge reductions were strictly prohibited for certain types of offenses (drugs, armed robbery, weapons, offenses, and burglaries) and certain types of defendants (those on probation or who appeared to be habitual offenders), or where there was a strong likelihood of conviction at trial. Where primary charge reductions could be made (there were strong norms against any), assistants could not make them without consulting the arresting officer, and the offered reduction could not be below that offered by the prosecutor at the district court (if such an offer were made). The prosecutor made it very clear that these policies had teeth. Within six months of their creation, an assistant reduced a marijuana charge and was fired immediately. Other assistants also were fired for subsequent violations; others told of being called on the carpet for close calls, a practice almost unheard of in most other offices we studied.

Peoria had a more informal set of control mechanisms, but it was implemented on a case-by-case basis. Assistants simply had to record plea offers in each file and have the head or first assistant approve them. Any deviation from the recorded offer had to be approved by them as well. Dauphin had a similar arrangement. All pleas had to be approved by the head, in writing. In contrast to the other counties, however, this procedure was initiated by the judges, not the prosecutor's office. The judges were concerned about the lack of uniformity and rapid turnover among young assistants. What the head prosecutor did establish, however, was a strong preference against primary charge reductions, a policy strongly supported by the judges. He also actively discouraged sentencing agreements. This also was reinforced by informal, but well-known, judicial norms. Judges generally refused to accept pleas stating a specific term of imprisonment; the most they would sometimes accept would be "county time" (which could range up to two years) and, sometimes, a term of probation.

While the approach to the formation and control of plea offers in

St. Clair, Saginaw, and Erie differed somewhat, they all fit nicely within the laissez-faire model. The counties had only the most general type of policies on plea offers and no formal mechanism to monitor the agreements actually reached. In essence, individual assistants controlled the offers even though they worked within the prevailing norms of the court community. Of the four, Saginaw probably had the loosest structure, largely because of their policy of vertical prosecution. Assistants who were assigned to conduct a preliminary hearing in a case were assigned the case permanently. Thus, the assistant had a virtual monopoly of information on a case, as no one else in the office had ever made an individual assessment of its merits after the warrant was issued. This made it less likely that an assistant's judgment would be second-guessed. In addition, the head prosecutor felt very strongly that assistants should not engage in "suicide missions," that is, try cases they had very little chance of winning. He felt it important to maintain an image of invincibility at trial in order to maintain credibility in plea cases. The irony, of course, is that the policy encouraged assistants to offer concessions in cases that were not sure things at trial, in a situation in which there was no independent check on an assistant's judgment of what was a sure thing. This is in stark contrast with the prosecutorial policies on charge concessions noted in Oakland, Kalamazoo, and Dauphin. While the offices in St. Clair and Erie left the assistants' discretion virtually unencumbered, the smaller size of the offices meant that the assistants worked under informal constraints. This was especially true in Erie, where a crusader's spirit prevailed with the election of the present prosecutor. Nonetheless, even in Erie the assistants did not operate under the type of controls used in the other counties.

Montgomery cannot be easily classified within our analytic scheme, but it lies somewhere between the mixed and the laissez-faire models. In some ways it had more in common with Oakland than the laissez-faire counties. The Montgomery prosecutor had firm, well-known policies with respect to cases like theft and residential burglary. Assistants had a far better idea of what was expected and knew that they were being watched. On the other hand, the enforcement of policies was not as heavy-handed as in Oakland. Moreover, the Montgomery prosecutor did not have to get offers approved; reviews of pleas were systematic but post hoc.

THE STRUCTURE OF THE LOCAL DEFENSE BAR

Even under the best conditions an analysis of the structure of the local defense bar would yield few insights into the overall orientation toward work within a court community. Much of the work is done by solo practitioners and is characterized by idiosyncratic strategies and tactics adopted to the local terrain. The contours of that terrain are determined by the mix of judicial and prosecutorial practices and policies just reviewed. Defense work is reactive because, with few exceptions, attorneys can have little impact upon the shape of this terrain. Even the head of the public defender's office, if one exists, does not enjoy the clout of his or her counterparts. He or she is not likely to be a powerful or respected elected official but rather someone who depends upon someone else for both appointment and tenure, as well as budget. Neither does the head public defender exercise control over key aspects of the dispositional process such as charging, case scheduling, and sentencing. But, despite the relative impotence of the defense bar in landscaping the terrain, they are active players on it. No analysis of the court community's infrastructure can be complete without a review of the defense bar.

The extent to which felony criminal work is concentrated in the hands of a small group of attorneys is one of the most important structural characteristics of the defense bar. It can affect the cohesiveness of the courthouse community, the functioning of the system, and perhaps even the quality of justice. The extent to which defense work is privately or publicly funded is also important, and in some cases, can affect the level of concentration. This level is affected by both public policies and private markets. Clearly, wealthy defendants are more likely to hire private defense attorneys. This leads to a more diffuse defense bar. However, even in counties with large proportions of indigent defendants (those defended by publicly paid attorneys), a highly concentrated defense bar is not insured. Much depends upon the structure of the indigent defense system.

A good deal of variance in both the private-public mix and the level of concentration was uncovered across our counties; these data are reported in Table 6.5. Overall, nearly 57 percent of the sampled felony defendants in the counties were represented by publicly paid defense attorneys. However, the mix in the Michigan counties was much more heavily tilted toward publicly paid attorneys than those in the other states, perhaps because, as will be seen later, this work is parceled out to private attorneys. The Michigan proportions averaged about 75 percent and were fairly consistent across the three counties. In Illinois and Pennsylvania, the ring counties used fewer publicly paid attorneys than the other jurisdictions. Slightly more than one-third of Montgomery's defendants and about 43 percent of DuPage's defendants had publicly paid counsel, compared to an average of around 50 percent in the autonomous and declining counties. The second row of Table 6.5 shows the number of attorneys who represented these defendants. The numbers are quite small in all but two of the counties. Whereas an average of about 10 attorneys represented indigent defendants in the other counties, 76 attorneys in Oakland and 78 in Saginaw

Table 6.5. **Structure of Defense Bar**

	DuPage (Ring)	Peoria (Autono-mous)	St. Clair (Declin-ing)	Oakland (Ring)	Kalamazoo (Autono-mous)	Saginaw (Declin-ing)	Mont-gomery (Ring)	Dauphin (Autono-mous)	Erie (Declin-ing)
Percent of all cases represented by publicly paid attorney	42.8 N=614	62.9 N=921	56.0 N=912	67.7 N=748	80.2 N=671	77.2 N=616	34.0 N=506	48.1 N=1,014	45.1 N=588
Number of attorneys accounting for the bulk of indigent defense cases*	7	8	13	76	10	78	11	9	14
Degree of concentration in criminal defense bar: percent of cases handled by public defender plus 15 most regular private attorneys**	53.9 (22)	82.4 (23)	77 (28)	N.A. (91 attorneys handled 74.7 percent of cases)	90.4 (25)	N.A. (93 attorneys handled 91.9 percent of cases)	46.0 (26)	71.2 (24)	71.7 (29)

* This figure includes all public defenders who regularly handled a felony caseload; the small number of defenders who handled an occasional case was not included.
** The number in parentheses indicates the number of attorneys embodied in the percent of the caseload figure cited directly above it.

were appointed counsel for indigent defendants, according to our case samples.

The level of concentration of the local defense bar is indicated in the third row of Table 6.5. It shows the percent of cases handled by the 15 "most regular" private attorneys in each county plus the percent handled by the public defenders. The raw number of attorneys is depicted below in parentheses. In five of the counties, fewer than thirty attorneys represented more than 75 percent of the sampled defendants—Peoria, St. Clair, Kalamazoo, Dauphin, and Erie. In DuPage and Montgomery, the proportion of cases handled by regulars was much smaller because publicly paid attorneys handled only 43 and 34 percent of the cases, respectively, and because no private attorneys dominated the markets. In Oakland and Saginaw, the defense bar is quite diffuse because of the large numbers of lawyers representing both indigent defendants and those who could pay for legal services.

If we examine the structure of the indigent defense system in these counties, we see a number of important differences. Perhaps the most basic is their location on a private-public continuum. At the private end are systems in which members of the local bar are chosen or appointed on a case-by-case basis and paid to represent poor defendants. At the other end are public defender offices with full-time staffs working under a more or less centralized administration. Between these poles are quasi-public models in which a law firm or group of attorneys, often on a part-time basis, handles indigent defendant cases on a contractual basis with the court or county.

One can see some obvious implications of these distinctions for the work orientations discussed earlier. A wholly private system with largely blind appointments (with the exception of personalized appointments in very serious cases) could be expected to appeal to a formalistic orientation. Although it is cumbersome, it avoids the stigma attached to public defender offices by providing indigents with private counsel who have few visible ties to the court system. The sense of autonomy is maximized in such a system. A quasi-public system would have appeal to those torn between formal and efficiency considerations. A smaller number of publicly paid attorneys could facilitate the handling of cases while minimizing costs. The semiprivate nature of the attorneys would still give the aura of independence to the indigent defense, which is so crucial from a formalistic orientation. The bureaucratic model would have most appeal to those with a pragmatic orientation or, under some conditions, those concerned with efficiency. Although it does not maximize autonomy, it can be an economical, reliable way to provide large numbers of indigents with a criminal defense, depending upon its internal structure. Large numbers of attorneys do not have to be accommodated, and organizational problems are localized and handled by one administrator. It is perhaps the easiest way to provide indigent defense, especially in large and medium-sized counties.

Despite the general appeal of these different systems to different work orientations, we must be careful in drawing too many inferences. There are many reasons for adopting one form of indigent representation over another, and not all are tied to broad work orientations. Jurisdiction size may make certain forms of private representation impractical, except in serious cases. A depressed local market for legal services may lead to demands to spread out the indigent criminal work to the private bar. Finally, there are so many variations within these three general models that one particular variant of a seemingly inconsistent model may well meet the requirements of a particular orientation. Thus we must look below the surface.

Oakland and Saginaw both adopted the private model, as is evident in the data presented in Table 6.5. Despite the fact that Oakland was the largest of our nine counties, it used the most cumbersome indigent defense system, but the one that placed the most emphasis upon a sense of autonomy. The Oakland judges appointed counsel individually, some using largely sequential appointments. This individualized method of appointments made the system somewhat more manageable, but the potential for conflicts and bottlenecks was still great. In Saginaw, an Office of Assigned Counsel was used to assign cases centrally in a largely systematic manner, except for serious cases. The relatively small size of Saginaw's defense community made this system manageable. A point to be kept in mind about Saginaw's system is that it was adopted in response to a critical report that suggested the county move to a public defender system. It had used a private system in which judges made appointments to favored local attorneys, a variant of the private model more consistent with a pragmatic orientation.

Both Peoria and Kalamazoo adopted variants of the quasi-public model. Peoria employed a part-time head who contracted with seven part-time attorneys who worked out of their offices. They were given a salary plus reimbursement for office expenses. This provided Peoria with a highly cost-efficient, professionally oriented, indigent defense system, one that meshed nicely with the two judges who handled criminal cases on a full-time basis. Kalamazoo had a contract system in which it made an agreement with a consortium of local attorneys to handle all indigent defendants. Although more expensive than Peoria's system, it did alleviate the need to maintain a public building, hire an administrator and staff, and become involved in hiring and other personnel matters. It also gave the aura of independence and professionalism to the indigent attorneys, even though chapter 5 suggested that this image was not entirely accurate. Both Peoria and Kalamazoo's system blend some of the benefits of the private models with the economies of the public model.

Montgomery, Dauphin, and Erie had bureaucratic public defender offices because state law mandated it. That St. Clair adopted such a system comes as no surprise. A bureaucracy whose activities can be easily routinized and integrated into the court community is a traditional response to the problem of providing indigent defense. Indeed, many have observed that such a bureaucracy becomes so integrated that its defense attorneys become indistinguishable from other state employees, especially the prosecuting attorneys. This is especially the case where the public defender is housed in or near the courthouse. Nevertheless, this approach seems entirely consistent with the largely pragmatic orientation evidenced in other sectors of their courthouse communities.

What is somewhat surprising is that DuPage also had a public defender's office. The practices of both the bench and the prosecutor's office in DuPage had strong formalistic overtones, and one would perhaps have expected some more innovative form of indigent representation. One could, of course, point to DuPage's size as a reason for using a public defender's office, except that Oakland is larger and adopted a private model. Size may have reinforced the inertia that perpetuated DuPage's public defender's office, but what is probably a more significant factor is that DuPage was dominated by a single, strong local political party. The office, whose head is an appointed official, provides a useful and important source of patronage. Indeed, if the nine counties are examined, it can be seen that of the four counties without a public defender's office, none had a dominant local party. Four of the five counties with a public defender's office had a strong local party, but three of the four are in Pennsylvania, where a public defender's office is mandated by state law.

In our discussion of prosecutor organizations it was noted that although their method of personnel deployment could say something about their work orientation, certain structural factors sometimes forced an office's hand. Although this is equally true with respect to indigent defense systems, we can still gain some useful insights. Figure 6.2 reports the representation and assignment practice for indigent defense attorneys in the different counties. Although Oakland used continuous representation, it left the appointment of defense attornies to the discretion of individual judges. This permitted judges' favoritism in indigent appointments. Many adopted a sequential method of appointments, but others gave preferential treatment to a select group of attorneys. Kalamazoo and Saginaw use continuous representation and case-by-case assignments.

It is interesting to note that Peoria has a quasi-public model somewhat similar to Kalamazoo's, yet it uses discontinuous representation and assigns assistants to individual judges. This, of course, is a more efficient use of public defender resources from a systemic perspective. It integrates the public defenders with Peoria's specialized judges and prosecutors who are

Figure 6.2. **Deployment Practices of Indigent Defense Systems**

Assignment Policies

	Judges	Cases
Representation Practices Continuous	Oakland	Dauphin Erie Kalamazoo Saginaw
Discontinuous	DuPage Peoria	Montgomery St. Clair

also assigned to individual judges. DuPage deployed its public defenders in the same way as Peoria, but the different settings lead us to a somewhat different interpretation of DuPage. Unlike Peoria's part-time public defenders who worked out of their own offices, DuPage public defenders were full-time employees of a central office and permitted to maintain a private practice. Their assignment to individual judges—who had a full civil docket in addition to their criminal docket—fit the assistant public defenders purposes quite nicely. It provided them with ample time to develop their private practices. Thus, assignment practices in DuPage reflected pragmatic, as well as efficiency, considerations.

All four counties (St. Clair, Montgomery, Dauphin, and Erie) using a master calendar system assigned public defenders to cases, by necessity, just as in the case of prosecutors.

SUMMARY

In discussing the various practices, policies, structures, and options utilized by these nine court communities, the variety of possible infrastructures available to criminal courts—as well as their implications—is, we hope, clearer than when we began. It should also be clearer how decisions made in one sector of the court community interface with those in another. When judges choose specialized or mixed dockets, or when they adopt a master calendar or an individual calendar, the ramifications are felt throughout the court community. These choices affect how the prosecutor's office deploys its personnel and how effectively it can utilize them. These decisions may make one type of indigent defense system more attractive than another, as well as determine how its personnel are utilized. They can also affect the strategies that defense attorneys can construct for their clients. Decisions made by the prosecutor in areas such as screening, the organization of plea offers, and personnel deployment are felt in other sectors as well. They can make the private practice of criminal law less profitable by skimming the cream before it ever reaches the system and by limiting the options and flexibility of defense attorneys in plea negotiations. These prosecutor policies can also affect the magnitude of the judges' workload, how efficiently they can process their cases, and even their level of involvement in plea cases.

The preceding analyses have also demonstrated that the adoption of one structure or another has different implications for the attainment of a variety of different objectives or values such as limited discretion, the appearance of autonomy and evenhandedness, flexibility, cooperation, systemic integration, and meeting the day-to-day needs and desires of practitioners. The value of hearing a variety of different cases or appearing before a variety of different judges for the professional development of lawyers and judges is as clear as the problems such practices create for the smooth, efficient flow of cases. The advantages of personalized case assignment procedures and master calendars for those who see advantages in flexibility are apparent. The benefits and costs of a well-structured case-screening mechanism and centralized procedures to regulate plea offers were evident as well.

These insights were some of the benefits of developing the different work orientations and analyzing the various counties in light of them. The review of the infrastructure in the different counties also underscored the points made earlier about the difficulties in moving from the structure of work in a county to statements about the prevailing values and views within nine court communities. Many of our observations were conflicting, and they showed, with more specificity, the array of factors that affect the formation of a court system's infrastructure. In addition to whatever impact work orientation exerted, the relevance of such things as state laws, supreme court rules, county size, wealth, long-established traditions, and the strength of local political parties was observed.

We cannot say much more about what determines the shape of a court community's infrastructure. What we are going to be concerned with here, among other things, is the impact of these infrastructures upon the tenor of justice in these counties, particularly as manifested in their guilty plea process. We turn now to a consideration and assessment of that process.

III

THE GUILTY PLEA PROCESS

7

FAIRNESS, CRIMINAL COURTS, AND THE GUILTY PLEA PROCESS

The process by which disputes are handled goes to the heart of our conception of justice. As Justice Douglas stressed in the *McGrath* case: "It is not without significance, that most of the provisions of the Bill of Rights are procedural. It is procedure that spells much of the difference between rule by law and rule by whim or caprice. Steadfast adherence to strict procedural safeguards is our main assurance that there will be equal justice under law" (*Joint Anti-Fascist Committee v. McGrath,* 341 U.S. 123, 179 [1951], concurring opinion).

There is a great deal of contention over what constitutes a "just" resolution to a grievance, a petition, a criminal case, and many other forms of disputes. A sentence in a particular burglary case may seem very appropriate to some people while overly lenient or punitive to others. The same can be said about the amount of damages in a civil suit. There is much more agreement over the elements of fair procedure to be used in arriving at a resolution than the substantive fairness of the outcome. These elements are an integral part of what Huntington (1981) and others refer to as the "American Creed." As Fellman once noted:

> The nation agrees upon many things, and it is observable that a very broad consensus exists in connection with the basic elements of fair procedure. There are, to be sure, some differences of opinion about the precise scope of a few procedural guarantees, such as the Fifth Amendment protection against self-incrimination. There are grave differences of opinion on such matters as the construction of the permissible limits of free speech. But on the whole Americans of most shades of political opinion agree, at least in the abstract, upon the basic rules of fair play

which prevail in the field of criminal justice. On these matters the national and state constitutions say substantially the same things, in about the same language. (1976, 10)

This study grows out of a recognition of the centrality of the notion of procedural fairness. Through making an empirical inquiry into the methods used by the courts to process defendants, we want to begin to assess the tenor of justice at the trial level, the degree of fairness or consistency that exists, and the importance of different factors that affect the courts' outputs. The effort encounters a number of barriers. There are, for example, questions about the standards to which the courts should be held. Despite the considerable unanimity over what is "fundamental fairness," there is normally more agreement over what is unfair in practice than what is required of due process. After discussing the high level of agreement over the notion of abstract procedural rights, Fellman writes, "The actual administration of these rights is another matter, of course, since in this regard the picture over the country is uneven. For the translation of legal doctrine into concrete results depends upon the temper of the community, the nature of its prejudices and values, the character of its scapegoats, the state of the economy, the quality of its bench and bar, its educational system, and related nonlegal factors. Here there is much room for debate" (1976, 11).

Justice Frankfurter has written eloquently on more than one occasion about the ambiguities inherent in due process. More than thirty years ago he wrote:

> It is now the settled doctrine of this Court that the Due Process Clause embodies a system of rights based on moral principles so deeply embedded in the traditions and feelings of our people as to be deemed fundamental to a civilized society as conceived by our whole history. Due process is that which comports with the deepest notions of what is fair and right and just. The more fundamental the beliefs are the less likely they are to be explicitly stated. But respect for them is of the very essence of the Due Process Clause. (*Solesbee v. Balkcom* 338 U.S. 9, 15-16, 1950)

In a somewhat later case he noted that:

> Since due process is not a mechanical yardstick, it does not afford mechanical answers. In applying the Due Process Clause judicial judgment is involved in an empiric process in the sense that results are not predetermined or mechanically ascertainable. But that is a very different thing from conceiving the results as ad hoc decisions in the opprobrious sense of ad hoc. Empiricism implies judgment upon variant

situations by the wisdom of experience. (*Irvine v. California* 347 U.S. 128, 147, 1954)

Even if the ambiguities over the substance of procedural rights were able to be resolved, an assessment of justice based upon their prevalence would be overly formalistic and not particularly meaningful, as anyone familiar with the day-to-day operation of criminal courts would know. One of the reasons for the rather vacuous nature of such an approach is the prevalence of uncontested resolutions of criminal cases: guilty pleas. While procedural formalities act as a backdrop in the resolution of such cases, most are not directly relevant. The extent to which these noncontested dispositions loom over the larger issue of assessing fairness in the dispositional process can be seen in Table 7.1. It reports the distribution of known dispositions in our counties and is based on a pool of cases created by merging the nine county samples. Contested trials account for less than 8 percent of all dispositions, whereas guilty pleas and diversions together account for more than 81 percent of all dispositions and 93 percent of all convictions. Dismissals account for about 11 percent of the cases. The disposition data broken down by county (Table 7.2) show some inter-county variation in this pattern, but the large picture remains unchanged.[1] This is especially true if diversions are viewed as a form of guilty plea, which they are. They are simply a form of uncontested disposition for cases that meet certain criteria. In counties without a diversion program (as was true of our Illinois counties), most—if not all—of the cases probably result in guilty pleas with a sentence of probation. Viewing diversion as a form of guilty plea, we see that these dispositions accounted for between about 74 percent of the dispositions in a county (Peoria) to almost 90 percent (Montgomery). Most, however, hovered around 80 percent of all dispositions.

Table 7.1. **Trial Court Distribution of Dispositions (All Counties)**

	Number of Cases	Percent of All Known Dispositions
Dismissals	767	10.9
Trial acquittals	151	2.1
Trial convictions	402	5.7
Guilty pleas	4,823	68.4
Diversion	908	12.9
Totals	7,051*	100.0

*716 cases were disposed of at the lower court or had unknown dispositions. The total number of cases is 7,767 rather than the 7,475 reported in chapter 3 because the Dauphin Accelerated Rehabilitative Disposition cases had to be weighed to reflect the fact that we only sampled every third ARD case.

Table 7.2. **Percent of Trial Court Dispositions by County**

	DuPage	Peoria	St. Clair	Oakland	Kalamazoo	Saginaw	Mont-gomery	Dauphin	Erie
Dismissals	7.4 (48)	17.7 (165)	14.5 (144)	9.4 (82)	6.3 (42)	16.0 (100)	4.8 (32)	7.7 (81)	12.4 (73)
Trial acquittals	1.7 (11)	3.1 (29)	2.1 (21)	1.3 (11)	3.4 (23)	1.3 (8)	.7 (5)	2.8 (29)	2.4 (14)
Trial convictions	3.9 (25)	5.1 (47)	8.5 (85)	4.7 (41)	5.7 (38)	5.1 (32)	5.1 (34)	6.2 (65)	6.0 (35)
Guilty pleas	87.1 (565)	73.9 (687)	74.7 (744)	66.4 (580)	84.0 (561)	75.5 (471)	65.4 (440)	44.0 (462)	53.2 (313)
Diversions	—	—	—	18.2 (159)	.6 (4)	2.1 (13)	24.1 (162)	39.3 (413)	26.0 (153)
Don't know	259	114	168	42	51	58	14	8	6
Total number of cases	908	1,042	1,162	915	719	682	687	1,058	594

These data underscore what many empirical researchers already knew: Any assessment of the procedural fairness of the dispositional proce as opposed to evaluations of the substantive fairness of the case's resolutic n— Was the defendant guilty? Was the sentence appropriate?—must center upon the guilty plea process. Indeed, our entire assessment is limited to the guilty plea process. Although this obviously limits the scope of our diagnosis, it is justifiable because the fate of so many defendants is de- termined by the discretionary deliberations that are a part of this process. These discretionary deliberations are largely beyond the reach and view of written law and are so crucial to the dispositional process that they overshadow other facets of it. These other facets become ancillary to the plea process and are often tailored to conform to its needs and demands. Thus, although our diagnosis may not be complete, we will have at least covered the most important organs and the central nervous system.

Models of the Guilty Plea Process

At an earlier time it would have been sufficient to present the data in Tables 7.1 and 7.2 as an indictment of the dispositional process. Further tests would have been unnecessary, and a somber diagnosis rendered. However, a certain ambiguity now surrounds the guilty plea process. Until recently an implicit—and sometimes not so implicit—presumption of most criminal court researchers had been that guilty pleas were the result of plea *bargaining,* in one form or another. This term, of course, invoked images of a Turkish bazaar, extensive horse-trading, and back-room deals. While such tactics undoubtedly characterize the procurement of some guilty pleas, we do not know the extent to which these practices actually prevail. Indeed, the presumed prevalence of bargaining has been so strong that for a while researchers labeled many interactions in the guilty plea process as different forms of "bargaining," even though they had little relationship to the term *bargaining* as it is normally used. Thus, we began to discover such things as "implicit bargaining," and bench trials that are known as "slow pleas."

A review of the literature reveals two quite different conceptions of the guilty plea process. They differ fundamentally in their answer to one key question, What makes the plea process work? While most observers agree that some form of trial penalty exists to encourage pleas, they differ over how plea packages are put together. These differences form the basis for two competing models. One could be termed the "concessions" model, the other the "consensus" model. Adherents of the first are normally vociferous critics of plea bargaining. Although they span the ideological spectrum, they are in general agreement that charging manipulations and sentencing concessions grease the wheels of justice. In contrast, the consensus model stresses the importance of shared understandings in lubricating the court's machinery. Concessions and explicit bargaining have a role to play, but they are restricted to a small subset of cases involving lengthy sentences, evidentiary deficiencies, or some other type of problem.

Because these models portray criminal court proceedings in fundamentally different ways and provide us with some substantive grounding to structure our inquiries concerning fairness, we pause to discuss them in some detail. We then outline our approach to assessing the plea process.

The Concessions Model

This model has its roots in the crime surveys of the 1920s and forms the basis for most popular conceptions of the guilty plea process. In the late seventies, Krislov listed several sets of objections to plea bargaining; three of them could be used to describe the concessions model:

> At the simplest level the objection is to the notion of cow buying or haggling over the price. To some it is objectionable because it is unseemly in itself. Others feel that it is unjust because it produces differential results. And finally, there are those who argue that the accused should not participate in defining the punishment.
>
> A second family of objections argues that because plea bargaining takes place *in camera* it undermines the appearance of justice. The privacy of the proceedings not only permits collusion but, even more, suggests to outsiders the possibility of collusion. This latter is an objection over and above the unseemliness of what actually occurs.
>
> The final argument against plea bargaining is that punishment is ad hoc rather than regular and predictable. (1979, 575-76)

Alschuler, in his concessions-oriented criticisms of the guilty plea process, objects to the injection of improper considerations into the plea deliberations. In this view, evidentiary flaws, legal rights, prior records, witness defects, backlog and scheduling problems, personal relationships and debts, and other factors become grist for the plea-bargaining mill. As Alschuler notes:

> The flexibility often praised by the defenders of plea bargaining encourages ... the introduction of thoroughly improper, even corrupt considerations that they would not for a moment defend. One important fact is that many people are lazy, and bargaining makes it easy for them to split the difference. ... Most people also like to be liked and to enjoy comfortable relationships with co-workers, and this factor, too, interferes with the rational analysis of each party's interests that is seen as the basic justification of compromise. (1981, 693)

While much of the concessions model is based on observations and impressions from early crime survey research on criminal courts (Bettman, 1931; Nardulli, 1978), it is buttressed by more recent studies (Alschuler, 1968, 1975, 1976; Buckle and Buckle, 1977; Nardulli, 1978; Utz, 1978). Moreover, some adherents of the concessions model who have recently looked at criminal court dispositions over time have concluded that the role of bargained concessions has increased. Friedman, for example, states that "in the most recent period [1950-70] plea bargaining took center stage. Defendants with lawyers at their sides, relied less on understandings, more on outright negotiations" (Friedman, 1979, 256). Sounding a similar theme, Alschuler (1979) claims that high rates of guilty pleas during the 1920s left little room for further increases in absolute levels. Consequently, he argues, prosecutors faced with the floodtide of crime in recent years "may have found it necessary to offer greater concessions simply to keep their rates constant" (Alschuler, 1979, 235). He notes, for instance, that his interviews with older prosecutors and attorneys revealed "almost universal" agreement that the concessions made by prosecutors increased in scope and number during their working lives.

The Consensus Model

The concessions model has been the dominant view for the past fifty years and was useful in focusing attention on the most undesirable aspects of the dispositional process. However, it has fostered a suspicion, perhaps misleading, that bargaining and exchange can be found in every nook and cranny of the courthouse and deflects attention from the pulls of routine and common perceptions. Thus a continued, unqualified adherence to the model and an extension of its exchange perspective to encompass all facets of the disposition process may not be justified. Suggestions that explicit bargaining has grown apace with crime and that concessions have gotten larger leave the impression that courthouses resemble the trading floors of stock exchanges and other kinds of markets where "fixers" and "cop out lawyers" continue to ply their trade. Feeley's comments are pertinent at this point:

> Discussion of plea bargaining often conjures up images of a Middle Eastern bazaar, in which each transaction appears as a new and distinct encounter, unencumbered by precedent or past association. Every interchange involves higgling and haggling anew, in an effort to obtain the best possible deal. The reality of American lower courts is different. They are more akin to modern supermarkets, in which prices for various commodities have been clearly established and labeled in advance. Arriving at an exchange in this context is not an explicit

bargaining process—"you do this for me and I'll do that for you"—
designed to reach a mutually acceptable agreement. To the extent that
there is any negotiation at all, it usually focuses on the nature of the
case, and the establishment of relevant "facts.".... In a supermarket
customers may complain about prices, but they rarely "bargain" to get
them reduced. (1979, 462)

Feeley's contrasting images highlight how misdemeanor courts differ
from conventional beliefs about the fashioning of guilty pleas. Some recent
work suggests that, in many respects, felony courts also operate more like
supermarkets than bazaars (Mather, 1974, 1979; Rosett and Cressy, 1976;
Heumann, 1978, 1979) in that they are more orderly than the concessions
model would suggest. Mather (1979, 2, 3), for example, contends that
"there are rules for the plea bargaining process . . . embedded in the social
and cultural experience of the courtroom." Rosett and Cressy develop this
ordered view even further. They contend that:

Even in the adversary world of law, men who work together and
understand each other eventually develop shared conceptions of what
are acceptable, right and just ways of dealing with specific kinds of
offenses, suspects and defendants. These conceptions form the bases for
understandings, agreements, working arrangements and cooperative attitudes. Norms and values grow and become a frame of reference which
prosecutors, defense attorneys, judges and experienced offenders all use
for deciding what is fair in each case. Over time, these shared patterns
of belief develop the coherence of a distinct culture, a style of social
expression peculiar to the particular courthouse. (1976, 90, 91)

Much of the claim to order made by adherents of the consensus view
rests upon the existence of strong, well-established going rates. Going rates
are a county-specific range of acceptable sentences for a given offense.
Although they vary across counties, they bind the plea discussions in a
given county and provide a measure of predictability to sentencing that
renders the machinations implicit in the concessions model unnecessary,
even futile, at least for most cases. As a prosecutor in Detroit suggested
to Heumann: "the critical thing is that everyone, the defense attorney,
the defendants, the judges, and the prosecutors know what the current
value is. I mean as long as you take a position and make it known and
enforce it, then everyone will say, 'Well, okay, so it used to be I could
get probation for armed robbery, now I'm going to have to go to the
slammer for two years. . . .' As long as everyone understands that, you
know, people will still plead, I mean, it's curious. . . . You still have a
tremendous number of pleas like you did in the past" (1979, 209-10).

Going rates, like supermarket prices, reduce the uncertainty and the need to bargain over what every case is worth. Because similar cases receive similar kinds of outcomes, the frequency and costs of negotiations are cut sharply. Open, direct, explicit bargaining involving extensive swapping becomes an exception to the rule, contrary to earlier speculations. Heumann, for example, notes that: "Generally, only a few words have to be exchanged before agreement is reached. The defense attorney mutters something about the defendant, the prosecutor reads the police report, and concurrence on 'what to do' generally, but not always, emerges" (1978, 35). According to Rosett and Cressy, strategic maneuvering is normally absent from the process. "Undeniably, prosecutors and defenders sometimes use the adversary tactics of poker and chess in an attempt to win concessions from each other. . . . But in practice, most cases are disposed of in cooperative agreements reaching a consensus on facts and, therefore, on appropriate punishment" (1976, 15).

Courthouse actors often simply take the going rate and drastically truncate their interactions because of what Maynard (1984) calls a "concerting of expectations." In his analysis of the discourse of bargaining, he found that many of the cases he observed were concluded by one party offering a disposition and the other agreeing to it. Equally important, Maynard discovered that only in a small number of cases was there a visible compromise.

> That each recipient "takes" rather than "leaves" his counterpart's offer may be due to the "concerting of expectations" that occurs implicitly before an offer is made. . . . The concerting of expectations . . . means simply that participants are able to read situations in like manner and infer what resolution will be mutually acceptable. Such a process in plea bargaining is surely aided by the participants' knowledge of the courtroom subculture. The establishment by legal practitioners of "going rates" for run-of-the-mill, "normal crimes". . . in local jurisdictions and the administration of these rates as a matter of course . . . is a well-documented practice. (1984, 81)

Maynard concludes (98), "it is clear that settling cases by agreement is not the same as 'compromise' " and points out that in the literature on bargaining "this is considered to be a different bargaining game altogether."

The concessions paradigm does not necessarily imply that courthouse norms are nonexistent or inconsequential. Still, its adherents tend to minimize the extent to which these norms define the scope and nature of bargaining in criminal cases. The common distinction between implicit and explicit bargaining retains the concession model's viability by making implicit bargaining more or less synonymous with going rates. But the fit between the two concepts seems unsatisfactory if bargaining amounts to nothing more than taking the going rate.

A less easily described distinction between the concessions and consensus models may be seen in their view of why a defendant pleads guilty. Both models take for granted the existence of a trial penalty of some sort that will provide a major impetus for pleading guilty. The consensus model, however, does not include a trial penalty in cases where there is genuine doubt about important factual issues since no norms may have been violated. More important, a consensus perspective suggests that a good number of guilty pleas will be forthcoming even in the absence of a general trial penalty, largely because of the absence of factual issues or disputes in so many criminal cases. Thus, coercion plays a smaller role in the consensus model than in the concessions model.

Mather, for example, remarks that even when a penalty for going to trial is a remote foreboding, defendants still prefer the certainty associated with pleading guilty over the unlikely prospects of acquittal. She adds, "The benefit of certainty and wish to get the case over with cannot be quantified like that of a sentence differential but they can still be of significant value to defendants facing criminal charges" (Mather, 1979, 72). Although research on this point is limited, evidence exists that indicates a fairly large proportion of defendants plead guilty just to "get it over with." Baldwin and McConville (1979) interviewed 121 defendants in the United Kingdom and found that 29 percent of them reported no pressure or deals led them to enter guilty pleas. Indeed, only slightly more than 18 percent recalled explicit offers. The remaining 53 percent merely assumed some kind of agreement had been reached, or they pleaded guilty without an explicit offer because of pressure from their attorneys. Moreover, according to recent studies of jurisdictions where plea bargaining has been banned, guilty plea rates failed to plummet despite the limitations on charge concessions or sentence bargaining. Rubenstein and White raised a number of interesting questions on this in their evaluation of the ban in Alaska:

> So why do defense attorneys continue to advise their clients to enter guilty pleas? The answer seems to be that some cases are "triable" while others simply are not; they are "naturals" for a guilty plea. . . . But when all is said and done, most defendants continued to plead guilty even if they had to walk into open sentencing for the crimes with which they were originally charged—the classic "leap from an unknown height." Defendants probably changed their pleas because they perceived that in view of the strength of the evidence against them going to trial would be a useless act. (1979, 379-80)

Heumann explains that defense attorneys quickly discover after they start their criminal law practice that most cases offer few litigation opportunities. The newcomer "learns that the reality of the local criminal court differs from what he expected, and that compelling reasons to negotiate cases are often a product of this 'reality' " (Heumann, 1978, 154). Concessions, sanctions, rewards, penalties, benefits, and costs are part and parcel of how neophytes are taught the advantages of cooperation and of pleading guilty, as the concessions model claims. However, Heumann argues (154) that matters are more complex than this because "independent of rewards and sanctions newcomers will plea bargain most of their cases." Thus, the absence of factual ambiguity in most criminal cases looms large as an explanation for the defendant's decision to plead guilty within the consensus paradigm.

ASSESSING THE GUILTY PLEAS PROCESS

The contrast between the concessions and consensus models leads to several questions and observations that will help us in our efforts to understand and assess how criminal courts operate. A fundamental question is, Which model is most consistent with the reality of criminal courts? Although criminal court processes always involve a blend of consensual and manipulative interactions, it is important to obtain some rough estimates of the role of each within the dispositional process. It would be far too simplistic to expect to find that one model or the other accurately portrays criminal court operations. However, a specification of the actual blend will go a long ways toward helping us assess the tenor of justice dispensed by our nine courts.

If the empirical evidence indicates that exchange or bargaining interactions dominate criminal court operations, then all the fears of those who cherish the ideals of due process would be realized. The indiscriminate manipulation of the powers entrusted to public officials to coerce defendants into yielding important constitutional rights is anathema to those who claim that "steadfast adherence to strict procedural safeguards is our main assurance that there will be equal justice under law." The very possibility of such manipulations breeds contempt and resentment—instead of remorse and resolve—on the part of the defendant and undermines the justice system's credibility and legitimacy in the eyes of the public.

Strong empirical support for the consensus perspective would lead to somewhat different and certainly more involved conclusions. The impact of formal due process strictures—the type articulated in landmark Supreme Court decisions and legal treatises—upon the formation of pleas would be no greater if the vast majority of them were the result of a "concerting of expectations." There should be no mistake about this. Order would prevail within a given court community based upon widely shared norms and perceptions. But that local culture, that order, is not the result of our most learned and articulate jurists ruminating over, extending, and applying the hallowed principles of the Anglo-Saxon legal tradition. Rather it is produced by practical people with varying degrees of imagination, skill, and resources who face a continuing parade of fairly mundane problems, and who are restricted in their actions by the local political and socio-economic setting. That local order belongs to the genre of bureaucratic routine, not hallowed legal dogma. Its aim is not the realization of cherished abstract principles but the elimination of uncertainty and of the need not to reinvent the wheel, as well as to accomplish limited goals utilizing scarce resources within a given setting.

Regardless of the nature and origins of the shared norms and perceptions that may structure the guilty plea process, it should be stressed again that their existence and vitality would lend some certainty and consistency to the dispositional process. To the extent that these norms curb the blatant manipulation of official powers and are applied to individuals on a uniform basis, they can be considered to meet minimal definitions of fairness to a far greater extent than a system based upon manipulation and exchange.

If we consider these observations in light of the contrasting images of the plea process depicted in the concessions and consensus models, the faint outlines of a realistic and meaningful approach to assessing the procedural fairness of that process begin to emerge. We need to begin with an examination of structure of charging and sentencing decisions. These are the primary levers of power that public officials use to influence the defendant's decision to waive his or her rights to a formal adjudication, with all of its procedural safeguards. The supposed structure of these decisions varies considerably in the two models of the guilty plea process; a picture of their actual structure would shed much light on the fairness of the process.

Basic to the concessions model is the assertion that the plea process is characterized by pervasive and significant charge reductions due either to calculated overcharging or prosecutorial infidelity to the public trust. Extensive charge manipulations involving substantial reductions would support the view that guilty pleas are characterized by considerable horse-trading and the inference that give-and-take oils the wheels of justice. They would suggest that coercion plays an important role within the process and call the integrity of the system into question. This support is limited and questionable, however, unless it is buttressed by findings of wide-ranging sentencing disparities (for the initial, "untainted" charges). Without such findings, the data on charge manipulations would be vulnerable to the accusation that they are wholly symbolic, made only to mollify defendants and to assure them that they have received something in exchange for their plea.

In contrast to the concessions model, the consensus model would predict high levels of consistency with respect to both charging and sentencing. Charge and count modifications will be relatively infrequent, and instead of rampant sentence disparities, a set of going rates would minimize variations in sentences for comparable cases and circumstances. If charging modifications are infrequent, it could be concluded that common understandings and perceptions among court participants underlie the process, and that participants are chiefly concerned with pigeonholing defendants, not with negotiating over relative advantages. But charging consistency must be accompanied by sentencing consistency. Otherwise it could be argued that beneath the placid surface of charge constancy a lively trade in guilty pleas—with sentences as currency—is being conducted.

We discuss high levels of consistency in the charging and sentencing decisions in only general terms because any attempt to specify a priori levels would be wholly artificial. The criminal court system is highly complex and is composed of largely autonomous units that must cater to a variety of interests while handling large numbers of defendants of varying backgrounds charged with a variety of different acts. Any assessment of consistency must be prepared to yield a certain amount of slack, while at the same time recognizing unacceptable inconsistencies if they are present. Moreover, it should be stressed again that we do not expect absolute levels of consistency or manipulation, but rather want to clarify the mix of practices with some empirical precision.

One last point should be stressed. This approach relies upon the assessment of outcomes to say something about the nature of the process, a tactic that frequently requires a leap of faith. In this case we feel that the leap is fully justified. The study of trial courts has long relied upon qualitative assessments of the dispositional process—based upon observations and interviews, as well as preconceptions, but seldom buttressed by hard data. Our approach enables us to quantify the level of charge changes and sentencing disparities that flow from the process. Both measures lend themselves to straightforward quantification and enable us to gauge accurately the flow of changes and the level of disparity throughout the system. Although the evidence would be indirect, findings of high levels of charge consistency from arrest to sentence and the existence of prominent clusters of sentence, by offense, would put the burden on concession adherents to respecify the role of manipulation and concessions in the process. If they do not emerge in these key measures, then where would they emerge? How important could they be? If high levels of charge reductions and wide sentencing disparities emerge, then consensus adherents would be forced to rethink the role of common perceptions. Why would charge reductions be necessary if there is a concerting of expectations and few questions of facts exist? How important can going rates be if sentences are widely disparate?

If high levels of inconsistency are found, our diagnoses would be highly simplified, if also discouraging. An assessment could be rendered on such a set of results. However, if we find largely ordered processes in which charge manipulations are the exception, not the norm, and sentencing patterns are clustered tightly, we would have to take the analysis a step further. Common sense tells us that there will be some charge reductions in such a complex setting and that some sentencing disparities will inevitably exist. Thus, we must question the allocation of any existing concessions. While we may not have a generally accepted set of criteria that would justify the granting of concessions, we certainly can identify unacceptable criteria and examine their role in the allocation process.

With this general plan in mind, we can now discuss in concrete terms our approach to measuring charge changes, how we detected and measured the impact of going rates, and the consistency indicators used to examine the allocation of charge changes and sentence deviations.

Measuring the Incidence and Significance of Charge Changes

Changes in the charges pending against a defendant can have an impact upon his or her decision to plead guilty because, irrespective of any sentencing agreements, reduced charges can have an impact upon the defendant's legal liability at sentencing. But we must be cautious in interpreting whatever charge modifications occur, and we should be careful in equating one modification with another. While some changes (a reduction of rape to battery or armed robbery to robbery) can be significant and have important sentencing implications, others may be symbolic or largely so (a reduction of burglary to larceny in a building or dropping three counts of theft in a four-count indictment).

In addition to being careful to make the distinction between real and symbolic reductions, we also must guard against being too flippant in our assessment of symbolic reductions. It is doubtful that the dismissal of an extraneous count or two on a multicount indictment has much of a coercive impact upon a defendant's decision to plead guilty, but the actual impact is problematic. They are, after all, a bird in the hand and could be especially important in counties that do not permit sentencing agreements in plea cases. Moreover, symbolic reductions can affect the public's perceptions of justice. Outsiders cannot differentiate between real reductions and symbolic ones, and media reports of routine charge reductions conjure up images of a "Middle Eastern bazaar" in the county courthouse. What is as unfortunate about this image as the meaningless nature of most reductions is that they may not even be the result of bargaining. Just as a concerting of expectations may lead to strong going rates for common crimes, they may also lead to the routinization of count drops in multicount cases. Little give-and-take may be required.

To assess the actual incidence of charge changes, and to sort out the various types, we developed three measures. The first is a very general measure that captures any changes in the set of charges between arrest and conviction. As we recorded only the first four charges on our case-file forms, our measures are limited to those four charges. Because the data reveal that less than 1 percent of the cases had as many as four charges, the loss of information due to this limitation is minimal. This general measure reflects any changes in any counts, including a handful of charge enhancements and some cases involving enhancements at the indictment stage followed by reductions at the conviction stage.[2]

The second charge modification measure concerned count drops. There were actually several versions of this variable. One measured whether or not a count drop occurred, another measured the actual number of counts dropped, and a third expressed the number of counts dropped as a proportion of the counts charged. Finally, we determined whether there was a primary charge reduction. The primary charge is the central, and most serious, charge listed in an indictment or information filed against a defendant. It is normally easy to determine, because most cases involve either one count or a set of charges such as burglary and possession of burglary tools, rape and aggravated battery, or battery and resisting arrest.

The measures of count drops and primary charge reductions provide us with a limited means of differentiating among the various types of charge reductions in terms of their significance. Using them, we can only infer in the most general way the sentencing impact of the different types of charge reductions (i.e., whether or not they are largely symbolic). But if we examine the *changes* in the seriousness of the offenses charged, using the offense seriousness variable derived in chapter 3, we can obtain a more concrete assessment of the sentencing implication of various charge concessions. We can determine whether a reduction is likely to be worth one month in jail or closer to one year in jail. The measure of offense seriousness is tied strongly to sentencing practices in a county. Indeed, the offense seriousness score assigned to each offense is equal to the average sentence, in months, given to the defendants convicted of that offense in each county sample. For the merged pool of cases from all county samples, the correlation between the seriousness of the most serious offense convicted upon and sentence is .7. Thus, there is a strong correspondence between the offense seriousness scores and sentencing, as well there should be given the nature of the offense variable's derivation.

Although we had offense seriousness scores for a large number of different offenses, the nature of this analysis requires that we pare the analysis down to the most frequent offenses handled by the courts. Two reasons dictate this paring. First, the seriousness estimates for more frequent offenses are considered more stable because the estimates are based upon a larger number of cases. Stable estimates are crucial because the whole analysis is based upon the differences in these estimates. Estimate errors would simply be compounded in the calculation process if infrequent offenses were included.

Second, by concentrating on frequent offenses we can be more certain that we are in fact capturing real reductions. The inclusion of a large number of miscellaneous offenses would introduce unnecessary ambiguity and uncertainty. For example, it is unclear whether a charge change from gambling to disorderly conduct, or from conspiracy to commit theft to attempted theft, is a real reduction. We have less serious problems assessing changes from rape to aggravated battery, burglary to theft, or attempted murder to aggravated battery.

Both of these problems are reduced if we limit ourselves to the more standard criminal offenses. Moreover, the cost of this refinement, in terms of cases eliminated, is not high. The offenses included in this analysis are listed in Table 7.3, along with the proportion of the total cases they represent at the first appearance and at sentencing. By limiting the analysis to these cases, we eliminate less than 9 percent of the cases at the initial appearance and about 15 percent at the sentencing stage.

Limiting the analysis to this subset of offenses did not eliminate all the problems encountered in this analysis. Another problem concerned the handling of multiple-count cases. The calculations required for a single-count case involving, say, a reduction from burglary to theft, were simple, and their accuracy depended only upon the accuracy of the seriousness estimates. But two or three count cases in which a second or third count was dropped or reduced caused additional problems. Reductions (or enhancements) of nonprimary offenses could not be ignored. At the same time, it would be inflationary to evaluate modification of these secondary and tertiary offenses at face value. The net impact upon sentence of a burglary offense as a second or third charge is much less than if it were the only charge. For example, most defendants charged with only one count of burglary may get eight months in a county. However, if a defendant is convicted of rape *and* burglary, that burglary is not likely to add eight months to the defendant's sentence.

To integrate the seriousness of the nonprimary offenses into an overall seriousness score for each case, weights had to be assigned to each offense. To determine these weights, variables depicting offense seriousness for the first, second, and third offense charged at the conviction stage were entered into a regression equation with minimum confinement time, in months (probation coded 0), as the dependent variable. Only the first three offenses

Table 7.3. **Offenses Used in Charge Modification Analysis**

Offense	Percent of Cases at First Appearance	Percent of Cases at Sentencing Stage
Murder	1.6%	1.0%
	(124)	(76)
Manslaughter	.4	.5
	(28)	(38)
Rape	2.0	1.1
	(152)	(87)
Armed robbery	4.1	3.2
	(310)	(247)
Unarmed robbery	1.2	1.3
	(93)	(99)
Aggravated battery	3.6	2.9
	(277)	(222)
Simple battery	1.4	2.2
	(104)	(166)
Aggravated assault	2.5	1.8
	(188)	(138)
Simple assault	.3	.4
	(22)	(30)
Possession hard drug	8.0	7.8
	(612)	(598)
Burglary	17.1	14.1
	(1,306)	(1,082)
DWI	7.6	7.5
	(582)	(577)
Theft	16.9	18.3
	(1,296)	(1,401)
Fraud	4.3	4.4
	(332)	(336)
Arson	.8	.7
	(64)	(57)
Vandalism	2.0	2.5
	(150)	(189)
Unlawful use of weapon	2.8	2.5
	(214)	(189)
Disorderly conduct	.9	1.1
	(72)	(85)
Kidnapping	.5	.5
	(42)	(35)
Credit card crime	.5	.4
	(39)	(28)
Resisting arrest	.2	.2
	(19)	(18)

Table 7.3. (continued)

Offense	Percent of Cases at First Appearance	Percent of Cases at Sentencing Stage
Receive stolen property	1.0	.8
	(80)	(65)
Interfering with officer	1.1	1.0
	(87)	(80)
Possession of marijuana	1.8	1.8
	(140)	(137)
Delivery of marijuana	.8	.9
	(63)	(66)
Miscellaneous sex act	1.0	1.0
	(80)	(78)
Possession of controlled substance	.5	.5
	(37)	(40)
Building larceny	2.3	1.7
	(178)	(133)
Car theft	1.3	1.1
	(98)	(81)
Insufficient funds	.7	.7
	(55)	(55)
Lesser sex offense	.7	.6
	(54)	(48)
Attempted murder	.7	.5
	(50)	(39)
Attempted armed robbery	.3	.4
	(25)	(27)
Attempted burglary	.6	.6
	(47)	(47)
Attempted theft	.2	.4
	(18)	(33)
	91.7%	85.4%
	(7,035)	(6,627)

were included in the analysis because only 3 percent of the cases involved convictions on more than three counts; if there was no second or third offense, the offense seriousness variable was scored 0. The B-coefficient for OFFSER1 (the most serious offense at conviction) was 1.0; for OFFSER2, it was .15; and for OFFSER3, it was .18.

The implications of these results are quite straightforward. In computing a summed, weighted case-seriousness variable that incorporates the three most serious charges, it makes sense to assign the second and third offenses weights of .15 and .18, respectively. For each case, the weighted, summed case seriousness variable would equal 1*OFFSER1 + .15*OFFSER2

Table 7.4. **Basic Charge Modification Measures**

Variable Name	Variable Meaning and Coding
CHRGCHNG	The existence and type of any charge modification between arrest and sentence: 0 = complete consistency 1 = count drop only 2 = primary charge reduction only 3 = a count enhancement followed by a reduction 4 = a primary charge enhancement followed by a reduction 5 = charge enhancement not followed by a reduction
CHRGRED	The existence of any type of charge reduction: 0 = no reduction 1 = any type of reduction, permanent enhancements and ambiguous charges coded missing
CTRED	The existence of a reduction in the number of counts only: 0 = no reduction 1 = some reduction, permanent enhancements coded as missing
PRIMRED	The existence of a reduction in the primary charge facing the defendant: 0 = no primary charge reduction 1 = a primary charge reduction, permanent enhancements, and ambiguous charges coded missing
MAGNITUDE	Magnitude of the charge reduction in months of projected sentence; enhancements and ambiguous changes coded missing

+ $.18*OFFSER3$. If no second or third offense existed, the value of the offense seriousness variable would be 0 and it would make no contribution to the overall score. A simple example will illustrate. If a defendant is charged with one count of burglary (county-specific seriousness score = 10 months) and one count of simple battery (county-specific seriousness score = 3), the summed, weighted case-seriousness score would be 10.45 ($1 * .10 + .15 * 3 + .18 * 0$). Using this algorithm, a case-seriousness score was assigned to each case in which *all offenses charged* involved one of the offenses listed in Table 7.3. This led to the elimination of additional cases, but we are still dealing with more than 72 percent of all guilty plea cases (4,038 out of 5,600).

Table 7.4 summarizes the principle measures of charge changes used in the following analyses.

Detecting Going Rates

Our assessment of the plea process must extend beyond the incidence and significance of charge reductions because, if courthouse participants expend their time and resources negotiating sentences, then charge manipulations are superfluous, and hence less frequent than supposed. This possibility is troublesome because, although it is entirely plausible, it is also difficult to examine. The difficulty is alleviated somewhat by the realization that if sentencing is in fact the critical issue, then there should be marked sentencing disparities. If bargaining and negotiation are rife throughout the courthouse "bazaar," and bartering over sentences is the *sine qua non* of the process, sentences ought to vary widely as combinations of personalities and skills shift from one case to the next. At a minimum there should be wide disparities within charge categories. If they do not exist and sentences are tightly clustered within each offense type, it would be difficult to maintain the position that sentencing concessions grease the wheels of justice. To determine the role they do play, we must grapple with the notion of going rates.

Although intuitively and theoretically attractive, a critical problem with the concept is defining it empirically. Thus, an ordinary or typical theft case may be "worth" probation, a burglary one or two years in prison, or an armed robbery may have a going rate of three years in prison. These are norms or averages. But what are the cut-off points in defining a going rate? An unstated assumption is that the distribution around these norms is narrow, but how narrow? For that matter, how dispersed can the cluster of sentences be before the idea loses its meaning? And why should it be assumed that each offense has only one going rate or cluster of sentences, especially given the varying criminal records of defendants? If charges do indeed have more than one going rate, how can one be distinguished from another?

The procedure used here requires a rather detailed explanation because two major problems had to be overcome before starting the analysis. The first dealt with the offenses that could be used. The analyses had to rest on frequently appearing offenses to an even greater extent than the analysis of the magnitude of charge modifications. To use offenses with only a handful of cases could either inflate the number of clusters (three cases of attempted theft receiving probation might qualify as a cluster, for example) or deflate them because the small number of cases prevented a pattern from emerging. Accordingly, only offenses totaling at least ninety cases in the pooled sample at the sentencing stage were included. Behind this criterion was the thought that in most counties ten cases would be enough to permit the formation of a sentence cluster (if one existed). Where the actual number of cases dropped below this criterion, the offense was excluded from the calculation for that county unless a strong cluster emerged. If Table 7.3 is reexamined, it can be seen that fourteen offenses (the two marijuana categories were merged into one) meet the ninety-

Table 7.5. **Hypothetical Distribution of Sentences for Burglary Offenses (at Arrest)**

Months of Incarceration	Number of Cases	Percent of All Cases
0 (Probation or some other nondetentive punishment)	50	50
1	2	2
2	—	—
3	3	3
4	17	17
5	13	13
6	4	4
7	—	—
8	—	—
9	—	—
10	—	—
11	—	—
12	1	1
13	—	—
14	—	—
15	—	—
16	—	—
17	—	—
18	8	8
19	—	—
20	—	—
21	—	—
22	—	—
23	—	—
24	2	2
	100	100

cases requirement. These accounted for slightly more than 66 percent of all sentenced cases.

The second problem centered on the definition of the spans for the clusters. Table 7.5 portrays this problem in a simplified way. It reports a hypothetical distribution of sentences for the offense of burglary. With sentence length measured in months, it can be seen that defendants who were given probation constitute one cluster, those given between four and five months define a low cluster, while those given eighteen months constitute a high cluster. The low cluster in the example is what might be termed an interval cluster, while the probation and high clusters are point clusters. The fact that probation is so common means that many felony charges will have two sentencing clusters, one for probation and one for incarceration. Only a handful of the more serious offenses will have high clusters. Obviously, the meaning of low or high depends entirely on the spread of the overall distribution and the distance between the clusters; they relate only to the sentencing pattern for a particular charge in a specific county.

To identify and define these clusters, the distribution of *guilty plea* sentences was examined for each qualifying offense (as defined by the original primary offense at *arrest*) within each county to see if patterns such as those depicted in Table 7.5 existed. It should be stressed that sentences were grouped by *arrest* offense because this *maximizes* the potential for disparities to emerge. If sentences were grouped by charge at conviction, the cases receiving primary charge reductions would be excluded from the set of defendants originally charged with a given offense. The identification of clusters was a difficult process that had to be sensitive to competing concerns. Obviously, the wider the span allowed for interval clusters, the greater the number of cases that would fall within a cluster. This could lead to a conclusion that more consistency existed than was justifiable. At the same the actual distribution of sentences might be obscured by unrealistically stringent criteria. Thus the working definitions used in the search process needed a measure of slack.

The following procedure was used. If an offense had less than ten sentenced cases, the cases were categorized as "indeterminate," unless a strong cluster emerged. The probation cases were assigned to a "probation cluster"; with only a few exceptions (armed robbery), all offenses in each county had a cluster of cases given probation. The distribution of the remaining cases was then examined to determine if there were any other discernible clusters. In some instances there were none. These were categorized as "no cluster above probation." In most instances a unimodal distribution existed for the remaining detention cases. If the modal category accounted for at least 10 percent of all cases, defendants given that sentence were assigned to a low-cluster category.[3] Next, the distribution of sentences around the modal incarceration sentence was examined to see if the low cluster encompassed a span of sentences surrounding the mode or just the mode (i.e., three to five months instead of four). While the vast majority of all clusters defined were point clusters (about 90 percent), we still had to be extremely careful in defining interval clusters. One could expand indefinitely the range around the mode and consume increasingly larger numbers of cases. To control this, we generally limited our intervals to three months (only 3 of 160 clusters exceed a span of 3) and computed a ratio of cases to months (number of defendants encompassed in a span of sentences/width of the span of sentences, in months) in analyzing whether a cluster was a point or an interval. Where the "span ratio" was greater than three, the span was considered "tight" enough to be considered a cluster.[4]

A discussion of Table 7.5 will illustrate this procedure. It is clear from Table 7.5 that at least two clusters exist. The probation category includes half of the defendants, and another seventeen received four months. These seventeen cases are 34 percent of the remaining cases, after the fifty probation cases are removed. As we examine the distribution of cases around four months, we see that another thirteen defendants received five months. Because these two groups "look" like a cluster and the span is only two months, we compute a span ratio to see if the four to five month grouping qualifies as an interval cluster. The span ratio is computed by dividing the number of cases in the categories (17 + 13 = 30) by the span of months in the interval (2). We get a span ratio of 15 (30 divided by 2 = 15). As we continue down the distribution of sentences, we see what might be termed a high cluster at 18 months. Eight defendants received 18 months in jail, and they account for 16 percent of all non-probation cases. No other cases are close to 18 months, so it is simply a point cluster.

Based upon the distribution in Table 7.5, the fifty probation cases were assigned to a probation cluster category, the thirty cases that were given four or five months were assigned to a low-cluster category, and the cases given eighteen months were assigned to a high-cluster category. Cases that fell into the "valleys" between the "peaks" (clusters) were assigned to one of three categories: between probation and low, above low (or between low and high), and above high. In a few instances, no clusters existed, and cases in these distributions were assigned to a "no-cluster" category. Table 7.6 summarizes the various cluster categories used.

Table 7.6. **Categories of the Sentencing Cluster Variable**

Category	Case Description
Probation cluster	Probation cases where a cluster exists
Between probation and low	Jail cases in the "valley" between the probation and low cluster
Low cluster	Jail cases lying on or around the first peak meeting span criteria
Above low cluster	Jail cases in the valley between the low and high clusters or above the low cluster
High cluster (optional)	Jail cases lying on or around the second peak meeting span criteria
Above high cluster (optional)	Jail cases above the high cluster
No cluster or no cluster above probation	Randomly distributed cases

Table 7.7. **Distribution of Cluster Spans**

Span of Cluster (difference between high and low sentence, in months)	Including Probation			Excluding Probation		
	Number of Charge-Based Clusters	Percent of All Clusters	Percent of All Cases	Number of Charge-Based Clusters	Percent of All Clusters	Percent of All Detention Cases
0 (point cluster)	143	89.4	91.4	58	77.3	50.6
1	2	1.2	.3	2	2.7	1.6
2	7	4.4	3.5	7	9.3	19.9
3	5	3.1	2.5	5	6.7	14.2
4	—	—	—	—	—	—
5	1	.6	.6	1	1.3	3.2
6	2	1.3	1.8	2	2.7	10.5
	160	100	100 ($n=3,241$)	75	100	100 ($n=563$)

The data presented in Table 7.7 reveal how successful the above procedure was in identifying tight clusters of sentences. Because probation clusters are so dominant, the data in Table 7.7 are reported in two ways: with the probation clusters included and excluded. If probation clusters are included, "point" clusters account for about 90 percent of the clusters and cases as just mentioned. Only about 2 percent of the clusters had spans in excess of three months (about six weeks either side of a mid-point), and these clusters accounted for about 2 percent of the cases. If we exclude the probation clusters, the point clusters account for about 77 percent of the clusters and about half of the cases. The three clusters above three months account for 4 percent of the clusters and about 14 percent of the cases.

The actual sentence range for each offense in each county along with the number of cases in the clusters can be found in Appendix IV. An inspection of this appendix can provide a much better feel for results of the procedures just described.

Consistency Indicators

It was mentioned earlier that an issue independent of the overall levels of charge manipulation and sentence dispersion in our assessment of the plea process is the way in which charge changes and sentence deviations are allocated. If they are handed out on a discriminatory basis or in a way that discourages a defendant from exercising legal rights, then it could be said that reductions are used predominantly to pursue unjustifiable ends (to reward certain classes of defendants or to discourage certain types of activity). An alternative view is that they are allocated on the basis of prosecutorial policies or court community norms ("always reduce stray counts on a multiple-count indictment," for example), individual views, or collective assessments of the equities of a particular situation. Such factors should lead to relatively unbiased allocations of concessions.

Our aim here is not to develop a sophisticated statistical model of the concession process. Rather it is simply to assess whether factors considered by most to be unacceptable play a significant role in the allocation of concessions. Three sets of such factors seem particularly pertinent to this analysis. One can be referred to as social fairness factors and includes considerations that relate to a defendant's socioeconomic status or social characteristics. We examine four social fairness indicators in the analysis: the type of attorney representing the defendant (public-private), whether the defendant was confined at the time of disposition, and the defendant's race and sex. While the defense attorney type and confinement status variable are "tainted" indicators of socioeconomic status (other factors such as charge and criminal record may affect them), they are the best available to us. Moreover, the use of some statistical controls (to be discussed later) will enhance their utility for the purposes of the analysis. Clearly, if charge drops are used in a discriminatory manner to the disadvantage of "have nots," then defendants who are represented by public counsel and/or who are confined at the point of disposition would be less likely to receive a reduction, or as significant a one. Much the same can be said of the race variable, which captures the effects of both racism and economic disadvantage. Blacks should receive fewer and less significant reductions. The sex variable was included to determine whether the largely male-dominated court community treated males and females in a similar manner.

The second set of factors includes evidence indicators. These are important because many critics of plea bargaining assert that concessions are made only in weak cases which, if pursued to trial, might result in acquittals, or at least have a greater chance of acquittal than most. The lure of concessions, compounded by real or perceived trial penalties, would discourage these cases from going to trial. Our ability to examine whether a case is evidentially weak is limited because of the difficulty of quantifying and comparing the strength of various types of evidence. We can tell when there are eyewitnesses, but we do not know who they are, what they saw, or how impressive their testimony might be. A statement by the defendant might be viewed as a confession, but not necessarily to the charges filed. The value of certain types of evidence may also vary from case to case.

With these limitations in mind, we employed four evidence indicators plus a composite "deadbang" measure (named for those cases in which there is no doubt of the client's guilt). The four individual indicators were: the existence of a confession, the existence of physical evidence, the existence of two or more eyewitnesses ("single finger" cases are not always viewed as necessarily "solid"), and the existence of a positive identification. An examination of the patterns of these variables and an assessment of their different uses led to the development of a composite, deadbang measure that attempts to isolate cases with both eyewitness testimony and either a confession or some physical evidence. For this deadbang measure all cases that had at least two eyewitnesses *or* a positive identification and a confession *or* physical evidence were coded 1. All other cases were coded 0. Approximately two-thirds (65 percent) of the guilty plea cases were classified as "deadbangers" on the basis of this alogrithm. Such a composite measure is important because it captures several evidentiary dimensions. Assessments of a case based upon unidimensional measures may be misleading because, although a case may seem strong in one area (physical evidence), it may be lacking in another (eyewitness). Because of the high intercorrelation between the deadbang measures and the individual ones, the deadbang measure was analyzed separately.

The final set of factors examined here include what might be referred to as "resistance" indicators. They include the use of legal motions and delaying tactics by the defense and are important because such activities often run counter to accepted court community norms, at least in certain situations. The use of motions, especially those considered frivolous, and delaying tactics interfere with the efficient and informal processing of cases. The legalistic and logistical problems that these tactics cause may damage what is an otherwise sound prosecution. To discourage such tactics, prosecutors may be less forthcoming with charge reductions when they are used.

We use two resistance indicators: the filing of one or more legal motions and a trichotomized, county-specific delay variable.[5] The legal motion variables were dichotomized because so few cases had more than a handful of motions and their impact was not curvilinear (i.e., filing two or three motions had about the same effect as filing one). Although these are the best available indicators of this phenomenon, we should be sensitive to their inherent shortcomings. Not all motions are considered frivolous, nor are they equally detrimental to the state's case. Moreover, some lengthy delays are neither needless nor due to defense tactics. Thus, the results must be interpreted cautiously.

Table 7.8. **Summary of the Consistency Indicators**

Variable Name	Variable Description and Coding
	Social Fairness Indicators
PRIVDC	Was the defendant represented by a private defense counsel? (public = 0; private = 1)
CONFINED	Pretrial detention status (released = 0; confined = 1)
DRACE	Defendant's race (white = 0; black = 1)
DSEX	Defendant's sex (male = 0; female = 1)
	Evidence Indicators
CONFESS	Was there a confession? (no confession = 0; confession =1)
PHYSEVID	Was any physical evidence available? (no evidence = 0; evidence = 1)
TWOEYES	Were there two or more eye witnesses? (less than two eyewitnesses = 0; two or more eyewitnesses = 1)
POSID	Existence of a positive identification (no ID = 0; ID = 1)
DEADBANG	Was this a deadbang case? (not deadbang = 0; deadbang = 1)
	Resistance Indicators
MOTIONS	Were there legal motions filed? (no motions = 1; motions = 1)
DELAY	Delay (short = 1; medium = 1; long = 3)

Table 7.8 summarizes the consistency measures. With our arsenal of instruments laid out, we can now use them to assess the nature of the plea process with an eye toward the questions raised by the concessions/consensus perspectives.

NOTES

1. The large number of "Don't Knows" in Illinois is accounted for by lower court dispositions. They are included as missing because they were not trial court dispositions.

2. Where there was a change in charges we compared the scores on the offense seriousness measure (described in chapter 3). When the new charge had a lower

score, the change was classified as a reduction; when the score on the new charge was higher, it was classified as a charge enhancement.

3. This figure of 10 percent may seem low as a cutoff point, but it usually accounted for a much higher percentage of the incarceration cases—20 to 25 percent. For example, if probation accounted for 60 percent of all sentences for an offense, then a second sentence category, say three months (which accounted for 10 percent of all cases), actually accounted for a quarter of all cases remaining after the probation cases are removed. In a few instances (where probation accounted for a large proportion of the sentences), a low cluster was defined even if the percentage of cases dropped slightly below 10 percent (8-9 percent). This only occurred where the overall distribution of incarceration cases indicated clearly that a cluster existed.

4. The span ratio of 3 was a wholly arbitrary cutoff point, inductively constructed after a preliminary examination of the data. Patterns that looked like a cluster generally had span ratios well above 3 (the mean for interval clusters was 7); those that were spotty normally had ratios below 3. While the criteria were subjective, no independently determined standards for such a procedure exist. Although arbitrary, the criteria lent an element of objectivity to the classification procedure, permitted replication, and greatly facilitated the classification procedure. Moreover, because these procedures affected only a small proportion of the cases (about 10 percent), their arbitrariness has only a marginal effect upon the number of cases falling within a cluster.

5. Because case processing times varied so much by county, we classified cases in each county into one of three roughly equal categories, based upon the number of days that elapsed between arrest and dispositions.

REFERENCES

Alschuler, Albert W. 1981. "The Changing Plea Bargaining Debate." *California Law Review* 81:69.

———. 1975. "The Defense Attorney's Role in Plea Bargaining." *Yale Law Review* 84:1179.

———. 1979. "Plea Bargaining and Its History." *Law and Society Review* 13:211.

———. 1968. "The Prosecutor's Role in Plea Bargaining." *University of Chicago Law Review* 36:50.

———. 1976. "The Trial Judge's Role in Plea Bargaining, Part I." *Columbia Law Review* 76:1059.

Baldwin, John, and Michael McConville. 1979. "Plea Bargaining and Plea Negotiation in England. *Law and Society Review* 13:282.

Bettman, Alfred. 1931. "Criminal Justice Surveys Analysis Vs. National Commission on Law Observance and Enforcement." *Report on Prosecution* 31:4.

Buckle, Leonard, and Suzann R. Buckle. 1977. *Bargaining for Justice: Case Disposition and Reform in Criminal Courts.* New York: Praeger Publishers.

Feeley, Malcolm. 1979. "Perspectives on Plea Bargaining." *Law and Society Review* 13:199.

Fellman, David. 1976. *The Defendant's Rights Today.* Madison: University of Wisconsin Press.

Friedman, Lawrence M. 1979. "Plea Bargaining in Historical Perspective." *Law and Society Review* 13:247.

Heumann, Milton. 1978. *Plea Bargaining: The Experiences of Prosecutors, Judges, and Defense Attorneys.* Chicago: University of Chicago Press.

————. 1979. "Thinking About Plea Bargaining." In *The Study of Criminal Courts: Political Perspectives,* ed. Peter F. Nardulli. Cambridge, Mass.: Ballinger Publishing.

Huntington, Samuel. 1981. *American Politics: The Promise of Disharmony.* Cambridge, Mass.: Harvard University Press.

Krislov, Samuel. 1979. "Debating on Bargaining: Comments from a Synthesizer." *Law and Society Review* 13:573.

Mather, Lynn M. 1979. *Plea Bargaining or Trial? The Process of Criminal Case Disposition.* Lexington, Mass.: D. C. Heath.

————. 1974. "Some Determinants of the Method of Case Disposition: Decision-Making by Public Defenders in Los Angeles." *Law and Society Review* 8:187.

Maynard, Douglas W. 1984. "The Struture of Discourse in Misdemeanor Plea Bargaining." *Law and Society Review* 18:75.

Nardulli, Peter F. 1978. *The Courtroom Elite: An Organizational Perspective on Criminal Justice.* Cambridge, Mass.: Ballinger Publishing.

Rosett, Arthur I., and Donald R. Cressy. 1976. *Justice by Consent: Plea Bargains in the American Courthouse.* Philadelphia: Lippincott.

Utz, Pamela J. 1978. *Settling the Facts: Discretion and Negotiation in Criminal Court.* Lexington, Mass.: D. C. Heath.

8

THE GUILTY PLEA PROCESS: AN EMPIRICAL EXAMINATION

As our earlier discussion suggests, the issues of fairness and consistency in the guilty plea process are multifaceted. Even though our plan of analysis is fairly straightforward, the complexity of the issues makes the analysis complicated and at times difficult to follow. We cannot expect simple portrayals of complex social processes; nor do we choose to analyze superficially the important and controversial questions raised by this analysis. The existence of nine different counties, while enhancing the scope and richness of our analysis, further complicates the presentation of the results and their implications.

To enhance our ability to keep our "eye on the doughnut, not upon the hole," we begin with an overview; we merge all nine county samples into one analysis pool. Toward that end, we examine the various measures of charge modifications described in Table 7.4, compare reductions in guilty plea and trial cases, and then examine the impact of the three sets of consistency indicators (see Table 7.8) upon the allocation of charge concessions. Next, we turn our attention to the role of going rates. We examine the distribution of guilty plea cases that fall within the sentence clusters described earlier (Table 7.6), and examine the consistency and fairness of the pigeonholing process (i.e., placing defendants in one cluster or another). We also look at the sentencing implications of charge reductions and the existence of a trial penalty.

The next main section deals with county-level differences in the plea process. An examination of the role of charge reductions in guilty plea cases reveals four different patterns for the nine counties. We examine the strength of going rates by county type and the impact of our consistency indicators in these various settings. Finally, the impact of charge reductions upon sentences and the role of the trial penalty is compared across the different types of counties.

CHANGES IN LEGAL EXPOSURE: CHARGE REDUCTIONS AND GUILTY PLEAS

The modification of a defendant's legal exposure at sentencing can have an important effect upon the decision to plead guilty. This exposure depends upon the severity and range of penalties associated with the charges lodged against the defendant, charges upon which he or she could be convicted and sentenced after a trial. While the going rate for an offense normally limits the *probable* sentence, its outermost boundary or *potential* sentence is set by statute. Modifying charges can, therefore, change potential exposure in ways that constitute tangible benefits or threats to defendants. Because of the differences in potential and probable sentences — and the possibility that some charge reductions may be largely symbolic — the analysis of charge reduction is fairly complicated.

We begin by examining the incidence of some types of charge modification. An examination of our most general charge modification variable (*CHRGCHNG*) reveals four distinct patterns of change in guilty plea cases: (1) no change in the charges; (2) a "pure" reduction in the number of counts or seriousness of offenses; (3) a "mixed" modification, with an enhancement of counts or charge seriousness followed later by a reduction; and (4) a straightforward enhancement in exposure through increases in the number of counts of charge seriousness. Diagram 8.1 reports the frequency of these patterns.

Complete consistency — no modifications in *any* count or charge from the time of arrest through final disposition — occurred in 60 percent of the cases. Pure reductions were made in just over one-quarter of the cases (26.7 percent). Enhancements took place in roughly 13 percent of the cases, although the lion's share of these were "mixed" cases since 71 percent of them were later mitigated through reductions. Charge enhancements normally took place when the indictment or information was filed; reductions were made in the trial court. Comparisons of the arrest and conviction charges showed that this two-step process produced real reductions, and they should be combined with the "pure" reduction category to gain an accurate picture of charge concessions.

Together these two categories of reductions accounted for 36 percent of the entire pooled sample of cases, at first glance a rather sizable proportion. This should be qualified by the observation that the charge concessions primarily affected secondary or tertiary offenses (i.e., count

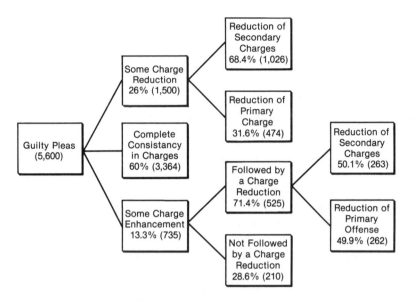

Diagram 8.1. **Charge Modifications from Arrest to Disposition,
Guilty Plea Cases Only**

drops), not the primary charge. For example, 68.4 percent of the pure
reductions entailed alterations in these secondary charges. For the mixed
cases, the proportion was 50.1 percent. Altogether, count drops occurred
in 29.9 percent of the cases; the average number of counts dropped (for
the cases where a count drop occurred) ranged between 1 and 2 (mean =
1.7; median = 1.3). The number of counts dropped accounted for half of
the counts charged (mean proportion of all counts dropped = .55; median
= .50). Only about 15 percent of the cases involved a reduction in the
primary offense. It also bears mentioning that the number of true enhancements amounted to only 210 cases, or slightly less than 4 percent
of the pooled sample. For this reason, and the fact that such enhancements
do not normally flow from the negotiating process, the following discussion
concentrates on charge reductions.

Depending upon one's views, the data on charge reduction may show
either too much charging manipulation or too little. According to the
latter view, the reduction of secondary offenses is insignificant and wholly
symbolic, and therefore deceives most defendants. Although such an assessment is premature at this point, we cannot even begin to address such
issues without comparing charge changes in guilty plea cases with those
in trial convictions. A certain level of adjustment is bound to occur in a
process as complex as the criminal justice system. Hence, charge reductions

Table 8.1. **Incidence of a Charge Reduction by Mode of Conviction**
(from Arrest Charge to Sentence)

Type of Reduction	Guilty Pleas	Trial Convictions
CHRGRED (any charge reduction)	36.0 *** (5,560)	30 *** (370)
CTRED (count reduction only)	29.9 ** (5,353)	23.1 ** (375)
PRIMRED (primary charge reduction)	15.1 * (5,564)	10.9 * (387)

* Significant at .05 level.
** Significant at .01 level.
*** Significant at .001 level.

may not be unique to plea cases but simply inevitable, at least to some extent. Table 8.1 reports data on the incidence of a charge reduction by mode of conviction.

Reductions were significantly more likely to occur, statistically speaking, in guilty plea cases than in the trial cases regardless of which measure is examined. But it also is quite evident that charge modifications were not unknown in trial convictions, largely because of the dismissal of certain counts or acquittals. Some type of reduction was made in 30 percent of the trial cases, only 6 percent less than for reductions after guilty pleas (36 percent). The difference narrows when we focus on reductions in the primary charge: 10.9 percent of the convictions in trial cases were on reduced primary charges compared to 15.1 percent following guilty pleas. The difference in the incident of a count drop by mode of conviction was about 7 percentage points (29.9 percent for guilty pleas and 23.1 percent for trial cases).

The fundamental similarity in charge reduction patterns of guilty plea and trial cases introduces a certain element of ambiguity to the data reported in Table 8.1. The fact that yawning gaps do not appear by mode of conviction suggests that at least some of the charging concessions that purportedly limited the defendant's legal exposure at sentencing might have occurred even if a plea had not been submitted.

An examination of the magnitude of these concessions may erase some of this ambiguity. As noted earlier, our measure of magnitude (MAGNITUDE) is based on changes in weighted seriousness scores that are tied to the sentencing patterns of individual courts. Thus they give us a rough estimate of a reduction's projected sentencing implications. We can also compare them with reductions made after a trial.

Table 8.2 reports data on the *MAGNITUDE* variable, which registers changes in weighted seriousness scores between arrest and conviction charges. Almost a quarter of the guilty plea cases in the subset of offenses for which we have *MAGNITUDE* scores received a reduction in one of the first three arrest offenses. The mean projected sentencing value of these reductions was 7.6, months but that figure is highly skewed by a handful of extreme cases. As the median value of 1.4 months indicates, half of those pleading guilty had charge reductions worth somewhat less than two months in projected sentence. Almost 80 percent of the defendants received reductions worth less than six months.

To obtain an accurate interpretation of these data, it should be kept in mind that the absolute level of charge reductions is limited by the projected sentence of the total package of charges. For this reason, it is important to note that the last two columns in Table 8.2 report the reductions as proportions of the summed seriousness scores. The mean value of these proportions is .39, and the median is .24. According to the median figure, then, the projected sentences of half of the defendants who pleaded guilty and received some form of charge reduction was cut by one-fourth.

These proportions seem somewhat more significant. However, it should be kept in mind that they represent less than one-quarter of all guilty plea cases. Moreover, if these statistics, as well as the others reported in Table 8.2, are compared with the reduction of charges in trial cases, it is not at all clear that the charge reductions in guilty plea cases are real concessions. No significant differences occur between plea and trial cases in terms of the proportion of cases receiving some charge reduction (in this subset of cases) or the magnitude of charge reductions.

Consistency in the Allocation of Charge Reductions

The preceding analyses shed some light on the level of consistency in the charging process in our nine counties. The role of charge reductions in the guilty plea process is not as paramount as many assume, especially if reductions in primary charges are examined. Most charge reductions involve count drops that have only marginal implications for sentence. Moreover, the incidence of charge reductions in a guilty plea case is not much different from that in trial cases. Despite these findings, another dimension to the question of consistency needs to be examined: the allocation of reductions. Who gets the benefit of the reductions that do occur? Do prosecutors use their discretionary charging powers in a punitive

Table 8.2. *MAGNITUDE* Variable by Type of Conviction (Arrest Charges Compared with Sentence Charges)

Type of Conviction	Percent of All Cases Involving a Reduction	Average Weighted Modifications (in Months)		Percent of All Weighted Changes That Are Less Than 6 Months	Average Weighted Modifications as a Proportion of Weighted Changes	
		Mean	Median		Mean	Median
Guilty pleas	23.9* (965)	7.6*	1.4	79	.39*	.24
Trial convictions	22.0* (62)	11.6*	1.1	79	.40*	.35

* Not statistically significant.

or discriminatory way? To address these questions, we examine the re-lationship between three sets of consistency indicators introduced in chapter 7 (social fairness, evidence, and resistance) and our measures of charge reduction.

We examined the impact of these three sets of factors upon four measures of charge reductions (*CHRGRED, CTRED, PRIMRED, MAG-NITUDE*) by using multiple regression to do an analysis of covariance. In these analyses we controlled for the effects of the seriousness of the charge, the nature of the defendant's criminal record, and the existence of a multicount indictment, and then examined the impact of the con-sistency indicators. The first two control variables are fairly straightforward and self-explanatory. The impact of variables such as attorney type and confinement status may be misleading if offense and record are not con-trolled, because they are likely to be intercorrelated. Any variance shared by these sets of variables must be attributed to the control variables in an analysis such as this. The multicount indictment variable is used as a control variable because it is the strongest determinant of a charge reduction (r = .54). Because most charge reductions are simply count drops, a multicount indictment is a necessary condition.

Table 8.3 outlines the hypothesized effect of the eleven consistency indicators (column 1) for the four measures of charge reduction, as well as the results (significance levels, *B*-coefficients) of the analysis of co-variance. To simplify matters we report only findings that were statistically significant in the *hypothesized* direction. Findings that show that women do better than men, or that legal motions translate into more reductions, may be interesting, but they unduly complicate the presentation and assimilation of the results of this fairly limited analysis and interfere with the achievement of its objectives. What we want to obtain here is simply an appreciation of the role that certain specified influences play in the allocation of charge reductions.

A glance at Table 8.3 shows that these influences played only a sporadic and minor role in the allocation of charge reductions. Of the forty-four effects examined, only six significant hypothesized effects were found; three of those involved the count-drop variable. Only the physical-evidence variable had a consistent effect. The clients of private attorneys had a probability of receiving a count reduction that was only five points greater than indigent defendants (B = .05). Released defendants received sentence reductions worth an average of about 2.5 months greater than incarcerated defendants. Defendants who confessed were only slightly less likely (B = .04) than others to get a count drop. Defendants in cases that were deficient in physical evidence were more apt to receive some charge reduction. There was a difference of nine percentage points on the

Table 8.3. **Consistency Indicators and Charge Reductions
in Guilty Plea Cases**

Consistency Indicator	Hypoth-esized Effect	CHRGRED	CTRED	PRIMRED	MAGNI-TUDE
PRIVDC	+	—	** (.05)	—	—
CONFINED	−	—	—	—	*** (−2.5)
DRACE	−	—	—	—	—
DSEX	−	—	—	—	—
CONFESS	−	—	** (−.04)	—	—
PHYSEVID	−	*** (−.09)	*** (−.09)	*** (−.05)	—
TWOEYES	−	—	—	—	—
POSID	−	—	—	—	—
DEADBANG	−	—	—	—	—
MOTIONS	−	—	—	—	—
DELAY	−	—	—	—	—

* Indicates a significance level at or beyond .05.
** Indicates a significance level at or beyond .01.
*** Indicates a significance level at or beyond .001.
— Indicates no statistically significant impact.

CHRGRED and CTRED variable and a five-point spread on the PRIMRED variable.

The generally spotty and weak patterns of association between the various consistency indicators suggest that they play a relatively insignificant role in the charge reduction calculus. Indeed, it would be difficult to conclude that blacks, women, or indigents did worse in obtaining reductions than others. Moreover, while cases that are lacking in available physical evidence appear to do slightly better in obtaining some form of charge reduction, the composite measure (DEADBANG)—which blended the two basic evidentiary dimensions—revealed no pattern of association with charge reduction. Thus, no consistent or straightforward relationship between evidence and charge reduction is apparent. Even if we viewed the impact of the physical evidence variable in a highly charitable light, its relatively minor impact would not justify a conclusion that there is widespread charge manipulation aimed at sweetening the pie for evidentially weak cases.

The minimal impact of these consistency indicators is underscored by the fact that in no instance did they, as a group, add more than one percentage point to the explained variance (R^2) of any of the charge reduction measures. Reasonable minds can quibble about what is an acceptable level of bias. However, even if the level of bias were much higher than reported here, it would not be appropriate to attribute the bias to plea bargaining unless the bias did not exist in trial cases.

To check whether the patterns reported above were different in trial cases, an interaction analysis was conducted. Using data presented in Table 8.3, we took each consistency indicator that showed a significant impact and computed an interaction term between it and the method of conviction (0 = guilty plea; 1 = trial); that term was then entered into the regression analysis. If the impact of the consistency indicator was significantly different in trial cases than in guilty plea cases, the interaction term would be statistically significant. No significant differences were found.[1] The failure of the interaction analysis to uncover significant differences between trial processes and guilty plea processes, in conjunction with the weak and somewhat perplexing pattern of findings reported in Table 8.3, suggests that the types of bias many feared to be operating in the guilty plea process are not important considerations in charge reductions. These findings are, then, generally supportive of the picture presented earlier in Diagram 8.1.

GOING RATES AND GUILTY PLEAS

The argument that common perceptions and understandings characterize the guilty plea process to a greater extent than horse-trading and explicit bargaining would seem to hold up well in the face of the results of the charge reduction analysis. Count drops and — to a far lesser extent — changes in primary charges occurred with some regularity in the courts, but the magnitude of these changes with respect to their likely impact on sentencing was marginal at best. When they did occur, they typically shaved less than two months off probable sentences. More surprising, perhaps, than the somewhat spotty occurrence and marginal effects of these modifications is the fact that similar patterns often prevailed in both guilty plea and trial conviction cases. Finally, the allocation of charge concessions did not seem to be dictated by blatantly discriminatory criteria or punitive motives.

Nonetheless, any comprehensive assessment of the guilty plea process must await the analysis of sentencing patterns. Charge reductions may be infrequent and evenly distributed because they do not mean very much. Real negotiations may focus on sentences, and it may be that the most serious manipulations, disparities, and biases exist at that stage. To examine this possibility, we must look at the proportion of cases within the clusters

Table 8.4. **Distribution of Sentencing Clusters by Type of Conviction**

Sentencing Cluster	Percent of Qualifying Guilty Plea Cases*	Percent of Qualifying Trial Conviction Cases*
Probation cluster	66.0 (2,666)	39.0 (90)
Between probation and low cluster	4.8 (192)	12.1 (28)
Low cluster	10.7 (433)	11.7 (27)
Between low cluster and high cluster	5.4 (220)	15.6 (36)
High cluster	4.1 (165)	3.9 (9)
Above high cluster	3.8 (154)	9.1 (21)
No cluster or no cluster above probation	5.2 (212)	8.6 (20)
Total	100.0 (4,042)	100.0 (231)

* These data excluded 1,072 cases that were convicted but that involved nonregular offenses.

described in chapter 7. The first column of Table 8.4 reports this information for defendants who pleaded guilty.

When the three major clusters (probation, low, high) are combined, they include just over 80 percent of the guilty plea cases (80.8 percent). This finding strongly suggests that going rates play a prominent role in determining sentences in guilty plea cases. The fact that the probation cluster had 66 percent of the cases does not diminish the significance of these findings; the simple reality is that many felony cases involve first offenders or people convicted of routine crimes who receive minimal punishment. What is not apparent from this table—but may be seen in the detailed findings reported in the Appendix IV—is that proportionately fewer cases are located in clusters as the charges mount in seriousness and sentencing latitude becomes greater. The correlation between offense seriousness and being in a cluster is −.29, indicating that sentence disparities are concentrated in more serious cases.

One other point concerning these findings should be noted. Available evidence suggests that this estimate of the importance of going rates is not inflated seriously by restricting the analysis to the most frequently handled offenses. An analysis of 947 of the 1,072 excluded cases (the other

125 were in a "miscellaneous" category) revealed that 711, or 75.1 percent of the 947, received either probation or the modal confinement sentence. These were excluded because the number of offenses handled in the county samples were considered too small to yield stable results. We still feel that the numbers underlying the 75.1 percent statistic are too small to yield a highly accurate estimate, but report them simply to demonstrate that our selection procedure did not have a marked impact upon our estimate of sentencing consistency.

Are the sentencing norms represented by these clusters as effective in constraining sentencing after a trial conviction? The short answer is *no*. Although more than 80 percent of the plea cases fell within one cluster or another, only 54.8 percent of the trial cases did, a difference that is statistically significant well beyond the .001 level. As the second column of Table 8.4 indicates, the probation cluster includes proportionately fewer cases and the "off-cluster" categories include more, raising the possibility of a trial penalty that moves defendants who fail to plead guilty "over the hill" (or peak, as it were).

Consistency in the Application of Going Rates

Table 8.4 paints a portrait of sentencing that is dominated by a small handful of going rates for specific offenses, but it cannot reveal whether the pigeonholing process was consistent. The assignment of going rates to defendants could be distorted by bartering. An examination of the criminal records of the defendants in various clusters is a first step toward understanding and assessing the consistency of this assignment procedure. The trichotomized criminal record variable described in chapter 3 was used to do this. This variable was then cross-tabulated with the three cluster categories to produce Table 8.5.

Table 8.5. **Composition of Sentence Categories by Defendant's Prior Record (Guilty Plea Cases Only)**

Sentencing Cluster	No Prior Record	Moderate Criminal Record	Serious Criminal Record
Probation cluster	65.0 (1,431)	25.0 (550)	10.0 (220)
Low cluster	31.0 (104)	33.1 (111)	35.8 (120)
High cluster	11.0 (8)	35.6 (26)	53.4 (39)

In general, the matches were consonant with what might be expected, as there was a moderately high association between criminal record and cluster placement. This is scarcely surprising. But the important point to be made is that the classification of defendants was not grossly distorted by unreasonable decision rules. For instance, 65 percent of the probation cluster comprised first offenders, whereas only 10 percent of the defendants had serious criminal histories. The low cluster has fairly equal representations of each set of defendants, suggesting that other factors such as aggravating or mitigating circumstances, bargaining positions, or victim-defendant relationship may affect placement in this grouping. Because these defendants had neither the least serious nor the worst criminal records, there may have been more ambiguity concerning the appropriateness of sentences and more room for disagreement. A look at the high cluster shows that there is no uncertainty about this group because it is almost a mirror image of the probation cluster. This third cluster is dominated by more serious offenders: 53.4 percent of the defendants had extensive criminal histories. Only 11 percent of the defendants in the high cluster were first offenders.

The close correspondence between criminal record and cluster placement provides an opportunity to assess the impact upon sentence of the consistency indicators used to assess the allocation of charge reductions. The data in Table 8.5 suggest that the defendant's criminal record raises certain expectations concerning sentencing. More specifically, most first offenders who plead guilty expect some form of probation. Those who have a prior record can expect some incarceration depending upon the offense, the severity of situational factors surrounding it, the length of the defendant's record, and other factors as well. Those getting below the low cluster in a county can be considered to have received a good deal, those above it, a bad one.

To simplify the analysis of the consistency indicators, we eliminated the 104 cases that were placed in the high cluster, leaving us with two sets of expectations. The most basic is, Did a first offender get a detention sentence (No = 0; Yes = 1)? It is captured by a *FRSTJAIL* variable. The second expectation is, Did a defendant with a record receive a sentence below the low cluster (-1), within the low cluster (0), or above the low cluster ($+1$)? This is measured by a variable labeled *SENTNORM*. A related question is, How far above or below the cluster were the off-cluster sentences? To quantify this variable (labeled *NORMDEV*), we simply subtracted the actual sentence a defendant received from the cluster parameters. An example will illustrate. If the low cluster for burglary in a county is four to six months, a defendant who received a sentence of two months will receive a score on this measure of -2 ($2 - 4 = -2$).

Table 8.6. **Consistency Indicators and Sentences in Guilty Plea Cases**

Consistency Indicator	Hypothesized Effect	FRSTJAIL	SENTNORM	NORMDEV
PRIVDC	−	** (.04)	—	—
CONFINED	+	*** (.32)	*** (.48)	*** (10.0)
DRACE	+	—	—	—
DSEX	+	—	—	—
CONFESS	+	—	—	—
PHYSEVID	+	—	—	—
TWOEYES	+	—	—	—
POSID	+	—	—	—
DEADBANG	+	—	—	—
MOTIONS	+	—	—	—
DELAY	+	—	—	—

* Indicates a significance level at or beyond .05.
** Indicates a significance level at or beyond .01.
*** Indicates a significance level at or beyond .001.
− Indicates no statistically significant impact.

A defendant who received a sentence of eight months would receive a +2 (8 − 6 = +2). For point clusters, the floor and ceiling are the same.

To analyze the impact of the consistency indicators upon these sentencing variables, we used the same technique (analysis of covariance using multiple regression) and reporting procedures (only significant differences in the hypothesized direction) that were used in the charge concession analysis. Offense seriousness and the severity of the defendant's criminal record were used as control variables. The results are reported in Table 8.6. Only four of 33 hypothesized influences were uncovered, and only the pretrial detention variable had a strong and consistent impact upon the sentencing measures. The first-offender clients of private attorneys were more apt to get probation but the difference in probabilities was only 4 points.

The effects of the pretrial confinement variable are, by far, the most significant and troublesome in this analysis. First timers who are confined before trial are less apt to get straight probation; confined prior offenders are less apt to get a good deal than released prior offenders. Obviously, some of the effects of the pretrial detention variables are because of contextual factors that obscure their meaning. Some defendants who are detained before their disposition will receive a sentence equivalent to their pretrial incarceration and will be released on probation at the time of their plea. However, even if this accounts for some of the difference in probation rates, it would not account for the tendency of repeat offenders to receive worse deals. Because offense and criminal record are controlled, one could make a strong argument that the impact of pretrial detention reflects the effects of socioeconomic bias in the system, as reflected in the defendant's weakened bargaining position and the participants' biased perceptions of the threat posed by lower-class defendants. However, it is difficult to counter the argument that detained defendants are being detained primarily because our control variables do not capture the participants' views of certain aspects of the case or the defendant. Quite possibly it could be that these attributes would have led to a longer sentence regardless of pretrial detention. The truth of the matter undoubtedly lies somewhere between the two views. Detention status probably reflects both types of effect.

The cumulative impact of the consistency indicators upon the explained variance in the three sentencing variables was significantly greater than in the case of the charge reduction variables, wholly because of the strong impact of the confinement variable. It alone added 6.5 percent, 8 percent, and 2.3 percent, respectively to the R^2's. The strong role of this variable and the impact of the defense-attorney-type variable raise some serious questions about the consistency of the pigeonholing process. It thus becomes important to ask whether these biases are unique to the guilty process or also characterize sentencing decisions in trial cases.

We use the same interaction analysis employed in the charge reduction analyses to see if the four effects reported in Table 8.6 also exist in trial cases. Only one interaction was uncovered: a positive interaction between the confined variable and the dummy trial variable with respect to the NORMDEV measure. This indicates, of course, that the bias against confined defendants is *stronger* in trial cases than in plea cases and that the earlier findings cannot be attributable to inequities in the plea process.

THE IMPACT OF CHARGE CONCESSIONS UPON SENTENCES AND THE EXISTENCE OF A TRIAL PENALTY

The sentencing expectations used in the consistency analysis can be used to address two remaining issues that are crucial to our assessment of the guilty plea process. The first deals with whether the various forms of charge reductions translate into real sentencing breaks; the second concerns the existence of a trial penalty. The cluster analysis provides us with a direct means of assessing the first. The various clusters were constructed on the basis of arrest charges, without reference to the final charge. Thus, the question is whether those defendants who received a

Table 8.7. **The Impact of Charge Reductions upon Sentencing Expectations**

Type of Reduction	FRSTJAIL	SENTNORM	NORMDEV
CHRGRED	—	—	—
CTRED	—	—	—
PRIMRED	—	*** (−.22)	*** (−8.0)

*** Indicates a significance level at or beyond .001.

reduced charge were more apt to get probation or, for repeat offenders, more apt to get a below-cluster sentence.

We use the same approach employed in the analysis of the consistency indicators to examine these two sets of questions. In this case, however, we control for offense seriousness, criminal record, and detention status, the latter because of the strong impact revealed in Table 8.6. The results are reported in Table 8.7; it reveals that only the measure of primary charge reductions (PRIMRED) had a significant impact and then only with respect to repeat offenders. Repeat offenders who receive a reduction in the primary charge are more apt to get a below-cluster sentence; the average benefit is about seven months. This is, however, somewhat misleading because not every defendant who received a primary charge reduction received a sentence below the low cluster. About a quarter of those receiving such a reduction received a sentence within or above the low cluster. For those receiving a below-cluster sentence, the average break was closer to a year.

One last point should be made about the data in Table 8.7. While the impact of the charge reduction upon the sentence of first offenders failed to survive the controls, all three findings indicated that defendants who received some form of charge reduction were *less* apt to get probation. This suggests that charge reductions may, in some situations, be used as a palliative for somewhat stiffer sentences.

The final question to be addressed here concerns the existence of a trial tariff, or penalty. Are first offenders convicted after a trial less likely to receive probation than those who plead guilty? Are repeat offenders less likely to get a good deal? Data on these questions are presented in Table 8.8. They show a qualified "yes" to the questions. Defendants who are convicted after a jury trial do significantly worse than others, even after controlling for offense seriousness, criminal record, and detention status. The B-coefficient indicates that the probability of a first offender receiving some detention time is seventeen points higher after a jury trial. Repeat offenders are significantly more likely to get a sentence above the

Table 8.8. **The Impact of Mode of Conviction upon Sentencing Expectations**

	FRSTJAIL	SENTNORM	NORMDEV
Was the defendant convicted after a bench trial or on a plea? (plea = 0; bench trial = 1)	—	—	—
Was the defendant convicted after a jury trial or on a plea? (plea = 0; jury trial = 1)	** (.17)	*** (.26)	*** (15.9)

** Indicates a significance level at or beyond .01.
*** Indicates a significance level at or beyond .001.
— Indicates a no statistically significant impact.

low cluster if convicted after a jury trial; sentences for these offenders are, on average, almost sixteen months greater than those who pleaded guilty (after controlling for offense, record, and detention status). Those who are convicted after a bench trial do not do significantly worse than those who plead guilty.

OBSERVATIONS ON THE "BIG PICTURE"

If we look at the results that emerge from the analysis of the pooled data set, it appears that the role of shared perceptions and accepted norms is far greater than the visible results of bargaining and that the plea process is not overly dependent upon explicit, concrete exchanges or manipulations. Consistency prevails to a surprising extent, and not merely because we may have expected a high level of inconsistency. Primary charge reductions in guilty plea cases are the exception rather than the norm, and the overall level of charge reduction is not much different than in trial cases. Those that are given in plea cases do not appear to be allocated in a capricious manner. County-specific going rates are a major force in sentencing and appear to be a highly effective restraint in limiting disparities. While the pigeonholing process seemed to be fairly rational in placing defendants within various sentence clusters, the analysis of the consistency indicators (primarily the detention status variable) revealed more undesirable effects than in the charge reduction analysis. However, the impact of these factors in plea sentences did not differ from their impact in trial sentences. Thus it is difficult to attribute their role in sentencing to any particular facet of the plea process.

Perhaps the most disturbing findings—from the defendant's per-spective—concerns the impact of the charge reduction variables upon sentencing and the existence of a trial penalty for jury cases. Only primary charge reductions—the most infrequent type—had a significant impact upon a defendant's sentence. This, of course, suggests that most charge reductions are merely symbolic manipulations of the process. Their actual effect—either coercive or inducive—upon a defendant's decision to plead guilty, however, is difficult to establish. Most pleaded guilty without any type of charge concessions, and the dropping of a count or two may have little actual impact on a defendant's calculus. The jury trial penalty suggests that defendants, or at least some, do pay a price for the full exercise of their rights. Even though a penalty-free bench trial may be available, the perceptions of a trial penalty may be a more potent incentive for a defendant to plead guilty than the illusory benefits of a charge reduction.

The role of the trial penalty in the defendant's decision to plead guilty should not, however, be overplayed. In most situations the possibility of a trial is remote, not only because of its possible costs, but also because of the lack of benefits. A trial entails uncertainty, work, money, and time, but—from most defendants' perspective—little prospect of gain. The high levels of consistency in the plea process as revealed by our data probably indicate, as much as anything, how little there is to quibble about, factually or legally, in most cases. This is certainly not news to criminal court observers. However, our data show that an important consequence of this is that the process of deciding what to do with the culpable is so routinized that manipulation plays only a minor part in the process. Just as pleas are not largely the result of concessions, the vast majority are probably not the result of a perceived trial penalty. Although all of these factors play a part, most pleas probably result from the fact that, given the circumstances surrounding most cases, they appear to be the best way to proceed, simply because there was so little to contest.

These observations are the result of looking at the big picture. But to what extent does this picture obscure what is happening in the individual counties? We selected these counties because of some very fundamental differences among them, and Section II develops these differences at some length. To what extent are these differences reflected in their plea process? What insights into the nature of the plea process can these differences yield? It is to these questions that we now turn.

COUNTIES, CONCESSIONS, AND CONSISTENCY

Table 8.9 reports by county on the incidence of charge reductions in guilty plea cases. It is evident that a large measure of variance exists

Table 8.9. **Percent of Guilty Plea Cases Involving Some Type of Charge Concession by County**

	DuPage	Peoria	St. Clair	Oakland	Kalamazoo	Saginaw	Mont-gomery	Dauphin	Erie
Percent any type of charge reduction	52.8 (542)	43.1 (622)	39.9 (699)	36.5 (712)	15.8 (549)	69.0 (465)	41.7 (592)	10.4 (836)	59.1 (445)
Percent reduction of the primary charge	12.2 (559)	21.4 (677)	21.1 (740)	17.6 (712)	12.8 (547)	43.2 (470)	10.9 (597)	4.9 (872)	8.6 (463)
Percent cases involving count drops	46.2 (528)	37.6 (548)	22.0 (654)	28.5 (708)	12.2 (542)	38.3 (459)	42.0 (591)	8.9 (832)	59.0 (440)·
Ratio of primary reductions to total reductions (row 2:row 1)	1:4.3	1:2	1:1.9	1:2.1	1:2.3	1:1.6	1:3.8	1:2.1	1:6.9

across counties, regardless of which measure is examined. The most general measure (column 1) shows that reductions vary from about 10 percent in Dauphin County to nearly 70 percent in Saginaw; four hover between 35 and 45 percent. If we look at primary charge reductions (row 2)—the only type of charge reduction with significant sentencing implications— a much narrower range of variation exists. Excluding Saginaw, which is clearly a deviant case (43.2 percent had primary charge reductions), the level of primary charge reductions ranges from about 5 percent in Dauphin to 21 percent in Peoria and St. Clair; four counties hover around 10 percent. Thus, even leaving out the deviant case (Saginaw), a good deal of variation in primary charge reductions exists. A quick comparison between the two measures of charge reductions reveals very little systematic correspondence; being high on one does not mean being high on the second, and vice versa. This is captured in the ratio of primary charge reduction to any type of charge reduction (row 4). While the norm seems to be about one primary charge reduction to every two charge reductions, DuPage, Montgomery, and Erie have considerably higher ratios. Saginaw is somewhat lower (1:1.6) because it reduces so many primary charges.

These disparities lead us to focus on differences in the incidence of count drops, which account for the drop off between the overall level of charge reductions and primary charge reductions. While, as demonstrated earlier, these reductions may have no more than symbolic importance, they can underscore important differences in the nature of plea systems and should be considered. Significant differences emerge in count-drop patterns in our nine counties (row 3). Dauphin and Kalamazoo, consistent with earlier patterns, seldom drop counts. However, Erie, Montgomery, and DuPage, which seldom reduce primary charges, have the highest incidence of count drops. Saginaw, which has the highest total as well as primary charge reductions, has a relatively moderate level of count drops. Peoria, St. Clair, and Oakland have relatively moderate levels of count drops; the same is true for their overall measure of charge reductions.

Charge Bargaining Modes

While the data discussed thus far are far more complicated than the simple picture presented earlier, a hard look at Table 8.9 reveals four basic patterns. They are shown in Table 8.10. While other factors are important in analyzing plea systems, these patterns form a good basis for beginning the construction of a more comprehensive typology. The first might be termed a *minimalist system*; it includes Kalamazoo and Dauphin. Both counties have identical rankings in each of the four categories listed in Table 8.10, rankings that suggest that charge reductions play a minimal role in the guilty plea process. These two counties have the lowest incidence of

Table 8.10. **Summary of Charge Reduction Patterns**

	DuPage	Peoria	St. Clair	Oakland	Kalamazoo	Saginaw	Mont-gomery	Dauphin	Erie
Incidence of any type of charge reduction	H	M	M	M	L	H	M	L	H
Incidence of a primary charge reduction	L	M	M	M	L	H	L	L	L
Ratio of primary charge reduction to incidence of any type of charge reduction	H	M	M	M	M	L	H	M	H
Incidence of a count drop	H	M	M	M	L	M	H	L	H

H = High
M = Medium
L = Low

overall charge reductions and two of the lowest rates of primary charge reductions. Because they have such a low level of overall reductions, they rank medium in terms of the ratio of primary charge reductions to total reductions. They also have the lowest incidence of count drops.

DuPage, Montgomery, and Erie can be included in what might be termed a *symbolic system*. With one exception (Montgomery is ranked only "medium" on the overall level of charge reduction dimension, as well as the count-drop dimension, while the others are ranked "high"), these counties have identical rankings on the four criteria included in Table 8.10. While these counties have high rates of overall charge reduction, most of the reductions are largely symbolic. This is reflected in the uniformly low rate of primary charge reductions and the correspondingly high ratio of primary charge reductions to overall charge reductions. These counties rely heavily on count drops, which accounts for the high rate of overall reductions; they ranked highest on the incidence of count drops. The high degree of frivolous reductions suggests that these counties have more in common with the minimalist counties than with those that rely more extensively on charge reductions.

The third discernible pattern reflects what might be called a *middling system*; it includes Peoria, St. Clair, and Oakland. They rank "medium" on every dimension and have a healthy mix of count drops (22–38 percent) and primary charge reductions (18–21 percent), which add up to a moderate overall rate of reductions (36–43 percent). This moderate nature of the charge reductions can best be seen when contrasted with Saginaw, which illustrates a concessions-oriented (*maximalist*) mode. Saginaw has an extremely high rate of reductions (69 percent), with more than 43 percent of the guilty pleas made to a reduced primary charge—about eight times Dauphin's rate. Because of the readiness of Saginaw prosecutors to reduce the primary charge, the ratio of primary reduction to overall reduction was low; not much emphasis is placed on count drops.

The data summarized in Table 8.10 suggest the existence of several very different types of guilty plea processes, which means that charge reductions take on different forms and operate at different levels in different counties. Do these differences have broader implications for the tenor of justice in these counties? Does the laxity evidenced by relatively high levels of meaningful charge reductions encourage, or at least tolerate, unacceptable biases in how those reductions are allocated? Does the concession-oriented mentality evidenced in the charging practices of those counties extend to sentencing, or does it alleviate the pressure to grant sentencing concessions? Phrased on a more concrete level, does Saginaw represent the wide-open, freewheeling type of plea bargaining uncovered by the crime survey researchers during the 1920s and decried by legal reformers since then? Or does the high level of charge reductions represent merely rain

dancing? Are Kalamazoo and Dauphin reflective of a new breed of jurisdiction that take a no-nonsense approach to screening, charging, and
disposing of cases? Where do the symbolic counties fall? Do they operate
like the minimalist counties, using count drops in a preconceived but
meaningless manner to placate defendants and fend off demands for sentence concessions? Where do the middling counties fall? Finally, what led
to such different patterns of charge reductions?

The above are only a few of the questions raised by the findings
summarized in Table 8.9, and they fall into two categories: What implications do the different charge reduction modes have for other aspects of
a county's plea process? What accounts for the observed differences? We
address the first set of questions here and deal with the second set in
chapter 9. The answers to these questions will raise yet others, some of
which deal with the role of criminal court actors in the plea process and
will be addressed in Section IV.

We are concerned here with the impact of the different patterns of
charge reductions on other aspects of the guilty plea process. First, we
want to know their impact on the going rates in a system; that is, Is the
structure of sentencing patterns affected by the charge reduction mode?
Next, we will examine the impact of charge reduction modes upon the
allocation of concessions. Here we will want to know whether biases are
more apt to affect charge or sentence allocation within one type of system
or another. Third, we will scrutinize the impact of charge reductions upon
sentencing across the different modes. Does their impact upon sentence
fade or increase with levels of use? Finally, we will examine the role of
the trial penalty in these different settings. If some systems rely more on
the role of consensus than on concessions in the procurement of pleas,
then the role of the trial penalty should be reduced correspondingly.

Before we begin to address these various aspects of the guilty plea
process, we should ask a more fundamental question. Do policies and
practices concerning charge reduction affect the role of the guilty plea in
the dispositional process? If so, in what way? Table 8.11 reports data on
the level of guilty pleas as a percent of all trial court dispositions, and

Table 8.11. **Guilty Pleas, and Patterns of Charge Reductions**

	Minimalist Counties (Kalamazoo, Dauphin)	Symbolic Counties (DuPage, Montgomery, Erie)	Middling Counties (Peoria, St. Clair, Oakland)	Maximalist Counties (Saginaw)
Guilty plea rate	83 (1,979)	86 (1,910)	77 (2,826)	74 (650)

contains several surprises. The level of guilty pleas is related inversely to the role of charge reductions. The highest rates of guilty pleas (83 percent, 86 percent) were found in the counties with the lowest rates of primary charge reductions; the county with the highest incidence of primary charge reduction (Saginaw) had the lowest rate of guilty pleas (74 percent).

With these data in mind, we can begin to address the questions just outlined.

Charge Reductions and Going Rates

One could fashion several different arguments concerning the role of charge reductions and the strength of sentencing norms. On the one hand, it could be argued that if consensus in fact is the grease that allows the wheels of justice to turn smoothly (in at least some jurisdictions), then a high level of sentencing consistency should characterize jurisdictions that engage in only minimal charge reductions. This logic could be extended a step further: If the consensus perspective is correct, then a high level of sentencing consistency should exist even in the face of high levels of charge reductions. These reductions could be dismissed as mere palliatives given to defendants as inducements to plead; consensus would still govern the all-important sentencing decision. On the other hand, a concessions orientation would suggest low levels of sentencing consistency, and perhaps, an inverse relationship—or no relationship—between charge reductions and sentencing consistency. An inverse relationship would be expected because pressures on sentencing concessions would be expected to mount in the face of charge rigidity. No relationship would be expected if charge reductions were also accompanied by marked and uneven sentencing concessions.

We use as our measure of the level of sentencing consistency in a county the proportion of guilty plea cases that fell within one of our three types of sentence clusters. The data on these measures are represented by county type in Table 8.12. While a higher level of consistency seems to exist in the minimalist and symbolic counties (in a pattern similar to that in Table 8.11), no strong or consistent pattern exists in the data. An examination of the data by county reveals that the proportion of cases falling within a cluster has more to do with the state where the county is located than in its mode of charge reduction. In every county outside of Michigan, the percent of cases falling within a cluster was between 79 and 90 percent. Largely because the Michigan counties treat first offenders more harshly, their figures ranged from 61 percent in Kalamazoo to 63 percent in Saginaw and 68 percent in Oakland. Thus, there seems to be no direct, straightforward relationship between charge reduction made and the impact of going rates.

Table 8.12. **Sentencing Consistency and Mode of Charge Reduction**

	Minimalist Counties (Kalamazoo, Dauphin)	Symbolic Counties (DuPage, Montgomery, Erie)	Middling Counties (Peoria, St. Clair, Oakland)	Maximalist Counties (Saginaw)
Percent of defendants pleading guilty that fell within a sentencing cluster	81.5 (1,080)	86.4 (1,162)	76.9 (1,633)	75.2 (295)

The Allocation of Concessions

Our primary concern here is with the existence of undesirable influences upon the allocation of concessions within the different county types. We again use the three sets of consistency indicators to detect the impact of these influences. As was the case in the analysis of the role of going rates, several conflicting views seem to pertain. According to one view, it could be argued that counties that make wide use of charge concessions, especially symbolic ones, make them available to all on an equitable basis because the concessions are not viewed as scarce commodities. The more stringent counties may use them only for specific purposes, not all of which are desirable. For example, they may be granted only in cases involving evidentiary problems or only in selected situations where the defense has been cooperative. The alternative view, of course, is that high levels of charge concessions are reflective of a wide-open, unregulated process into which biases can creep. In low-use counties, concessions may be granted only in response to the equities of the case, permitting little if any bias.

To examine these various possibilities with respect to charge concessions, the eleven consistency indicators introduced in chapter 7 were used in a series of regression analyses with the three charge reduction dummy variables (*CHRGRED, CTRED, PRIMRED*) as dependent variables. Discrete versions of offense seriousness, criminal record, and the existence of a multicount indictment were used as control variables.[2]

The results of the consistency indicators regression analyses are reported in Table 8.13. Once again reality is more complex than anticipated, and neither of the simple expectations just discussed is supported totally. At the same time, a comparison with the data in Table 8.13 reveals some interesting insights. If we examine the two minimalist counties, we find only one significant difference in the hypothesized directions, and it involved the *CONFESS* variable. Its impact suggests that those who have

Table 8.13. Consistency Indicators and Charge Concessions, by Mode of Charge Reduction

Consistency Indicator	Hypothesized Effect	Minimalist Counties			Symbolic Counties			Middling Counties			Maximalist Counties		
		CHRGRED	CTRED	PRIMRED	CHRGRED	CTRED	PRIMRED	CHRGRED	CTRED	PRIMRED	CHRGRED	CTRED	PRIMRED
PRIVDC	+	—	—	—	—	—	—	—	*	—	—	—	—
CONFINED	—	—	—	—	—	—	—	—	—	—	—	—	—
DRACE	—	—	—	—	—	—	—	—	—	—	—	—	—
DSEX	—	—	—	—	—	—	*	*	—	—	—	—	—
CONFESS	—	—	—	***	***	***	—	—	—	—	—	**	—
PHYSEVID	—	—	—	—	***	**	**	—	—	***	—	—	—
TWOEYES	—	—	—	—	—	—	—	—	—	—	—	—	—
POSID	—	—	—	—	—	—	—	—	—	—	—	—	—
DEADBANG	—	—	—	—	—	—	—	*	***	—	—	—	—
MOTIONS	—	—	—	—	—	—	—	—	—	—	—	—	—
DELAY	—	—	—	—	—	—	—	—	—	—	—	—	—
		(n=1,166)	(n=1,172)	(n=1,172)	(n=1,045)	(n=1,049)	(n=1,040)	(n=1,390)	(n=1,330)	(n=1,434)	(n=300)	(n=299)	(n=289)

*, **, *** Indicate a significant impact in a positive direction at .05, .01, .001 level.

— Indicates no significant impact in the expected direction.

not confessed are more apt to receive a rare primary charge reduction, perhaps as an inducement to plead guilty. None of the other evidence variables, however, suggest such a result. An examination of the symbolic counties reveals three significant findings in the expected direction. Two involved the "hard" evidence variables (*CONFESS, PHYSEVID*) and showed a greater willingness to give reductions in evidentially weaker cases. Only the effects of the physical evidence variable extended into primary charge reductions. The confession variable affected only symbolic reductions.

The middling counties evidence a rather weak, sparse, and loosely knit set of findings, at least with respect to primary charge reductions. The only strong, expected finding that affects nonsymbolic reductions is the impact of the physical evidence variable upon the reduction of primary charges. However, males were marginally more likely than females to receive a primary charge reduction. The confession and physical evidence variables show a tendency for evidentiary deficiencies to lead to symbolic reductions in the middling counties. Saginaw, the single maximalist county, had the weakest pattern of significant results. Only one moderately strong, expected finding was uncovered, and it affected only symbolic reductions (the *CONFESS* variable on the *CTRED* variable). These findings would suggest that in counties that make wide use of charge reductions, their allocation is generally not based upon undesirable criteria.

Table 8.14 summarizes the impact of the consistency indicators upon the three measures of sentencing expectations used earlier (*FRSTJAIL, SENTNORM, NORMDEV*). Although significant findings in the expected direction are sparse, a few general patterns emerge that are worth noting. First, although the *CONFINED* variable has the strongest and most consistent impact throughout the counties, its troublesome interpretation makes it difficult to say much about its substantive implications. A second less evident pattern concerns the distribution of statistically significant effects across county types. They are less frequent in counties that reduce charges most frequently. If we eliminate the pretrial detention status variable, we find only three weak statistically significant effects (at .05 level) in the four counties that rely most heavily on reduction (Peoria, St. Clair, Oakland, Saginaw). All three are in Saginaw and all affect repeat offenders only; two involved the eyewitness variable, the other the race variable.

The existence of statistically significant effects is considerably more widespread in the minimalist and symbolic counties. As the table shows, private defense attorneys are more likely to get probation for their first-offender clients in these counties. There is a slight tendency for repeat offender blacks to get longer sentences in the minimalist counties, while first-offender blacks in the symbolic counties were less likely to get probation. Also, although the effect is by no means universal, the impact of several of the evidentiary variables suggests that where the evidence

Table 8.14. Consistency Indicators and Sentencing Expectations, by Mode of Charge Reduction

Consistency Indicator	Hypothesized Effect	Minimalist Counties			Symbolic Counties			Middling Counties			Maximalist Counties		
		ABV/PROB	PRIORLOW	CLUDEV	ABV/PROB	PRIORLOW	CLUDEV	ABV/PROB	PRIORLOW	CLUDEV	ABV/PROB	PRIORLOW	CLUDEV
PRIVDC	−	**	—	—	***	—	—	—	—	—	—	—	—
CONFINED	+	***	***	***	***	***	***	***	***	***	—	***	***
DRACE	+	—	—	*	**	—	—	—	—	—	—	—	*
DSEX	+	—	—	—	—	—	—	—	—	—	—	—	—
CONFESS	+	*	—	—	—	—	—	—	—	—	—	—	—
PHYSEVID	+	**	—	—	—	—	—	—	—	—	—	—	—
TWOEYES	+	—	—	—	*	***	***	—	—	—	—	*	*
POSID	+	—	—	—	*	—	*	—	—	—	—	—	—
DEADBANG	+	—	**	—	—	—	—	—	—	—	—	—	—
MOTIONS	+	—	**	—	**	—	—	—	—	—	—	—	—
DELAY	+	—	—	—	—	—	—	—	—	—	—	—	—
		(n=474)	(n=470)	(n=467)	(n=436)	(n=515)	(n=512)	(n=565)	(n=888)	(n=856)	(n=74)	(n=193)	(n=193)

*, **, *** Indicate a significant impact in a positive direction at .05, .01, .001 level.
— Indicates a significant impact in the expected direction.

is weaker, the sentence is generally shorter. This can be seen in some of the effects of the confession, eyewitness, positive identification, and dead-bang variables. Although the results are far from conclusive, the data suggest that certain pressures imposed by rigid policies on primary charge reduction may manifest themselves in sentencing concessions. However, even if this is the case, the pressures are weak and sporadic; no large, systematic pattern of findings peculiar to these counties is discernible.

Sentencing Expectations

Table 8.7 reveals that the only type of charge reduction to have a general and significant effect upon sentencing expectations was a primary charge reduction. Such a reduction was associated with more lenient sentences, as defendants would expect. This relationship, and those involving the other charge reduction variables, were examined by county type to see if modal patterns of charge reductions had any impact upon the sentencing implication of the reductions. The short answer is no, with one proviso. A primary charge reduction had a negative impact upon the *NORMDEV* variable across all county types; it had no impact upon *FRSTJAIL* in any of them. The only significant difference appears with respect to the trichotomous *SENTNORM* variable. Primary charge reductions (*PRIMRED*) had a negative impact upon it only in the middling counties. Also, count drops were accompanied by marginally *longer* sentences for repeat offenders in the minimalist counties; in Saginaw, first offenders who received count drops were less likely to receive probation. Thus, in some instances it appears that count drops are used as a palliative to help defendants swallow longer sentences.

Our final point of comparison concerns the role of the trial penalty in the different types of counties. It is expected to play less of a role in the counties that evidence low use of charge reductions, if this marginal reliance is indicative of the central role of consensus in the guilty plea process. Where consensus plays a central role, a lower incidence of "unnecessary" trials is likely to occur, and fewer sanctions will have to be levied. This notion is supported to some extent by the data presented in Table 8.15, which shows the results of the jury trial variable upon sentencing expectations (the bench trial variable had no significant impact). The jury trial variable has only one weak impact upon the sentencing expectations in the minimalist and symbolic counties. Indeed, this effect is wholly due to Dauphin; no other low-use county evidences any jury trial effect. In contrast, the jury trial was associated with longer sentences in all three sentencing measures in Saginaw, and with longer sentences for repeat offenders in the middling counties.

These analyses of the impact that the charge reduction mode has

Table 8.15. Summary of the Impact of the Trial Variables (Bench, Jury) upon Sentence Expectations, by Mode of Charge Reductions

	Minimalist Direction and Level of Significance	Symbolic Direction and Level of Significance	Middling Direction and Level of Significance	Maximalist Direction and Level of Significance
FRSTJAIL				
Bench trial	—	—	—	—
Jury trial	—	—	—	—**
SENTNORM				
Bench trial	—*	—	—	—
Jury trial		—	—	—**
NORMDEV				
Bench trial	—	—	—***	—
Jury trial	—	—	***	—***

*, **, *** Indicate a significant impact in a positive direction at .05, .01, .001 level.
— Indicates no significant impact in the expected direction.

upon various aspects of the plea process reveal a few interesting and some surprising insights. They do not, however, show any clear patterns that would clarify the answers to the questions raised earlier. One of the most surprising findings was the inverse relationship between the prevalence of charge reductions and the rate of guilty pleas. Even though the differences were not great, the counties in which significant charge reductions were most rare had the highest incidence of guilty pleas. This, of course, suggests that consensual processes may in fact be more prevalent in these counties. At the same time, however, a close inspection of the data on sentence clusters reveals no marked difference across county type in the role of going rates. Moreover, the results of the consistency analyses suggest that undesirable influences upon the allocation of concessions were, if anything, slightly more prevalent in the minimalist and symbolic counties, especially with respect to sentencing. But, again, the patterns were not strong. The examination·of the impact of charge reductions upon sentence showed no distinct patterns across county type, but the role of the jury trial penalty seemed to be less significant in the minimalist and symbolic counties. This again is a sign of stronger consensual influences in these counties.

Our county-specific examination of the charge reduction and sentencing patterns stands in stark contrast to the clean and simple big picture that emerged from the pooled analysis. But that reality is so complex should come as no surprise. Moreover, it can be used to our advantage if an examination of these various patterns yields some insights into the determinants of charge reduction and sentencing practices. The data presented in Section II will prove useful for this examination; we begin with an analysis of charge reduction patterns.

NOTES

1. Because there were so few trial cases involving reduced charges that went to trial, we did not conduct the interaction analysis for the magnitude of the charges variable.

2. Because of the high intercorrelation between the *DEADBANG* variable and the other evidence variables, their impact was examined separately.

9

COURT COMMUNITIES, CHARGE REDUCTIONS, AND THE GUILTY PLEA PROCESS

Viewed broadly, the findings presented in chapter 8 suggest strongly that, although a plea-oriented dispositional process is not dependent upon a high level of charge reductions, they do characterize some systems in varying degrees and in different ways. The different patterns of charge reductions observed, in particular, suggest that they are not inevitable consequences of nontrial dispositions, but, rather, may be the result of conscious policies, practices, structures, or other such influences. We can obtain a better sense of this by examining the patterns described in chapter 8 in light of the environmental and contextual characteristics described in Section II. This is an important task even if most manipulations are symbolic and disparities are less manifest than thought previously—as the previous analyses suggest—because of the symbolic implications of the reductions that do exist. This analysis can also provide us with a more in-depth picture of other aspects of the guilty plea process that operate within these counties. This, in itself, will enhance our understanding of how the guilty plea process works.

If we reflect upon the observations garnered from our fieldwork, we can point to myriad factors that arguably have some effect upon the role of charge concessions in a county's guilty plea process. But the large number of potential influences and the small number of counties make a rigorous specification of the causative agents impossible. Our observations also make it clear that there are many paths to the same destination. Nonetheless, an empirically based, but intuitive, analysis makes it quite clear that several sets of factors are very influential and limit the potential routes to a few well-travelled paths. First, the organization of the court's infrastructure, or at least key facets of it, has direct implications for the prominence of charge reductions in a county. Also important are some prosecutorial policies and practices that are unrelated to work orientations. The most notable of these are charging practices. In some counties, the structure and orientation of the defense bar, especially the indigent defense system, appears to have an impact upon the overall level of charge reduction. The defense bar's role, however, is often clouded by the overriding significance of more immediate factors. Much the same can be said about ecological influences. Their impact, although important to note, is uncertain at best and normally is channeled through prosecutorial practices and policies. Thus we can not say much about the role of environmental influences.

Because of the difficulties we encountered earlier (chapter 6) in neatly categorizing some county subcomponents in terms of overall work orientations—as well as the need for greater specificity—we disaggregate the notion of work orientation in this analysis. That is, we deal here primarily with the organization and implications of specific functions (such as docketing, screening, and organization of plea offers) rather than with the overall work orientation of the court community, or even the bench or prosecutor's office. Despite this, we must not lose sight of the fact that the organization of these specific functions has meaning at a more abstract level. This will facilitate our understanding of the more general influences that pervade criminal courts, as well as their possible impact upon the guilty plea process.

Before delving into a discussion of the various county types, it will be useful to introduce a concept that captures some important differences in plea systems, differences that have been implicit in our discussion of the infrastructure in different counties. It is the notion of *plea agenda*. By plea agenda, we mean the items "on the table" (charge, sentence, judge) when the parties sit down to discuss the settlement of a case. If we think about the calendaring systems adopted by the judges in the different counties and how they mesh with other judicial and prosecutorial norms and policies, we can see that the plea agenda varies quite a bit across counties. Charges are theoretically always subject to discussion because prosecutors can always file new ones. But, as we demonstrated in chapter 6, strong policies existed against meaningful charge reductions in some counties (Oakland, Kalamazoo), whereas judges and prosecutors in other counties (Dauphin, Erie) had strong aversions to such reductions. In still other counties, formal mechanisms made reductions difficult to secure (DuPage).

Sentencing practices also varied from county to county. In some, sentence agreements were the norm (DuPage, Peoria, Kalamazoo, Montgomery). The judges in these counties essentially ceded their power to set sentences in plea cases. One important distinction should be made among these four counties: In DuPage, Peoria, and Montgomery, the prosecutors were anxious to set sentence; in Kalamazoo, they were indifferent. Kalamazoo prosecutors would prefer to submit a blind plea, but would make explicit agreements on the defense's initiative. In one county (Oakland), sentencing agreements of any type were prohibited by the prosecutor's policies; in others (Saginaw, Erie), by the judges' practices. In still other counties (Dauphin, St. Clair), sentence agreements by prosecutors were discouraged but were permitted under certain circumstances. Finally, in counties where some type of master calendar was used (St. Clair, the Pennsylvania counties), the identity of the judge could be part of the plea agreement.

The structure of the plea agenda for different counties is reported in Table 9.1.

The impact that the structure of the plea agenda has upon charge reductions is somewhat complex and contingent upon other aspects of the plea process. All other things being equal, the broader the agenda, the less likely charge reductions are to occur. In most instances, the sentence and the identity of the judge would be viewed as more crucial than the charge, and this would deflect whatever pressures existed for reductions away from the charges. However, where the prosecutor's office gives high priority to attaining sentence agreements, they may be more willing to yield charge reductions. We would not necessarily expect more concessions in counties where the charges were the only item on the plea agenda, especially where the prosecutor screened cases carefully and had a tightly structured plea-offer system.

The difficulties involved in assessing the role of these various factors in the plea process of such a small number of counties make any rigorous quantitative examination impossible. The best we can do is proceed on a county-by-county basis, trying to mold an explanation of the different patterns from the available information. In doing so, it makes sense to begin with the extremes and work inward.

SAGINAW

As was shown in chapter 8, Saginaw had the highest level of meaningful charge reductions and was clearly a deviant case among our counties. It was also one of the most perplexing in trying to apply our notion of work orientations. We saw a puzzling mix of formalist and pragmatic orientations embodied in the various structures used to handle the court's work, a mix that underscored the maze of divergent factors influencing

Table 9.1. Structure of the Plea Agenda, by County

	DuPage (Ring)	Peoria (Autonomous)	St. Clair (Declining)	Oakland (Ring)	Kalamazoo (Autonomous)	Saginaw (Declining)	Montgomery (Ring)	Dauphin (Autonomous)	Erie (Declining)
Prosecutor policies on charge reductions	Determined by indictment committee	Determined on case-by-case basis between assistant and first assistant	None, at discretion of assistant	Strong on-the-nose plea policy	Strong on-the-nose plea policy	None, at discretion of assistant	None, at discretion of assistant	No formal policy, but strong sentiment against	None, at discretion of assistant
Are sentences normally part of plea agreement?	Yes	Yes	Only at defense attorney's insistence; no agreement to probation	No, prosecutor policy	Yes	No	Yes	Variable*	No, judge's policy
Can the identity of the judge be part of the plea agreement?	No	No	Yes, in some cases	No	No	No	Yes	Yes	Yes, in some cases

* The head prosecutor actively discouraged them, and the judges refused to accept specific recommendations for penitentiary times. They would sometimes accept recommendations for county time or probation.

the structure of work in court communities. While the data presented in chapter 8 do not help us understand the unique amalgam of structures in Saginaw, a brief review of some of these structures does help us understand the reasons for the prominent role of charge reductions in Saginaw.

The Saginaw prosecutor's office was the most difficult to make sense of in light of our typology of work orientations. Its screening process was quite formalistic in its structure, but its operation was less so during the time-frame covered by our case sample. It permitted a good deal of prosecutor shopping, of which the police regularly took advantage. This undoubtedly led to the initiation of cases that would have been pruned in other systems. Saginaw's plea offer system was also pragmatic in its orientation; much discretion was vested in individual assistants, who could control charges but not sentences or judges. The inability of the prosecutors to affect sentence (which was set after the plea and pre-sentencing investigation) or judge (who was assigned randomly) undoubtedly increased the pressure to yield charge concessions. Also, the level of the assistant prosecutor's discretion over charges in Saginaw was enhanced by Saginaw's system of vertical prosecution. Assistants who were assigned to conduct a preliminary hearing in a case were assigned the case permanently. Thus, the assistant had a virtual monopoly of information on a case, because no one else in the office ever made an assessment of its merits after the warrant was issued. This made it less likely that an assistant's judgment would be second-guessed, a fact that led to further charge inflation as assistants laid the groundwork for later reductions. More than 46 percent of the cases in Saginaw experienced some type of charge enhancement at the indictment level; the next highest county was DuPage with 17 percent.

One final point about the prosecutor's plea policies in Saginaw deserves note. The head prosecutor felt very strongly that assistants should not engage in suicide missions, that is, try cases they had very little chance of winning. He felt that it was of primary importance to maintain an image of invincibility at trial. This, he thought, would maintain assistants' credibility in plea cases. The irony, of course, is that the policy encouraged assistants to offer charge reductions in cases that were not sure things at trial. There was no independent check on an assistant's assessment of the case's trial prospects. Thus, the policy enhanced the opportunities to grant charge reductions.

One last aspect of Saginaw's infrastructure should be mentioned even though its impact upon charge reduction practice is uncertain: the county's diffuse criminal defense bar and formalistically oriented indigent defense system. The county has no public defender's office and, like Oakland, spread its indigent assignments throughout a large segment of the local bar; more than a hundred attorneys regularly received a small number of assignments. Unlike Oakland, where judges controlled appointments, the assignments were done on a largely random basis. This enhanced the autonomy of the Saginaw defense attorneys and may have led it to be more assertive in demanding charge reductions. Also, the large number of attorneys handling a small number of cases may have impeded the development of a level of consensus required to operate a guilty plea system largely independent of tangible charge concessions. The insecurities involved in handling criminal cases only infrequently may lead defense attorneys to demand something concrete in exchange for a plea, to placate themselves as well as their clients. This need, interacting with the loosely structured charging and plea policies in Saginaw's court community, may well have led to the high level of charge reductions uncovered there. It is unclear, however, whether the diffuse defense bar was a necessary condition for these practices to emerge, or whether the loose prosecutorial organization would have been sufficient.

THE MINIMALIST COUNTIES

If we begin our analysis of the minimalist counties with Kalamazoo, a number of telling differences can be seen from Saginaw, especially with respect to the organization of the prosecutor's office. These differences go a long way in explaining the difference in the role of charge reductions in the two counties. The prosecutor's office in Kalamazoo, it will be recalled, was oriented very formalistically. Most important facets of the process were centralized to some extent, and the discretion of individual assistants was subject to a number of checks. As we saw in chapter 6, assistant prosecutors in Kalamazoo did not have a monopoly of information on cases, in stark contrast to Saginaw. Others set sentencing recommendations and evaluated the case at different points in its life.

These strict plea-offer procedures were coupled with the very stringent screening and charging procedures used in Kalamazoo. Next to St. Clair, Kalamazoo probably pruned more cases than any other county. They used a reasonable likelihood of conviction standard in both the decision to initiate proceedings as well as the charge. Kalamazoo had the lowest incidence of multicount indictments, 16 percent (see Table 6.5). In addition, the head prosecutor instituted a very strong, "on-the-nose" plea policy (i.e., pleas to the initial charge); all primary charge reductions had to be approved by the trial chief, who served as the system's lightning rod. This policy was due to the philosophy and orientation of the Kalamazoo head prosecutor, who differed fundamentally from Saginaw's head prosecutor in a number of regards. Kalamazoo's head was a former deputy sheriff from Wayne County. As a former outsider, he was very concerned with the symbolic aspects of the court's work. Whereas the Saginaw prosecutor felt strongly about suicide missions and their impact upon prosecutorial credibility within the court community, Kalamazoo's prosecutor felt strongly about charge reductions and their impact upon the public's perception of justice. This accounted for his strong policy concerning on-the-nose pleas.

In contrast to their emphasis upon on-the-nose pleas, the Kalamazoo prosecutors did not feel strongly about achieving sentencing goals in plea cases. Although they could not agree to a sentence below the bottom line, they were pleased to agree to a blind plea on the initial charges and let the judge worry about an appropriate sentence. The relative lack of concern over achieving sentencing agreements among Kalamazoo prosecutors made it easier to stick to their position on charge. This position, of course, was strengthened by their stringent screening and charging practices. In truth, there was not much to give in Kalamazoo; getting what there was to give was difficult as well. This is, undoubtedly, the primary explanation for the marginal role of charge reductions in Kalamazoo.

This notwithstanding, we would be remiss if we did not at least mention the structure of the indigent defense system, which represented more than 80 percent of all Kalamazoo defendants (Table 6.7). It was a contract system, and the contract was held by a group of local attorneys, primarily former prosecutors who had close ties to the court community. They had negotiated a quite lucrative contract, with the implicit understanding that they would not engage in overly legalistic, nit-picking tactics. The extent to which this posture carried over into plea discussions is unclear. It is also unclear whether even extremely adversarial tactics could have secured charge reductions from a prosecutor's office structured such as Kalamazoo's was. But the contrast with Saginaw, which had an autonomous indigent defense system and more loosely structured prosecutor's office, is clear.

Drawing parallels between the infrastructures of Dauphin and Kalamazoo does not help us much in understanding the similarities in the minimal role played by charge reductions in their plea processes. This is especially true with respect to prosecutor offices. Whereas Kalamazoo's office clearly had a formal orientation, Dauphin was more difficult to categorize, although it had some pragmatic leanings (Table 6.6). Whereas in Dauphin the police initiated cases and filed charges, Kalamazoo had a very cautious approach to screening and charging. Whereas Kalamazoo had a very centralized plea-offer system, the Dauphin prosecutor pursued a more laissez-faire approach, although it was clearly not as unstructured as in some other counties studied. It was only at the insistence of the judges that the office began to approve in writing the sentence offers of its young assistants.

These differences notwithstanding, there were some similarities between the Dauphin and Kalamazoo prosecutors' offices. Perhaps the most important was the Dauphin head prosecutor's aversion to primary charge reductions and the fact that he actively discouraged sentencing agreements. This latter point was reinforced by informal, but well-known, judicial policies. They generally refused to accept pleas stating a specific term of imprisonment; the most they would sometimes accept would be county time (time served in the county jail)—which could range up to two years—and, sometimes, an unspecified term of probation. There was no elaborate set of internal checks to enforce the Dauphin prosecutor's feelings for on-the-nose pleas, but the arresting officer and the victim, if one existed, had to be notified.

The importance placed upon on-the-nose pleas in Dauphin and the general absence of sentence on the plea agenda undoubtedly helped Dauphin prosecutors resist pressures to grant charge concessions, as it helped Kalamazoo prosecutors. So did the relatively low incidence of multicount indictments filed by the police, 27 percent (Table 6.5). But where Kalamazoo's efforts in this regard were bolstered by a carefully pruned caseload that was lacking in Dauphin, Dauphin prosecutors were aided by their ability to affect case assignments to judges. The master calendar system in Dauphin made it possible to route plea cases to a particular judge, with the assistant prosecutor's consent. This possibility, and its perceived importance, overshadowed and minimized the importance of charge reductions.

As important as the possibility of plea-routing in Dauphin, however, is the fact that the Dauphin head prosecutor could determine, to a large extent, the judge who would hear the trial if plea discussions failed. Plea-routing and the prosecutor's power to affect the trial judge put the Dauphin prosecutors in a profoundly stronger position than those in Kalamazoo. While there was a good deal of homogeneity in the Dauphin bench, there was one judge most defense attorneys desperately tried to avoid; other judges were considered good for certain types of cases (property offenses, driving while under the influence), others less good. Thus the identity of the judge was considered important. Also, Dauphin had what was termed a Miscellaneous Court, universally known as "Junk Court." Among other things, this court accepted felony guilty pleas at all times except during criminal trial terms. By precedent, the judge in front of whom no one wanted to practice never sat in Junk Court; the other judges rotated. The attorneys knew who the judge in Junk Court was at the beginning of each week; if he was acceptable, the case could be sent there immediately upon arraignment. This, of course, was done on the defense attorney's initiative, who was then in no position to secure charge reductions. The defendant simply pleaded guilty as charged. After arraignment, the best deal a defense attorney could normally obtain would be to have the case pleaded in front of a specific judge (or *not* in front of a specific judge) and perhaps have the prosecutor "stand mute" at sentencing (i.e., offer no extenuating circumstances or recommendations).

It is extremely difficult to even speculate about the role of the defense bar, especially the public defender's office, upon the minimal role of charge reductions in Dauphin. It does not suffice to say that the defense bar had close ties to the rest of the court community because that holds true in many counties. Nor is it meaningful to point out that the public defender pursued a very cautious policy because of the need to maintain good relations with the county board and judges. Some of the most forceful advocates of defendants' rights were found in the Dauphin public defense bar. Thus the bar probably had little to do with the role of charge reductions in Dauphin, which were largely determined by the mix of practices and structures just outlined.

THE SYMBOLIC COUNTIES

We move now to the symbolic counties because their charge reduction practices are closer to the minimalist counties than any other category, largely because the use of count drops means so little in terms of sentencing. In trying to understand how the symbolic counties differed from the minimalist counties, it is useful to begin by contrasting DuPage with Kalamazoo. Both head prosecutors were outsiders and were much less concerned with internal court community matters than many of their counterparts. A casual glance at the relevant aspects of the infrastructures in these two counties also reveals several parallels. Both used formalistically oriented screening mechanisms involving trial assistants, even though Kalamazoo probably pruned more cases. Both had the most centralized plea-offer mechanisms of our counties, and in neither was the judge part of the plea agenda. Both counties used blind assignments and individual dockets.

Despite these parallels, we can point to two important differences, and possibly a third, that are plausible explanations for the greater use of count drops in DuPage than in Kalamazoo. First, unlike in Kalamazoo, the DuPage prosecutors were extremely concerned with attaining the sentencing objectives set for each case by the Indictment Committee. The Kalamazoo head prosecutor tolerated acceptable sentencing agreements but did not push for them, preferring a blind plea in which the judges imposed a sentence at a later point. In DuPage, the prosecutors did not trust this responsibility to the judges, many of whom they thought were too lenient. This concern with sentencing affected their charging philosophy, which differed markedly from Kalamazoo's. While the trial assistants who initiated cases and set charges were not in the habit of "issuing dogs"—

inflating the primary charges—they did engage in a conscious strategy of count multiplication. Their incidence of multicount complaints, 65 percent (Table 6.5), was second highest among the nine counties. These additional counts provided them with something to give in their efforts to achieve other goals in plea discussions.

The charging practices of DuPage prosecutors were criticized vehemently by DuPage defense attorneys, especially members of the private bar. This underscores another fundamental difference between Kalamazoo and DuPage, but one that has a problematic impact upon the plea process. We simply cannot determine whether DuPage's practice of count multiplication and reduction was because of their efforts to achieve sentencing goals or was done to appease defense attorneys. We think that the attainment of sentencing objectives is more crucial because they were very important to DuPage prosecutors. Also, the manipulation of counts probably fooled few defense attorneys.

The symbolic mode of charge reduction in Montgomery was not the result of a conscious policy as in DuPage. Indeed, the Montgomery prosecutors had no control over the high level of multicount complaints— 70 percent, the highest among the nine counties (Table 6.5)—upon which a defendant was arrested. These were wholly determined by one of the forty-odd police departments in Montgomery County. None of the Pennsylvania counties, it will be recalled, screened cases. Nor was Montgomery's charge reduction made as a result of the county's desire to implement hierarchically defined sentencing objectives. This alleviated the need for a centralized plea offer system such as existed in DuPage. Montgomery prosecutors were concerned with setting sentences, but the office hierarchy was content with leaving that largely to the discretion of individual assistants, even though some clear-cut policies on sentencing did exist for some offenses.

The relaxed, communal atmosphere in Montgomery's court community probably made the imposition of centralized controls unnecessary to attain these modest sentencing goals. But even more important to their attainment was the rather involved, sequential case assignment procedures used in conjuction with Montgomery's master calendar system. With the agreement of both the prosecutor and the defense attorney, a plea agreement could be routed to a judge of choice. Indeed, much of the plea discussions in Montgomery concerned to whom the case would be routed. In this sense the plea agenda in Montgomery was more inclusive than in DuPage, or, indeed, in any of the counties. Charge, sentence, and judge were all part of the discussions, usually beginning with sentence and then proceeding to agree upon a judge who would find it acceptable. This is significant because, in the vast majority of cases, sentence and judge are of much more concern to most defense attorneys and defendants. Securing agreement on them deflected attention from meaningful charge reductions. Given the importance of the screening and charging process we observed in Saginaw and Kalamazoo, we perhaps would have expected a much higher level of primary charge reductions in Montgomery (10.9 percent, Table 8.9). We do not see this, probably because discussions were focused on more significant aspects of the Montgomery plea agenda: judge and sentence. Also, some of the judges in Montgomery objected strongly to primary charge reductions. The extraneous secondary charges tacked on by the police were dropped routinely, undoubtedly as symbolic concessions.

The problem of clarifying the factors that affect the emergence of a symbolic mode of charge reduction is compounded even further by examining Erie. The complexities underscore the point made earlier that there are many routes to the same destination. An examination of the various plea-related practices in Erie illustrates this point. While the failure of Erie prosecutors to screen and initially charge cases led to a high level of multicount complaints in a manner similar to Montgomery and DuPage, the other key similarity shared by these two symbolic counties—the importance attached by prosecutors to obtaining sentencing agreements—was not shared by Erie. Indeed, Erie's judges would accept no sentence agreement and uniformly insisted upon a pre-sentencing investigation, which meant that sentences were generally not set until a month after disposition. Thus, all pleas were, to a degree, blind.

The absence of sentencing agreements on the plea agenda is not the only point upon which Erie differs from DuPage and Montgomery. The latter two counties differed significantly with respect to the structure of the plea process; Erie fit in the mold of neither. While Montgomery's prosecutor was the consummate insider who ran a somewhat pragmatic office, Erie's was an insurgent committed to change (like DuPage's), who ran a pragmatic operation (somewhat like Montgomery's). While Erie used a master calendar system, unlike DuPage's, plea-routing was not as pervasive as in Montgomery. The court administrator controlled judge assignments and made an effort to balance caseloads across the judges. Nonetheless, most requests for a specific judge could be met.

The contrasts between Erie and the other two symbolic counties notwithstanding, we can point to a number of factors that shed light on Erie's symbolic pattern of charge reductions. First, as an extension of the insurgent prosecutor's get-tough campaign, he had a strong dislike for primary charge reductions, a dislike that was shared by the judges. We do not term this a formal on-the-nose plea policy because the Erie prosecutor did not issue formal policies, and there was no enforcement mechanism. It was effective nonetheless. A second point concerns sentencing practices in Erie. One wonders whether the plea process in Erie, a process in which the defendants are not routinely given a sentence commitment or a primary charge reduction, could be maintained without strong sentencing norms. Such norms prevailed in Erie: 86 percent of the sentence fell within one cluster or another, one of the highest among our nine counties (see Table 10.1). Also it was one of the more lenient counties, as will be seen in chapter 10.

THE MIDDLING COUNTIES

In attempting to understand the charge reduction patterns in the middling counties it makes sense to begin with Peoria and Oakland and compare them with Kalamazoo. There are many parallels among these three counties, yet charge reductions, especially primary charge reductions, played a significantly larger role. Even though the prosecutor's office in Kalamazoo was formalistically oriented, whereas those in Oakland and Peoria were more efficiency oriented, these offices were, like Kalamazoo's, far more outward-looking than many of their counterparts. These concerns were simply manifested in different ways. For example, whereas Kalamazoo had one of the most formal, centralized plea-offer mechanisms, Peoria and Oakland adopted more flexible plea-offer mechanisms. They were, nonetheless, much more centralized than the more pragmatically oriented counties. Also, Oakland, like Kalamazoo, had a strong on-the-nose plea policy. No one talked about such a policy in Peoria, but it was clear that when the current prosecutor took over eight years before our study, he took a hard line against pervasive charge reduction practices (much like the Erie prosecutor). It simply was not much of an issue at the time of our study.

These similarities notwithstanding, we can point to a number of differences among Kalamazoo and Peoria and Oakland that can plausibly account for the differences in charge reduction patterns. The differences concern the screening and charging practices of the counties. There is little question that Kalamazoo pruned more cases than either Peoria or Oakland. Moreover, although there is little evidence that Peoria and Oakland engaged in calculated overcharging and count multiplication, they were not as conservative in charging as Kalamazoo. One of the reasons for this is institutional. In Kalamazoo, trial prosecutors initiated charges; they had to try whatever "dogs" were issued. In Peoria and Oakland, experienced prosecutors initiated charges, but they were not trial attorneys and would not have to try any cases that were charged inappropriately.

The upshot of these differences in the early stages of prosecution was that there was probably more junk among the cases handled in Peoria and Oakland than in Kalamazoo. This probably created more opportunities, and perhaps more legitimate reasons, for primary charge reductions. Differences in the plea agenda in Peoria also exacerbated whatever pressures existed for meaningful charge reductions. Individual calendars limited the plea agenda in all three counties to charge and sentence. But in addition to strong on-the-nose policies, neither Kalamazoo nor Oakland were overly concerned with obtaining sentence agreements. Indeed, they were prohibited by the Oakland prosecutor. Sentencing agreements were accepted frequently in Kalamazoo, but prosecutors did not expend resources in obtaining them because they were initiated by the defense. In Peoria, on the other hand, the prosecutors did try to achieve sentencing objectives. In some cases, they may have had to "give" on charges to achieve those sentencing objectives.

We can point to no meaningful differences in the defense bars of these three counties to explain the difference in charge reduction patterns. Oakland's bar was far more diffuse than those in Kalamazoo and Peoria, but the indigent defense system in each was more autonomous than in the public defender counties, at least superficially. But given the ties of Oakland attorneys to the Oakland judges, the overall conservatism of the Peoria bar, and the contract system used in Kalamazoo, none of these defense bars, in the aggregate, was as adversarial as the DuPage private bar or that in St. Clair.

The empirical coupling of St. Clair with Peoria and Oakland is as puzzling as that of Erie with DuPage and Montgomery. St. Clair is much more pragmatic in its overall work orientation, and the unreformed nature of its political environment, documented in chapters 4 and 5, would lead us to expect more pervasive charge reductions. The St. Clair prosecutor's office pursued very laissez-faire plea practices, and St. Clair had a relatively fiesty defense bar. Thus, the question to be addressed with respect to St. Clair is not why its plea patterns failed to resemble Kalamazoo's, but why they didn't resemble Saginaw's.

To explain this, we can point to several aspects of St. Clair's infrastructure. The first, and most crucial, again relates to screening and charging practices. As noted in chapter 6, the combination of initial screening and grand jury screening in St. Clair probably resulted in a more closely pruned caseload than even in Kalamazoo. St. Clair was the only county in which defense attorneys complained about the conservative charging practices of the prosecutor. Next to Kalamazoo, St. Clair had the lowest level of multicount complaints, 21 percent (Table 6.5), of the nine counties. Thus, there was little junk in St. Clair's system and little "give" to be gotten as far as charges were concerned. Making charge reductions even more difficult to obtain in St. Clair was the structure of its plea agenda. Although sentence agreements by assistant prosecutors were not prohibited by the office (except for agreements to probation), the St. Clair prosecutors were not concerned with achieving sentencing objectives. They were content to let the judge set sentences. Thus, unlike in places such as DuPage, it was the defense attorneys in St. Clair who had to push to achieve sentencing agreements. This, of course, drained whatever defense resources may have been available to secure charge reductions. In addition, it was sometimes possible to route pleas to one of the three St. Clair criminal court judges, with the agreement of both parties. Plea-routing was not as prevalent in St. Clair as it was in Montgomery and Dauphin, but it did work to further deflect pressures for charge reductions in some cases.

In light of these observations, we must restate the initial question. We should not ask why charge reductions were so low in St. Clair but, rather, Why were they so high? The conservative screening and charging practices and the structure of the plea agenda in St. Clair would lead us to expect minimal levels of charge reduction. The fact that they were so high suggests that the overall pragmatic orientation and laissez-faire plea-offer procedures played a role in the structure of St. Clair's plea process.

ATTEMPTS AT A SYNTHESIS

To generalize about the factors affecting charge reductions, we must first distinguish between their two primary components: primary charge reductions and count drops. Beginning with count drops, we must again stress their symbolic nature and question their significance in the guilty plea process. In some ways count drops given by prosecutors as part of a plea agreement are similar to toasters given by banks as part of an agreement to sell long-term certificates of deposit. They are nice to have, but they are not the reason for the purchase, nor do they add much to the overall value of the package. Few people would commit $5,000 to a C.D. for a two-year period to get a toaster, but one would rather have it than not. A higher rate of interest would be preferable, but such rates are usually determined by factors beyond the control of individual investors. Most plea agreements, like most financial dealings, are entered into for reasons unrelated to acquisition of tokens.

If count drops have an important role in the guilty plea process, it may not be as a sham to induce hapless defendants into pleading guilty, but as a prosecutorial tool to achieve sentencing objectives. That is, in the way toasters and other trinkets may sometimes disguise deficiencies in financial services or returns, so may count drops disguise marginally higher sentences. This was unquestionably the motivation behind the DuPage prosecutor's conscious policy of issuing multicount complaints and granting a high percentage of count drops (46 percent, see Tables 6.4 and 8.9.)

Indeed, if we exclude Saginaw as a deviant case, three of the four counties with the highest level of count drops were the three counties in which the prosecutors were concerned with obtaining sentencing stipulations in plea agreements—DuPage, Peoria, and Montgomery. Erie, where sentencing agreements were not permitted, had the highest incidence of count drops, but those were largely because of the relatively high level of multicount complaints issued by the police. The large number of multicount complaints that were beyond the control of Erie prosecutors may have resulted in a generous count-drop policy because it is so costless and, perhaps, because the office had so little else to offer. However, as demonstrated in counties such as Kalamazoo and Dauphin, such inducements are not necessary to obtain a high level of pleas. However, it should be recalled that Erie prosecutors could not influence the selection of the trial judge, as Dauphin prosecutors could. Moreover, they were not dealing with a highly pruned caseload, as in Kalamazoo. Count drops may be more prominent when these other factors are not present and where multicount complaints are the norm.

If a high incidence of count drops is due to a combination of charging practices and sentencing objectives (or limitations), the factors affecting the level of primary charge reductions are far more complicated. The situation may be best summarized by noting again that there appear to be many routes to the same end. But, despite the multiplicity of routes, it is clear that the principal point of origin lies with the screening and charging practices of the prosecutor. Unfortunately, an understanding of these practices in and of themselves will not yield a conclusive picture of primary charge reductions. Much depends upon how these practices mesh with the plea agenda and the control of plea offers. Of less certain importance is the orientation and structure of the criminal defense bar, especially the public defender's office.

To illustrate these points, it is useful to begin by comparing Kalamazoo, St. Clair, DuPage, and Saginaw. Kalamazoo and St. Clair had the most stringent screening and charging practices. But Kalamazoo backed up its practices with a highly controlled plea offer process and little concern for achieving sentencing agreements. Moreover, it had a group of contract attorneys who worked under some institutional barriers to rigorous, aggressive representation. St. Clair prosecutors were also not concerned with obtaining sentencing agreements, but they adopted laissez-faire plea practices and faced a fiesty defense bar. Consequently, they yielded a significantly higher level of primary charge reduction than Kalamazoo (21.1 percent as opposed to 12.8 percent, see Table 8.9). DuPage did not prune cases to the extent that Kalamazoo and St. Clair did, yet was as successful as Kalamazoo in limiting primary charge reductions (12.2 percent compared to 12.8 percent, see Table 8.9). But it used trial assistants to determine appropriate charges and rigidly controlled plea offers. They did this even though they faced a very hostile private defense bar and aggressively tried to control the sentencing process. In none of these four counties was the judge a prominent part of the plea agenda (the judge was relevant in some instances in St. Clair).

The reverse side of screening and charging practices, of course, can be seen in Saginaw. There the warrant process was somewhat pliable and permitted prosecutor-shopping to an extent. Trial prosecutors were assigned cases early on, and they took advantage of this by routinely inflating the charges at the indictment stage. Sentencing agreements were prohibited by Saginaw judges. The result was the widespread use of primary charge reductions. Oakland and Peoria are in the middle, on all counts. They screened cases, but they were not as stringent in screening and charging as Kalamazoo and St. Clair. They centralized their plea offers to a degree, but not to the extent we observed in DuPage and Kalamazoo. The result was moderately high levels of primary charge reductions.

The picture that emerges from these counties is that screening and charging practices are central to an understanding of primary charge reductions. Stringent practices can eliminate junk cases and the opportunities for meaningful charge reductions, but the extent to which they do depends upon other factors such as the centralization of plea offers, the breadth of the plea agenda, and, perhaps, the orientation of the defense bar. But then we encounter the Pennsylvania counties. They left the initiation of cases and charging to the police and had pragmatically oriented plea practices, yet had overall rather low rates of primary charge reductions. For an explanation of these low rates, we must point to the prominent place of the judge on the plea agenda. But we do not know whether the primary charges were inflated routinely by the police in these counties. If they were not, then we cannot say much about the impact that securing an agreement on the judge has upon limiting primary charge reductions. The strong but lenient sentencing norms in the Pennsylvania counties may also have something to do with the low level of primary charge reductions in the Pennsylvania counties. We turn now to an examination of sentencing practices.

10

GOING RATES AND SENTENCING SEVERITY: ENVIRONMENTAL AND CONTEXTUAL DETERMINANTS

Thus far we have been largely concerned with consistency in the guilty plea process, both with respect to charges and sentencing. Significant differences in charge manipulation practices across counties were uncovered, and some of the reasons for these different patterns were addressed in chapter 9. However, as noted in chapter 8 (Table 8.12 and the accompanying discussion), far less variance in sentencing consistency was noted. This can be seen in Table 10.1. In the six non-Michigan counties, between 79 and 90 percent of all guilty plea cases fell within one cluster or another; in the Michigan counties, the range was between 61 and 68 percent. The overall higher level of sentencing and the less frequent use of probation in the Michigan counties accounted for the lower levels of consistency in them.

The relatively narrow differences in sentencing consistency in these counties makes them of less interest for further analysis. However, the observation that the Michigan counties sentenced somewhat more harshly than the other six emphasizes a heretofore neglected point: differences in the severity of going rates across counties. Two counties may evince very comparable consistency levels in their sentencing patterns but may sentence at markedly different levels. For example, the low cluster for burglary may be five to six months in one, but nine to ten months in the other. These constitute an important dimension of a county's plea process, but differences would be lost if we focused only on intra-county sentencing consistency. Severity levels have important implications for both defendants

Table 10.1. **Sentencing Clusters by County**

	DuPage (Ring)	Peoria (Autono-mous)	St. Clair (Declin-ing)	Oakland (Ring)	Kalamazoo (Autono-mous)	Saginaw (Declin-ing)	Mont-gomery (Ring)	Douphin (Autono-mous)	Erie (Declin-ing)
Probation cluster	73.2 (341)	65.1 (365)	78.5 (507)	41.1 (172)	38.3 (159)	47.5 (103)	81.4 (341)	78.8 (495)	67.3 (183)
Between probation cluster and low cluster	3.0 (14)	5.0 (28)	2.9 (19)	5.3 (22)	6.8 (28)	14.7 (32)	2.4 (10)	4.1 (26)	4.8 (13)
Low cluster	14.2 (66)	9.8 (55)	7.9 (51)	14.1 (59)	15.0 (62)	12.4 (27)	1.2 (5)	9.7 (61)	17.3 (47)
Between low cluster and high cluster	4.9 (23)	3.4 (19)	4.0 (26)	4.3 (18)	15.4 (64)	12.0 (26)	2.4 (10)	3.2 (20)	5.1 (14)
High cluster	3.2 (15)	4.1 (23)	3.1 (20)	12.7 (53)	7.7 (32)	3.7 (8)	0 (0)	.8 (5)	3.3 (9)
Above high cluster	1.5 (7)	4.1 (23)	.5 (3)	14.4 (60)	9.9 (41)	7.8 (17)	0 (0)	.13 (2)	.4 (1)
No cluster or no cluster above probation	0 (0)	8.6 (48)	3.1 (20)	8.1 (34)	7.0 (29)	1.8 (4)	12.6 (53)	3.0 (19)	1.8 (5)
Percent of cases falling within one cluster or another	90.6 (404)	79.0 (443)	89.5 (578)	67.9 (284)	61.0 (253)	63.6 (138)	82.6 (346)	89.3 (560)	87.9 (239)
Total	446	561	646	418	415	217	419	628	272

and citizens. More severe sentences mean more restraints on the freedom of defendants, may impede their rehabilitation and reintegration into society, and impose significantly greater economic costs on the county and state. More lenient sentences, on the other hand, may impair the deterrent impact of the criminal law and could jeopardize the security, or at least perceived security, of local citizens.

For these reasons, we are concerned here with examining differences in severity across counties and detailing the differences that exist. Moreover, we want to offer an explanation for those differences. Several problems, largely methodological, are encountered in attempting to achieve these objectives. For example, one would quickly become overwhelmed in trying to compare average sentences, and/or the proportion of people given probation in nine counties for the thirteen offenses used in our cluster analysis in chapter 8. Thus, with the loss of some specificity, we will use a more general approach to detecting differences in sentencing severity. Another problem concerns our ability to outline the general factors that influence severity. The difficulty here is that we have only a limited number of counties with which to deal. While this will place some limits on what we can say and will necessitate a somewhat cumbersome approach, we are still able to generate some statistically based insights into these questions.

We will outline our approach to these problems after we examine sentencing patterns in a more general fashion.

SENTENCING SEVERITY: A GENERAL VIEW

Graph 10.1 portrays the proportion of the guilty plea cases in all nine counties that were given at least one of four basic sentence forms: a penitentiary commitment, a jail term, probation (including diversion), or a monetary punishment (restitution or a fine). The shaded portion of the bars indicates the proportion of cases given some punishment in addition to the basic, most severe one. For example, all county jail sentences were accompanied by some term of probation (29 percent), a combination of probation and a fine (17 percent), or some other form of punishment (34 percent). Fifty-five percent of all probation cases were also given a fine or some other type of sanction; 9 percent of penitentiary sentences were given an additional form of punishment, usually a term of probation to be completed after being released. Graph 10.1 indicates that probation (including diversion) is by far the most common basic sentence form, accounting for close to 60 percent of all sentenced cases. Penitentiary and jail are each used in roughly 17 and 20 percent of all cases, respectively. Money punishments account for the remaining 3 percent of the cases.

percent of all sentences

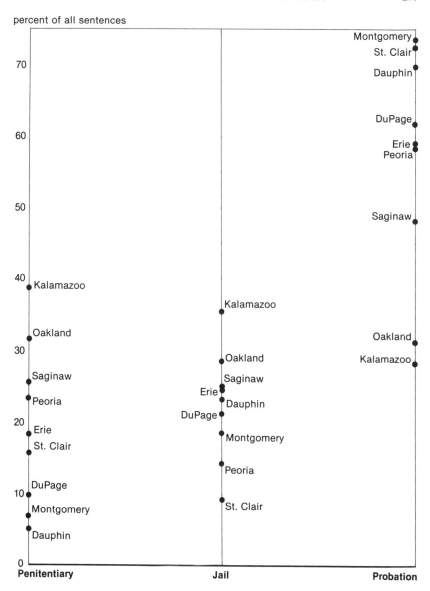

Graph 10.1. **The Distribution of Basic Sentence Forms,
Guilty Plea Cases Only (n = 5,944)**

A close examination of Graph 10.1, however, reveals that this pattern does not characterize all counties. It reports the proportion of sentenced cases in each of three basic sentencing forms by county. The money

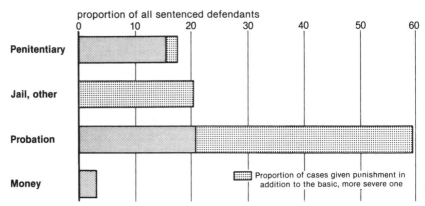

Graph 10.2. **The Distribution of Basic Sentence Forms, by County**

category from Graph 10.2 is excluded because of a lack of variance across counties. While DuPage County gave almost 7 percent of sentenced cases solely a monetary punishment, most of the other counties hovered around 2–4 percent.

Several observations can be made on the basis of Graph 10.2. First, in Kalamazoo, penitentiary commitment is the modal form of punishment, followed by jail confinement. In Oakland, an equal proportion of defendants are given penitentiary sentences and probation; almost as many are given a jail sentence. Dauphin, Montgomery, and DuPage are the least likely to send defendants to the penitentiary. Dauphin and Montgomery were among the most likely, along with St. Clair, to use probation. St. Clair, Peoria, and Montgomery are the least likely to use the local jail; Oakland and Kalamazoo are the least likely to use probation.

While the patterns embodied in Graph 10.2 are suggestive about which counties hand out the most severe sentences, one must be extremely cautious in interpreting the data. They are raw numbers that do not control for differences in the types of cases handled or for the criminal records of the defendants, which together are the primary determinants of sentences within these counties. Moreover, these data are only crude indicators of sentencing severity because they ignore, for example, differences in the length of confinement sentences. To identify meaningful differences in countywide sentencing tendencies, these problems must be overcome. Fortunately, analysis of covariance using stepwise multiple regression (Cohen and Cohen, 1975, chapter 9) permits us to control simultaneously for the impact of offense and criminal record while examining differences across county. The dependent variable used in this analysis is *JAILMIN*, the minimum amount of time a convicted defendant was required to be incarcerated, coded in months (nonconfinement sentences coded 0).[1] This

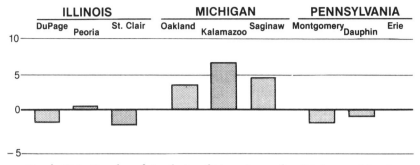

Graph 10.3. **Results of Analysis of Covariance for Minimum Months in Confinement (n = 5,578)**

is a straightforward and sensitive measure of a sentence's severity, one that is comparable across counties. While somewhat more crude than the sentence cluster variables used earlier, it is more suitable for present purposes because it includes all offenses and detects differences in a straightforward and comparable manner.

The analysis of covariance was conducted by merging the cases from all nine counties into one analysis pool. The variable depicting the seriousness of the most serious offense *at arrest* was entered in the first step of the regression analysis, followed by the criminal record variable. Then dummy variables representing each (K-1) of the counties were entered to determine the difference in the residualized sentence variable across counties.[2] The B-coefficient for the eight dummy variables—which depicts the average residualized difference, in months of confinement, of a county from the reference group (in this case Erie County)—can be used to compare differences in sentencing severity.[3]

The B-coefficients for the eight county dummy variables from the analysis of covariance controlling for offense seriousness and criminal record are presented in Graph 10.3.[4] While these figures are all referenced to the Erie mean, they can be compared to one another to determine relative sentencing levels. The analysis of covariance does not provide information per se on the statistical significance of the differences across the counties reported in Graph 10.3. Independent analyses, however, reveal some significant differences; the most important are across states. The Michigan cases received much more severe sentences than those from other counties—about five months more overall. There is no significant difference between Illinois and Pennsylvania counties when offense and criminal records are controlled. However, each county in Michigan sentences more severely than do those outside of Michigan.

While the data reported in Graph 10.3 do reveal some statistically

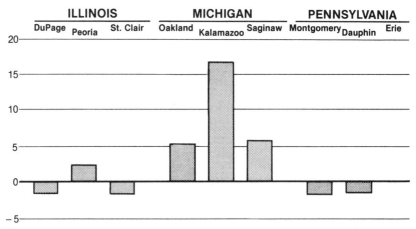

Graph 10.4. **Results of Analysis of Covariance for Minimum Months in Confinement, Repeat Offenders Only (n = 3,216)**

significant intercounty differences in severity, the range of variation is actually quite limited, especially if the Michigan counties are excluded. One of the reasons for this somewhat limited variance is the fact that so many of the defendants pleading guilty in these counties were first offenders who were normally given probation (no time in confinement). Overall, 80 percent of first offenders were given probation, and in only two counties (Oakland, 63 percent and Saginaw, 69 percent) did the percent of first offenders receiving probation dip below 75 percent. To gauge the impact of these cases upon severity patterns, we conducted an analysis of covariance for repeat offenders only.

The results of this analysis are reported in Graph 10.4 and, as suspected, a good deal more variation in severity patterns emerges. Even though no change in rank ordering emerges, the earlier differences became magnified. Michigan looks much more severe than the other states, and Kalamazoo evidences a distinctly severe sentencing pattern, followed by the other two Michigan counties. Among the non-Michigan counties, Peoria emerges as somewhat more punitive when only repeat offenders are examined.

What the differences between Graph 10.3 and 10.4 tell us is that to understand differences in severity across counties, we may have to pay particular attention to repeat offender cases. It is in these cases that the environmental and contextual factors with which we are concerned are most likely to make themselves felt. We now turn to a discussion and examination of these factors.

EXPLAINING DIFFERENCES IN SEVERITY
ACROSS COUNTIES

We could end our quantitative analysis at this point and begin to speculate, much as we did in chapter 9, about the factors that account for the observed differences in severity. However, we have the option here of conducting a more rigorous analysis into the factors influencing severity. In chapter 9, we were concerned with explaining differences in charge reduction *patterns,* patterns that were necessarily defined at the county level. Thus we had only nine observations with which to deal. Here, however, we are concerned with sentence severity, which can be defined as the deviation of a sentence in a particular case from a pooled, offense-specific mean. The greater the positive deviation, the more severe the sentence, and vice versa. The advantage of this situation is that we have thousands of observed sentences that we can use to examine the impact of county characteristics, our primary concern.

The availability of several thousand cases for analysis is important because, unlike in chapter 9, we are able to control statistically for the impact of certain county characteristics while examining the effect of others. However, our ability to do this is limited by the fact that although we have more than five thousand observations (more than three thousand involving repeat offenders), we have only nine sources of variance for county-level characteristics. This can cause problems of multicollinearity among variables defined by county characteristics and, if too many are entered into a regression equation, it becomes progressively more unstable (i.e., parameter estimates will vary as different variables are entered or removed from the equation).

These limitations impede our ability to mount a truly definitive macro-level analysis of sentencing severity because a relatively large number of environmental and contextual factors are plausible determinants of severity. Preliminary bivariate analyses revealed that, in reality, only a handful have any direct impact upon severity. However, the number of plausible variables was still too large for a valid simultaneous analysis given the relatively small number of counties. As a way of reducing these statistical problems, we separate the analysis of environmental variables from the analysis of contextual variables. Moreover, within each of the separate analyses we were very sensitive to correlations between variables and fluctuations in parameter estimates as different variables were entered or removed from the regression analysis. More of this will be discussed in the presentation of the results.

In one sense, using this bifurcated approach is artificial: The two sets of variables coexist and may be somewhat interrelated in the real world. Nonetheless, this approach will provide us with some insights into the types of environmental and contextual variables that may affect sentencing. These findings can be used to produce better site-selection strategies in future studies, studies that we hope will include more sites, thereby significantly reducing some of the statistical problems we encountered in this study. In interpreting the results of the two analyses that follow, readers must be careful not to assume that the results are simply additive. Further research may confirm that these are independent sources of influence, but until more counties can be examined simultaneously, we can only speculate on the real pattern of interrelationships.

We can now turn to a discussion and analysis of the environmental and contextual determinants of sentence severity.

Environmental Determinants of Severity

Table 10.2 lists some environmental determinants of sentencing severity. It includes social, political, structural, and legal factors, as well as some that are related to the linkages between the courts and their environment. Despite the variety of factors included, it is not intended to be seen as an exhaustive list, nor does it even exhaust the data we have on our nine counties. The variables simply reflect our best judgment about where to begin a fairly limited analysis of environmental influences upon sentencing severity.

The first factor listed in Table 10.2 is the severity of the social strains in the county (*STRAINS*). This variable was chosen because in heterogeneous counties, especially those suffering from some economic malaise — or where crime is highly concentrated in a major city or among an identifiable population grouping — sentencing decisions may take on political overtones. Sentencing may be more severe in heterogeneous counties than in prosperous suburban counties with no serious crime problems. The political ideology of the counties (*CONSRVTSM*) is considered important because if judges do in fact try to reflect the views of their constituents, those in more conservative counties are more likely to sentence similarly situated defendants more severely. The crime problem (*PERSCRM*) factor is expected to have a similar impact. In counties where crime is a serious problem, judges may feel more compelled to sentence severely than do judges in counties with minimal crime problems. We use a measure of only crimes against persons because we feel it is a much better gauge of the type of crime about which people feel most strongly.

Neither the political ideology of the county nor the seriousness of the crime problem is expected to have a similar impact in all counties. Rather, their impact is expected to vary with the nature of the political linkages between the court and its political environment. Indeed, the severity of the crime problem is considered to be a key factor in the level of public scrutiny. Nonetheless, because of the relatively small number

Table 10.2. **Summary of Environmental Factors**

Environmental Factor	Variable Name	Expected Impact	Source and Range on Coding of Variable
County-Level Variables			
Severity of social strains	STRAINS	+	Peoria, St. Clair, Dauphin coded as most strained (3); DuPage, Montgomery coded as least strained (1); others coded 2*
Seriousness of crime problem	PERSCRM	+	Ten-year average of FBI crimes against persons from Table 4.8; range = 201 to 860
Political ideology	CONSERVTSM	+	Weighted conservatism scores from Table 4.7; range = −31 to 47.5
Media outlets (countywide newspapers and television stations)	MEDIA#	+	Level of media concentration from Table 4.3; range = 0 to 4
Local jail capacity	JAILSIZE	+	Capacity per arrest for violent crime from Table 4.10; range = .14 to .29
State-Level Variables			
Penitentiary capacity	PENITSIZE	+	Capacity per adult arrest for serious UCR crime from Table 4.13; range = 69 to 127
Severity of sentencing code	STATCODE	+	Average standardized offense-specific score from Table 4.15; range = −.10 to .13
State sentencing norms	SENTNORM	+	Average rank from Graph 4.3; Michigan = 3, Illinois = 2, Pennsylvania = 1

* Peoria, St. Clair, and Dauphin are included in the most strained category because all have fairly high crime levels, especially in their major city. Moreover, the county's minorities are also highly concentrated in the major city. Finally, blacks made up more than half of the court system's felony defendants (as represented in our case samples) in all three counties. DuPage and Montgomery are listed as least strained because of their homogeneous population and their low, diffuse crime levels. The other counties have one or more moderating influences, which leads us to classify them in the middle.

of counties and the distribution of the political and linkage variables it is impossible to conduct a meaningful interactive analysis using variables defined at the county level. Insufficient variation exists when the various combinations of characteristics are made. Despite this, we do examine the independent role of one measure of political linkages, the number of media outlets in a county (*MEDIA#*). Although as a linkage variable it is expected to be primarily important in conjunction with measures of such phenomena as county political ideology and the severity of the crime problem, we can also project some independent linear impact. Thus, where media are highly concentrated in a county, sentences are expected to be more severe.

The impact of the local jail capacity (*JAILSIZE*) does not depend upon any political linkages. It is important because where capacity is low, it has a constraining impact upon the ability of judges to give jail time to marginal offenders. High capacity levels, in contrast, may determine whether some of these other factors play a role. If jail capacity is a significant constraint, the courts may not be able to react to some of the pressures they experience. This will be discussed in more detail later.

At the state level three factors are considered relevant—the severity of the state sentencing code (*STATCODE*), penitentiary capacity (*PENIT-SIZE*), and the severity of statewide sentencing norms (*SENTNORM*). The expected impact of each is self-evident. However, as our discussion in chapter 4 indicated, the Michigan counties stand out on all three dimensions (as they do in Graphs 10.3 and 10.4). The three factors are intertwined in our data to such an extent that we cannot unravel them, especially since we have only a handful of states. Nonetheless, it is clear that Michigan's maximum penalties are more severe, it has more relative penitentiary capacity, and, for a long time, has sentenced more people to the penitentiary.

As just noted, we could not use county-level linkage variables effectively as components of multiplicative terms to conduct an interactive analysis, even though environmental factors were not expected to have simple linear relationships to sentencing. However, the political linkages between a county and its environment are not the only factors affecting the impact of external influences upon sentencing decisions; case attributes do also, especially the seriousness of the offense and the prior record of the defendant. Because the realm of possible outcomes for these serious cases is larger, courtroom actors have more latitude with which to respond to get-tough pressures. They are also the types of cases most likely to generate such pressures. Cases such as murders, rapes, robberies, home burglaries, and big drug busts attract media attention and are the type of cases about which citizens are concerned, especially in communities faced with a serious local crime problem. Also, structural constraints such as confinement capacity are most relevant for the more serious crimes.

A comparison of Graph 10.3 and 10.4—which show that the inclusion of first offenders suppressed intercounty differences—suggests the utility of confining the macro-level analyses reported here to the subset of pooled cases involving only repeat offenders. We will do this while reporting, in a footnote, identical analyses involving all cases. We test for the existence of interaction between offense seriousness and the environmental variables through the use of interaction terms.[5] In these analyses we use *GRANSER*1 as our measure of offense seriousness. As described in chapter 3, it is based upon the average sentence given to the primary offense charged in a case in all nine counties. It is in a very real sense then a pooled estimate of offense seriousness. This is used instead of county-based averages because we seek to analyze sentence deviations from these pooled means and explain them in terms of county characteristics. A county-specific measure of offense seriousness, as used in chapter 8, would absorb and obscure intercounty differences in sentencing.

Using multiple regression analysis with *JAILMIN* (the minimum months of confinement variable used in the analysis of covariance reported in Graphs 10.3 and 10.4) as the dependent variable, we produced Equation 10.1 (R^2 = .246; adjusted R^2 = .243; n = 3,216). We used only cases involving defendants who had at least one previous arrest.[6] The numbers in the parentheses below the *B*-coefficient for each variable are the *F* value and the beta weight, respectively. Because our pool of cases is not technically a sample, tests of statistical significance based on probability theory are not strictly applicable. However, to guide us in determining which findings are most significant and to enhance the stability of the reported results, we will adhere to accepted conventions concerning probability levels. With the number of cases being used here, an *F* value of at least 3.8 is needed for a finding to be significant at the .05 level; 6.0 is needed for a level of .01; and 10.8 is needed for a level of .001.

$$JAILMIN = .18 - 2.0 * GRANSER1$$
$$(68.2; -.8)$$
$$+ 3.7 * CRIMRCD + 7.4 * PENITSIZE$$
$$(98.3; .15) \qquad (2.3; .04)$$
$$+ .5 * MEDIA\# - .02 * CONSVRTSM$$
$$(1.9; .04) \qquad (1.0; -.02)$$
$$- .007 * PERSCRM + 4.9 * PENTISIZE * GRANSER1$$
$$(8.8; -.07) \qquad (135.0; .95)$$
$$+ .0007 * PERSCRM * GRANSER1$$
$$(15.5; .15)$$

$$+ .13 * MEDIA * GRANSER1$$
$$(15.7; .16)$$
$$+ .006 * CONSVRTSM * GRANSER1$$
$$(13.3; .08) \qquad (10.1)$$

In this analysis we first controlled for the pooled version of offense seriousness for the most serious offense at arrest (GRANSER1) and the severity of the defendant's criminal record (CRIMRCD). We then entered the linear version of each of the environmental variables listed in Table 10.1 in order of their statistical significance. Not surprisingly, GRANSER1 and CRIMRCD were the most important variables in the equation, explaining 12.2 percent and 2.5 percent of the variance, respectively. In contrast, the environmental variables altogether explained just under 10 percent of the variance (9.8 percent). Most of this was because of the variable measuring state prison capacity (PENITSIZE) and its corresponding interaction term; no other variable explained more than one-half of 1 percent of the variance.

Before we assess the impact of individual variables in detail, we should address several technical points. First, several of the variables listed in Table 10.2 had to be removed because they were intercorrelated with other variables and their inclusion would have resulted in misleading and unstable results. For example, the variable measuring social strains (STRAINS) had a correlation of .84 with the variable measuring the level of personal crime (PERSCRM). Because PERSCRM was used in constructing STRAINS and had a stronger impact upon sentence (see Table 10.4), STRAINS was eliminated. Although JAILSIZE has the second-strongest bivariate and partial correlation with the sentencing variable (see Table 10.4), a high intercorrelation with CONSRVTSM (−.84) and a moderate one with PENITSIZE (.47) forced us to eliminate it. At the point it would have entered the equation it had a tolerance level of only .15, which indicates that all but 15 percent of the variance in JAILSIZE could be explained by independent variables already in the equation. This was considered far too low, so it was eliminated from the analysis. Finally, because of high intercorrelations (.98) between PENITSIZE and the variable measuring the severity of the state sentencing code (STATCODE) and the variable measuring the severity of statewide sentencing norms (SENT-NORM), the STATCODE and SENTNORM variables could not be included in the final equation. This decision will be discussed later.

The other variables in the regression analysis were fairly independent of one another, and a relatively stable equation resulted. This can be seen in Table 10.3, which reports the intercorrelation among all independent variables, and especially in Table 10.4, which reports various information on the independent variables at different stages of the regression analysis.

Table 10.3. Bivariate Correlations Among Environmental Variables

	PERSCRM	PENITSIZE	JAILSIZE	MEDIA#	STRAINS	SENTNORM	STATCODE
PERSCRM							
PENITSIZE	.07355						
JAILSIZE	.33665	.47449					
MEDIA#	.51685	−.31627	.18110				
STRAINS	.86170	−.08051	.32776	.74636			
SENTNORM	.19182	.97829	.49062	−.30397	−.01442		
STATCODE	−.26805	.82296	.31806	−.27518	−.24262	.68737	
CONSIDEO	−.23979	−.18871	−.84698	−.16966	−.40952	−.19887	−.11620

Table 10.4. **Summary of Impact of Environmental Variables**

Environmental Variable	Bivariate Correlation with *JAILMIN*	Partial Correlation with *JAILMIN* after Controlling for *GRANSER*1 and *CRIMRCD*	Net Linear Effect (Partial Correlation with *JAILMIN* at Point Entered into Equation)	Tolerance Level at Point Entered into the Equation
STRAINS	.01	.01	(−.10)*	(.09)*
PERSCRM	.05	.04	−.02	.66
CONSERVTSM	−.05	−.01	.05	.89
MEDIA#	.01	−.01	.07	.89
JAILSIZE	.18	.15	(.13)*	(.15)*
PENITSIZE	.25	.23	.23	.98
STATCODE	.24	.22	(.06)*	(.17)*
SENTNORM	.24	.21	(−.06)*	(.02)*

* Indicates variable was never entered into the equation; statistic is for point at which the last variable (*PERSCRM*) was entered into the equation.

Table 10.4 reports three correlation coefficients between the independent variables and the dependent variable: the bivariate coefficient, a partial correlation coefficient (net of only the control variables—*GRANSER*1, *CRIMRCD*), and a second partial (net of all variables already entered into the equation). The tolerance levels are also reported. Ideally, a highly stable analysis would show very little changes in the correlation coefficients at these different stages; in reality, some changes almost always occur because of correlation among variables. Very little change in the absolute values of the coefficients occurs here. *PENITSIZE* is very stable, whereas *MEDIA#*'s final impact is actually strengthened (from .01 to .07) because of a moderate negative correlation (−.37) with *PENITSIZE*. *PERSCRM* and *CONSVRTSM* actually change signs after the two control variables are entered, but the absolute change is quite small. The tolerance levels are all quite high; only *PERSCRM* (.66) is much below .90.

With these technical points clarified, we can now look in greater detail at the impact and meaning of the individual variables. The variable depicting the level of social strains was not included in the final equation because of a high correlation with *PERSCRM*, because *PERSCRM* had a stronger net effect upon *JAILMIN*, and because crime rates were a criteria in constructing the *STRAINS* variable. Nonetheless, it should be stressed that both *STRAINS* and *PERSCRM* have a negative net linear impact upon sentence, not a positive one as hypothesized. *PERSCRM*, however, interacts with *GRANSER*1 to have a positive impact upon *JAILMIN*. This means that courts located in counties that have high levels of personal crime sentence repeat offenders convicted of minor offenses less severely than courts in counties that rarely encounter serious crimes. By the same token, repeat offenders convicted of more serious crimes are punished more severely in high-crime counties.

Several factors may explain these findings. Because crime is likely to be a more volatile political issue in counties with severe crime problems, court officials may prefer to consume available jail and prison capacity by sentencing a smaller number of more violent offenders to longer periods of confinement, while less serious crimes are given little or no punishment. To do otherwise would require giving less time to offenders convicted of more serious crimes. This might not be as politically satisfying as giving a few severe sentences in highly visible cases. Also, where a court's docket has a healthy mix of more and less serious cases (as would be the case in counties with a relatively high level of violent personal crime), less serious offenses may simply not look as "bad" as they would to judges who handle largely routine offenses.

The number of media outlets in the county (*MEDIA#*) and the political conservativism of the county (*CONSVRTSM*) had fairly straight-forward and similar effects upon sentencing. Both had positive linear impacts, and both interacted with offense seriousness. Thus, the notion that the level of media scrutiny in a county can have some effect upon sentencing patterns receives empirical support here. Moreover, for repeat offenders convicted of serious offenses, the impact of the media appears to be even greater. The same can be said of the political views of the county populace. The more conservative these views, the longer the sentences, especially for repeat offenders convicted of serious crimes.

The role played by crime, conservativism, and the media in setting levels of severity in criminal courts is extremely important because it suggests the importance of the court's political environment in its day-to-day operation. We hope that future studies involving more counties will examine the interplay among all three of these factors and further elucidate the political influences that pervade the court community. At the same time, the importance of these factors should not be overplayed. Altogether their net linear addition to the explained variance in sentencing severity is just barely over one-half of a point (.6); if we add the amount contributed by their interaction terms (.9), their total contribution is just 1.5 points. This pales in comparison to the combined effect of *PENITSIZE* and its interaction term (8.1).

PENITSIZE was, by far, the strongest environmental variable analyzed in the analysis. It suggests the primacy of structural factors and constraints upon sentencing. Defendants cannot be placed in cells that do not exist and, apparently, use will be made of the penitentiary spaces available. This has profound implications especially in an era of state prison overcrowding. It suggests that county-specific going rates may be, in some way, tagged to available state prison spaces and that additional spaces may be consumed by adjustments to these going rates.

Despite the allure of these findings and their implications, we must be very cautious in interpreting the role of penitentiary capacity (*PENIT-SIZE*) in this analysis. As noted, *PENITSIZE* is almost perfectly correlated with *SENTNORM* (the variable reflecting the long-term incarceration trends depicted in Graph 4.3) and *STATCODE* (which measures the severity of the state sentencing code). Although these three variables cannot be included in the regression simultaneously because of multi-collinearity, either of the other two variables could replace *PENITSIZE* in Equation 10.1 without affecting it materially.

PENITSIZE was chosen for several reasons. It was preferable to *STATCODE* because its effect was thought to be theoretically much more direct; *STATCODE* was based upon statutory sentencing maximums, which are seldom imposed. Thus, while the severity of the code and changes in it may send signals to local decision makers, it is not expected to have a very direct effect on sentencing behavior. The choice between *PENITSIZE* and *SENTNORM* was more difficult. One could argue that the penitentiary systems in Michigan and Illinois are large because of historically high demand for penal space. Differences in demand, in turn, could be caused by deep-set cultural and/or political factors. We cannot refute that argument and, indeed, differences in penitentiary systems and sentences may be a reflection of differences in legal cultures. Nonetheless, several considerations led us to use *PENITSIZE* rather than *SENTNORM* or a more abstract variable incorporating both, such as punishment culture.

The most important of these was the apparent role played by penitentiary capacity in the severity of sentencing norms depicted in Graph 4.3, at least for the post–1970 period. The post–1970s' jump in the incarceration rates of the three states was apparently affected by the prison construction programs of the three states. Michigan added six facilities, and it experienced the steepest increase in incarceration levels. Illinois added two new facilities, and it had a much more moderate jump in incarceration rates; Pennsylvania added none and had the slightest change. Although the cross-sectional nature of this study makes it impossible to make any causal statements about the role of penal capacity, it would seem safe to conclude that, at least during times of public concern with law and order, the relative size of penitentiary systems has an effect upon sentencing levels.

Despite the argument concerning the importance of penitentiary space in influencing the severity of going rates, it would be overly simplistic— even absurd—to assume that judges and prosecutors simply count available penal spaces in determining who should be incarcerated. The role played by detention capacity in criminal court sentencing decisions is expected to be much more subtle and circuitous. Court community going rates for various crimes are in part influenced by, and are adjusted to conform to, available detention capacity. This is especially easy to see in the case of county jail space, even though statistical problems make it impossible for us to discuss anything here about its role in sentencing severity. It is a fairly fixed and inelastic resource. Most jails are relatively old and cannot be enlarged either quickly or easily to accommodate passing whims or short-term crime waves. Going rates reflect these facilities. If a jail is relatively small, minor offenses will not normally be punished by jail time, or at least not much of it. If detention capacity remains constant in the face of significant increases in convictions for serious crimes, going rates for less serious offenses may actually drop. The court community's hierarchy of offenses and sentencing norms will reflect what can be done under existing constraints.

Over time, increases in capacity can also affect going rates. Increases in capacity may be due to the need for new facilities or may be in response to political pressures to get tough. In either case, the additional facilities enhance the bargaining position of prosecutors and increase the options available to judges. When increases in penal resources are due to law and order political pressures, the judges and prosecutors will be receiving signals from both the local community and the legislature to make good use of the additional space. The impact of these political pressures upon sentencing will be limited if there is not an increase in capacity. Increases in capacity unaccompanied by political pressures are also expected to increase sentencing levels, largely because of changes in bargaining positions and sentencing options. Thus, changes in detention capacity can be seen as both a necessary and sufficient condition for increasing sentencing levels. Its impact is thought to be greatest when increases in capacity are accompanied by political pressures to get tough.

Contextual Determinants of Severity

We saw in chapter 9 the importance of contextual factors such as the structure of discretion, office policies, and the locus of sentencing power upon the role of charge reductions in the plea process. It is reasonable to expect that some of the same factors will play a similar role in the determination of severity levels. These factors are important because they can affect the structure of interactions among participants, their allegiances, and their bargaining options. Table 10.5 lists some of the contextual factors thought to be relevant to severity levels. Most of the contextual influences, especially those concerned with the impact of structural factors, are related to work orientations. Although we again disaggregate this notion for

Table 10.5. **Summary of Contextual Factors**

Contextual Factor	Variable Name	Expected Impact	Source and Range on Coding of Variables
Does judge have effective control over sentencing?	*JUDGSENT*	+	From Table 9.1; 1 = Judge controlled sentencing in guilty plea cases, .5 = Variable situation, 0 = Prosecution controlled sentencing in guilty plea cases
The level of charge concessions in a county	*CONCLEVEL*	−	1 = Minimalist counties, 2 = Symbolic counties, 3 = Middling counties, 4 = Maximalist counties
Existence of prosecutor screening	*PSCREEN*	+	From Table 6.5; 1 = Screening, 0 = No screening
Platoon deployment of prosecutor	*PROSDPLY*	−	From Figure 6.1; 1 = Assigned to judge, 0 = Assigned to cases
Platoon deployment of indigent defense counsel	*IDCDPLY*	+	From Figure 6.2; 1 = Assigned to judge, 0 = Assigned to case
Availability of plea routing	*ROUTING*	−	From Figure 6.3; 1 = Routing possible, 0 = Routing not possible
Degree to which plea bargaining is centralized in prosecutor's office	*PLEACNTL*	+	From data in Table 6.6; 3 = Highly centralized, 2 = Centralized, 1 = Not centralized*

* DuPage and Kalamazoo were coded 3; Peoria, Oakland, and Dauphin were coded 2; the rest were coded 1.

purposes of analysis, the existence of pragmatically oriented structures is expected to be associated with lower sentencing levels; formalistically oriented arrangements are expected to be associated with higher sentencing levels.

The first contextual variable listed in Table 10.5 concerns the locus of sentencing power. It will be recalled from chapter 9 (Table 9.1) that prosecutors, through the widespread use of sentencing agreements, control sentencing in plea cases in several counties. In other counties sentencing agreements were not used because of prosecutorial or judicial prohibition. Finally, in two counties (St. Clair and Dauphin), sentencing agreements were discouraged but were used in some cases. These different practices are considered relevant to severity levels because they change the context of the sentencing decisions markedly. Where a sentence agreement is common practice there may be downward pressures exerted by the need to secure the defendant's consent. While unreasonable judicial sentencing practices in counties where judges control sentencing could jeopardize the smooth operation of the plea process, they still have more leeway than in counties where they are presented with a sentencing agreement that has the consent of all parties. Thus, a negative relationship is hypothesized between *JUDGSENT* and the *JAILMIN* variable.

The level of charge concessions variable listed in Table 10.5, *CONC-LEVEL*, corresponds to the four county categories discussed in earlier chapters (Minimalist, Symbolic, Middling, Maximalist). It is relevant because the level of charge concessions may say something about the court community's overall orientation or approach to the handling of criminal cases, much like their infrastructure. Care in the allocation of charge concessions may carry over into the setting of sentences. The widespread use of charge concessions may indicate a more pragmatic approach to the dispositional process, which may also be reflected in the setting of sentences. Thus a negative relationship between *CONCLEVEL* and *JAILMIN* is expected.

Where the prosecutor's office screens out cases (*PSCREEN*), weak and/or trivial cases can be weeded out. This is thought to enhance the credibility and bargaining position of prosecutors over time, and a positive relationship with *JAILMIN* is hypothesized. The use of platoon-type deployment of prosecutors and indigent defense attorneys (assignment to judges not cases) is relevant because such deployments can have an effect upon an attorney's allegiances. Being assigned to a specific courtroom should strengthen work-group ties and weaken ties to sponsoring organizations or clients. This should lead attorneys to be more reasonable in sentencing interactions. Thus, the prosecutor deployment variable (*PROSD-PLY*) is expected to have a negative impact, while the indigent defense counsel deployment variable (*IDCDPLY*) is expected to have a positive impact.

The availability of plea routing (*ROUTING*) and the extent to which plea offers are centralized in the prosecutor's office (*CENTRALIZED*) are relevant because they affect the ability of attorneys to maneuver. Where the possibility of routing exists, defense attorneys can use their skills and abilities to obtain a more lenient judge; thus a negative relationship is

Table 10.6. **Bivariate Correlations Among Contextual Variables**

	JUDGSENT	CONCLEVEL	PSCREEN	ROUTING	PROSDPLY	IDCDPLY
JUDGSENT						
CONCLEVEL	.17					
PSCREEN	−.16	.49				
ROUTING	.28	−.24	−.72			
PROSDPLY	.37	.55	.51	−.10		
IDCDPLY	−.43	.11	.33	−.45	.18	
PLEACNTL	−.25	−.53	.34	−.61	−.17	.42

hypothesized. Where the discretion of prosecutors is limited, as in centralized plea-offer systems, the probability of significant, last-minute concessions is much less, regardless of the defense attorney's strategic and psychological tactics.

Because of the prominence of interaction terms involving GRANSER1 and various environmental factors, and the fact that interaction with offense seriousness seemed plausible for at least some contextual variables, interaction terms similar to those used in the environmental analysis were included here. Equation 10.2 (R^2 = .238; adjusted R^2 = .236; n = 3,216), reports the final results. Again, this equation is just for repeat offenders.[7] The figures in parentheses report the F values and the beta weights for each term. All terms were significant beyond the .001 level except PSCREEN, which was significant only at the .05 level. Table 10.6 reports the bivariate correlation among the contextual variables, and Table 10.7 summarizes the interim results.

$$JAILMIN = -2.6 + 2.6 * GRANSER1$$
$$(83.8; 1.0)$$
$$+ 3.5 * CRIMRCD - 1.3 * ROUTING$$
$$(90.7; .15) \qquad (1.4; -.03)$$
$$+ 6.1 * JUDGSENT + .42 * CONCLEVEL$$
$$(21.5; .11) \qquad (.6; .02)$$
$$- .1 * ROUTING * GRANSER1$$
$$(87.4; -.30)$$
$$- .36 * CONCLEVEL * GRANSER1$$
$$(56.9; -.42)$$
$$-.65 * JUDGSENT * GRANSER1$$
$$(39.2; -.20) \qquad\qquad (10.2)$$

As was the case in Equation 10.1, the two control variables—offense

Table 10.7. **Summary of Impact of Contextual Variables**

Contextual Variable	Bivariate Correlation with JAILMIN	Partial Correlation with JAILMIN after Controlling for GRANSER1 and CRIMRCD	Net Linear Effect (Partial Correlation with JAILMIN at Point Entered into Equation)	Tolerance Level at Point Entered into the Equation
JUDGSENT	.12	.06	.01	.89
CONCLEVEL	−.03	−.06	−.11	.93
PSCREEN	.14	.13	(.04)*	(.37)*
ROUTING	−.18	.18	.18	1.0
PROSDPLY	−.02	−.05	(.02)*	(.68)*
IDCDPLY	−.08	−.05	(−.05)*	(.20)*
PLEACNTL	.13	.15	(−.06)*	(.09)*

* Indicates variable was never entered into the equation; statistic is for point at which last variable (CONCLEVEL) was entered into the equation.

seriousness (GRANSER1) and criminal record (CRIMRCD)—were the strongest determinants of severity. GRANSER1 added .122 points to the R^2 and CRIMRCD added about .025; the contextual variables, including their interaction effects, added about .09 points. This is very similar to the 9.8 percent of the variance accounted for by the environmental variables. Here, however, no one dominant variable emerges. The most potent is the availability of plea-routing variable (ROUTING); its linear component adds .027 to the R^2. The linear component of CONCLEVEL (the level of charge concessions variable) adds about 1 percent to the R^2, while the linear component of JUDGSENT added no significant variance. It only had an interactive effect.

None of the other contextual variables contribute to the equation, for a variety of reasons that can be gleaned from Tables 10.6 and 10.7. The variable PLEACNTL, for example, has a fairly healthy correlation (bivariate and net of the control variables) with JAILMIN, but high correlations with ROUTING (−.62) and CONCLEVEL (−.53) leave it with a tolerance level of only .09 after these stronger variables enter into the equation. Much the same could be said of PSCREEN (the variable indicating whether the prosecutor's office screened cases); a correlation of −.73 with ROUTING and .49 with CONCLEVEL reduce its tolerance to .37. The two deployment variables (PROSDPLY and IDCDLY) simply had weak correlations with JAILMIN at all points in the analysis.

If we looked simply at Equation 10.2 and the data on ROUTING, JUDGSENT, and CONCLEVEL in Table 10.6, we would have ample reason to be satisfied with the results of the contextual analysis. Although most of the contextual variables had no independent impact upon severity, the three that did affected *JAILMIN* in the expected direction, with one partial exception. Where pleas can be routed to judges of choice, sentences were less severe; the more common the use of charge concession, the less severe the sentence. The interpretation of the *JUDGSENT* variable is more complicated, however. Although its linear version had no significant effect, the interaction terms with *GRANSER1* did. An inspection of the *B*-coefficients for the final equation suggests, however, that in less serious cases (those with *GRANSER1* scores of about 10 or less), defendants do receive somewhat more severe sentences in counties where judges control sentence. In more serious cases, however, sentences are actually lower than in counties where prosecutors control sentences. Thus it appears that a cost might be associated with the certainty of a plea agreement that stipulates the sentence, at least in more serious cases.

These results seem firm because the three contextual variables reported in Equation 10.2 are highly independent of one another. In no case was the tolerance level of a variable below .93 when it was entered into the equation, and a highly stable equation resulted. However, if the results in Equation 10.2 are examined in depth, one of the findings is doubtful. Most of the counties that permit plea routing are in Pennsylvania, which has the lowest level of penitentiary capacity. Indeed, if the *PENITSIZE* variable is added to the contextual analysis as a control variable, the independent effect of *ROUTING* is affected drastically. The beta weight of its interaction term with *GRANSER1* drops from .30 to −.09, and the direction of its effect is reversed. The effect of the *CONCLEVEL* variable is actually enhanced with the inclusion of *PENITSIZE,* whereas the status of *JUDGSENT* is largely unchanged. This reanalysis casts significant doubt on what we can say here about the real impact of *ROUTING. PENITSIZE* is causally and logically prior to it and must be given deference when trying to untangle joint effects. However, there is no inherent collinearity between these variables, and later studies using more, and better selected, sites will be able to sort out the independent effects of each.

SUMMARY

The severity of sentencing practices is as important a component of the guilty plea process as the charge reduction practices described and analyzed earlier. Moreover, the various analyses in this chapter have established that important variations in the severity of sentencing practices exist in the nine counties studied here, especially if we focus on the handling of repeat offenders. Far more difficult than the documentation of differences in severity is the delineation of factors that account for those differences. The most that we can say with certainty from the data available is that most of the significant differences in sentences are across states. Michigan sentenced much more severely than Illinois and Pennsylvania. Only in Michigan did relatively large within-state differences in severity emerge.

Cautious attempts were made to use regression analysis to ferret out factors associated with differences in severity. The most significant variable uncovered was the penitentiary size variable, and it has a good deal of intuitive appeal. Despite the strength of PENITSIZE's impact in the regression analyses, its real relationship to sentencing patterns is undoubtedly far more complicated than we can know on the basis of this limited study. More structured examinations need to be done into the role of both jail and penitentiary capacity in sentencing decisions.

Although most of the observed differences in severity occurred across states, some county-level variables also emerged in the regression analyses. Several of these (MEDIA#, CONSIDEO) suggest that the court community's political environment may have important implications for sentencing severity. Here again, however, a more refined understanding of these political linkages must await more broadly based research. The confounding effects of state-level environmental influences make conclusions concerning contextual influences more problematic. But, as noted earlier, our limited sample sites are simply too constraining to reject with any certainty the possible significance of contextual factors such as the availability of plea routing. Indeed, given the constraints upon what can be said about these various factors, perhaps the most important contribution of these analyses will be the stimulation of further debate and research. This is no small contribution because, up to this point, there has been very little discussion of these matters in the research on criminal courts.

NOTES

1. In Illinois, which has a determinate sentencing law and day-for-day sentence reduction for good behavior, all penitentiary sentences were halved. Michigan and Pennsylvania have indeterminate sentencing laws, but they also have statutory provisions that prohibit parole before the minimum sentence is served. Thus the minimum penitentiary times across all three states are meaningful and comparable. Two dispositions unique to Michigan and Pennsylvania, deferred prosecution and accelerated rehabilitative dispositions (ARDs), are comparable to probation in Illinois and were, therefore, coded 0. One last point should be noted: Kalamazoo and Dauphin had a handful of sentences in excess of one hundred years. Because

these distorted some analyses, they were recoded to twenty years, the next highest code in each of the counties.

2. Dummy variables are coded 1, 0 (or some other dichotomous scale); 1 usually depicts the presence of a given characteristic (being a Democrat, being a Protestant), while 0 usually depicts the absence of a given characteristic (not being a Democrat, not being a Protestant). Dummy variables can be used to quantify and, therefore statistically control for, a nominal scale, such as religion (Protestant, Catholic, Jew, other), political affiliation (Democrat, Republican, Independent, other), or criminal offense (murder, rape, robbery, etc.). When dealing with a set of K dummy variables that exhaust all possibilities in a data set, multiple regression permits one to enter only K-1 of the dummy variables. Entering the Kth variable does not permit a unique solution to the underlying set of simultaneous equations and adds no additional information to the analysis (Cohen and Cohen, 1974, 172–73). No additional information is added because in dummy variable analysis the B-coefficient for a given variable represents the mean value of the dependent variable for all cases belonging to the category represented by the dummy variable (the mean value for all Democrats or all Protestants, or all murder cases). The value of the intercept (A) is the mean value on the dependent variable of the cases not represented by the dummy variable. Thus, when a nominal scale has K categories represented by K-1 dummy variable, the value of the A intercept is the mean value on the dependent variable for the Kth category.

3. Before the results of this analysis are presented, a few comments are in order concerning how this sentence analysis compares with the analyses of sentence presented in chapter 8. This will be helpful in putting these results in a comparative perspective as well as in understanding what is being done here. First, although earlier analyses dealt with only a subset of offenses, here we are dealing with all offenses. We were restricted earlier to a subset of most frequent offenses because we were concerned with identifying within county clusters; here we are concerned only with deviations from pooled means and are therefore not confined to the most frequent offenses. Second, in chapter 8, we separated first offenders and repeat offenders and analyzed deviations from probation clusters and low clusters, respectively. Here we merged all offenders into one analysis and, again, examine individual deviations from pooled, offense-specific means. The reason for this is that, in order to get some parsimonious sense for general patterns of severity across counties, it is necessary to use all defendants, at least initially.

4. The analysis of minimum months of confinement was also conducted without the most extreme sentences (murder and rape cases), but the results were virtually identical.

5. An interaction term is simply a variable arrived at by multiplying two, or sometimes three, variables. For example, a two-way interaction term between media concentration and offense seriousness would be computed as follows: $MEDIA\#$ * $GRANSER1$. To test for significance of the interactive effect (i.e., that counties with more media outlets sentence more severely than others as the severity of

the offense increases), one must first "force" into the regression equation the two linear terms (*MEDIA#, GRANSER1*) then permit the interaction term to enter. The test for the interaction lies with the significance (*F* value) of the interaction term. Because of the high level of collinearity between the interaction term and the two linear terms, the *B*-coefficient of the linear terms often changes considerably when the interaction term is entered. These *B*-coefficients may become much smaller and even "flip" (reverse their sign); the *F* values often drop below acceptable levels of significance. These changes are unavoidable. However, the terms must be left in the equation in order to gauge the joint impact of the variables. To interpret the joint effect of the variables, the *B*-coefficient of all terms must be considered (i.e., if the linear term has a negative sign but the interaction term has a positive sign, the overall effect of the interaction is determined by the combination of the two terms). The significance of the interactive effect, however, depends solely on the *F* value of the interaction term (Cohen and Cohen, 1975, chapter 8). One other point that should be stressed in interpreting interaction terms is that their *B*-coefficients can be deceptively small because of the large range that can be produced by multiplying two interval variables.

6. The equation for the analysis involving all defendants is reported as follows:

$$(R^2 = .188; \text{ adjusted } R^2 = .186; n = 5,578)$$

$$JAILMIN = -2.0 - .4 * GRANSER1$$
$$(14.0; -.19)$$
$$+ 5.4 * CRIMRCD + 7.8 * PENITSIZE$$
$$(384; .24) \qquad (6.0; .05)$$
$$+ .77 * MEDIA\# - .003 * PERSCRM$$
$$(16.6; .07) \qquad (6.5; -.04)$$
$$- .15 * CONSVRTSM + 2.1 * PENITSIZE * GRANSER1$$
$$(1.4; -.02) \qquad (86.9; .51)$$
$$+ .003 * CONSERVTSM * GRANSER1$$
$$(10.6; .05)$$

It is quite similar to the equation involving just repeat offenders, with one general exception. The interaction effects are not as strong. Indeed two of the four (those involving *MEDIA#* and *PERSCRM*) drop out altogether. This, of course, suggests that what is particularly effective in stimulating environmental influences are both serious cases *and* defendants with long criminal records.

7. The regression equation for all guilty plea cases is reported as follows:

$$(R^2 = .18; \text{ adjusted } R^2 = .18; n = 5,578)$$

$$JAILMIN = 3.4 + .76 * GRANSER1$$
$$(85.1; .36)$$

$$+ 5.4 * CRIMRCD + 1.6 * JUDGSENT$$
$$(38.3; .24) \qquad (3.4; .03)$$

$$- .75 * ROUTING - 1.1 * CONCLEVEL$$
$$(1.0; -.02) \qquad (8.5; -.05)$$

$$- .50 * ROUTING * GRANSER1$$
$$(65.6; -.19)$$

$$+ .07 * CONCLEVEL * GRANSER1$$
$$(4.9; .08)$$

This equation is somewhat similar to the one for just repeat offenders, but there are also important differences. One concerns the CONCLEVEL variable. It did not have a significant linear impact upon severity and, unlike in Equation 10.2, it has a *positive* interaction with GRANSER1. It seems safe to conclude from these differences that CONCLEVEL makes a meaningful difference only in repeat offender cases. Counties that differ in charge concession practices may not differ much in how first offenders are handled. Also, the JUDGSENT variable, although mildly positive as hypothesized, is not statistically significant, nor is the interaction term with GRANSER1.

REFERENCE

Cohen, Jacob, and Patricia Cohen. 1975. *Applied Multiple Regression/Correlation Analysis for the Behavioral Sciences.* New York: John Wiley and Sons.

IV

INDIVIDUALS IN THE GUILTY PLEA PROCESS

11

CRIMINAL COURT ACTORS AND THE GUILTY PLEA PROCESS: THEORETICAL OBSERVATIONS AND ANALYTICAL APPROACHES

The severity analysis in chapter 10 notwithstanding, our efforts to examine and assess the guilty plea process have been largely devoted to the discussion, development, and analysis of a set of measures that tap charge and sentence consistency. Despite a handful of contrary findings and some deviant counties, the empirical analyses revealed a surprisingly high level of consistency in the plea process in these middle-sized jurisdictions, especially in light of what we are led to expect by concessions-oriented critiques of plea bargaining. Moreover, with the exception of bail status—the impact of which is subject to multiple interpretations—none of the consistency indicators routinely revealed bias or vindictiveness in the manner in which concessions were alloted. This leads to the suggestion that the charge reductions and sentence disparities that do exist in these counties are not, in large part, the result of illegitimate or unjustifiable factors such as racial bias, bargaining strength, socioeconomic status, and sexism. Rather, they may be due, in large measure, to legitimate efforts to tailor dispositions to meet the needs or equities of individual cases, leading to idiosyncratic deviations, not patterned ones.

Such a conclusion is premature. We have not yet examined one extremely important possible source of patterned, illegitimate influences upon the plea process, influences emanating from the principal criminal court actors. What might be interpreted, on the basis of prior analyses, as unpatterned discrepancies resulting from good faith efforts to individualize justice may, in fact, be attributable to the decision makers involved in handling the case. That is, to the extent that the beliefs, attitudes, and operating styles of these actors systematically affect the allocation of reductions and disparities within the plea process, then they cannot be interpreted as the result of good faith efforts aimed at tailoring the disposition to fit the circumstances of the defendant and the cases. Rather, such a pattern would suggest that who handles the case can be as important as what it involves.

That the attributes of individual actors should systematically affect the disposition of cases in a system imbued with as much discretion as the criminal process is not beyond plausibility. A range of justifiable charges exists in many situations, and there are few legal checks on prosecutorial discretion. It is not unimaginable that different prosecutors in the same county could approach charging and charge reduction in systematically different ways. Much the same can be said about sentencing. Many different and conflicting sentencing goals exist, and reasonable minds can differ over what type of sentence is required to attain any one goal. Thus, it can be expected that actors of different persuasions could systematically generate different patterns of outcomes.

Despite the reasonableness of these expectations, and the importance of these notions to the thought of many judicial scholars, no significant body of corroborated empirical evidence exists that supports the proposition that the attributes of these actors are strong determinants of outcomes in plea cases (or any other type of cases). This dearth of evidence is due, in part, to the complexities of measuring and detecting such influences and in part to the relative infancy of empirical investigation in this area. In truth, not much is systematically known one way or the other about the role of these actors.

The availability here of a large amount of data on individual actors in a variety of different court systems makes it possible for us to contribute to the existing body of literature in a fairly rigorous and systematic fashion. The significance of these analyses is enhanced when the fairly orderly picture that emerges from earlier analyses presented here is contrasted with both conventional wisdom and learned theoretical speculation concerning the role of criminal court actors in a setting of almost unbridled discretion. Thus, this and the next chapter will be devoted to addressing the impact of these actors upon the allocation of charge concessions and sentencing disparities in guilty plea cases. We want to get a better understanding of the magnitude of their impact and the types of attributes that are most important in understanding the allocation of "breaks"— symbolic or otherwise. We also want to enhance our understanding of the conditions under which individuals are most likely to make a difference in the formation of plea packages.

In structuring our analysis of the role of decision makers in the plea process, we separate judges and prosecutors from defense attorneys because they are quite different sets of actors that require distinctively different approaches. Almost without exception judges and most prosecutors are full-time public actors given formal control over very important decisions in the criminal process (charging, ruling on motions, deciding guilt or innocence, sentencing). They are vested with virtually unfettered discretion in making those decisions. While both are charged with the very diffuse responsibility of serving the state, albeit in different ways, neither has a specific client who must be satisfied in every case.

The situation of defense counsel is quite different and considerably more complex. Unlike judges and prosecutors, they have no direct control over most fundamental decisions that affect the plea process. Moreover, they are a more diverse lot organizationally. Some are paid publicly, and some are retained privately. Among those who are paid publicly, some are full-time public defenders, some are part-time defenders, still others are appointed counsel. All have a specific client who is likely to be markedly affected by the outcome of the case. Also the relationship of these defense attorneys to the court community varies considerably. Full-time public defenders are as much a part of the court community as prosecutors; nonregular defense attorneys have a much more distant relationship. These different roles and relationships raise substantively different questions concerning the role of the defense attorney that require a somewhat different analytic approach.[1]

JUDGES AND PROSECUTORS

Because of the important powers and wide discretion vested in the public actors, much of the historical concern over the role of individual influences upon the criminal process has focused upon them, especially judges. Judges have been the center of attention because of the presumption, often mistaken, that they are the most influential actors in the dispositional process. This is especially true because most earlier research on the role of individuals has been concerned with the sentencing decision, where the judge is believed to be paramount because of his or her formal authority. As late as 1974, Gaylin, for example, asserted that "Sentencing is the province of the judge. It is he who decides whether the convicted man will be allowed to return to his everyday life, relatively free of punishment, whether he will be fined an insignificant or a crippling amount, whether he will go to jail and the amount of time that he will spend there" (15).

This emphasis, of course, ignores the role of the prosecutor (as well as the defense attorney) in sentencing, a role that can be very significant in the plea process of some counties. Also, if we broaden our theoretical perspective to include the charging decision, then the importance of the prosecutor is even greater. The prosecutor's formal powers over charging are similar to the judge's formal sentencing power. Because of the rough similarities between the formal position of the judge and prosecutor, and the dearth of work on the role of individual prosecutors, we will be largely concerned here with a brief review of thought as it has developed with respect to the judges. In many respects, it can be directly extended to prosecutors; in others, some modifications will be required.

The role of judicial influences upon the dispositional process has usually been presumed to be quite significant. For example, in his landmark study of judicial attitudes upon sentencing Hogarth notes that:

> A universal criticism of sentencing is the apparent disparity of sentences imposed by different judges for cases which do not appear to be substantially different from one another. The imposition of unequal sentences for the same offence, or for offences of comparable seriousness, without a clearly visible justification, amounts, in the public mind, to judicial caprice. Accused and counsel openly "jockey" for lenient judges and the notion that the criminal justice system is fairly and evenly applied is thereby shown to be a myth. The report of the President's Commission on Law Enforcement quotes, with approval, the statement made by Mr. Justice Jackson, when he was Attorney-General of the United States: "It is obviously repugnant to one's sense of justice that the judgement meted out to an offender should depend in large part on a purely fortuitous circumstance; namely, the personality of the particular judge before whom the case happens to come for disposition." (1971, 6)

Gaylin, somewhat more colorfully, notes that:

> A judge is, even on the bench, a human being, and therefore subject to the same lack of controls and disciplines as are we all. If the conditions of his life outside the court can introduce factors that will influence his decisions, so can his exposure to the defendants in the court produce emotions which modify judgment. This can generate compassion, identification, sympathy, but also antagonisms. More often than not these can be buried and hidden from view but, buried or not, they will be reflected in his decisions on sentences. Consciously or unconsciously, the animosity that may develop during this period can find the satisfaction of retribution to a degree beyond what most of us are allowed in satisfying our personal hostilities. What is interesting is how many cases there are where even with the knowledge of this awesome power

to strike his offender down, the judge simply cannot control his own passions. (1974, 40)

Consequently, "Whatever pettiness, whatever malice, bigotry, fear, paranoia, resentment, vengefulness, and spite are generated in hearts of men can be demonstrated in the sentencing decisions of judges" (1974, 42). Many of these allegations could be extended to prosecutors, especially in counties where they control the sentencing decision in plea cases.

To document the significance of such factors, Gaylin engaged in some in-depth interviews with a set of judges, and he analyzes some of the differences in the way that they approach sentencing. However, he never bothers to examine whether these differences in perspective are translated into actions. Instead he merely contends that "There is no question that the simplest computer program could define a consistent pattern of sentencing which would separate these four judges. That means that any one defendant, independent of his personal history and his particular crime, will be meted out a punishment based on the idiocyncrasies of the particular judge into whose hands he is delivered. There will be considerable differences" (1974, 163).

Gauging Decision-Maker Impact

Gaylin's sanguine attitude is not shared by most who have actually attempted to document empirically the impact of judges' personal attributes upon sentencing. Most such studies, especially earlier ones, have failed to support adequately the view that differences in judges' attributes make much of a difference in sentencing.

We will not pause here to review the earlier research on this question. It ranges from the earlier, simplistic work of Gaudet (1938; 1946) and Green (1961) to the more sophisticated work of Hogarth (1971), Gibson (1977; 1978; 1979; 1980; 1981) and others. Several reviews of these works already exist and will not be repeated here.[2] Our primary concern lies with what prior studies, and critiques of them, tell us about what is needed for a thorough assessment of the impact of judges and, by extension, prosecutors upon the charging and sentencing decision in plea cases. Although we are less concerned here with contributing to the development of theory on judicial decision making, we need to learn from this literature in order to avoid the pitfalls that have hampered earlier efforts. Overly simplistic assumptions and approaches that have hampered prior efforts to explain judicial decision making will have an equally deleterious effect upon our effort to assess these actors' roles in the allocation of charge reductions and sentencing disparities.

Early research into judicial attributes and decision making was plagued by the researcher's failure to obtain independent measures of judicial attitudes and overly simplistic theoretical models that posited a direct relationship between attitudes and decisions. Glendon Schubert (1965; 1974) developed a more sophisticated theoretical model of judicial behavior, one that began to recognize the interaction between judicial attitudes and case stimuli. This is crucial because, as Gibson notes in a review essay that closely parallels the approach we took into our fieldwork:

> Attitudes alone cannot determine behavior; before attitudes even become relevant, they must be stimulated. Consequently, there has long been a concern for the influence on decisions of stimuli emanating from the cases themselves.
>
> Judges' attitudes specify the substantive objectives—what they prefer to do—but that is not all there is to the process of decision making. Some sort of decision-making process or framework or formula must also be established. Specifically, decision makers must create a stable decision-making framework that specifies the sources and types of relevant information and the rule or procedure through which the information is weighted and combined to form a decision. The imperative for forming such a framework derives primarily from resource shortages—especially time and information—which compel decision makers to adopt economical and standardized processes. The decisional formula directs the decision maker to reliable and readily available informational sources, or cues. (1983, 13, 15)

Thus, meshing of facts and attitudes is the first step toward developing a more refined understanding of the role of judicial attributes in decision making. But the recognition of the role of facts as stimuli also underscores the inadequacy of a simplistic attitude-fact model of decision making. Almost every decision-making situation is likely to involve a complex set of facts that is likely to evoke conflicting responses. These facts may emanate from the case at hand or the context of the decision. In any event, the attitude-fact model of decision making is unable, by itself, to provide insights into how these conflicting stimuli are integrated into a decision. It cannot tell us how conflicting facts are normatively evaluated and blended into a situation.

What can perform this function is role theory. It can be integrated with attitude theory to produce a more sophisticated model of the role of individuals in decision making because, in Gibson's terms:

> Role theory provides a useful way of understanding the manner in which these normative prescriptions and proscriptions influence behavior. Role theory begins from the premise that individuals acting in relative isolation act differently from how they act in a context,

and thus role theory provides a means of moving beyond an exclusive focus on individuals to consider the influence of the institutional constraints on decision making. Contexts are always associated with expectations emanating from others who share the context. All social behavior is contextual and therefore constrained at least in part by expectations. Behavior within institutions, as a subset of social behavior, is especially sensitive to these contextual influences. Institutions typically have formal and relatively explicit informal expectations that are reinforced through incentive and sanctioning mechanisms. Institutional expectations always serve to limit choice and discretion on the part of the members of the institution. Thus, according to role theory, the ways in which individuals accommodate themselves to the institutional expectations affect their institutional behavior. (1983, 17)

In other words how a decision maker views his or her role or, stated differently, approaches his or her role-specific tasks, is likely to affect what attitudes are evoked and what facts are most likely to be the most potent stimuli. Other factors are also relevant. Perhaps the most important of these is personality type. Differences in such traits as self-esteem, willingness to innovate, styles of leadership and interpersonal relationships, and receptivity to role expectations can have a direct effect upon decisions in some cases. In others they can affect the impact of a decision-maker's preferences upon decisions, especially group decisions. Also important are factors emanating from the institutional context, such as the court community's infrastructure, and environmental constraints, such as political or legal culture (Gibson, 1983, 27-32). Our concern with these will be restricted to contextual factors. Their role is much more direct, and we have already discussed a number of structural variants that have direct implications for the exercise of discretion by judges and prosecutors.

Analyzing Judge and Prosecutor Effects

What does this brief review mean for our effort to assess the impact of judge and prosecutor attributes? On a very basic level, it means that an analysis of simple correlations between decision-maker attributes and our measures of charge reduction and sentence is not likely to yield definitive results concerning the role of individuals in the plea process. Rather these attributes will have to be analyzed in conjunction with other factors that are likely to stimulate them, and/or that constrain (or enhance) the impact of the decision-makers' preferences. Also, in conducting the analyses and interpreting the results, we must be sensitive to the contextual and environmental factors that envelope the plea process in the different counties.

In more concrete terms, the analysis of judges and prosecutors upon the formation of plea packages will be organized as follows. We will begin at a very basic level by estimating the simple linear impact of each actor upon the charge reduction and sentence measures in plea cases. While this simple, straightforward approach will not yield conclusive results, it is a necessary beginning point. Moreover, if done properly, the basic linear results will be of great interest to those who are concerned that the idiosyncrasies of the decision makers are a blatant source of inconsistencies within the plea process. If "who you get" is as important as "what you did," many of the niceties just noted may be irrelevant for the simple purposes of assessing the impact of these actors upon the plea process. If large, broadly based effects exist, they will be evident from the outset.

Two different methods will be used to assess linear impacts. The first is a dummy variable approach. Using analysis of covariance with appropriate control variables, a set of dummy variables depicting each relevant actor (judge or prosecutor) in a county will be entered into the second stage of the regression (after the control variables). The contribution of this set of dummy variables to the R^2 will determine the maximum linear contribution of that set of actors for the county under examination.

The dummy variable analysis can yield insights into the relative importance (in R^2 terms) of the decision makers, but it does not tell us much about the characteristics of the decision maker that are important. Nor are the dummy variables of much use in the more sophisticated, interactive analyses suggested earlier. Therefore, a second method to be used in gauging the linear effects of decision-maker attributes will employ a set of attitudinal and background measures that tap specific traits. The most relevant attitudinal measures for these purposes are the Belief in Punishment and the Regard for Due Process measures described in chapter 3 and Appendix I.

Judges and prosecutors who hold strong views on the utility of punishment would be less likely to yield sentencing concessions and more likely to react to situational factors they view as requiring sentences above the norm. Judges and prosecutors with a less strong Belief in Punishment are likely to be "set off" by far fewer factors. The same views may carry over into charge reductions. To the extent that these views are strong enough to overcome the strength of established norms and the pulls of routine, significant differences should emerge across judges. The expected impact of Regard for Due Process is somewhat more ambiguous but is worth pursuing nonetheless. On the one hand, we could posit that a high Regard for Due Process would lead to closer adherence to established norms (i.e., justice is equivalent to getting the standard package). On the other hand, one could argue that actors with a high Regard for Due Process would be more likely to acquiesce in arrangements whereby the defendant actually received some type of concession. Those with a low Regard for Due Process may be more inclined to be manipulative and coercive in the use of the levers that they control. Thus, these actors, especially prosecutors, can be expected to press for advantage whenever they can, leading to more severe sentences and fewer charge reductions.

Although some view background variables as surrogates for values and attitudes (Gibson, 1983, 25), these variables do constitute more concrete measures of interpersonal differences. Also, several are of some intrinsic interest. Thus, we will also examine the linear effects of a small set of these variables. For judges, we will examine the effect of their political affiliation, their length on the bench, the extent of their ties to the community, and whether or not they were ever a prosecutor. For prosecutors, we will be concerned with the same variables, except for the variable depicting prior status as a prosecutor. The political affiliation measures are relevant because conventional wisdom holds that Republicans would be less defendant-oriented than Democrats. The tenure in office variable is of interest because newer members may feel a greater need to prove themselves to colleagues by being tougher, especially in the case of prosecutors. Actors with strong local ties, and judges who were previously prosecutors, may be more community oriented than others, and less inclined to yield real breaks.

The next phase of the analysis will introduce case factors as stimuli and examine whether they interact with some of the decision-maker attributes in affecting the charge and sentence measures. Although this will make the interpretation of the analyses more complex, this type of analysis is more likely to yield a truer picture of the decision-maker's role in the plea process, as our brief review of the literature makes clear. We could not claim to have made an in-depth examination of their role without introducing these more involved analyses.

Although the number of case characteristics that may act as stimuli is formidable, we limited ourselves to a handful of factors that prior analyses suggested might be most important. For the *charge reduction* analysis, we will look to the existence of a multicount indictment, the defendant's prior record, and the defendant's bail status. The multicount indictment variable is important because without more than one count the options of the decision maker are more limited. With several counts pending, more can be done by those inclined to offer charge reductions. The defendant's prior record and bail status are important because they impart something about the gravity of the case and his or her bargaining position. Some people may view some defendants as not meriting a reduction, or at least in no position to demand one.

The prior record and bail status variables will also be employed in the *sentencing analysis,* for similar reasons. Instead of the multicount indictment variable, however, we will use offense seriousness in an interaction term with the various attribute measures. Offense seriousness is important because emotions run deeper in such cases, and there is more latitude for manipulation. If the going rate for an offense is two to three months in the county jail, not much downward pressure can be exerted, certainly not as much as when the norm is between fifty and sixty months. Moreover, while beliefs about appropriate punishments may not be very relevant in the handling of minor offenses, they may be very important in serious ones.

The third phase of the analysis will introduce other attributes of the decision makers as a factor affecting the translation of their preferences into actions. Our prior discussion of both role perception and personality type suggests that some decision makers may be more likely than others to see their preferences reflected in decisions, especially when those decisions are made jointly. We have several measures that are relevant here and that can provide some insights into the role of the judge and prosecutor within the plea process. One that is common to both is our measure of Machiavellianism (see chapter 3). As noted earlier, high Machs are more manipulative and purposeful in getting what they want. Thus, high Machs who also had strong views about punishment would be expected to be more successful in translating their preferences into sentences in plea cases.

Another relevant attribute common to both judges and prosecutors is our measure of Responsiveness (see chapter 3). Responsiveness refers to the extent to which individuals accommodate the needs of others. Judges and lawyers often feel they are a part of a larger courthouse community, identify with its fortunes, and think it is in their long-run interests to respect local practices and customs. At times these attachments override formal role expectations and personal preferences, prompting responsive actors to deal pragmatically with others in order to preserve amicable ties within the courthouse. Thus the individual views of more responsive actors may be less salient than those of less responsive ones.

Two-role specific measures are also relevant here. One important difference across judges is the extent to which they involve themselves in pretrial negotiations. Whereas some judges keep their distance from pretrial proceedings, others spurn this traditional hands-off role and actively immerse themselves in working out the details of dispositions. Greater involvement by judges, as well as anticipation of their involvement by attorneys, means that their sentencing views probably will be incorporated more directly in plea packages than those of their aloof brethren who remain above the fray. Therefore, our measure of Judicial Involvement (see chapter 3) should play an important mediating role between preferences and outcomes. An equally important attribute for prosecutors is their trial competence. In many cases the failure to resolve a case successfully through plea discussions means that a trial may result. A prosecutor's reputation as a skilled trial attorney, therefore, may be an important bargaining resource in the negotiations. More skilled prosecutors may well be able to realize their preferences than less skilled ones, resulting in longer sentences and fewer reductions.

Table 11.1 summarizes the logic and structure of the planned analyses for judges and prosecutors.

Integrating Contextual Factors

While Table 11.1 is useful in summarizing the basic thrust of our planned analyses, it says little about how the contextual factors will be integrated into the decision-maker analyses. We know from earlier chapters that there is a good deal of variance with respect to these factors and that they can be influential. But we also know from chapter 10 the types of constraints that exist in doing truly rigorous comparative research with only nine sites. Thus, we are able only to look at the pattern of findings that result from the county-by-county analyses and compare them with the basic contextual features of the counties in the hopes that useful insights will emerge.

If we look at the prior analyses (especially those reported in chapters 9 and 10) in light of the present task, several contextual factors seem to be most relevant. They relate primarily to prosecutorial charging practices, the prosecutor's centralization of plea offers, the structure of the plea agenda, and the dominant pattern of charge reduction in the county. Not all of these factors are relevant for each analysis, but each gives rise to certain expectations about whether individuals are likely to make much of a difference on a particular aspect of the plea process in a county. Table 11.2 summarizes these data.

In row 1 of Table 11.2, we report charging practices as measured by the incidence of multicount indictments. Where a relatively high level of multicount indictments exists, individual prosecutors have more leeway in plea discussions. Thus, a greater potential for decision-maker impact exists for prosecutors in the area of charge reduction. The incidence of multicount indictments is highest in Montgomery, Erie, and DuPage, followed by Peoria, Oakland, and Saginaw.

Prosecutor policies affecting plea offers must be considered because some offices severely restrict the discretion of trial assistants, discretion that is essential if large discrepancies across individuals are to emerge. DuPage, for example, had a committee that set all plea offers—charge and sentence. Any deviation from that offer had to be approved by the committee. A formal review of all dispositions served as a check against departures from the bottom line. Kalamazoo had an equally elaborate, centralized system for restricting

Table 11.1. **Logic and Structure of the Judge and Prosecutor Analyses**

Phase 1: Linear Analyses	Phase 2: Interactive Analyses, Case Stimuli Measures		Phase 3: Interactive Analyses, Other Decision-maker Attributes	
Judge and prosecutor dummy variable analysis Analysis of Belief in Punishment, Regard for Due Process, and Social Background Measures	*Charge Concession Analysis* Belief in Punishment, Regard for Due Process, with a) existence of a multi-count indictment b) defendant's prior record c) defendant's pretrial confinement status	*Sentence Disparity Analysis* Belief in Punishment, Regard for Due Process, with a) offense seriousness b) defendant's prior record c) defendant's pretrial confinement status	*Judges* Belief in Punishment, Regard for Due Process, with a) Machiavellianism b) responsiveness c) involvement	*Prosecutors* Belief in Punishment, Regard for Due Process, with a) Machiavellianism b) responsiveness c) trial competence

Table 11.2. **The Structure of the Guilty Plea Process, by County**

	DuPage	Peoria	St. Clair	Oakland	Kalamazoo	Saginaw	Mont-gomery	Dauphin	Erie
Charging practices, (percent of cases involving multicount indictments)	45	38	21	35	16	34	70	27	48
Prosecutor policies affecting plea offers	Highly central-ized	Central-ized	Laissez-faire	Central-ized	Highly central-ized	Laissez-faire	Laissez-faire	Central-ized	Laissez-faire
Locus of sentencing power in guilty plea cases	Attor-neys	Attor-neys	Mixed	Judge	Attor-neys	Attor-neys	Attor-neys	Mixed	Judge
Availability and use of plea routing	Not avail-able	Not avail-able	Limited	Not avail-able	Not avail-able	Not avail-able	Wide-spread	Wide-spread	Limited
Dominant pattern of charge reductions	Sym-bolic	Mid-dling	Mid-dling	Mid-dling	Minimal-ist	Maximal-ist	Symbolic	Minimal-ist	Symbolic

the discretion of assistants. Initial offers were set in the warrant office, and systematic, numerical evaluations of the viability of the cases were made at different points during the case. Moreover, all charge reductions had to be approved by the "hard-nosed" chief of the criminal division. Peoria, Oakland, and Dauphin also had centralized plea-offer systems, but they were not as elaborate as those in DuPage and Kalamazoo; they largely involved a supervisor approving all offers before a plea agreement could be finalized. The remaining counties had what could be termed laissez-faire systems. Large amounts of discretion were vested in individual assistants, who were normally guided by only the most general policies. The impact of assistant prosecutors is expected to be greater in these counties (St. Clair, Saginaw, Montgomery, Erie) because the assistants are not constrained by any significant centripetal influences.

Just as important as the degree of discretion enjoyed by assistant prosecutors is the locus of sentencing power in plea cases. In some counties, prosecutors and defense attorneys agree on both charge and sentence, and judges routinely respect the agreement. In other counties, either because of prosecutorial policies or the judges' refusal to relinquish their prerogatives, sentence agreements are not the norm. An understanding of the locus of the sentencing power in a county's plea process is important because it affects expectations concerning which actor (the judge or prosecutor) is likely to make the most difference, as well as how much difference. For example, if assistant prosecutors cannot agree to sentences, we would not expect their views to make much of a difference in sentencing. On the other hand, if judges had a free hand in sentencing (i.e., they set sentences after the plea was formally entered), we would expect that their effect would be greatly magnified.

Row 3 of Table 11.2 shows that sentencing agreements are the norm in DuPage, Peoria, Kalamazoo, Saginaw, and Montgomery. The judges in Erie refused to accept sentencing agreements, and those in Dauphin usually refused specific sentencing commitments. The head prosecutor in Oakland did not permit his assistants to agree to specific sentences, whereas in St. Clair, sentencing agreements were only discouraged. St. Clair assistants were strictly forbidden to agree to probation, but they were permitted where a sentence agreement was essential to a plea involving incarceration. Perhaps most interesting is a comparison of row 3 with row 2; the latter shows information on plea centralization. Only Saginaw, Montgomery, and, to some extent, St. Clair, have laissez-faire prosecutorial policies combined with significant prosecutorial control over sentence agreements. In every other county, the discretion of assistant prosecutors is checked by the centralized plea policies of the office or by the judge's control over sentences, an observation to which we will return.

Another important characteristic of county plea systems is the availability and use of plea routing. Plea routing enables the attorneys to route a case that is to be pleaded to a judge of choice, one who will either be favorable to the agreement or one to whom the defense attorney can go with a blind plea (i.e., a plea with no sentence agreement). This is important because, in counties where judges can be selected, the plea agenda is quite different. Bargaining resources may be expended in getting the right judge, and therefore more concrete concessions, such as charge reductions, may be less frequent. Plea routing is not available in systems that employ individual calendars. It is frequently available where a master calendar is used, but even then in some counties a court administrator has control over the flow of cases to judges and impedes the routing process. Untrammeled plea routing occurred in only two counties, Montgomery and Dauphin (see Table 11.2), and the identity of the judge was a major component of most plea agreements in both counties. This observation was particularly important in Montgomery because, due to prosecutorial discretion and control over sentencing, the role of prosecutors could be expected to be most clear in that county.

Finally, the role of charge reductions in plea cases must be noted. Analyses of the incidence of such reductions—primary charge reductions and secondary county drops—in our nine counties revealed four dominant patterns (see Tables 8.9 and 8.10). Dauphin and Kalamazoo were characterized as minimalist counties because they have a very low incidence of primary charge reductions (5-13 percent) and a low incidence of count drops (9-13 percent). DuPage, Montgomery, and Erie were characterized as symbolic counties because, although they had a low incidence of primary charge reductions (9-13 percent), they had a high incidence of count drops (38-59 percent). Peoria, St. Clair, and Oakland were termed middling counties because they had moderate rates of primary charge reductions (17-21 percent) and moderate rates of count drops (22-38 percent). Saginaw was labeled a maximalist county because more than 43 percent of its plea cases involved a primary charge reduction, and 38 percent had some type of count drop.

These differences are important for the present analysis because factors that restrict the granting of charge reductions, or lead to the use of largely symbolic count reductions, can affect the impact of decision makers. Where charge reductions are more widespread, we would expect the role of decision makers to be greater.

DEFENSE ATTORNEYS

At first glance one would think that the approach developed with respect to judges and prosecutors could be simply extended to assess the impact that defense attorney attributes had upon the plea process, using the subset of attorneys for which data were available. Measures such as Belief in Punishment, Machiavellianism, and Trial Competence could be seen as having similar import for their machinations. Unfortunately, such an extension would obscure several important points. First, while the judges and prosecutors are decision makers, at least with respect to those aspects of the process with which we are concerned, defense attorneys are not. Only the prosecutor can actually file new charges, and only the judge can officially impose sentences. It would be naive to think that defense attorneys played no role in these decisions. But it would be equally naive to blindly extend an approach designed to assess the impact of decision makers to actors who play a more indirect role.[3]

Also, to focus primarily on the preferences and attitudes of the defense attorneys would be to ignore those concerns that have historically preoccupied criminal court scholars: the effect of the defense attorney's ties to the court community upon case outcomes. The defense bar is structured quite differently from the judicial and the prosecutorial subcomponents of the court community, which are dominated by regulars. The urbanization of America has permitted some private attorneys to specialize in the practice of criminal law, and the establishment of indigent defense systems has resulted in a regulars' defense bar in many areas. But its size and importance varies considerably from system to system. In some, regulars dominate criminal defense practice, in others a large number of "one timers" play a significant role. In every instance, however, there will be much more variance in the defense attorneys' ties to the court community than is the case with judges and prosecutors.

These developments have led observers to question how well the clients of different types of attorneys fare in the plea process. Interestingly, they have come to markedly different conclusions with respect to this question. One view that has emerged views regular defense attorneys, or insiders, as manipulators of the plea process whose clients benefit by their machinations; another sees insiders as "cop-out artists" who betray their clients' interests. Both are clearly concession-oriented perspectives on the plea process; they differ simply in the direction of the deviations they predict. The third view sees regulars as creators and protectors of routine and is a consensus-oriented perspective. Unfortunately, the little empirical work that has been done in this area has not clarified matters.[4] A brief review of the different perspectives will facilitate our efforts to assess the impact of defense attorneys.

Defense Attorneys and the Plea Process

In the view of those who consider defense attorneys as manipulators, attorneys who have close ties to the local court community take advantage of their personal relationships with judges and prosecutors, as well as their political connections, to obtain maximum consideration for their clients. These ties are their stock-in-trade since, according to this view, the attorneys are sorely lacking in professional skills and knowledge. In return for the favorable treatment they receive, these attorneys are expected to make campaign contributions to individual judges, or the local party, and/or distribute graft among the various public actors in the system.

This perspective was first put forward by the pioneers of empirical research in criminal courts, the crime survey researchers.[5] These surveys, conducted in a variety of American cities and counties during the 1920s, were an attempt to diagnose the ills of American criminal justice through extensive empirical examinations of a variety of criminal justice agencies, including the courts. In the first crime survey, *Criminal Justice in Cleveland*, Reginald Heber Smith and Herbert B. Ehrmann described the connection they found between the "professional criminal lawyer" and the prevailing ills of the justice system:

> Another factor to be considered . . . is the professional criminal lawyer. A poll of the bar of Cleveland shows that most lawyers dislike criminal practice, partly because of a feeling that it is detrimental to civil practice and partly because of professional ignorance or dislike of the required technique. The result is that a large part of the lucrative practice in the criminal courts goes to a small number of special-ists. . . . Moreover, many of this small group of professional criminal lawyers are in politics. Were the system as invulnerable as Achilles, these political criminal lawyers would find the penetrable heel. (1921, 233-34)

One need not go as far back as the 1920s to uncover concern that insiders are manipulating the system of justice to the benefit of their clients and themselves. In many ways, such a view reflects today's conventional wisdom concerning how at least some criminal courts work. Although this conventional wisdom may have its roots in the findings reported in the crime surveys, as well as personal experiences—or, more likely, reports of others' experiences—it is reenforced from time to time in highly publicized scandals. None, however, reached the magnitude of the recent multiyear undercover investigation in Cook County, Illinois, popularly referred to as Operation Greylord.[6] As Andrew H. Malcolm noted in the *New York Times*:

> Suspicions—assumptions might be more accurate—of court corruption have long permeated life in Chicago and encompassing Cook County as a whole. "You'd see the same defense attorneys appearing before the same judge over and over," recalled a local political veteran who asked

not to be identified, "and that same judge seemed to find for that defense attorney over and over again. And you'd wonder. But a few suspicions are not very powerful in a place like this."

Chicago did not invent the political mixture of patronage and the judiciary, but it did perfect it. Judges were handpicked for election or appointment by the ruling Democrats in a secret "slate-making" session, a delicate process of balancing Chicago's myriad political sectors. Often, a position on the slate was a reward for party work. . . . If a relative or a friend was charged with some infraction, a phone call "downtown" could see that the case was assigned to a "friendly" judge, someone who understood how things worked. And this system also seemed susceptible to corruption by the large amounts of money associated with the growth in narcotics trade. (Dec. 18, 1983, 17)

Underlying the notion that the clients of regular defense attorneys do better than the clients of others is the assumption that the advantages enjoyed by these insiders (or the favors owed them) will be translated into benefits for their clients. This assumption was challenged in a series of works that began to appear in the late 1960s.[7] These expounded a view of the courts as quasi-autonomous, self-perpetuating organizations to which regular defense attorneys, both private and public, have close ties. This view promoted the idea of regulars as cop-out artists who "sold out" their clients. In such a system, the quality of the attorneys' work life, as well as their standard of living, depends heavily on their relations with co-workers. In exchange for benefits accruing to them, benefits controlled by judges and prosecutors, these regulars have to perform a function: to sell their clients on a deal worked out with the permanent members of the work group. Because of the ties and indebtedness to their co-workers, most of the negotiating done by regulars is with their clients. Outsiders are not encumbered by such ties and obligations. Also, because the regulars frequently do not have exceptional trial skills, or indeed any other professional resources with which to enhance their bargaining power, prosecutors are less pliable in their negotiations with them. Both factors translate into bargaining advantages for nonregulars, leading to the expectation of better deals for their clients.

Albert Alschuler, in one of his classic articles on plea bargaining, addresses the role of the criminal defense bar in depth and adds some refinements that are important for rigorous empirical analysis. "[Plea bargaining] subjects defense attorneys to serious temptations to disregard their clients' interests — temptations so strong that the invocation of professional ideals cannot begin to answer the problems that emerge. Today's guilty-plea system leads even able, conscientious, and highly motivated attorneys to make decisions that are not really in their clients' interests"

(1975, 1180). To understand how this happens, one must distinguish between public defenders and private practitioners and understand the economics of private criminal practice. With respect to private attorneys, Alschuler notes that:

> There are two basic ways to achieve financial success in the practice of criminal law. One is to develop, over an extended period of time, a reputation as an outstanding trial lawyer. . . . If, however, one lacks the ability or the energy to succeed in this way or if one is in a greater hurry, there is a second path to personal wealth — handling a large volume of cases for less-than-spectacular fees. The way to handle a large volume of cases is, of course, not to try them but to plead them.
>
> These two divergent approaches to economic success can, in fact, be combined. Houston defense attorney Percy Foreman observed that the "optimum situation" for an economically motivated lawyer would be to take one highly publicized case to trial each year and then to enter guilty pleas in all the rest. (1975, 1182)

This observation leads Alschuler to distinguish between the more conscientious members of the regular criminal defense bar and the writ runners, pleaders, or cop-out artists. It is this latter group that is most likely to be indebted to the permanent members of the court community and who do the greatest disservice to their clients. The attorneys whom Alschuler interviewed were unanimous in the belief that these cop-out artists compromised a significant portion of most defense bars. While attorneys' estimates of the number of cop-out artists varied from jurisdiction to jurisdiction, their large clientele made them a significant force — and a significant problem (Alschuler, 1975, 1184-85).

In addition to distinguishing between types of private attorneys, Alschuler distinguishes public attorneys from private ones. Unfortunately, Alschuler makes no direct comparison between the various types of private attorneys he identifies and public defenders. It is clear from his discussion, however, that the clients of public defenders will not necessarily do worse than those of all private attorneys, especially considering the systematic differences in the types of cases they handle (Alschuler, 1975, 1206-24). In short, Alschuler believes that an average public defender may do better than the private cop-out artist, but less well than the more competent private attorney. However, when making comparisons across roles, attention must be given to both the individual traits of the attorneys and the type of indigent defense system. These individual and contextual factors aside, the ambiguity surrounding the issue of how public defenders fare relative to others is largely institutional. In Alschuler's view, while the public defender is "subject to many of the same pressures and temptations as the private attorney, he is free of others; and he also confronts some pressures, problems, temptations, limitations, and opportunities of his own. His institutional position apparently gives him both advantages and disadvantages in the plea-bargaining process" (1975, 1210).

In his analysis of these advantages and disadvantages, Alschuler contends that public attorneys are not subject to the economic pressures that lead private attorneys to engage in trade-outs (selling out the interests of one client for another). They are, however, saddled with a heavy caseload that they must move, and that may make it more difficult to secure favors (1975, 1211-19, 1223). This heavy caseload also leads to a good deal of interactions with prosecutors, which in turn may lead to a mutual perception of how cases should be handled, as well as to feelings of mutual trust. Alschuler quotes Edward Bennett Williams, who analogized the public defender/prosecutor situation to one involving two wrestlers who fight one another every night in different cities (1975, 1210). Their primary concern is that no one gets hurt too badly. In other words, public defender cases may involve both fewer "bad deals" and fewer "good deals." By the same token, cases involving private, attorneys would produce a greater deviation from the norm. Among privates, the nonregulars and conscientious regulars would be more apt to get good deals, and the cop-out attorneys would be more apt to get bad deals. Whatever the actual breakdown, it is clear that Alschuler would expect outsiders to do better, overall, than insiders.

The third perspective on defense attorneys is premised on the belief that the real role of regulars is to participate in the creation and perpetuation of the norms that govern standard dispositions within a specific court community. This view posits no systematic differences across attorney types and is really an extension of the notion that public defenders are less apt to obtain dispositions that deviate much from the norm. Once a consensus has been forged within the community, there is little desire, or incentive, to invent or improve upon it. Not only would that take time and effort, but also by adhering to the standard disposition for the routine case, "no one gets hurt too badly." These norms are also the basis for plea discussions with outsiders. Deviations occur, to be sure, but are related more to the exigencies of a particular case than to the relationship between the defense attorney and the court community.

The view of insiders as creators and protectors of routine can be seen in Galanter's discussion of how lawyers representing "one-shotters"(OS) fare in a situation dominated by "repeat players." He describes several distinctive features of such encounters:

> The demands of routine and orderly handling of a whole series of OSs may constrain the lawyer from maximizing advantage for any individual OS. Rosenthal (1970:172) shows that "for all but the largest

[personal injury] claims an attorney loses money by thoroughly preparing a case and not settling it early."

For the lawyer who services OSs, with his transient clientele, his
permanent "client" is the forum, the opposite party, or the intermediary
who supplies clients. (1974, 117)

Galanter also notes that the episodic nature of relations with their
OS clients leads to a stereotypic and uncreative brand of legal service,
and cites a similar observation by Carlin and Howard made in 1965 (1974,
117). This merely underscores the importance of creating and adhering
to routine in such a setting. It is the basis for the efficient handling of
large numbers of seemingly similar cases. Deviations and exceptions can
only undermine the strength of the governing norms, creating work and
enhancing uncertainty for all concerned.

In thinking about the importance of consensus and routine, the
comments of Rossett and Cressy are worth noting again: "Even in the
adversary world of law, men who work together and understand each
other eventually develop shared conceptions of what are acceptable, right
and just ways of dealing with specific kinds of offenses, suspects, and
defendants. These conceptions form the bases for understandings, agreements, working arrangements, and cooperative attitudes. Norms and values
grow and become a frame of reference which prosecutors, defense attorneys,
judges, and experienced offenders all use for deciding what is fair in each
case" (1976, 90-91).

Analyzing Defense Attorney Effects

To empirically examine the role of defense attorneys in the plea
process in such a way as to be responsive to the concerns of those works
just reviewed, especially those concerns raised by Alschuler, we had to
use our available data to construct a number of different categoric variables.
We first created a trichotomous defense counsel variable. One category
included public defenders; the other two covered nonregular private attorneys and regular private attorneys. Two criteria were used to differentiate regular privates from nonregular privates. The most important
criterion was the number of cases they represented in our case samples.
This criteria enabled us to make fairly easy decisions with respect to most
private attorneys; a large majority represented only one or two cases. At
the other end of the continuum, a handful of attorneys represented eight
to ten defendants or more. Members of the latter group of attorneys
normally accounted for about 1 percent of the cases in their respective
county sample, and this 1 percent figure was used as the criterion, to
define regular private attorneys.[8] In addition to this 1 percent criterion

we used a list of private regulars compiled from field discussions with judges and prosecutors. There was a great deal of overlap between the two sets of regulars. However, if the 1 percent criterion did not define an attorney listed by the judges and prosecutors as a regular, that attorney was included as a regular.[9] This led to the reclassification of fifty attorneys out of the more than nine hundred who represented defendants in one of our samples, or between four and five in each county.

A thorough examination of the role of defense attorneys requires that we go beyond the distinctions discussed previously and differentiate among types of regulars. To do this we again employ our measures of Responsiveness and Trial Competence. Responsiveness and Trial Competence define two of the most important dimensions of what might be termed a criminal defense attorney's operating style. An attorney can be nice (highly responsive), good (a respected trial lawyer), both, or neither. By combining our measures of Responsiveness and Trial Competence, we can categorize our regular attorneys in a way that addresses some of the concerns raised by Alschuler and permits us to analyze in a more refined way the role of regular defense attorneys.

To combine these two variables, we categorized attorneys, by county, into two groups (high, low) on each variable (Trial Competence, Responsiveness). The attorneys were categorized on the basis of their ranking with respect to other attorneys in a county, without reference to the number of cases each handled. Those above the mean for the defense attorneys on the Responsiveness scale in a county were scored High; the others Low. The same procedure was used on the Trial Competence variable. They were then combined into one of four categories: Not Nice, Not Good (NG NG); Nice, but Not Good (N, NG); Not Nice, but Good (NN, BG); Nice and Good (NAG).

A summary of the variables to be used in the defense attorney analysis is reported in Table 11.3. Because of the nature of the hypotheses to be examined here, the defense attorney analysis will not be as complex as those involving judges and prosecutors. The expectations concerning defense attorney ties are simply more straightforward and less contingent than those involving judge and prosecutor attitudes, personality traits, and operating styles. We will simply be using analysis of covariance (with the same set of dependent variables and covariates described above) and the set of dummy defense attorney variables listed in Table 11.3. Moreover, we will be sensitive to the same type of contextual considerations noted in the discussion concerning Table 11.1. Many of the factors discussed there have as important implications for the receipt of concessions as for their allocation.

We can now turn to an examination of these various actors' roles, hopefully with a better understanding of what we are looking for and how we may find it.

Table 11.3. **Summary of Measures Used to Capture Differences in Defense Attorneys**

Variable Name	Variable Meaning	Variable Coding
PRIVDC	Is the defense attorney privately retained or publicly paid?	1 = privately retained; 0 = publicly paid (public defender, contract attorney, assigned counsel)
REGULAR	Is the defense attorney a regular or a nonregular?	1 = regular; 0 = nonregular
NG, NG	Is the defense attorney categorized as Not Nice, Not Good?	1 = Not Nice, Not Good; 0 = All Others
N, NG	Is the defense attorney categorized as Nice, Not Good?	1 = Nice, Not Good; 0 = All Others
NN, BG	Is the defense attorney categorized as Not Nice, but Good?	1 = Not Nice, but Good 0 = All Others
NAG	Is the defense attorney categorized as Nice and Good?	1 = Nice and Good; 0 = All Others

NOTES

1. Methodological reasons also require a separate analysis for prosecutors and judges. The methodological problems flow from the differing relationships of defense attorneys to the court community. Even in a modest-sized county it is not uncommon through the course of the year for hundreds of defense attorneys to represent at least one client in the felony court system, even though the bulk of the clients may be handled by only ten to twenty attorneys. This is in contrast to the three to eight judges and five to ten prosecutors who may handle the bulk of all felony cases within a county. What this means on a practical level is that it was not possible to collect the amount of in-depth information on all defense attorneys that was collected on the judges and prosecutors. There were far too many defense attorneys handling far too few cases to justify such data collection procedures. Hence, individual-level data on only the regular defense attorneys was collected, and this requires different analytical procedures in assessing their role within the plea process.

2. Some of these reviews can be found in Green (1961, 100 et seq.); Hogarth (1971, 7 et seq.); and Gibson (1983).

3. We do not want to press this point too far because we are fully aware that when we examine the impact of prosecutors upon sentence and judges upon charge reductions, we are applying the decision-maker model to actors who play only an indirect role. However, depending upon the structure of the plea process, the distinction across is less sharp in some counties than others. This is a point that we will keep in mind as we interpret the data analysis.

4. For three studies that come to different conclusions about the effect of different types of attorneys see Smith and Ehrmann (1921, 229-375); Nardulli (1978, 169-72, 210-13); and Phillips and Ekland-Olson (1982).

5. A review of this tradition and its findings can be found in Nardulli (1978, chapter 1).

6. Operation Greylord was a multiyear federal investigation of Cook County's court system that involved the use of undercover agents, hidden tape recorders, and phony crimes. It resulted in the indictment and conviction of several judges, lawyers, police officers, and lesser law enforcement officials. An extensive journalistic review of the investigation can be found in *Chicago Lawyer* (Jan. 1984). The entire issue is devoted to Operation Greylord.

7. These works include Blumberg (1971); Skolnick (1967); Mileski (1971); Feeley (1972); Cole (1970); Mohr (1976); Nardulli (1978).

8. More troubling than the differentiation between regulars and nonregulars was the categorization of a group of private attorneys that represented between four and seven defendants in a county sample (about .5 percent of the cases in a county sample). These "semi-regular" attorneys accounted for 7.6 percent of all defendants in the merged pool of county samples, except in Saginaw, which has an assigned counsel system for indigent defense, and where these semiregulars accounted for more than 54 percent of the cases. A separate semiregular category was created because of the concern that these semiregulars might be skilled trial attorneys doing both civil and criminal trial work. However, preliminary comprisons on outcomes indicated that the semiregulars were not dissimilar from nonregulars. For this reason they were finally coded as nonregulars.

9. Attorneys defined as regulars on the basis of representation in the case samples, but not noted by judges and prosecutors, were not reclassified as nonregulars. Especially in the larger counties, regulars could easily be overlooked by the other participants; the case samples provided us with a rigorous basis for identifying the private regulars. We modified this list with the "reputational regulars" because we felt that the reputational method revealed relationships and perceptions that might not be picked up in the case sample method.

REFERENCES

Alschuler, Albert. 1975. "The Defense Attorney's Role in Plea Bargaining." *Yale Law Review* 84:1180.

Blumberg, Abraham. 1967. *Criminal Justice.* Chicago: Quadrangle Books. *Chicago Lawyer* 7 (Jan. 1984).

Cole, George. 1970. "The Decision to Prosecute." *Law and Society Review* 4:33-43.

Feeley, Malcolm. 1973. "Two Models of the Criminal Justice System: An Organizational Perspective." *Law and Society Review* 7:407-26.

Galanter, Marc. 1974. "Why the Haves Come Out Ahead: Some Speculation on the Limits of Legal Change." *Law and Society Review* 9:95.

Gaudet, F. J. "The Differences Between Judges in the Granting of Sentences of Probation," *Temple Law Quarterly* 19 (April 1946).

————. "Individual Differences in the Sentencing Tendencies of Judges." *Archives of Psychology* 22 (June 1938).

Gaylin, Willard. 1974. *Partial Justice: A Study of Bias in Sentencing.* New York: Alfred A. Knopf.

Gibson, James L. 1977. "Discriminant Functions, Role Orientations and Judicial Behavior: Theoretical and Methodological Linkages." *Journal of Politics* 39:984-1007.

————. 1980. "Environmental Constraints on the Behavior of Judges: A Representational Model of Judicial Decision Making." *Law and Society Review* 14:343-70.

————. 1983. "From Simplicity to Complexity: The Development of Theory in the Study of Judicial Behavior." *Political Behavior* 5:7.

————. 1978. "Judges' Role Orientations, Attitudes, and Decisions: An Interactive Model." *American Political Science Review* 72:911-24.

————. 1981. "Personality and Elite Political Behavior: The Influence of Self-Esteem on Judicial Decision Making." *Journal of Politics* 43:104-25.

————. 1979. "A Role Theoretic Model of Criminal Court Decisionmaking." In *The Study of Criminal Courts: Political Perspectives,* ed. Peter F. Nardulli. Cambridge, Mass.: Ballinger Publishing.

Green, Edward. 1961. *Judicial Attitudes in Sentencing.* London: Macmillian.

Hogarth, John. 1971. *Sentencing as a Human Process.* Toronto: University of Toronto Press.

Malcolm, Andrew H. 1983. "Chicago's Inquiry Shows Court's Hidden Side." *New York Times,* Dec. 18, 17.

Mileski, Maureen. 1971. "Courtroom Encounters: An Observation Study of a Lower Court." *Law and Society Review* 5:473-538.

Mohr, Lawrence. 1976. "Organizations, Decisions, and Courts." *Law and Society Review* 10:621-42.

Nardulli, Peter F. 1978. *The Courtroom Elite: An Organizational Analysis of Criminal Justice.* Cambridge, Mass.: Ballinger Publishing.

Phillips, Charles David, and Sheldon Ekland-Olson. 1982. " 'Repeat Players' in a Criminal Court: The Fate of Their Clients." *Criminology* 19:530.

Rosenthal, Albert. 1971. "Client Participation in Professional Decisions: The

Lawyer-Client Relationship in Personal Injury Cases." Unpublished dissertation, Yale University.

Rossett, Arthur, and Donald Cressy. 1976. *Justice by Consent: Plea Bargains in the American Courthouse.* Philadelphia: Lippincott.

Schubert, Glendon. 1965. *The Judicial Mind: The Attitudes and Ideologies of Supreme Court Justices, 1946-1963.* Evanston: Northwestern University Press.

———. 1974. *The Judicial Mind Revisisted: Physchometric Analysis of Supreme Court Ideology.* New York: Oxford University Press.

Skolnick, Jerome. 1967. "Social Control in the Adversary System." *Journal of Conflict Resolution* 11:52-70.

Smith, Reginald Heber, and Herbert Ehrmann. 1921. "The Criminal Courts." In *Criminal Justice in Cleveland,* ed. Roscoe Pound and Felix Frankfurter. Cleveland: The Cleveland Foundation.

12

CRIMINAL COURT ACTORS AND GUILTY PLEA CASES: A QUANTITATIVE ASSESSMENT

The impact of judges, prosecutors, and defense attorneys upon the shape of plea packages is, as chapter 11 suggested, an extremely important issue in the study and assessment of criminal court processes. These actors are a potentially important source of undesirable influences upon the plea process, one that prior analyses reported here would not have detected. The primary concern of this chapter is to examine their impact in the manner outlined in chapter 11. We first look at judges and prosecutors. Before describing their impact upon plea packages, we stop to examine the differences across judges and prosecutors within the various counties. The impact of defense attorneys is the second major concern of the chapter. After a review of the structure of the defense bar in the nine counties, we examine the impact of the different attorney types upon our charge reduction and sentence measures. Finally, in a concluding section we try to summarize, interpret, and explain the implications of the results.

JUDGES, PROSECUTORS, AND THE ALLOCATION OF PLEA CONCESSIONS

Before delving into the results of the various analyses, we address a preliminary matter: the degree of the variance in judge and prosecutor traits within counties. Examining the diversity in decision makers is especially important in a study focusing on middle-sized jurisdictions, where a handful of judges and prosecutors may dominate the felony

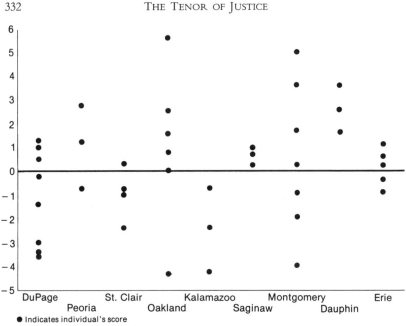

Graph 12.1. **Judge's Belief in Punishment Scores by County**

disposition process. In such a setting, it is plausible that the selection and socialization process could, over time, mitigate individual differences in perspectives and attitudes. Without first checking such a possibility we could possibly misconstrue the meaning of our empirical results. Null findings could be attributed to a lack of decision-maker impact when, in fact, they are due to a relative uniformity in perspective. We would not expect significant differences in case outcomes if there are no significant differences in the relevant views or traits of the actors. A county-by-county examination of relevant decision-maker attributes may also enhance our ability to interpret the quantitative results. Disparate findings across counties that may be puzzling when viewed only in light of contextual differences may be clearer if the pattern of decision-maker traits is known. Indeed, the configuration of these traits may be viewed as just another type of contextual factor.

Although it would be far too cumbersome to present the range of data for each variable to be used in the multivariate analyses in the text, a few selected ones will serve our purposes well. Others will be presented in Appendix V. Graphs 12.1 and 12.2 display the range of scores for the Belief in Punishment variable for judges and prosecutors, respectively. These scores are the result of the factor analysis done on the standardized attitudinal variables described in chapter 3 and Appendix I; high scores

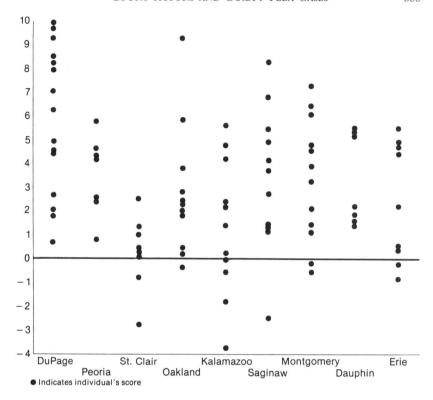

Graph 12.2. **Prosecutor's Belief in Punishment Scores by County**

indicate a strong belief in punishment as an appropriate response to criminal offenders, low scores indicate a weak belief. If we look at the judges (Graph 12.1), we see a healthy spread in the larger counties such as DuPage, Oakland, and Montgomery, but a tighter range in the smaller ones. All counties except Kalamazoo and Dauphin have some judges above and below the overall mean of 0. This overall mean is for all actors interviewed—judges, prosecutors, and defense attorneys. All Kalamazoo judges have negative scores, all Dauphin judges have positive scores. The ranges for the judge's Regard for Due Process (Appendix V, Graph V.1) follow a similar pattern as Belief in Punishment, except overall they are considerably tighter even in the larger counties. This undoubtedly reflects a greater consensus over the notion of due process than in the worth of punishment as a means of dealing with offenders.

The range of prosecutor scores for the Belief in Punishment variable is significantly wider than was the case for judges, as can be seen in Graph 12.2. Almost every prosecutor's office evinces a wide range of attitudes

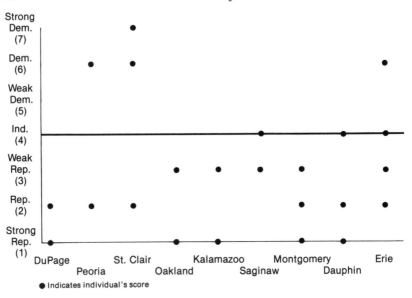

Graph 12.3. **Judge's Political Affiliation by County**

toward punishment, even the relatively smaller ones. Another basic difference between prosecutors and judges is that the wide variance in prosecutors is almost all above the overall mean. Negative scores are the
exception, undoubtedly reflecting the effects of the institutional role of
prosecutors. Prosecutor Regard for Due Process scores (Appendix V, Graph
V.2) were, again, more diverse than those for judges but not as diverse as
prosecutor punishment scores.

If we look at political affiliation for judges (Graph 12.3), we see little
variance, with some exceptions (Peoria, St. Clair, Erie). Most judges in
most of the nine counties are Republicans of one sort or another. Graph
12.4 shows more variance among prosecutors. They are more apt to label
themselves as Independents and Democrats than are judges. The opposite
pattern holds true if we examine years of experience (Appendix V, Graphs
V.3, V.4). It is not uncommon for some judges to be on the bench for as
little as two years, while others have served for ten to fifteen years. Only
a few prosecutors have served for more than five to six years. Nonetheless,
a reasonable amount of variance exists if it is recognized that most
prosecutor offices have fairly frequent turnover (i.e., the range in the
universe of prosecutor offices is generally tighter).

If we look at the judge's community ties measured by the number
of local activities and group memberships (Graph 12.5), we again see
mixed patterns of ranges. DuPage, Oakland, Saginaw, and the Pennsylvania
counties had a healthy range, whereas the others had less. Graph 12.6

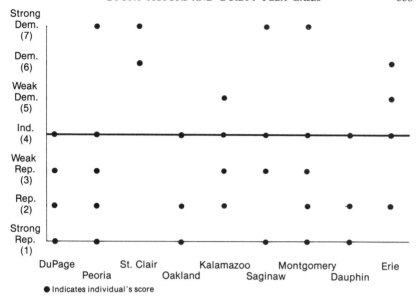

Graph 12.4. **Prosecutor's Political Affiliation by County**

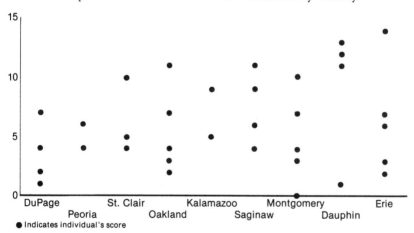

Graph 12.5. **Extent of Judge's Community Ties by County (Number of Local Activities and Group Memberships)**

demonstrates that prosecutor's organizational ties were, on the whole, less extensive than those of judges. Still, offices in DuPage, Kalamazoo, and Erie showed a good deal of variance in such ties. Part of the reason for the difference in community ties across these formal roles is that judges are elected officials and tend to be significantly older than prosecutors. Also, as shown in Graphs V.5 and V.6 in Appendix V, judges have spent

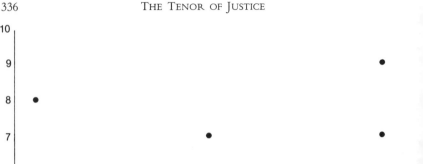

Graph 12.6. **Extent of Prosecutor's Community Ties by County (Number of Local Activities and Group Memberships)**

a larger portion of their life in the county they serve. Only judges in the ring counties showed much variance in the percent of life variable. In contrast, almost every prosecutor office had a wide range on this measure (Graph V-6).

The last background measure, whether or not a judge was formerly a prosecutor, does not lend itself to a graphic presentation. However, analyses showed that between 50-65 percent of the cases in the Illinois counties and two of the Pennslyvania counties (Dauphin and Erie) were handled by former prosecutors. The figures for Oakland, Saginaw, and Montgomery ranged between 18 and 28 percent. Only in Kalamazoo were there no former prosecutors. Thus, for the most part, we have adequate variance to examine the impact of this variable.

To summarize, we find what would appear to be sufficient ranges of variation on most decision-maker attributes in most counties. Perhaps the biggest problem comes with respect to the judge attitudinal measures and the political affiliation of both actors. The judge Regard for Due Process scores were fairly tightly clustered in most counties, and only the judges in the larger ring counties displayed a good deal of variance on the Belief in Punishment measure. Political affiliation is of some concern because most of the variation for both sets of actors was between Independent and Republican. Even here though we have variation, with respect to one actor or the other, in Peoria, St. Clair, Kalamazoo, Saginaw, Montgomery, and Erie.

There is little doubt that, with respect to some of the other variables, limited ranges exist in some counties. However, it is very difficult to know how much variation is needed before a variable is likely to emerge as an important factor in charge and sentence decisions. This is particularly true with respect to some of the measures with less concrete referents, such as the attitudinal measures. All that can be noted here is that we have enough variance in enough counties on each measure to guard against a misinterpretation of the findings. If certain traits emerge as more significant in counties where wide ranges of scores exist, then we will temper our conclusions with respect to counties with narrower ranges. If, on the other hand, decision-maker traits have a weak impact in counties with both wide and narrow ranges of variance, then it would be difficult to argue that restricted variance accounts for the weak showings.

The Linear Impact of Judges and Prosecutors: A Multivariate Assessment

The scope of the analyses undertaken to gauge the impact of judges and prosecutors upon different measures of the plea process was quite formidable. The presentation of the results in a coherent, comprehensible manner is no less challenging. In nine counties, we examined the impact of thirteen variables upon three measures of charge reduction (existence of any type of charge reduction, existence of a count reduction, existence of a primary charge reduction) and four sentence measures (Did a first offender get incarceration?; Did a repeat offender get a sentence above, at, or below the norm?; How far, in months, was the sentence from the norm? (for repeat offenders only); and minimum months of incarceration (probation coded 0). Also, two sets of interaction analyses were undertaken for each actor in each county.

Approximately ninety tables with thousands of entries were required to tabulate the results. These analyses were necessary to do a truly extensive analysis of decision-maker impact, one that insured that most obvious channels of influence were examined. But a detailed discussion of each of these analyses would be cumbersome and somewhat repetitive. It can also be counterproductive. Commentary upon such a broad array of data necessarily focuses upon deviations from the general pattern, and much analysis is devoted to explaining the deviations. Thus, the forest is lost for the trees.

To avoid this, we summarize the results from the data analyses here while reporting the details of the analyses in Appendix VI. In Appendix VI, we report the mean of the dependent variables (for dummy variables only),[1] the explained variance due to the control variables, the change in R^2 due to the individual-level variables, and the number of cases upon which each analysis is based, as well as the total possible number. Here, however, we simply report one statistic—the change in the adjusted R^2 due to the addition of the set of variables under consideration. Although this is normally not enough information to assess the relationship among a set of variables, it is the most succinct measure of a set of variable's impact upon the dependent variable. It also permits us to zero in on patterns without being distracted by details; further information on the results can be derived from an examination of the tables in Appendix VI.

The result of the judge and prosecutor dummy variable analyses are reported in Table 12.1. They reveal that the incidence of marked linear effects by these sets of actors upon our measures of charge and sentence are the exception not the rule. Indeed, if we begin by examining the linear impact of these actors on charge reductions, we see almost no marked effects. Of 54 analyses conducted, only 4 increased the explained variance by as much as 3 points. Half of the analyses revealed no significant effect or a negative one, due to the adjustment in the R^2 change for the number of variables entered. Interestingly, the pattern for prosecutors is as weak as the pattern for judges, even in counties such as St. Clair, Saginaw, and Erie, where controls over plea offers were weakest. Saginaw is particularly interesting in this regard. It granted a large number of charge concessions, especially primary charge reductions, with little centralized control over their allocation, yet no significant pattern emerges across individual prosecutors. Montgomery County had a fairly large and diverse set of prosecutors that dispensed many symbolic count drops with limited centralized supervision, but the prosecutor dummy variables account for only 3 percent of the variance in the *CHRGRED* and *CTRED* variables.

If we shift our analysis to an examination of the sentencing results, we see a greater frequency of adjusted R^2 changes in the 5-9 percent range (11 of 72) and one that is truly strong (.24 change in R^2). A few points should be made about these results. First, they are not broadly based effects. Of the 12 changes above .05, 8 (or 75 percent) affected the *FRSTJAIL* variable. None affected the more broadly based *JAILMIN* variable. This, of course, suggests that there may be a greater diversity of thought

Table 12.1. Summary of the Analyses of Covariance for Judge and Prosecutor Dummy Variables

	DuPage (Ring)	Peoria (Autonomous)	St. Clair (Declining)	Oakland (Ring)	Kalamazoo (Autonomous)	Saginaw (Declining)	Montgomery (Ring)	Dauphin (Autonomous)	Erie (Declining)
Impact of judge dummy variables (change in adjusted R^2) upon:									
CHRGRED	0	0	0	.03	.01	-.01	.01	.02	0
CTRED	0	0	0	0	0	.01	.01	.01	0
PRIMRED	.01	0	0	.02	.01	.03	0	0	0
JAILMIN	.03	.01	0	0	0	.01	.02	.01	.03
FRSTJAIL	.02	0	-.02	.06	.04	.06	.24	.03	.06
SENTNORM	.04	.01	0	.05	-.01	-.02	.04	.04	.06
NORMDEV	.01	.03	0	.03	-.02	.03	.03	.03	.07
Impact of prosecutor dummy variables (change in adjusted R^2) upon:									
CHRGRED	0	0	.01	.02	-.01	-.01	.03	.01	-.01
CTRED	-.01	0	0	0	-.01	0	.03	.01	0
PRIMRED	.01	-.01	.01	.02	-.01	.02	.01	0	0
JAILMIN	-.01	.02	0	0	0	-.01	.02	0	-.01
FRSTJAIL	-.02	0	0	.09	0	.05	.07	.03	.07
SENTNORM	.01	.04	.01	.04	-.01	-.02	.01	.03	.03
NORMDEV	0	.04	.02	.01	-.01	-.02	.07	-.02	-.01

concerning how first offenders should be handled. We also see moderately higher effects for judges in counties like Oakland and Erie, where the judges had clear control over sentencing. The one truly large impact in the analyses also affected the first-offender variable, but was due solely to the difference between two Montgomery judges; the others had fairly uniform rates of incarceration for first-offenders. One was an eccentric retired judge who handled 136 of 206 first-offender cases and gave only one offender any jail time. Another judge handled only 13 cases but gave 6 a jail sentence.

Our attempts to delineate more clearly the specific attributes of judges and prosecutors that have an effect upon the allocations of charge reductions and sentence concessions were by and large not very insightful. This was, of course, largely due to the fact that these actors did not have much of a linear impact upon plea outcomes, as we have just demonstrated. We report the aggregate impact of the attitudinal and background variables outlined earlier in Tables 12.2 and 12.3; results for the individual variables are again reported in Appendix VI. The negligible linear impact of the judge attitudinal variables with respect to both charge reductions and sentences can best be summarized by noting that of 63 sets examined, only 3 added more than 2 points to the adjusted R^2; none added as many as 4 points. The picture is similar for the judge background variables. Of 63 sets examined, only 4 added more than 2 points; only 1 set added as much as 4 points. Given these meager results, it is not really meaningful to discuss patterns.

The results for the prosecutor attitude and background variables are reported in Table 12.3; significant results are even more sparse. Only two of the sets of attitudinal variables have an impact greater than .02; both relate to Oakland prosecutors and the sentencing of repeat offenders. The impact of the sets of prosecutor background variables is only marginally more significant; 5 of 63 analyses uncovered increases in R^2 of greater than 2 points. Three of these involved Oakland and Peoria prosecutors and the sentencing of repeat offenders. This is somewhat puzzling because both Oakland and Peoria had moderately centralized plea offer systems, and the Oakland prosecutors were not even permitted to enter into sentence agreements. Another puzzling point is that only one moderately large effect (.05) is found with respect to charge reductions, which are wholly within the discretion of prosecutors.

The results of the linear analyses make it clear that judges and prosecutors do not constitute a patterned source of any large, straightforward disparities within the plea process in the counties studied here. Statistically significant findings were the exception and, when they did occur, they tended to be quite small. Few added more than a few points to the overall R^2. This was the case in counties with very diverse decision

Table 12.2. **Summary of the Analyses of Covariance for Judge Attitudinal and Background Variables**

	DuPage (Ring)	Peoria (Autonomous)	St. Clair (Declining)	Oakland (Ring)	Kalamazoo (Autonomous)	Saginaw (Declining)	Montgomery (Ring)	Dauphin (Autonomous)	Erie (Declining)
Impact of judge attitudinal variables (change in adjusted R^2) upon:									
CHRGRED	.004	0	0	0	0	0	—	.02	0
CTRED	0	0	0	0	.005	0	—	.01	0
PRIMRED	0	0	0	0	0	.026	—	0	0
JAILMIN	0	.01	0	0	0	0	—	0	.01
FRSTJAIL	0	0	0	0	0	0	—	0	0
SENTNORM	0	.01	.01	0	0	0	—	0	0
NORMDEV	0	.03	.02	0	0	0	—	0	.03
Impact of judge background variables (change in adjusted R^2) upon:									
CHRGRED	0	0	0	0	.002	0	—	.02	0
CTRED	0	0	0	.002	.01	0	—	.01	0
PRIMRED	.01	0	0	0	.01	.02	—	0	.02
JAILMIN	.01	.01	0	0	0	0	—	.005	.02
FRSTJAIL	.04	0	0	0	0	0	—	.10	0
SENTNORM	.03	0	.01	.03	0	0	—	0	0
NORMDEV	.02	.02	.01	0	0	0	—	0	.03

Table 12.3. Summary of the Analyses of Covariance for Prosecutor Attitudinal and Background Variables

	DuPage (Ring)	Peoria (Autonomous)	St. Clair (Declining)	Oakland (Ring)	Kalamazoo (Autonomous)	Saginaw (Declining)	Montgomery (Ring)	Dauphin (Autonomous)	Erie (Declining)
Impact of prosecutor attitudinal variables (change in adjusted R^2) upon:									
CHRGRED	0	0	0	0	0	0	—	0	0
CTRED	0	0	0	0	0	0	—	0	0
PRIMRED	0	0	0	0	0	.02	—	0	0
JAILMIN	0	0	0	0	0	0	—	0	0
FRSTJAIL				.04					
SENTNORM									
NORMDEV	0	0	0	.03	0	0	—	0	0
Impact of prosecutor background variables (change in adjusted R^2) upon:									
CHRGRED	0	0	0	.003	0	0	—	0	0
CTRED	0	0	.008	0	0	0	—	0	.05
PRIMRED	0	0	0	0	0	0	—	0	0
JAILMIN	0	0	.02	0	0	0	—	0	0
FRSTJAIL	0	0	0	0	0	0	—	.01	0
SENTNORM	0	.02	.03	.02	0	0	—	0	.03
NORMDEV	0	.05	.04	.015	.02	0	—	0	0

makers as well as more similar ones, in large counties as well as small counties. Also, the orientation of the infrastructure that the actors operated within seemed to make little difference in their overall linear impact, with only a few exceptions. Indeed, no consistent pattern of linear effects emerges with respect to any county or any variable or set of variables. Despite these findings, one might argue that the above analyses potentially diluted the effect of the attitudinal and background measures because they considered only guilty plea cases, that is, cases that resulted in a conviction. It might be the case that "tough" judges and prosecutors, or judges who were former prosecutors, are less likely to let cases slip away than other actors. That is, they may be more willing to grant a plea concession to get a conviction. This would increase their overall conviction rate but, when the entire pool of guilty plea cases is examined, the addition of "the ones that almost got away" may dilute what would otherwise be distinctly more severe patterns of case outcomes.

To check this, we examine the impact of the attitude and background characteristics upon a dummy, convict/not convict variable. The results are reported in Tables 12.4 and 12.5. We report the conviction rate for each county (the mean of the dependent variable) as well as the results for each variable. Several things are clear from these analyses. First, virtually no significant findings emerge in any county other than Dauphin and Erie. Moreover, the analyses reported in those two counties add only 2 to 5 points to the R^2. A second point is that the conviction dummy variable is highly skewed; most conviction rates are in the .8-.9 range. This, of course, makes the regression analysis somewhat suspect (see note 1). More important, these high rates indicate that few cases slip away, regardless of who handles them. Thus the fact we are only looking at convicted cases really does not undermine the implications of the results reported earlier.

The Interactive Effect of Judges and Prosecutors

In light of the more recent literature on judicial decision making, the preceding results may not be entirely unexpected. However, they constitute a very crucial addition to our understanding of the plea process. The view that Judge X or Prosecutor Y will routinely give you a better deal is simply not borne out in these analyses, despite the prominence of such thinking in many counties—especially those in which plea-routing was widespread. At the same time, it should be stressed that these results do not mean that some judges or prosecutors are never to be preferred or never make a difference. Some may be easier to work with, more accommodating in terms of scheduling, or to be preferred for other personal or professional reasons. Also certain judges or prosecutors may simply be

Table 12.4. The Linear Impact of Judicial Variables upon the Probability of a Conviction

	DuPage (Ring)	Peoria (Autonomous)	St. Clair (Declining)	Oakland (Ring)	Kalamazoo (Autonomous)	Saginaw (Declining)	Montgomery (Ring)	Dauphin (Autonomous)	Erie (Declining)
Mean response	.92	.79	.83	.90	.90	.84	—	.90	.86
Impact of judge's Belief in Punishment	0	0	0	0	0	0	—	-**	-***
Regard for Due Process	0	0	-*	0	0	0	—	-***	0
Net change in adjusted R^2 due to addition of attitudinal measures								.02	.02
Impact of judge's political affiliation	0	0	+*	0	0	0	—	0	-**
Length of time on bench	0	0	0	0	0	0	—	0	+*
Extent of community ties	0	0	0	0	0	0	—	0	+*
Percent of life in county	0	0	0	0	0	0	—	-*	0
Status as a former prosecutor	0	0	0	0	0	0	—	0	0
Net change in adjusted R^2 due to addition of attitudinal measures	0	0	.003	0	0	0	—	.035	.03

+ Indicates a positive relationship.
− Indicates a negative relationship.

* Indicates relationship significant at .05 level.
** Indicates relationship significant at .01 level.
*** Indicates relationship significant at .001 level

Table 13.3. The Linear Impact of Prosecutor Variables upon the Probability of a Conviction

	DuPage (Ring)	Peoria (Autonomous)	St. Clair (Declining)	Oakland (Ring)	Kalamazoo (Autonomous)	Saginaw (Declining)	Montgomery (Ring)	Dauphin (Autonomous)	Erie (Declining)
Mean response	.91	.80	.84	.90	.90	.82	—	.91	.86
Impact of prosecutor's									
Belief in Punishment	0	0	0	0	0	0	—	0	-***
Regard for Due Process	0	0	0	0	-**	0	—	+***	-***
Net change in adjusted R^2 due to addition of Attitudinal Measures	0	0	0	0	.01	0	—	.04	.028
Impact of prosecutor's									
political affiliation	0	0	0	0	0	0	—	+***	0
Length of time prosecutor	0	0	0	0	0	0	—	+***	0
Extent of community ties	0	0	0	0	+***	0	—	+**	0
Percent of life in county	0	0	0	+*	0	0	—	0	0
Net change in adjusted R^2 due to addition of attitudinal measures	0	0	0	.007	.03	0	—	.05	0

+ Indicates a positive relationship.
− Indicates a negative relationship.
0 Indicates no relationship.

* Indicates relationship significant at .05 level.
** Indicates relationship significant at .01 level.
*** Indicates relationship significant at .001 level.

better, or worse, for certain types of cases. Punitive views may be activated only in serious offenses or in cases involving "bad" defendants. These views may not make much difference in first-time, garden-variety burglary or theft cases. One of the basic implications of the literature on judicial decision making reviewed in chapter 11 is that, to obtain a clear understanding of the impact that the views of the decision maker have upon outcomes, these views have to be considered in conjunction with other factors. These other factors included such things as case attributes, other attributes of the decision makers, and contextual considerations. The analyses reported earlier suggested that the linear effects of judges and prosecutors seemed to vary little with differences in the court community's infrastructure. We turn now to a review of the results from our examination of the joint effects between the attitudes of our actors, case attributes, and other attributes of the decision makers.

While the expectation was that the impact of judge and prosecutor attitudes would emerge in certain subsets of cases (more serious offenses, repeat offenders, detained defendants) or under certain conditions (strong views coupled with strong trial skills or a highly manipulative personality), these expectations were not realized in any systematic way. The interaction analyses were quite involved and extensive; they required 56 tables with more than 2,500 entries to report. It is not feasible to report nor comment on them entirely, especially in light of the sparsity of statistically significant findings. To illustrate the general nature of these results, we report the interactions between the judges' and prosecutors' Belief in Punishment and case attributes for the two most generally based dependent variables of charge (*CHRGRED*) and sentence (*JAILMIN*).[2]

The results for the *CHRGRED* variable are reported in Tables 12.6 and 12.7. Significant interactions were rare and, where they did occur, were quite weak. Of the six significant interactions uncovered, only two added more than .01 to the adjusted R^2 (45 interactions were tested altogether), and both were in Erie. Parallel analyses for the *JAILMIN* variable are reported in Tables 12.8 and 12.9. A few more significant interactions occur, but most of the changes in R^2 that do occur are in the .01 to .02 range. Two are somewhat above that (in the .04 to .05 range), and one is well above it (Peoria judges in Table 12.8). However, nothing close to a consistent pattern emerges such that we could say "punitive judges make a difference in more serious cases in counties with _____ characteristics." With the exception of the interactions between the prosecutor's Belief in Punishment and offense seriousness, no consistent interactions (sign-wise) occur in more than two counties.

In four counties the prosecutor's Belief in Punishment variable interacted with offense seriousness. However, the interaction is negative — the opposite of what would be expected. This suggests that serious cases

Table 12.6. **Results of the Interaction Analysis among the Judge's Belief in Punishment Variable, Selected Case Characteristics, and CHRGRED**

	DuPage (Ring)	Peoria (Autonomous)	St. Clair (Declining)	Oakland (Ring)	Kalamazoo (Autonomous)	Saginaw (Declining)	Montgomery (Ring)	Dauphin (Autonomous)	Erie (Declining)
Did the judge's Belief in Punishment variable interact with:									
The multicount indictment variable	0	0	0	0	0	0	—	—	—***
The defendant's criminal record variable	0	+*	0	0	0	0	—	—	0
The defendant's bail status	0	0	0	0	0	0	—	—	0
Contribution to R^2	0	.01	0	0	0	0	—	—	.03
N	448	509	601	577	405	375	263	771	282

* indicates relationship at .05 level.
*** indicates relationship at .001 level.

+ Indicates a positive relationship.
— Indicates a negative relationship.
0 Indicates no relationship.

Table 12.7. **Results of the Interaction Analysis among the Prosecutor's Belief in Punishment Variable, Selected Case Characteristics, and *CHRGRED***

	DuPage (Ring)	Peoria (Autono-mous)	St. Clair (Declin-ing)	Oakland (Ring)	Kalamazoo (Autono-mous)	Saginaw (Declin-ing)	Mont-gomery (Ring)	Dauphin (Autono-mous)	Erie (Declin-ing)
Did the prosecutor's Belief in Punishment variable interact with:									
The multicount indictment variable	0	0	0	0	0	0	—	0	+***
The defendant's criminal record variable	-*	0	0	0	0	0	—	0	+***
The defendant's bail status	0	0	0	0	0	0	—	-**	0
Contribution to R^2	.01	0	0	0	0	0	—	.01	.03
N	421	511	515	615	462	381	225	674	269

+ Indicates a positive relationship.
− Indicates a negative relationship.
0 Indicates no relationship.

* Indicates relationship at .05 level.
** Indicates relationship at .01 level.
*** Indicates relationship at .001 level.

Table 12.8. **Results of the Interaction Analysis among the Judge's Belief in Punishment Variable, Selected Case Characteristics, and JAILMIN**

	DuPage (Ring)	Peoria (Autonomous)	St. Clair (Declining)	Oakland (Ring)	Kalamazoo (Autonomous)	Saginaw (Declining)	Montgomery (Ring)	Dauphin (Autonomous)	Erie (Declining)
Did the judge's Belief in Punishment variable interact with:									
The seriousness of the most serious charge at arrest	0	+***	0	0	−	+**	−	−	0
The defendant's criminal record variable	0	0	0	0	−	0	−	−	0
The defendant's bail status	−***	0	−**	0	−	0	−	−	+*
Contribution to									
R^2	.02	.143	.01	0		.01	−	−	.01
N	461	607	659	560	420	351	249	782	260

* Indicates relationship at .05 level.
** Indicates relationship at .01 level.
*** indicates relationship at .001 level.

+ Indicates a positive relationship.
− Indicates a negative relationship.
0 Indicates no relationship.

Table 12.9. **Results of the Interaction Analysis among the Prosecutor's Belief in Punishment Variable, Selected Case Characteristics, and** *JAILMIN*

	DuPage (Ring)	Peoria (Autonomous)	St. Clair (Declining)	Oakland (Ring)	Kalamazoo (Autonomous)	Saginaw (Declining)	Montgomery (Ring)	Dauphin (Autonomous)	Erie (Declining)
Did the prosecutor's Belief in Punishment variable interact with:									
The seriousness of the most serious charge at arrest	−*	0	−***	0	0	−***	−	0	−*
The defendant's criminal record variable	0	0	0	0	0	+*	−	0	0
The defendant's bail status	0	0	+**	0	0	0	−	+***	0
Contribution to R^2	.01	0	.05	0	0	.04	−	.02	.01
N	435	608	566	596	474	362	−	682	246

+ Indicates a positive relationship.
− Indicates a negative relationship.
0 Indicates no relationship.

* Indicates relationship at .05 level.
** Indicates relationship at .01 level.
*** Indicates relationship at .001 level.

handled by prosecutors who expressed more punitive views actually received less severe sentences than those expressing more lenient views. In two of the four counties (DuPage and Erie), this effect is quite weak; in neither does the individual prosecutor have much to do with sentencing in plea cases. However, the negative effect is quite strong in St. Clair and Saginaw, where assistant prosecutors can have an impact upon sentence. Further analysis showed that these findings were based on a fairly small subset of serious cases handled by a few rather punitive prosecutors. This is a hazard of engaging in such research in relatively small counties but, as was noted at the beginning of the chapter, several of the counties were considerably larger and their results were less subject to effects such as those observed here.

The second phase of the interaction analyses dealt with the joint effect of attitudes and other decision-maker attributes. The primary question addressed was, Does the impact of attitudes depend upon other aspects of a decision maker's operating or negotiating style (Machiavellianism, Involvement, Responsiveness, Trial Competence, etc.). The answer to the question based upon extensive interaction analyses is a resounding No! With respect to the *CHRGRED* variable, 48 interactions were tested between judge and prosecutor Belief in Punishment and these traits. No significant effects were found. With respect to the *JAILMIN* variable, two significant findings were uncovered, but only one above the .01 level. What this indicates is that the findings that did emerge are essentially random, and for this reason are not reported in tabular form. Results of the interactions involving the other measures of charge reduction and sentence disparity were quite similar to these.

DEFENSE ATTORNEYS AND THE RECEIPT
OF PLEA CONCESSIONS

Where the previous section dealt with the role of decision makers in the allocation of charge and sentence concessions, here we are concerned with the impact of the defense attorney's ties to the court community upon the shape of the plea package. This is a separate question, one quite independent of the results of the earlier analyses. Even though the overall thrust of the preceding results casts doubt upon the pervasiveness of individual-level effects, disparities across defense attorneys would not be detected by examining the allocation patterns across judges and prosecutors.

Although it is not as crucial here as it was in the judge and prosecutor analyses, it will be useful to first review the distribution of defense attorney types across counties. This will provide an understanding of the structure of the defense bar in the different counties beyond that provided in chapter

6 and help us view the empirical results in a broader context. Table 12.10 reports data on the number and percent 'of cases handled by nonregulars and regulars. Significant differences across counties are apparent imme-diately. The role of private, nonregular attorneys was greatest (60-65 percent) in two of the ring counties (Oakland, Montgomery) as well as in Saginaw, which had an assigned counsel system for indigents (as did Oakland). Nonregular privates played a rather minor role in Peoria, St. Clair, and Kalamazoo (16-23 percent of all trial cases), but a somewhat larger role (33-47 percent) in the remaining three counties. Private regulars represented the highest percentage of cases (33-36 percent) in the two counties with assigned counsel systems (Oakland and Saginaw). They represented the lowest proportion of cases (4-8 percent) in the two ring counties with geographically dispersed private bars and public defender offices (DuPage and Montgomery) and Kalamazoo, which assigns almost 75 percent of its cases to five contract attorneys who represent all indigent cases for the county. The private regulars in the other counties represented between 18 and 20 percent of the defendants except for Erie, where they handled only about 12 percent. The variance in the proportion of cases handled by public defenders (contract attorneys in Kalamazoo) is also considerable. As just mentioned, Kalamazoo has by far the largest portion represented by these public regulars, followed by Peoria and St. Clair (64 percent, 56 percent). In the remaining counties, these public attorneys represented between 44 and 48 percent of the cases, except in Montgomery, where the figure was only about 36 percent.

Table 12.11 reports the distribution of cases, and attorneys, in the various categories of the more refined variables for the regular attorneys (not nice, not good; nice, not good; not nice but good; nice and good) that were outlined in chapter 11 (Table 11.3). Some observations are worth making. First, the largest number of cases were handled by attorneys regarded as "nice" (see rows 2 and 4); the actual numbers of attorneys involved varied between eight and fourteen. However, the breakdown between "nice and good" and "nice, but not good" varied considerably across counties. There was a fairly good balance in the Illinois counties. But in Oakland, Kalamazoo, Dauphin, and Erie, the "nice and good" attorneys handled a much larger percentage of the cases than was true for the other county (or counties) in their respective states. As for those regulars evaluated as neither nice nor good—numbering between 4 and 7 attorneys in each county—they account for between 20 and 35 percent of the regulars' cases in most of the the counties. However, in Peoria, St. Clair, and Kalamazoo, their relative share is between 4 and 16 percent. Insiders considered "not nice, but good" numbered only between one and five but accounted for between 14 and 25 percent of the regulars' cases in five counties (St. Clair, Oakland, Saginaw, Dauphin, and Erie).

Table 12.10. Cases Handled by Regular and Nonregular Attorneys

	DuPage (Ring)	Peoria (Autono- mous)	St. Clair (Declin- ing)	Oakland (Ring)	Kalamazoo (Autono- mous)	Saginaw (Declin- ing)	Mont- gomery (Ring)	Dauphin (Autono- mous)	Erie (Declin- ing)
Percent of cases handled by:									
Private nonregulars (includes assigned counsel in Oakland and Saginaw)	47.3 (280)	16.1 (148)	23.0 (212)	66.4 (497)	17.5 (118)	64.8 (400)	60.5 (314)	33.5 (339)	43.1 (245)
Private regulars (includes assigned counsel in Oakland and Saginaw)	8.4 (50)	20.1 (185)	20.7 (191)	33.6 (252)	8.7 (59)	35.2 (217)	3.9 (20)	18.5 (187)	11.8 (67)
Public regulars (public defenders and Kalamazoo contract attorneys)	44.3 (262)	63.8 (588)	56.2 (518)	— —	73.8 (499)	— —	35.6 (185)	48.1 (487)	48.1 (256)
Number of cases with missing information	(57)	(9)	(75)	(151)	(5)	(33)	(154)	(38)	(20)

Table 12.11. **Cases Handled by Regular Defense Attorneys, by Type**

	DuPage (Ring)	Peoria (Autonomous)	St. Clair (Declining)	Oakland (Ring)	Kalamazoo (Autonomous)	Saginaw (Declining)	Montgomery (Ring)	Dauphin (Autonomous)	Erie (Declining)
Percent Not Nice, Not Good (NN, NG)	27.8	10.6	4.6	20.4	15.9	21.1	35.4	20.8	29.4
Number of cases	(67)	(65)	(25)	(42)	(85)	(37)	(57)	(133)	(82)
Number of attorneys	(7)	(5)	(5)	(5)	(6)	(5)	(6)	(4)	(7)
Percent Nice, Not Good (N, NG)	27.8	46.5	34.1	6.3	9.3	40.6	39.8	19.8	12.0
Number of cases	(67)	(285)	(187)	(13)	(50)	(71)	(64)	(127)	(33)
Number of attorneys	(4)	(3)	(8)	(1)	(2)	(5)	(6)	(4)	(2)
Percent Not Nice, But Good (NN, BG)	8.3	2.4	14.6	22.8	.7	25.1	6.8	17.8	19.2
Number of cases	(20)	(15)	(80)	(47)	(4)	(44)	(11)	(114)	(53)
Number of attorneys	(5)	(2)	(4)	(1)	(1)	(3)	(4)	(2)	(3)
Percent Nice and Good (NAG)	36.1	40.5	46.8	50.5	74.1	13.1	18.0	41.6	39.1
Number of cases	(87)	(248)	(257)	(104)	(397)	(23)	(29)	(267)	(108)
Number of attorneys	(10)	(6)	(9)	(9)	(7)	(3)	(6)	(7)	(8)
Total number of cases involving regular defense attorney	312	773	709	252	558	217	205	674	323
Cases with missing information on defense attorney	71	130	160	46	22	42	44	33	47
Percent of regulars' cases that are missing	22.7	16.8	22.5	18.2	3.9	19.3	21.4	4.9	14.5

Based on the data in Table 12.11, we should be sensitive to one last point. A handful of categories represent so few attorneys (one or two), or such a small number of cases (less than twenty-five), that they may not permit a valid analysis of a particular type of attorney's impact in a given county. It is a factor that must be kept in mind in assessing the results of the quantitative analyses.

Defense Attorneys and Guilty Plea Cases: An Empirical Assessment

The defense attorney analyses were considerably more straightforward and less involved than those for the judge and prosecutor and are easier to report. Thus, rather than merely providing a summary table, we present detailed results of the analysis of covariance for the two most broadly based charge and sentence measures (*CHRGRED* and *JAILMIN*); the data on the other dependent variables are reported in Appendix VII. The *CHRGRED* and *JAILMIN* results are contained in Tables 12.12 and 12.13, and the pattern of results is quite similar to those reported in earlier analyses. Despite the considerable variance within and across defense bars just described, the differences in attorneys have only sporadic implications for outcomes, especially sentences. Regular defense attorneys in St. Clair and Oakland do better in acquiring charge reductions. No other finding is recorded in more than one county, and in only three instances do any of the categoric regular attorney variables make a difference in charge reductions. Changes in adjusted R^2's are minimal (in the .01-.02 range); the results for the other charge reduction variables (Appendix VII, Tables VII.1 and VII.2) are similarly weak.

The impact of the attorney variables are even weaker in the *JAILMIN* analysis as only one finding emerges that is significant at or beyond the .01 level. Only minor differences occur if we examine the more refined sentence measures (Appendix VII, Tables VII.3, 4, 5). Private attorneys, for example, regardless of their standing as a regular, do less well than public defenders in Montgomery and Dauphin. No other variables have a similar impact in at least two counties and, with only three exceptions, no change in adjusted R^2 is greater than .03.

These results are fairly consistent with the view of regular defense attorneys as creators and protectors of norms. However, as was the case with the judge and prosecutor analyses, we must be careful to insure that the data reported in Tables 12.12 and 12.13, as well as in Appendix VII, are not the result of comparing "apples and oranges." While controls for case attributes are used in the multivariate analyses just reported, certain types of attorneys may be more likely to get their client exonerated entirely, a possibility that could potentially undermine the above findings.

Table 12.12. **The Impact of Defense Attorney Variables upon** *CHRGRED*

	DuPage (Ring)	Peoria (Autonomous)	St. Clair (Declining)	Oakland (Ring)	Kalamazoo (Autonomous)	Saginaw (Declining)	Montgomery (Ring)	Dauphin (Autonomous)	Erie (Declining)
Mean response (for dichotomous dependent variables only)	.54	.49	.41	.37	.16	.70	.40	.10	.60
Adjusted R^2 (for control variables)	.50	.33	.27	.30	.37	.06	.27	.14	.16
PRIVDC	0	0	+****	0	0	0	0	0	0
REGULAR	0	0	+****	+**	0	0	0	0	0
NN, NG (Not Nice, Not Good)	0	0	0	0	0	0	0	0	0
N, NG (Nice, Not Good)	0	0	0	0	0	0	0	0	0
NN, BG (Not Nice, But Good)	0	0	−*	0	0	0	0	0	0
NAG (Nice and Good)	0	0	0	−**	0	0	0	0	+**
Net change in adjusted R^2 due to addition of defense attorney variables	0	0	.02	.01	0	0	0	0	.01
Total possible N	427	444	531	545	520	413	406	770	389

+ Indicates a positive relationship.

* Indicates relationship at .05 level.

Table 12.13. **The Impact of Defense Attorney Variables upon** *JAILMIN*

	DuPage (Ring)	Peoria (Autonomous)	St. Clair (Declining)	Oakland (Ring)	Kalamazoo (Autonomous)	Saginaw (Declining)	Montgomery (Ring)	Dauphin (Autonomous)	Erie (Declining)
Adjusted R^2 (for control variables)	.24	.74	.63	.39	.48	.47	.12	.79	.39
PRIVDC	0	0	0	0	0	+*	0	0	0
REGULAR	0	0	-*	0	0	0	0	0	0
NN, NG (Not Nice, Not Good)	0	0	0	0	0	0	0	0	0
N, NG (Nice, Not Good)	0	0	0	0	0	0	+***	0	0
NN, BG (Not Nice, But Good)	0	0	0	0	0	0	0	0	0
NAG (Nice and Good)	0	0	0	0	0	0	0	0	0
Net change in adjusted R^2 due to addition of defense attorney variables	0	0	.003	0	0	.004	.01	0	0
N	469	571	650	554	570	424	415	836	378

* Indicates relationship at .05 level.
** Indicates relationship at .01 level.
*** Indicates relationship at .001 level.

+ Indicates a positive relationship.
− Indicates a negative relationship.
0 Indicates no relationship.

Table 12.14. **Probability of Conviction by Defense Attorney Types**

	DuPage (Ring)	Peoria (Autono-mous)	St. Clair (Declin-ing)	Oakland (Ring)	Kalamazoo (Autono-mous)	Saginaw (Declin-ing)	Mont-gomery (Ring)	Dauphin (Autono-mous)	Erie (Declin-ing)
PRIVDC	0	0	0	0	0	0	0	0	0
REGULAR	0	+***	0	0	0	+***	0	0	+***
NN, NG (Not Nice, Not Good)	0	0	0	0	0	0	0	0	0
N, NG (Nice, Not Good)	0	0	+**	0	0	0	0	0	0
NN, BG (Not Nice, But Good)	0	0	0	0	0	-*	0	0	0
NAG (Nice and Good)	0	-**	0	0	0	0	0	+*	0
Net change in adjusted R^2 due to addition of defense attorney variables	.00	.07	.03	.00	.02	.07	.03	.03	.07
N of cases	448	636	523	431	539	363	339	824	359

+ Indicates a positive relationship.
− Indicates a negative relationship.
0 Indicates no relationship.

* Indicates relationship at .05 level.
** Indicates relationship at .01 level.
*** Indicates relationship at .001 level.

Table 12.14 reports the results of a dummy variable regression analysis using a convict/not convict variable in conjunction with the defense attorney variables. While significant findings are relatively scarce, one pattern is important to note. The clients of regular attorneys in three counties (Peoria, Saginaw, and Erie) have higher conviction rates than clients of nonregulars. Moreover, the differences in the conviction rates are in the 14-19 percent range. Further analyses indicated that these differences were largely because of higher dismissal rates for nonregulars in these three counties. Also guilty plea rates in these counties were 20-25 percent lower for clients of nonregulars than for those of regulars. These findings have some import for the above results. The implication that nonregulars in Peoria, Saginaw, and Erie do not "do better" for their clients in plea cases is questionable because so many more clients are likely never to plead or be convicted.

SUMMARY AND OBSERVATIONS

In this chapter we examined the impact of criminal court actors upon a variety of measures—both general and refined—of charge reductions and sentence disparities in guilty plea cases. It would be difficult to identify more important features of a plea package, from either the defendant's or society's perspective. Moreover, we took great care in developing, and feel quite confident about, the measures we employed. The analyses themselves were multifaceted, designed to be both extensive and responsive to the concerns raised within the literature. We examined the linear impact of dummy variables and of more refined measures of individual traits, measures based upon the careful manipulation of data painstakingly collected during—and after—lengthy on-site interviews with the participants. With respect to judges and prosecutors, we also examined the joint effect of attitudes with case characteristics and other decision-maker attributes.

These analyses were conducted in diverse counties that varied considerably in how the plea process was organized. Moreover, they were not conducted before an examination of the diversity of the actors within each jurisdiction was undertaken. Although a large amount of variance did not occur with respect to every trait in every county, enough variance existed in enough counties to gauge the impact of each measure employed. Moreover, the results of the analyses did not appear to be tied systematically to the level of variance within a county. Finally, we also examined the effect of decision-maker traits upon disposition rates to insure that different types of actors were not dealing with systematically different pools of cases at the guilty plea stage. With a few exceptions involving defense attorneys, which were noted, this was not a significant problem.

The image of decision-maker impact that emerges from these analyses is one that is marginal at best, nil for the most part. Besides being very weak, many of the results that did emerge were almost random in their occurrence. That is, a particular actor or trait failed consistently to affect charge or sentence across all counties, or even in similar counties. The basic point to stress about the overall structure of the findings uncovered in the individual-level analyses is that they are consistent with the general patterns described in chapter 8. Patterned sources of disparity do not emerge consistently in the shaping of charges and sentences in these counties. At the same time, however, these results, particularly those that emerged from the interaction analyses of the judge and prosecutor variables, are not consistent with those that emerged from an earlier analysis (Nardulli, Flemming, and Eisenstein, 1984), one that used some of the same variables and data used here. Although the analysis was limited to sentencing (*JAILMIN*), one of its principal conclusions was:

> The findings demonstrate that the personal views and working styles of the principal actors shaped sentencing decisions in varying ways and to a nontrivial degree. The coefficient of determination (R^2) for a regression equation including only the contextual variables for offense seriousness and prior criminal record was .49, but adding just the two-way interaction terms involving individual-level characteristics (as in equation 2) enlarged the coefficient to .58, a net improvement of .09 in the coefficient and an 18% increase. By incorporating the three-way interaction terms in equation (4), the proportion of explained variance rose to .64, fully one-third greater than the coefficient for the original linear model. (1984, 925)

The incompatibility of that concessions-oriented conclusion with those that emerge from the results reported here requires a reasoned explanation; we must look to the differences in two analyses to provide it. One readily apparent difference is that the earlier analysis is a much more intensive and elaborate empirical examination. It included, in one equation, attitude measures for all three primary actors, plus a number of two- and three-way interaction terms incorporating case characteristics, other decision-maker attributes, structural variables, and work-group configurations. The final equation had twenty-four independent variables and interaction terms.

The more elaborate analysis undoubtedly contributed to some of the differences in the results. We could have, perhaps, increased the strength of some of the basic relationships examined here by merging variables on all actors into one equation and employing three-way interactions. But such a strategy would not have changed the results reported here considerably and would have entailed unacceptable costs. A more important cause of the differences in results lies with the basic design of the two analyses. Consider first the earlier analysis. It was a pooled analysis that merged cases from all county samples that met certain criteria. The criteria was that the case have been disposed of by a triad (a specific judge, prosecutor, and defense attorney) that handled at least five cases together in the county sample. This was to insure a sufficient level of familiarity among the participants. High levels of familiarity were considered desirable because it was thought that familiarity would increase the likelihood that participants understood one anothers' views and skills. This would increase the likelihood that these attributes would affect interactions and outcomes. The five-case criteria also added stability to the relationships observed, insuring that observed differences were not the result of a few deviant cases.

These were legitimate objectives to pursue in the early, exploratory phase of a research project such as this, but they were achieved at a considerable cost. Of the more than 5,500 guilty plea cases in the nine county samples, the final equation in the 1984 analysis was based on 784 cases, or less than 15 percent of those available. Very few private attorney cases were included, nor were many cases from DuPage, Oakland, Saginaw, and Montgomery. The diffuse structure of their defense bars produced few cases that met the five-case criteria. This is especially true of Saginaw and Oakland, neither of which had a public defender office.

Another factor should be stressed that limits the generalizability of the earlier results. It is the omnipresence of the offense seriousness variable in most of the interaction terms that emerged as statistically significant. Most effects that did emerge had an effect only in serious cases. This is reasonable because these cases provide the actors with the most leeway and motivation. But as suggested in some sentence projections in the 1984 article (Nardulli, Flemming, and Eisenstein, 1984, Table 2, 921) most effects—especially those for judges and prosecutors—did not emerge in cases whose seriousness index was less than or equivalent to burglary cases. The types of cases in which the various interactions began to have an effect were cases such as robbery, armed robbery, rape, arson, and murder. These cases accounted for approximately 20 percent of the sentenced cases in our nine county samples. Thus, interpersonal differences did not usually produce significant differences in approximately 80 percent of the small subset of cases analyzed.

The approach used in the present analysis differs considerably in scope and design from the 1984 article. We conducted the individual-level analyses within each of the county samples and in such a way as to minimize missing cases. Not pooling the data restricts the range of variance on the independent variables, but the sample specific approach is a closer approximation of reality as dispositions occur within individual court communities. Moreover, at this later stage of the research we could not—in light of the documented differences in court communities and plea systems we have seen—justify merging the various county samples for the purpose of conducting individual-level analyses. Nor could we, given the role of the individual-level analysis within the overall structure of this empirical assessment of the plea process, justify working with only 15 percent of the available cases.

The methodological benefits of proceeding as we have here notwithstanding, a better understanding of the evolution of this research will help explain the present approach, as well as the approach adopted in the earlier analysis. In striving to obtain a feel for the structure of the data in the early stages of this research, we constructed a "best case" analysis of the role that individuals played in the plea process. Despite the obvious limitations of the analysis, it suggested that individuals played a fairly prominent role in the sentencing process. On the basis of implications that flowed from the earlier results—implications that were very concessions oriented in nature—we attempted to extend the basic analysis to charge reductions. In the course of constructing our measures of charge reductions, it became evident that they were not widespread, nor were there patterned disparities in their allocation. This led us to reexamine sentences in plea cases, moving away from a regression-based analysis of selected cases to a more basic analysis of sentencing patterns. Here we again observed more consistency than we initially believed existed. Patterned disparities across case-level attributes again did not appear, with some exceptions.

This, of course, led us back to an examination of individuals as another potential source of patterned disparities in the allocation process. Our initial efforts had come full circle. But we could no longer justify an examination of the tip of the proverbial iceberg. Our explorations of its base—its structure and contours—revealed a different formation than we had anticipated initially. We could no longer be content with an analysis of selected individuals under special conditions. We wanted to know the shape of the gullies as well as the peaks. Moreover, while these formations may be different in structure, our assessment must be based upon a survey of the whole, not just its salients.

NOTES

1. The distribution of the dependent variable is important because we are using multiple regression analysis to analyze the impact of the decision-maker traits.

A dummy dependent variable indicates some of the underlying assumptions upon which multiple regression is based. However, there is general agreement among statisticians that as long as the dependent variable is not too skewed (i.e., not much more than a 70-30 or 80-20 split between the two categories), a regression analysis can be used reliably. For more on this point, see Gillespie (1977) and Knoke (1975). Because this is a crucial point, we report the mean of dummy dependent variables, which indicates the proportion of cases in the 1 category (all cases are coded 0 or 1). The breakdown of the *CHRGRED* dummy dependent variable is generally not a problem, except for in Kalamazoo and Dauphin, where charge reductions are rare. It is more of a problem for the *FRSTJAIL* and *PRIMRED* variable, which tend to be more skewed. This was one of the factors considered in not focusing on these variables in the textual discussions.

2. A few comments should be made about these analyses. First, trichotomized versions of the attitudinal variables were used. These are more appropriate when using a dummy dependent variable. Although collapsing variance is not always good, we probably have clearer distinctions among decision makers when we trichotomize. One consequence of this, however, is that because of the extreme views of Dauphin judges we have no variance in Dauphin on either the Belief in Punishment or the Regard for Due Process variable. A second necessary adjustment was that the trichotomized version of Regard for Due Process had to be inverted to calculate the proper interaction terms. We wanted to test the impact of more conservative actors in more serious cases. We could not do that when the high scores on the due process variable reflected more liberal views. One final difference should be noted. Because of the large number of tables required to report the results of the interaction analyses (fifty-six in all) and the fact that the results for the other charge reduction and sentence disparity variables are similar to those reported in the text, we do not include appendixes reporting the results for these other variables.

REFERENCES

Gillespie, Michael W. 1977. "Log Linear Techniques and the Regression Analysis of Dummy Dependent Variables: Further Bases for Comparison." *Sociological Methods and Research* 6:103-22.

Knoke, David. 1975. "A Comparison of Log Linear and Regression Models for Systems of Dichotomous Variables." *Sociological Methods and Research* 3:416-34.

Nardulli, Peter F., Roy B. Flemming, and James Eisenstein. 1984. "Unraveling the Complexities of Decision Making in Face to Face Groups: A Contextual Analysis of Plea-Bargained Sentences." *American Political Science Review* 78:912-28.

V

CONCLUSIONS

13

CRIMINAL COURTS, COURTHOUSE COMMUNITIES, AND THE GUILTY PLEA PROCESS: OBSERVATIONS AND IMPLICATIONS

We can usefully extend the iceberg metaphor a bit further as a way of thinking about what we have done here and what we can say about it. To find our way through the rather perplexing maze of structures, activities, and actors that dotted and enveloped the criminal court landscapes in our nine counties, we used a multidimensional map. We paid particular attention to those features most directly related to the guilty plea process. A variety of methodological instruments were used to record and gauge various features of these courts and their environs, as well as the people who operated them and the cases they handled. In some cases our recordings were only rough sketches of prominent but somewhat hazy features; in others, we had detailed drawings of more accessible and manageable objects. Our purpose was to obtain a better understanding of the terrain as well as to facilitate the work of those who will pass this way in the future.

What did we discover during our explorations? Do our discoveries provide new insights into the state of American justice, especially the guilty plea process? Does it hold implications for the reform of criminal courts? For the future direction of research on these courts? It is to these matters that we now turn.

CONCEPTUAL MAPS AND CRIMINAL COURTS

In developing the theoretical apparatus to be used for this research, we introduced a number of concepts. Not all of them proved useful for our inquiries. At the same time new insights were generated into the role of others. Our discussion of the role of these various concepts in the study of criminal courts, as well as their specific needs in terms of conceptual refinement, begins at the ecological level.

We find very little direct effect upon case outcomes of such environmental factors as the level of media concentration, the severity of the crime problem, various dimensions of the county's sociopolitical system, and detention capacity. While such things as media concentration and the severity of the crime problem had some effect upon the severity of going rates, only penitentiary capacity had a truly strong impact. But even in this instance its real impact was somewhat clouded by other state-level factors (sentencing codes, state-wide sentencing norms). These sparse findings do not mean that environmental influences are not important for understanding how criminal courts operate. To some extent the fact that these variables did not have a direct effect may be due to the design of this research, because the relatively small number of counties observed limited what we could do and find. A more likely explanation, however, is that ecological influences are more relevant for other aspects of the criminal court milieu than for case outcomes.

Most criminal court research up to now has used case outcomes as dependent variables; researchers have been primarily concerned with explaining differences in these outcomes. This is wholly understandable because these outcomes are the bottom line in the process, the output of most concern to society. But limiting research on criminal courts to case outcomes would be like limiting research on Congress to votes. We need to cast a broader net in the study of these courts; when we do, the relevance of environmental factors becomes clearer. In chapter 2 we alluded to the importance of the court community's social, political, and legal environment in affecting the composition of the court's caseload, the type of people likely to be recruited, and the nature of the constraints and expectations within which the court must work. In our analyses of the court communities in chapters 5 and 6, we observed some other effects as well.

A good example is the impact of various environmental factors upon the cohesiveness of various court communities, as well as upon the structure and reach of their grapevines. In counties like DuPage and Oakland, where political stakes were high and the outside communities were changing rapidly, wholly internal considerations were of less consequence to the prime actors. The reverberation of changes in the court's environment made it more difficult to maintain a vibrant grapevine. Unlike Montgomery, these counties did not have a strong centralized political party to exert centripetal forces, nor were there longstanding ties among a large component of the criminal court actors. Clearly, the situation was quite different in smaller, more stagnant communities of Erie, St. Clair, Dauphin, and Peoria.

It is also instructive to constrast a county like St. Clair with Peoria or Kalamazoo, or with DuPage or Oakland. Different types of individuals are drawn to serve within the local courts, bringing different values and expectations. They also work under different fiscal constraints. This is manifested in the types of people they recruit, the structure of their work, and in the norms they establish. The effects of the environment upon the structure and orientation of each court community are not always obvious if we view snapshots of these communities, nor do we always see clear links between orientation and case outcomes. But discussions with criminal court veterans who have watched these changes unfold over the years reveal the salience of environmental factors for courthouse communities. Students of criminal courts who ignore them because they fail to have a "statistically significant effect" upon case outcomes do so at their own peril and at great cost. Such a narrow perspective unduly handicaps our efforts to better understand these vital social institutions.

We move now to the next conceptual level, to contextual factors. We firmly believe that they are crucial to a better understanding of the milieu in which cases are processed and are legitimate objects of inquiry in their own right. Indeed, these factors should be the key component of any effort to broaden the scope of study in this field. Insofar as their impact upon case processing is concerned, much the same could be said about these contextual factors as was said about the ecological variables just discussed. This is especially true for the notion of a courthouse community. With respect to the court's infrastructure, however, we see much closer ties to case processing. Chapter 9, for example, suggests that such things as screening and charging practices, the structure of the plea offer mechanism, and the breadth of the plea agenda all had direct implications for the role of charge reductions in a county. Less clear results were obtained for the role of these contextual factors in determining the severity of going rates, but there is good reason to believe that a more broadly based study could demonstrate such a relationship. Also, the court community's infrastructure may have direct relevance for understanding other aspects of case outcomes, especially case processing time, across jurisdictions.

At this embryonic stage of its development, the potential utility of the notion of a courthouse community seems significant but is still unclear. Certainly it should be given more rigor and specificity. A more systematic analysis and mapping of court community norms and values could help identify key differences across court communities and perhaps lead to a fairly inclusive typology of court communities. It could also begin us on the path toward a better understanding of factors that affect the structure and work orientation of these communities, giving us a much better sense of the real role of ecological factors in shaping local justice. A more fundamental concern with the concept of a courthouse community that must be addressed is its applicability in larger jurisdictions. Will this concept be useful in the study of courts that permit greater specialization by private attorneys and that use public defender offices as well as a specialized criminal bench? Or will the relevant social unit be the court-room rather than the courthouse, as was perhaps the case in Oakland? If the situation varies from court to court, what factors affect the emergence of communities in these urban areas?

In thinking about the court community's infrastructure in conceptual terms, we can see the need for further refinement in a number of areas. First, we have to enhance our understanding of the key structures and practices within the criminal court domain. We feel we have developed a fairly comprehensive inventory here, especially for those structures and practices that affect the guilty plea process. But it is just a beginning. Certainly not all facets of the infrastructure have been discussed here, and undoubtedly other organizational variants also exist. Second, there is a need to refine our understanding of the relationship between various components of the court's infrastructure and the work orientations de-veloped in chapter 6. This is the key to understanding, beyond a purely technical level, the meaning and implication of these structural variants. Any such analysis must begin with a rigorous scrutiny of the work orientations that were developed here. These concepts are at an elementary stage of development, and they are limited by our observations in just nine counties within one sector of the United States. Broader fieldwork could yield refinements in the orientations we introduced and might also uncover additional orientations.

One last point should be made about contextual factors. It concerns the role of support agencies within the court community. They have been largely ignored here because we did not have the resources to deal with them effectively. This does not mean they are unimportant. Indeed, the existence and structure of pretrial release agencies, diversion programs, and work release and probation services may be every bit as significant as the components of the infrastructure that were reviewed here. They can have a marked effect upon the available options and the level of discretion enjoyed by the primary actors in the court community. It is also conceivable that their role and impact will vary across counties. Future comparative studies should make every effort to incorporate them.

We cannot be as optimistic about the role of individual-level concepts in future criminal court research. We initially believed that individuals play an important role in case processing, that differences in the attitudes, abilities, and orientations of actors would be reflected in different patterns of outcomes. Even if their impact varied across counties, we believed that we had enough structural variation in our court communities to undertake a comprehensive examination. We invested an inordinate amount of time and energy in thinking about important attributes and how to measure them, believing that the key to unraveling their real impact was better measures of more refined concepts.

Although we uncovered no broadly based, systematic pattern of individual-level effects within the guilty plea process, we are satisfied with the battery of measures we developed and implemented. They involved Q-sorts, a well-developed psychological test, and a background and attitude survey; they tapped operating styles, work-specific attitudes, and Machiavellianism, among other things. They were, without question, the most rigorously defined concepts used in this study.

We are fairly confident in our conclusion that individuals have no broadly based impact upon guilty plea cases. We do not believe that better measures would yield different conclusions, and the dummy variable analyses support this. One could contend that individuals have a more marked impact upon other facets of the process, but their level of discretion in such areas as charging, bail, and delay is probably not appreciably higher. It is conceivable that individuals could play a more prominent role in other jurisdictions. There is no way to refute such a contention, although we would not devote years of effort searching for such locales. Individual actors can make a difference in some cases under some conditions, and sometimes these differences can be considerable. Future research in this area, if it is to be undertaken, can most profitably be directed to the identification of the contingencies affecting the impact of these actors.

In conclusion, we return to a central theme of this book: A truly refined and comprehensive understanding of criminal courts can only be attained through the integration of concepts at all of the three levels of analysis addressed here. But we knew (or at least believed) that before we began our research. We also knew that this task required more than simply refining concepts at each level, it required integration. Some progress was made in this regard, in both the early theoretical chapters and in the empirical analyses. Perhaps the most significant contribution of this research, in terms of theoretical advances, is the development of the notion of a courthouse community. In the long run, this concept may both broaden the scope of inquiry into criminal courts and serve as a vehicle for integrating concepts across levels.

The emergence of this concept in our thinking about court processes is important because it is consistent with what is often referred to as the "new institutionalism" in political research. As Evans, Rueschemeyer, and Skocpol noted in the preface to a leading work in this movement:

> Until recently, dominant theoretical paradigms in the comparative social science did not highlight states as organizational structures or as potentially autonomous actors. Indeed, the term "state" was rarely used. Current work, however, increasingly views the state as an actor that, although obviously influenced by the society surrounding it, also shapes social and political processes. There is a recognized need, therefore, to improve conceptualizations of the structures and capacities of states, to explain more adequately how states are formed and reorganized, and to explore in many settings how states affect societies through their interventions—or abstentions—and through their relationships with social groups (1985, vii).

While neither the setting nor the terms in this excerpt are similar to our work, the parallels are evident. Our research demonstrates quite convincingly that the actions of local courts are not simple reflections of the societal forces that engulf them and the transient actors that operate them. Although both sets of influences are important, the court community as an institution is important in its own right. It acts to both mute and modify influences from these other sources and is deserving of considerable attention in future research.

CONSISTENCY IN THE GUILTY PLEA PROCESS

On a substantive level, our primary concern was with the consistency and fairness of the guilty plea process. We were driven by two different conceptions of that process: one stressed the centrality of concessions and manipulations, the other stressed the centrality of consensual, norm-bound behavior. Our first effort was directed at gauging the absolute level of charge reductions and sentencing disparities; this was a relatively simple, straightforward task, but one that virtually no prior researchers had done in a systematic way. Second, we wanted to know whether the concessions that did exist were patterned or unpatterned. Patterned disparities (disparities associated with defendant characteristics, case characteristics, or decision makers) would suggest that the plea process produced biased treatment, whereas unpatterned concessions would be consistent with the notion that they were allocated on a need-related basis.

What did we find? We found that although 40 percent of guilty plea cases received some type of a charge reduction, only about 15 percent received a primary charge reduction. The latter figure is the most significant because only they are associated with reduced sentences. With respect to sentencing, we found that 80 percent of the plea cases fell within one of our rather tightly defined sentencing clusters. Our analysis of consistency indicators and plea concessions revealed that only one of the eleven indicators examined in each analysis (*PHYSEVID* in the charge reduction analysis; *CONFINED* in the sentencing analysis) had any systematic effect upon the allocation of concessions.

When we examined our charge and sentence measures at the county level, we uncovered, as one might expect, a more complex pattern. Four different modes of charge reduction practices existed in the nine counties, but only Saginaw differed markedly from the image that emerged from the pooled analysis. With respect to sentencing disparities between 79 and 90 percent of all plea cases in the non-Michigan counties fell within one of our clusters. The figures for the Michigan counties ranged only between 61 and 68 percent. They were lower largely because of the markedly less frequent use of probation and a tendency to mete out a sizable number of exceptionally severe (above high cluster) sentences. These practices were made possible by Michigan's considerably more abundant detention capacity. This observation raises the issue of potential tradeoffs between consistency and severity, but we have too little data to say much on that score. We analyzed the consistency indicators for each of the four county types and found results roughly similar to the pooled analyses. Significant effects were sparse and largely unpatterned, especially by county type. Confined defendants routinely received sentences above the norm, and cases involving some evidentiary deficiency often received some type of charge reduction, although the pattern was not overwhelming (Table 8.13). Our county-by-county examination of the impact of individual actors upon the allocation and receipt of plea concessions revealed systematically negligible effects; significant findings were almost random in occurrence.

These results, examined in their entirety, lead us to the conclusion that consensus, court community norms, and shared perceptions are far more central to the guilty plea process than concessions, coercion, and bazaar-type behavior. There is no question that real charge and sentence concessions occur in the negotiation of some pleas. Some of these concessions undoubtedly are tantamount to coercion; bias may play a role in the granting of others. We readily admit that under some conditions some types of actors may be more willing to grant, or more able to negotiate, plea concessions. Nonetheless, the overwhelming weight of the evidence we have examined demonstrates that these types of influences are the exception, not the norm, in most counties. Most defendants plead guilty to the primary charge upon which they were arrested and get sentenced in a fairly uniform manner.

This is not a conclusion that we come to easily or one with which we began. Nevertheless our confidence in it is bolstered by a number of considerations, the first of which is the strength, simplicity, and breadth of the empirical data upon which it is based. Our findings are not based upon tenuous conclusions from sketchy data. Our measures of charge reductions and sentencing clusters were simple and straightforward. The same can be said about most of our consistency indicators. Few things in social science are easier to measure than race, bail status, attorney type, and case processing time. More ambiguity is involved in the measurement of some of the evidence and legal motion variables. The most complex were those concerning individual-level measures, but here our assessment was bolstered by the dummy variable analysis. Despite the directness of most of our measures, the ease with which strong patterns could be detected, and an examination of nine diverse counties, we do not detect the type of results one would expect if concessions and manipulation pervaded the guilty plea process. Modal distributions predominate the data, disparities are the exception.

A second point that reinforces our conclusions that real concessions are not widespread is the fact that our estimates of charge concessions and sentence disparities are generous. This is easy to see with respect to charge concessions. To say that every charge reduction is a plea concession, or that they all resulted from negotiations, is unwarranted. Some are simply justifiable adjustments of charges due to inappropriate charging. That such adjustments occur can be seen in the somewhat comparable level of charge reductions in trial cases (Table 8.1). Also, it is entirely conceivable that many of the charge reductions, especially count drops, are not bargained for but rather are part of the plea norms in a county. This is probably most likely in the symbolic counties. Count drops that were routinely offered as part of the standard deal are not the same thing as fiercely negotiated charge reductions or those that were granted in exchange for past favors. They are more similar to a clumsy shell game that fools no one.

As for sentencing disparities, we simply note that we used a very conservative approach to define clusters. More than 90 percent were point clusters, clusters that allowed for no spread in sentences. This is an exceedingly stringent definition of what sentencing consistency means, but it was necessary for the purposes of this research. More reasonable criteria would have yielded a more consistent picture of sentencing in Michigan. A second point worth noting is that it would be absurd to think that all off-cluster sentences are unwarranted disparities. Many were undoubtedly deserved deviations from the standard sentence; this conclusion is supported by the general failure of the consistency indicators to have much of an effect upon sentences.

The most unsettling empirical results reported here concerned the existence of a jury trial penalty. Our analyses revealed that those who exercised their right to a jury trial were more likely to receive more severe sentences. This, of course, colors the entire process because it suggests that an element of coercion exists, that individuals must plead guilty, often with no discernible concession, or face a stiffer sentence. Several things should be kept in mind here. First, we uncovered no significant bench trial penalty across county types or in the pooled analysis. Second, the analysis of the jury trial penalty suggested it was most likely to occur in counties where charge reductions were most prevalent, the middling and maximalist counties (Table 8.15). Third, it should be stressed that the results do not suggest that everyone who is convicted after a jury trial is penalized; in other words, a jury trial tariff is applied in only some cases. For example, the pooled analysis showed that a large majority of all first offenders convicted after a jury trial still received probation, the probability of getting some jail time was simply greater than for other cases—about 17 percent greater (Table 8.8). Thus, although we cannot say that trial penalties are nonexistent, they appear to occur only in some jury trial cases in some counties.

The fact that we do not find concessions, disparities, and trial penalties to be widespread in the plea process of most of our counties does not mean that those that do exist should be dismissed cavalierly. They can introduce inequities, and they affect real defendants and real victims in a direct manner. They also have a tremendous symbolic impact, albeit one that is greatly disproportionate to their actual frequency. Truly consequential charge reductions or large sentencing breaks in plea cases are to concessions-oriented critics of the plea process what jury trials are to those legalists who attempt to maintain the myth of an adversary disposition process. They only need a few to illustrate their point. The mundane and the routine are quickly forgotten; the exceptions are the stuff of court community lore. It is accounts of these cases that are told and retold, that make reputations for attorneys and judges, that become reported in newspapers and to academic journalists, and, finally, that become entrenched firmly in the conventional wisdom about the American criminal process. It is for these reasons that we must continue to be concerned with the concessions and disparities that do exist, regardless of their actual level.

COURT COMMUNITIES, GUILTY PLEAS, AND THE TENOR OF JUSTICE

Reasonable minds may differ over whether the level of consistency found within the plea processes in our nine counties is enough consistency. They may also differ over whether any type of trial tariff, however infrequently invoked, is justifiable. What we have to say about such value laden questions matters little. What we can do, however, is offer some ideas on why significant charge concessions and off-cluster sentences are the exception, not the norm, in the counties we examined. We can also offer our thoughts on what these findings mean for the tenor of justice in the criminal courts we studied.

Any attempt to fashion an explanation of the pattern of findings that emerged from our empirical analyses must start with an analysis of the individual actors within the dispositional process. It is their actions, individual or joint, that produce a flow of outcomes that are either consistent or disparate. If one contemplates the flow of commentary concerning these actors in the context of the debate over plea bargaining, especially in legal circles, the results reported here are all the more perplexing. Much has been made of the virtually unfettered discretion enjoyed by these actors, especially with respect to such decisions as charging and sentencing. This commentary has been reinforced by the outcome of many of the reforms imposed upon criminal court actors from the outside: In most cases the actors have been able to use their discretion to evade the intent of the reform, leading to charges of "lawless" behavior. In contrast, our research indicates that an internal order is produced by a set of effective internal checks upon actors whose discretion is, indeed, legally unfettered. Moreover, that internal order produces a high level of consistency in the handling of normal cases.

We see two main sources of internal checks upon individual discretion, the social dimensions of the court community and its infrastructure. Where a strong cohesive court community exists, the web of interpersonal ties and mutual needs that holds it together also creates norms and understandings that guide and restrict behavior. In a sense, court communities emerge because of the need to establish these understandings, as well as to meet other human needs. Once in place, these communities serve to perpetuate and reinforce these understandings. No one wants to reinvent the wheel with each new case. The problems, constraints, and cognitions governing how court actors approach garden-variety cases change very slowly. To be viable, court community norms and practices must evolve over time. But, in the short run, it is in the interest of all to establish, abide by, and enforce a common set of understandings about how normal cases should be handled and how defendants should be punished.

Systematic departures from these norms—either in the form of deviant actors or the differential treatment of certain types of attorneys— will serve to weaken the norms and understandings that are the court community's *raison d'etre*. The grapevine will disseminate disparate patterns throughout the court community, precipitating demands to correct the deviations (e.g., issue new policies, reassign individuals, threaten to publicize) or for equal treatment (i.e., redefine the norm to conform to the divergent pattern). Turmoil and problems may exist in the short run while adjustments are being made. Indeed, turmoil, with respect to one issue or another, may be a defining characteristic of some court communities. But such frays over isolated issues, even when they are a continuing phenomenon, are analogous to haggling over the trimming of a tree; they should not be allowed to obscure the shape of the forest. As long as the establishment and enforcement of norms serves the interests and needs of the courtroom actors, these norms will act as a check upon individual actors. When needed, formal or informal policies or mechanisms will emerge to insure that this function is performed, at least in court systems where some sense of community has emerged and is a viable force.

The court community's infrastructure affects the consistency of the plea process in a very different way from its social dimensions. Its impact does not depend upon the existence of a cohesive court community. Moreover, not all infrastructure will produce a high level of consistency in the plea process. Our discussions in chapters 6 and 9 suggest that certain practices, policies, and structures will minimize the opportunities and pressures for charge changes or sentencing accommodations in most counties. That is, court community leaders can structure the plea process to produce a high level of consistency, or they can structure it with other goals in mind, or no goals at all. The use of screening or the pretrial diversion of cases, careful charging practices, some degree of centralization in plea offers, strong on-the-nose plea policies, and other checks on the discretion of individuals can enhance the consistency of the plea process. Unfortunately, the question of which of these practices is most important or which combination will yield the highest level of consistency is one we cannot answer at this time.

What can we say about the nature of the internal order produced by these homogenizing influences? About the caliber of justice meted out by these court communities? Our fieldwork, empirical analyses, and deliberations suggest the existence of a system of bureaucratic justice. Although this characterization is neither novel nor original, we believe that the insights produced by this research, as well as the level of empirical support given those insights, is different from, and goes beyond, what prior researchers have concluded. By bureaucratic justice, we mean a system in which discretionary actions are governed by fairly rigid adherence to informal norms and procedures designed to pigeonhole defendants into a few rough groupings with as few exceptions as possible. Exceptions require work, create uncertainty, and breed more exceptions, further complicating work life. Bureaucratic justice is a system premised not on strict adherence to due process ideals, or committed to the refined, individualized treatment of individuals; nor is it one wedded to the swift and severe punishment of defendants based upon some conception of just desserts. Indeed, it is a justice not firmly committed to any consistent ideology but, rather, one premised on strict adherence to bureaucratic routine. That routine is structured by pragmatic people of limited imagination and experience dealing with large numbers of fairly routine cases in the context of limited resources and options.

The particular routine that emerges within a particular county is fashioned, over time, by prominent leaders in the court community within the constraints of a variety of contextual and environmental factors. Relevant here are such things as detention capacity, program availability, political expectations of the local community, prosecutorial practices and policies, the structure of the indigent defense system, and long-standing court community norms. Opinions will differ over the desirability of having such factors mold the internal order of a court community, as well as the process by which that molding occurs. The earthy nature of these considerations will cause indignation among many over the nature of bureaucratic justice, much like the way the crime survey researchers reacted to what they discovered in urban criminal courts in the 1920s. In addition, the ideological neutrality of bureaucratic justice will make few people happy. Because it is not based on due process ideals, it is consistent with the existence of a trial tariff, at least for those who request "unreasonable trials." Because it loathes exceptions, it alienates those who favor individualized justice. Bureaucratic justice is equally frustrating to law-and-order proponents who would isolate potentially habitual offenders early in their careers and treat them as exceptions deserving of harsh treatment. Thus, from diverse ideological perspectives the dictates of bureaucratic routine require that unequals be treated equally to a greater degree than is desired.

These criticisms notwithstanding, the type of order produced by a system of bureaucratic justice frequently minimizes the uncertainties and inequities that may accompany the widespread use of exceptions and distinctions. Bias and favoritism seem to be neutralized to a large extent. Bureaucratic justice conserves the resources that would be required to treat routine cases as though each were unique. The aura of consistency that emerges from a system of bureaucratic justice also enhances the legitimacy of the criminal court, if only because of the contrast with the image perpetuated by the myth of "bargain justice."

It is understandable to desire a system of justice that does more than routinely force defendants into a few rough, rigidly structured pigeonholes, one that goes beyond the mere muting of pernicious effects, a system that looks good only because we thought it would be worse. Unfortunately, it is unlikely that a more enlightened order will emerge in the near future. Nor, for several reasons, can we expect more from those who operate our criminal courts. First, our adversary legal system is designed to produce principles of law and enunciate legal rights only in contested matters. Uncontested matters—those that are the stuff of criminal courts—are the law's orphans. When issues of law and procedure emerge in contested matters, they float to the top of the legal system, where they are debated, considered, and resolved by prominent, knowledgeable jurists and scholars. Eventually an informed, considered resolution to the question is formulated, and the resolution is disseminated broadly. While history may show that these resolutions are not always correct, they are at least considered broadly and debated thoroughly. Uncontested matters are normally resolved within specific court communities in a manner that satisfies the affected parties, and/or with reference to some accepted local practice or tradition. Because these issues and resolutions never enter the broader legal arena, they are never considered widely or disseminated broadly. This limits the amount and type of information available to practitioners.

Second, most of the issues arising in criminal matters fall within what most observers would consider the legitimate purview of the actors' discretion. That is, they are not normally considered amenable to resolution by general decrees. As it has evolved, the highly decentralized American system of criminal justice purposely vests important discretionary matters in the hands of officials who are locally accountable. The fear of criminal prosecution as a tool of oppression wielded by some central authority has deep roots in American history. While such a fear is perhaps less justified today, the system has facilitated the establishment of largely autonomous court communities operating within broadly defined guidelines, but permitted, even expected, to develop their own mores.

A final reason why we cannot expect local courts to meet higher, more enlightened standards in the performance of discretionary tasks in uncontested matters is that their mission is so undefined and their technology is so uncertain. We, as a society, can provide them with few widely embraced, concrete standards by which to guide their behavior or to use in measuring the desirability of different approaches. If we could agree upon what a just disposition was, or who was potentially an habitual offender, or how to rehabilitate defendants, or even *if* we wanted to rehabilitate them, then perhaps enlightened methods prescribing how to achieve those ends could be promulgated and implemented on a wide scale. Until these and other matters are resolved, we are not justified in demanding too much of criminal courts with respect to how they govern their discretionary decisions in uncontested matters. Perhaps the most we can expect for the present is that they not be oppressive in the exercise of the powers vested in them and that established norms be applied in a consistent manner.

REFORMING THE GUILTY PLEA PROCESS

These observations temper our thinking about the reform implications of our research. We begin with the basic position that criminal courts are human institutions and will remain human institutions — notwithstanding the onslaught of technological advances in information processing and problem-solving. Advanced computer technology may help us sort out the judgments and value laden issues involved in everyday criminal court decisions, but they will never be able to resolve them for us. Our criminal courts are human institutions that deal with difficult issues; they are operated by people with limited cognitive abilities, imperfect analytic techniques, and personal biases. As such they will never operate flawlessly. This realization — in conjunction with our observations that the plea process in many counties is perhaps not as vile a dispositional system as conventional wisdom (and some scholarly work) would lead us to believe — makes it easier to talk about the reform, rather than the abolition of, plea-oriented dispositional processes.

This perspective is further reinforced by the parallel observation that the criminal trial is also a human institution. We do not advocate a wholesale movement to a trial-oriented dispositional process for a variety of reasons. One need only think about the current controversies in civil justice circles — the efforts to develop less rigid, less formalistic methods of dispute resolution — to realize that a shift to a trial-oriented disposition process would not be a panacea for the criminal courts. Despite the fact that criminal trials better meet the formal dictates of due process notions that have evolved over the years, they would actually eliminate many of the informal checks and balances upon individual discretion that we have noted here. We view this as a serious matter. Moreover, we believe that the trial functions well in its present capacity as an alternative form of dispute resolution for cases that present real factual disputes, as well as for those that raise value questions that require more direct participation by those outside the courthouse community — questions less appropriate for those whose expertise lies in the methodical processing of the routine.

We urge that the criminal trial's present role within the criminal process be preserved even though we agree, in principle, with Alschuler's assertion (1981) that our society can afford to provide every defendant with a trial. Although we strongly disagree with his estimates, the actual cost of such an experiment would be minimal in a society that routinely spends hundreds of billions of dollars for various public goods. Our objections go beyond a quick cost benefit analysis of such a proposal, even though we must question the actual benefits of providing trials in garden-variety cases that present few factual questions. Our primary concerns are with the long-run institutional costs of mandating a trial in every case.

Trials are clumsy instruments devised to insure that both sides of an argument over disputed facts are fully and fairly presented. But what will be the ultimate impact upon the structure of the trial process if it is routinely used to process cases with few factual issues? Will it desensitize fact-finders to real issues? Will it lead to procedural reforms or informal adaptations in the structure of the trial to reflect its new role within the dispositional process? The elaborate procedural safeguards that have evolved around the conduct of adversary trials have been tolerated, at least in part, because trials have been used so infrequently. To change their role would undoubtedly lead to changes in the structure of the trial, perhaps violating its institutional integrity. Our fear is that, if this occurs, the trial as we now know it will not be available for the types of cases for which it can be of most value.

These considerations make us eager to fine-tune the guilty plea process, to improve its ability to perform the valuable role it can play within the dispositional process, and to enhance its legitimacy in the eyes of society. At the same time, we must realize that criminal courts cannot be expected to succeed in matters where other social institutions have failed, or to resolve empirical and value-laden issues that society has been unable to resolve. Nor can they be expected to devise innovative technologies to cope with problems if they are denied the resources and flexibility to experiment. Therefore, our proposals are relatively modest. Also, they deal primarily with those facets of criminal courts that are most directly related to the guilty plea process and are relatively well grounded in the findings uncovered in this, and related, research. Our proposals deal directly with the makeup of the court system's infrastructure.

We believe that a court community's infrastructure can have a profound impact upon its guilty plea process. This infrastructure can, and should, be designed to minimize the level of manipulation within the system. This will enhance consistency, minimize coercion, and provide for the fair and equitable treatment of defendants. In the long run, this will enhance the legitimacy of the plea process in the eyes of the public. These goals can be attained in a variety of ways, and different structures may work better in some locales than others. But our research suggests two corrective actions that might be particularly effective: careful prosecutorial pruning of the caseload and minimizing the amount of discretion exercised by any one individual.

The experiences of Kalamazoo and Saginaw illustrate, among other things, the importance of carefully pruned caseloads. If every prosecutor's office carefully screened cases in accordance with well-defined criteria and eliminated procedures permitting prosecutor-shopping, the amount of "junk" flowing into the system would be reduced drastically. This would be obtained at the cost of a marginal number of additional convictions. Some might object to this trade-off, but we feel that these marginal cases often become prime candidates for special treatment of one sort or another. Their proliferation can lead to pressures for changes and concessions that unduly detract from the integrity of the justice process.

For similar reasons we feel that if—for cases that are to be prosecuted—charges are drafted carefully with input from experienced trial assistants, the consistency and integrity of the process would be further enhanced. The use of "reasonable likelihood of conviction" criteria in charging would, again, entail certain costs; in this case the loss of a number of convictions on more serious charges. But a consequence of loose charging practice is often prosecutorial overreaching that frequently leads to charge reductions at a later point in the process. Strong policies against charge inflation and count multiplication should be adopted. These tactics are not essential, as we have seen, to the maintenance of a plea-oriented dispositional process. They simply enhance the likelihood that some type of charge adjustment occurs, adjustments that serve to undermine the legitimacy of the process.

Efforts should also be made to control the discretion exercised by any one individual. This would minimize both the opportunities for manipulation as well as the likelihood of arbitrary actions, thus enhancing the exercise of the discretion that needs to be wielded. This proposal goes beyond the mere adoption of more centralized plea offers by prosecutor offices. We should aim for a more integrated plea-offer system, one that results in firm plea offers that cover all crucial aspects of the agreement but is not just the product of prosecutorial edict. Pleas are the dominant method of case disposition, and a firm plea offer put together at an early stage (either just before or after arraignment in the trial court) is perhaps the best way to organize the plea process. It would eradicate its most unseemly aspects, such as plea routing and last minute concessions.

While having a firm plea offer is the key to enhancing the legitimacy of the plea process, the key to enhancing its equitableness lies with the formation of the plea. Its formation is not, nor should it be, the exclusive province of the prosecutor. Judges should have a role in its formation, and defense attorneys should be able to present information to be considered by the judges and prosecutors. The discussions should be informed by a pre-plea report on the defendant's background. Judicial participation need not be limited to the judge hearing the case and, perhaps, should not be. There simply needs to be some institutional involvement by the judiciary to balance prosecutorial views. Judges could rotate in the participation of meetings to form plea offers, a permanent committee could be established, or professional sentencing officer(s) could be established.

The plea offer should cover charge and sentence, and it should follow the case to whomever it is assigned. These offers should be modified only under the most extenuating circumstances. If the defendant pleads guilty at all, it should be in accordance with the terms of the formal plea offer; the plea offer could also be admissible at the sentencing hearing after a trial. The existence of this offer will eliminate the motivation for plea-routing and permit counties to utilize the most rational and efficient case assignment procedures. Yet another advantage of this more formalized, better integrated plea-offer system is that it will probably lead to stronger more explicit and better informed sentencing norms. This is especially true in counties with highly decentralized plea systems.[1]

GENERAL DIRECTIONS FOR FUTURE RESEARCH

As we look back at what we have done, what we have found, and how we found it, and think about future directions for research on criminal courts, we come to one very basic conclusion: Empirically oriented criminal court research should move away from a preoccupation with "variance explained" models of case outcomes, whether those outcomes be sentence, bail status, case-processing time, or case disposition. Such models are undoubtedly the *sine qua non* of modern behavioral research. Unfortunately, collecting the type of data necessary to test even a mildly sophisticated statistical model of a single court system is costly and time-consuming. Obtaining the data on decision makers alone is a significant undertaking, not to mention the generation of data on a good-sized sample of defendants. But, is not rigorous scientific research on any complex social organization time-consuming and costly? Of course. But that misses the point. The point is that the prevalence of routine is so dominant in most criminal cases that not much of interest is happening at the micro level in most criminal courts. We will not learn much by continuing to conduct multivariate analyses of case, defendant, and decision-maker attributes. If something is going on, it is usually in a handful of exceptional cases. General statistical models trying to capture those contingent effects will become hopelessly complex; statistical models of just serious cases, or those that are exceptional in some other way, will not yield an accurate picture of how courts operate. In either case, such an approach will not further the aims of scientific research: a greater understanding of the world that surrounds us.

We do not suggest a total abandonment of studies that focus on case outcomes; they are still the bottom line of what criminal courts do. Instead, we suggest a move away from the preoccupation with deviation from system norms to a focus on differences in norms across court communities. A set of analyses like those presented in chapters 9 and 10, except more broadly based and sophisticated, would contribute far more to an understanding of how criminal courts operate than a proliferation of micro-level studies attempting to model the flow of cases through a system. Such a reorientation would move court researchers away from comfortable analyses of such variables as age, race, sex, and attorney and bail status. But it would open new vistas for court research and broaden the scope of research into these vital and complex institutions.

Such a reorientation of court research would lead scholars to cast a broader net because they would have to begin dealing more systematically with contextual and environmental variables. We would certainly need to know more about the impact of constraints imposed by environmental factors as well as the nature of the ties between court communities and their environment. Another prerequisite to a search for the determinants of routine would be a much better understanding of the notion of court communities and their infrastructures. We need to know with more precision how these structures differ from one another as well as how they change over time. Related to these questions is the need to know how court community practices are diffused across jurisdictional lines. We believe that a certain pendulum effect occurs within counties as they shift from one set of policies to another, as problems emerge with earlier innovations and reforms. Sometimes these "new" practices become adopted by other counties, and the cycle begins anew.

These and other questions that were outlined earlier in this chapter can feed a new generation of research into criminal court processes, thereby advancing our understanding of how they operate and how they fit into the world within which they operate.

NOTE

1. For the views of one of the authors on a method for enhancing the creativity and accountability of sentencing practices, see Nardulli (1984).

REFERENCES

Alschuler, Albert W. 1981 "The Changing Plea Bargaining Debate." *California Law Review* 81:69.

Evans, Peter, Dietrich Rueschemeyer, and Theda Skocpol. 1985. *Bringing the State Back In.* Cambridge: Cambridge University Press.

Nardulli, Peter F. 1984. "The Misalignment of Penal Responsibilities and State Prison Crises: Costs, Consequences, and Corrective Actions." *University of Illinois Law Review* 84:365.

APPENDIX I

DERIVATION OF THE ATTITUDINAL COMPOSITES

THE BELIEF IN PUNISHMENT SCALE

Repeated attempts at analyzing various combinations of punishment related variables resulted in a single-factor solution (Table I.1). It should be stressed that while a unidimensional solution (eigenvalue = 4.6) is produced, the factor loadings are not exceptionally high. None is as high as .7, although several come close. The correlations ranged from .21 to .56, although most were between .35 and .45.

Several explanations may account for the somewhat weak structure underlying the Belief in Punishment composite. It may be because of the fact that criminal court actors in different roles view the sentencing process in fundamentally different terms. To examine this possibility, the punishment-related variables were factor analyzed separately for each of the three roles. This procedure did not produce clear-cut results. The various loadings for the different roles tended to be weaker overall than the loadings reported in Table I.1. However, no distinctively different patterns emerged in any of the three separate analyses. The reason for the weaker overall loadings may well be that by separating the different actors, the range of variation in each of the individual variables was reduced significantly, which in turn weakened the correlations. Defense attorneys generally tended toward one extreme, prosecutors to the other, with judges in the middle. When the whole population is analyzed together, a stronger and more parsimonious solution results.

A second plausible explanation for the somewhat weak structure of

Table I.1. **Factor Loadings for Criminal Justice Attitude Variables on Belief in Punishment Factor**

Variable	Factor Loading	Interpretation of Factor Loading
CJ02	.62	Agree that punishment of criminals is required as repayment of debt to society.
CJ03	.64	Agree that probation should only be given to first offenders.
CJ06	.69	Agree that criminal rehabilitation advocates do not weigh seriousness of crime enough.
CJ11	.61	Agree that frequent use of probation wrongly minimizes gravity of crime committed.
CJ18	.52	Agree that failure to punish crime amounts to a license for it.
CJ22	.45	Agree that prisons should be places of punishment.
CJ23	.68	Agree that people charged with serious crimes should be kept in jail until trial.
CJ24	−.54	Disagree with the idea that sentencing according to individual need rather than on basis of the crime is important.
CJ27	.64	Agree criminals should be punished for crime whether or not punishment benefits criminal.
CJ28	−.64	Disagree that people with prior record but strong tie to community should not be detained prior to trial.
CJ30	−.67	Disagree that present treatment of criminals is too harsh.

the punishment variables is that the analysis suffers from conceptual ambiguities concerning the structure of views toward punishment. These views may be common across roles yet more complex than we realized when the questions were assembled. If the eleven items loading on the factor reported in Table I.1 have a common element, it is that the various items touch upon the respondents' belief in punishment as a tool to deal with criminal defendants. As such, they tap a very broad dimension. Two items (CJ23, CJ28) deal with pretrial detention, so the composite does not relate simply to sentencing. It does not really tap respondents' belief in the effectiveness of punishment in deterring crimes, nor does it necessarily say anything about who the respondents blame for the acts of the defendant. Viewed in their entirety, the questions seem to indicate that the factor simply measures the respondents' belief about whether punishment (incarceration in particular) is an appropriate way to give defendants their just desserts.

Although it is fairly general, the Belief in Punishment scale is appropriate for a study such as this, and the parsimonious nature of the factor solution may prove very beneficial in later analyses, which will become quite complex. The rather weak loadings suggest that views on sentencing may be more complex than the single-factor solution indicates. Future analyses may want to devote more resources at the item formulation stage to examine the strong possibility that punishment views are multidimensional. Belief in the effectiveness of incarceration, the accountability of defendants for their actions, the importance of simple incapacitation, and other dimensions may be fertile grounds for investigation.

THE REGARD FOR DUE PROCESS SCALE

The results of the factor analysis for the due process items were much stronger and more straightforward than those for the punishment items. These results are reported in Table I.2. Not only are the factor loadings considerably stronger, but all three items are designed to tap views on due process hung together (eigenvalue = 1.6). The interpretation of the composite also seems to be rather straightforward. Those scoring high on the scale reflect a greater concern with the procedural rights of the accused. They tend to support the Supreme Court's decisions expanding defendants' rights. In addition, they seem to be more concerned with threats to individual liberties than with threats to the community.

Table I.2. **Factor Loadings for Criminal Justice Attitude Variables on Regard for Due Process Factor**

Variable	Factor Loading	Interpretation of Factor Loading
CJ09	.85	Agree that Supreme Court's decisions expanding defendant's rights are basically sound.
CJ17	.55	Agree that it is better to free the guilty than convict the innocent.
CJ19	−.74	Disagree that court decisions protecting rights which might harm community should be curtailed.

THE CONCERN FOR EFFICIENCY SCALE

The factor analysis of the variables tapping views on efficiency did not yield particularly strong results. While four of the five efficiency

Table I.3. **Factor Loadings for Criminal Justice Attitude Variables on Concern for Efficiency Factor**

Variable	Factor Loading	Interpretation of Factor Loading
CJ04	.49	Believe that in handling cases efficiency is an end in itself.
CJ12	.54	Agree that court practices hampering expeditious processing of cases should be modified.
CJ25	−.42	Disagree with the idea that programs which speed up the litigation process produce unjust and improper resolutions to criminal cases.
CJ26	.51	Agree that criminal courts should be run like a business.

items did yield a single-factor solution with a minimally acceptable eigenvalue score (eigenvalue = 1.0), the individual-factor loadings are only moderate (Table I.3). This notwithstanding, the factor analysis does perform a useful function here. It reduces the various items into a single composite with a straightforward interpretation. Clearly, people scoring high on this composite evidence a high regard for efficiency and little tolerance for people or procedures that hamper the efficient processing of criminal cases.

Appendix II

Derivation of the Operating Style Composites

While the preparation and implementation of the Q-sort procedure was lengthy and expensive, it was well worth the effort. Many participants enjoyed this exercise far more than completing the attitudinal questionnaire. A wealth of data was produced, and virtually no one refused to participate in it. However, the exercise also produced a set of analytical problems, the most basic of which was how best to use the resulting data. In its raw form, the data base contained individual evaluations of a number of individuals by a number of other individuals on eight or nine questions. The purest use of these data might be an attempt to match individual evaluations of participants in a particular triad. For example, if Judge X, Prosecutor Y, and Defense Attorney Z handled case 0123, then only Judge X's evaluations of the two attorneys, Prosecutor Y's evaluations of Judge X and Defense Attorney Z, and Defense Attorney Z's evaluation of Judge X and Prosecutor Y would be matched with case 0123.

This approach offers a fairly direct means of assessing the impact of interpersonal relations upon case outcomes. However appealing this approach appears at first glance, it is fraught with methodological and technical problems. Thus, questions concerning such matters as the stability of individual evaluations, the potential for large numbers of missing data for individual cases, and the technical problems involved in matching triad-specific evaluations to individual cases led us to examine alternative ways of utilizing the data.

After extended consideration we chose an aggregated approach (averaging multiple assessments of an actor) to analyzing the Q-sort data, thereby eliminating a whole set of analytical problems and providing us with some insights into an actor's operating style. Despite this, we still encountered a number of methodological problems that we could not decide on an *a priori* basis. This led us to develop and compare different approaches to derivation of these measures.

One problem dealt with the issue of across-evaluator comparability. Evaluators were asked to rank individuals on a scale from 1-5, but we had no way of knowing whether the evaluators' "internal scales" were similar. Some may evaluate most individuals around a score of 2, whereas another may consistently evaluate the same set of individuals at about 3. To examine the nature and implications of any problems emanating from this possibility, two sets of mean scores were produced. One set was derived simply by computing the mean score for each person evaluated on each question. Raw scores were used to compute these means. A second set of means was computed by averaging scores that had been standardized by *evaluator.* This set of means .controlled for the evaluator comparability problem because each of the scores used in the computation of the standardized mean was expressed in terms of its deviation from the individual evaluator means. In other words, standardized scores were used to calculate these means. Both the raw and standardized means were then used in separate factor analyses to produce separate measures of operating style.

A second problem was the possibility that a given individual was evaluated very differently by evaluators who occupied different roles. This led us to develop a role-specific approach to the analysis of the Q-sort data in addition to a general, across-role approach. The reasons for the development of this approach will be clearer once the general approach is more fully described.

OPERATING STYLES: A GENERAL APPROACH

Table II.1 reports the results of the factor analyses used to produce the Judge's Responsiveness measure; the results using means derived from both the raw and standardized scores are reported. However, as Table II.1 shows, the structure of the results is very similar for both. The analysis using the standardized scores is somewhat stronger. What both analyses show is that the qualities of informality, accommodativeness, and reasonableness hang together quite tightly. The factor loadings are quite high, in the .6 to 1.0 range, with accommodativeness being the most important variable. Table II.2 reports the results of the factor analysis used to produce the Judge's Involvement composite. Again, the structure of the results is similar for both the raw and standardized mean variables. Here, however, the results for the raw score variables are somewhat stronger. The results are not quite as strong as those for Judge's Responsiveness but the factor

Table II.1. **Results of Factor Analysis for Judge's Responsiveness**

Variable	Factor Loading for Raw Mean Variables	Factor Loading for Standardized Mean Variables	Interpretation of Factor Loading
Informality	.60	.72	Attorneys feel it is easy to deal with the judge informally.
Accommoda-tiveness	1.0	1.0	Attorneys feel that the judge is willing to be accommodating and helpful with their problem.
Reason-ableness	.68	.80	Attorneys feel that the judge can be persuaded to change his mind.
Eigenvalue	1.8	2.1	

Table II.2. **Results of Factor Analysis for Judge's Involvement**

Variable	Factor Loading for Raw Mean Variables	Factor Loading for Standardized Mean Variables	Interpretation of Factor Loading
Informality	.56	.41	Attorneys feel it is easy to deal with the judge informally.
Active	.94	.90	Attorneys feel that the judge plays an active role in the disposition of a case.
Trial Preference	.59	.48	Attorneys feel that the judge tries to avoid trials whenever possible.
Eigenvalue	1.5	1.5	

loadings, especially for the raw mean variables are still quite respectable (.56 − .94).

Table II.3 reports the results of the factor analysis used to construct the Attorney Responsiveness composite. Again, both the raw and standardized mean variables were analyzed and are reported. As before, the structure of the loadings is remarkably similar. Moreover, both represent very solid solutions. The loadings are all above .90 except for the predictability variable, that is, trustworthiness, accommodativeness, and in-

formality all play a similar role in the construction of Attorney Responsiveness.

Table II.3. **Results of Factor Analysis for Attorney Responsiveness**

Variable	Factor Loading for Raw Mean Variables	Factor Loading for Standardized Mean Variables	Interpretation of Factor Loading
Trustworthiness	.91	.93	Others feel this attorney is trustworthy and keeps his or her word.
Accommoda-tiveness	.95	.96	Others feel this attorney is willing to be accom-modating and helpful with their problems.
Predictability	.62	.58	Others feel that this at-torney is very predictable in handling cases.
Informality	.92	.94	Others feel it is easy to deal informally with this attorney.
Eigenvalue	3.0	3.0	

OPERATING STYLES: A ROLE-SPECIFIC, AGGREGATED APPROACH

While the results reported in the previous section represent a parsimonious and reasonable first attempt at defining important dimensions
of operating style, one rather obvious and potentially troublesome problem
exists. The general approach combines the evaluations of people from
different roles into one overall measure of a given individual's Responsiveness, Trial Competence, Involvement, etc. Although this may be perfectly acceptable, it rests on two assumptions. The first is that people in
each role (judges, prosecutors, defense attorneys) view the various dimensions and subdimensions of operating style similarly, that is, that trustworthiness, informality, accommodativeness, etc. play a similar role in the
way each set of participants views Responsiveness. The second assumption—and it rests on the first—is that individuals across different roles
will evaluate a given individual similarly. That is, both judges and defense
attorneys in a given county will evaluate Prosecutor X's Responsiveness
in a similar manner. If that is not the case, some serious bias could result.
If judges and defense attorneys evaluate prosecutors in a systematically

Table II.4. **Correlations between Prosecutor and Defense Attorney Evaluations of Judges**

Familiarity	.43
	(53)
Informality	.56
	(53)
Active	.81
	(53)
Predictability	.44
	(53)
Trial Preference	.68
	(53)
Accommodativeness	.46
	(53)
Reasonableness	.47
	(53)
Overall Assessment	.53
	(53)
Docket Concern	.52
	(53)

different way, a prosecutor's aggregated score, which is a mean, will normally be biased toward the defense attorneys' view, because we interviewed far more attorneys than judges. Moreover, the nature of the bias may vary from county to county depending upon the ratio of judges to attorneys.

To examine this problem, the evaluation data were recalculated so that a mean was derived for each variable by role. For example, prosecutor means on each of the eight variables were recalculated using just judge evaluations and just defense attorney evaluations. Thus two sets of means were calculated for each set of participants. Only the raw scores were used in these calculations. Eliminating the standardized scores simplified matters greatly at a minimal cost—the two sets of measures produced highly similar results in the general approach just reported.

The correlations for the separate means are reported in Tables II-4 and II.5. there are some high (.81) to moderate (.43) correlations for the judicial evaluations. The correlations tend to be higher on more objective questions (Active, Trial Preference) and lower on those tapping social relations (Accommodativeness, Reasonableness). They do not appear to be high enough overall, however, to overcome the criticism that individuals in different roles evaluate judges differently. Moreover, the correlations are even lower when attorneys are evaluated. While the highest correlations in Table II.5 deal with a fairly objective trait, Trial Competence, there are extremely low correlations (.07, .15), and even one negative one. This suggests, of course, the need to examine the various evaluations in a role-specific manner.

Table II.5. **Correlations between Judge Evaluation and Prosecutor (or Defense Attorney) Evaluations of Prosecutors (or Defense Attorneys)**

	Prosecutor as Evaluatee	Defense Attorney as Evaluatee
Familiarity	.29	.44
	(94)	(171)
Trial Competence	.64	.61
	(94)	(171)
Trustworthiness	.26	.58
	(94)	(171)
Accommodativeness	.25	.46
	(94)	(171)
Predictability	.15	.32
	(94)	(171)
Informality	.07	.25
	(94)	(171)
Importance	.43	.44
	(94)	(171)
Overall Assessment	.44	−.35
	(94)	(171)

The Judge's Data

Table II.6 reports the results of the factor analysis for the role specific Judge Responsiveness variables. Two things stand out. First, the same variables hang together in the role-specific analyses as in the general ones. Second, the factor loadings across the prosecutor and defense attorney variables are remarkably similar. This suggests that both sets of participants

Table II.6. **Result of Role-Specific Factor Analyses of Judge Responsiveness**

Variable	Factor Loading for Prosecutor Evaluations	Factor Loading for Defense Attorney Evaluations	Factor Loading for Combined Roles (Raw Mean Variables)
Informality	.68	.62	.60
Accommodativeness	.86	1.0	1.0
Reasonableness	.64	.73	.68
Eigenvalue	1.6	1.9	1.8

APPENDIX II   395

Table II.7. **Results of Role-Specific Factor Analyses of Judge Involvement**

Variable	Factor Loading for Prosecutor Evaluations	Factor Loading for Defense Attorney Evaluations	Factor Loading for Combined Roles (Raw Mean Variables)
Informality	.29	.54	.56
Active	1.0	.91	.94
Trial Preference	.61	.38	.59
Eigenvalue	1.45	1.25	1.5

tend to view this attribute in a similar way. Moreover, the similarity of results in the three samples indicates that the responsiveness measure is fairly stable. When interpreted in light of the correlations reported in Table II.4, however, the results suggest that prosecutors and defense attorneys may rank the judges differently even though they define responsiveness similarly. This in itself may prove to be useful information.

Table II.7 reports the results of the role-specific factor analyses for the Involvement variables. The results here are not quite as similar to the general analysis as those reported in Table II.6. The Active variable is still the most central variable as was the case earlier (col. 3). However, the loading of the Informality variable for prosecutors is somewhat weaker than the original loadings, as is the loading for the Trial Preference variable for defense attorneys. The results suggest that the notion of Informality is somewhat more central to a defense attorney's definition of involvement than to that of a prosecutor. Similarly, a judge's trial preference is more central for a prosecutor than a defense attorney. However, the differences are not so great as to suggest that the concept of Involvement is not shared by both defense attorneys and prosecutors. Obviously, however, the measure used here is not as stable as the responsiveness measure.

Table II.8 reports the correlations between the role-specific composites and the general composites. Without exception, the correlations among the composite scores are much higher than those among the individual variables reported in Table II.4. What appears to be happening is that more disagreement emerges across roles where individuals are ranked on individual attributes. When all of the attributes defining a more abstract concept are considered together, the differences across roles are reduced significantly. Thus the correlations between defense attorney and prosecutor evaluations of Judge Responsiveness, Involvement, and Docket Concern are .54, .76, and .52, respectively. Moreover, when the general composites are compared with the role-specific ones, the correlations are all in the

Table II.8. **Correlations between the Role-Specific and General Composites for the Judge Measures**

	Judge's Respon- siveness — General	Judge's Respon- siveness — Defense Attorneys' View	Judge's Respon- siveness — Prose- cutors' View
Judge's Responsive- ness — General	1.0 (53)	.83 (54)	.83 (54)
Judge's Responsive- ness — defense at- torneys' view		1.0 (53)	.54 (53)
Judge's Responsive- ness — prosecutors' view			1.0 (53)

	Judge's Involve- ment — General	Judge's Involve- ment — Defense Attorneys' View	Judge's Involve- ment — Prosecu- tors' View
Judge's Involve- ment — general	1.0 (53)	.96 (54)	.92 (54)
Judge's Involve- ment — defense at- torneys' view		1.0 (53)	.76 (53)
Judge's Involve- ment — prosecutors' view			1.0 (53)

	Judge's Docket Concern — General	Judge's Docket Concern — De- fense Attorneys' View	Judge's Docket Concern — Prose- cutors' View
Judge's Docket Concern — general	1.0 (53)	.91 (53)	.82 (54)
Judge's Docket Concern — defense attorneys' view		1.0 (53)	.52 (53)
Judge's Docket Concern — prosecu- tors' view			1.0 (53)

.8 to .9 range. This, of course, indicates that the general composites are not terribly flawed and, in the interests of parsimony, may well prove to be acceptable indicators of the various concepts.

The Attorneys' Data

Table II.9 and II.10 report the results of the role-specific analyses of Responsiveness for both prosecutors and defense attorneys. A comparison of columns 1 and 2 with column 3 in each table demonstrates that, with one exception, the role-specific analyses are again very similar to the general results. The sole exception is the Informality variable for judges for both prosecutors and defense attorneys. Obviously, because of their role, judges do not view informality to be as central to the notion of responsiveness as do attorneys. Most prosecutors and defense attorneys, in most situations, would undoubtedly be as informal in dispositional discussions as the judge would permit. It provides them with some insights about the judge's position in their cases and gives them valuable information as to their options. Thus, from the judge's vantage point, the Informality of attorneys may be more of a constant, and therefore less relevant, than among attorneys.

Tables II.11 and II.12 report the correlations between the role-specific composites for the prosecutors and defense attorneys, respectively. Much

Table II.9. **Results of Factor Analyses for Prosecutor Responsiveness**

Variable	Factor Loading for Judge's Evaluations	Factor Loading for Defense Attorney's Evaluations	Factor Loading for Combined Roles (Raw Mean Variables)
Trustworthiness	.84	.89	.91
Accommodativeness	.88	.95	.95
Predictability	.61	.69	.62
Informality	.26	.99	.92
Eigenvalue	1.9	3.1	3.0

Table II.10. **Results of Factor Analyses for Defense Attorney Responsiveness**

Variable	Factor Loading for Judge Evaluations	Factor Loading for Prosecutor Evaluations	Factor Loading for Combined Roles
Trustworthiness	.91	.92	.91
Accommodativeness	.85	.94	.95
Predictability	.59	.45	.62
Informality	.46	.92	.92
Eigenvalue	2.1	2.8	3.0

Table II.11. **Correlations between the Role-Specific and General Composites for the Prosecutor's Measures**

	Prosecutor's Responsiveness — General	Prosecutor's Responsiveness — Judges' View	Prosecutor's Responsiveness — Defense Attorneys' View
Prosecutor's Responsiveness — general	1.0 (96)	.51 (96)	.97 (96)
Prosecutor's Responsiveness — judges' view		1.0 (96)	.29 (94)
Prosecutor's Responsiveness — defense attorneys' view			1.0 (96)

	Prosecutor's Trial Competence — General	Prosecutor's Trial Competence — Judges' View	Prosecutor's Trial Competence — Defense Attorneys' View
Prosecutor's Trial Competence — general	1.0 (96)	.79 (96)	.98 (96)
Prosecutor's Trial Competence — judges' view		1.0 (96)	.64 (94)
Prosecutor's Trial Competence — defense attorneys' view			1.0 (96)

the same pattern emerges here as emerged with respect to the judge correlations. The extent of disagreement across roles is much less for the composites than for the individual evaluation variables. The exception is prosecutor Responsiveness. Judges and defense attorneys clearly evaluate individual prosecutors differently. The correlation between the two role-specific composites is largely determined by defense attorney evaluations. The defense attorney measure is virtually identical to the general responsiveness measure ($r = .97$), while the judge measure is correlated much less strongly ($r = .51$). The correlations among the other role-specific composites and the general composites range from .76 to .98, with most in the .8 to .9 range.

Table II.12. **Correlations between the Role-Specific and General Composites for the Measures**

	Defense Attorney's Responsiveness — General	Defense Attorney's Responsiveness — Judges' View	Defense Attorney's Responsiveness — Prosecutors' View
Defense Attorney's Responsiveness — general	1.0 (171)	.76 (171)	.96 (171)
Defense Attorney's Responsiveness — judges' view		1.0 (171)	.56 (171)
Defense Attorney's Responsiveness — prosecutors' view			1.0 (171)

	Defense Attorney's Trial Competence — General	Defense Attorney's Trial Competence — Judges' View	Defense Attorney's Trial Competence — Prosecutors' View
Defense Attorney's Trial Competence — general	1.0 (173)	.81 (172)	.95 (173)
Defense Attorney's Trial Competence — judges' view		1.0 (173)	.61 (171)
Defense Attorney's Trial Competence — prosecutors' view			1.0 (173)

APPENDIX III

DERIVATION OF THE CONSERVATIVISM RANKINGS

Two different ranking measures of a representative's voting pattern were used to derive a raw "Conservativism score." The rankings of the Americans for Democratic Action (ADA) were used as a measure of liberal tendencies, and the rankings of Americans for Constitutional Action (ACA) were used as a measure of conservative tendencies.[1] Neither measure could be used independently because the components of the two rankings are not identical. One moderately liberal representative (ADA ranking of 70) may be ranked very low on the ACA scale (10, for example), while another with an identical ADA ranking may have a considerably higher ACA ranking (30, for example). To adjust for this possibility a composite ranking was constructed by subtracting an individual's ADA ranking for a session of Congress from his or her ACA ranking (both range from 0 to 100). This resulted in a raw Conservatism measure that had a possible range of -100 (very liberal) to 100 (very conservative).

Although these raw Conservativism scores were rough indicators of a county's ideological leanings, geopolitical factors made them incomparable. Congressional districts are not congruent with our counties and frequently include parts of several counties. Therefore, a person could be elected to Congress with only a small portion of the vote in any given county. This causes problems, because two counties may be represented by someone with raw Conservativism scores of 75, where one county gave the person 75 percent of its vote, while the other gave only 40 percent. To correct this, the Conservativism score given a representative for a session of Congress was adjusted by multiplying it by the proportion of the county's vote the representative received in the next election, if he

Comparative Average Conservatism Rankings

	DuPage (Ring)	Peoria (Autonomous)	St. Clair (Declining)	Oakland (Ring) 18th	Oakland (Ring) 19th	Kalamazoo (Autonomous)	Saginaw (Declining)	Montgomery (Ring)	Dauphin (Autonomous)	Erie (Declining)
1972										
Conservativism ranking	57	90.5	-44	54	54	51	40.5	73.5	74.5	-31.5
Proportion of county vote in election	.73	.65	.75	.52	.71	.54	.60	.61	.71	.73
Weighted conservative ranking	41.6	58.8	-33	28	38.3	27.5	24.3	44.8	52.9	-23
1974										
Conservativism ranking	32.5	85	-45	92	38.5	20	51	55.5	47.5	-58
Proportion of county vote in election	.66	.54	.80	.52	.63	.47	.60	.61	.49	.55
Weighted conservative ranking	21.4	46	-36	47.8	24.2	9.4	30.6	33.9	23.3	-32
1976										
Conservativism ranking	63.5	70.5	-46	-75.5	55.5	62.5	-57.5	75.5	60	-50.5
Proportion of county vote in election	.74	.56	.74	.68	.65	.53	59	.56	.47	.44
Weighted conservative ranking	47	39.5	-34	-51.3	36	33.1	-34	42.3	-28.2	-22.2
1978										
Conservativism ranking	52	66.5	-27.5	-45	60.5	37	-31.5	71.5	12	-13
Proportion of county vote in election	.75	.64	.76	.73	.72	.47	.47	.74	.47	.61
Weighted conservative ranking	39	42.5	-21		43.6	17.4	-14.8	52.9	5.6	-8
1980										
Conservativism ranking	58	79	-48.5	-65	62	-67	-36.5	86.5	-31.5	6
Proportion of county vote in election	.77	.61	.64	.66	.73	.53	.53	.74	.58	.41
Weighted conservative ranking	44.6	48	-30	-43	45.3	-35.5	-19.3	64.0	-18.27	2.5

or she ran. If the representative did not run, his or her rate totals in the last election were used as the weighting factor.

The raw Conservativism ranking, the percent of the vote received in the county, and the weighted measure are reported in Table III.1. Oakland has two scores because it is split into parts of two different districts, the eighteenth and nineteenth. To obtain Oakland's overall score, these two scores were averaged, a legitimate procedure because the raw number of votes cast in each district in Oakland is relatively close. The average of the weighted and unweighted scores of the five sessions is reported in Table 4.7.

We realize that there are a number of difficulties with using this approach to measure political ideology. One could argue, for example, that many people who vote for a candidate are not fully familiar with the candidate's political views, much less his or her ACA or ADA ranking. Moreover, even if voters are generally familiar with the candidate's views, the proportion of the vote may not be an accurate measure of support for that ideology: It would depend upon the views of the opponent. The more different the views of the opponent, the more meaningful the weighting factor. For example, in a highly conservative county where two highly conservative candidates split the vote, the procedure outlined here would underestimate the county's conservatism.

One could, of course, counter these arguments in a number of ways. With respect to the lack of knowledge, one could argue that political leaders involved in recruiting candidates are familiar with the candidates' views and their compatibility with the district. Also, this criticism fades in situations where a candidate has a long history of electoral support in a county. This is relevant because most of the counties studied here were represented by long-term representatives. All but Kalamazoo, Dauphin, and Erie were represented by people who had served at least four terms (Erlenborn, Michel, Price, Broomfield, Blanchard, Traxler, Schulze). The representative from Erie and Dauphin twice won reelection. The second criticism is more difficult to counter because little is known of the views of the representatives' opponents. However, given the longevity of most of these representatives, it would be a dubious campaign strategy on the part of their opponents to run an ideological clone.

NOTE

1. The data are reported in the *Almanac of American Politics* 1974, 1976, 1978, 1980, 1982, Michael Barone and Grant Vjifusa (Washington: Barone, 1974, 1976, 1978, 1980, 1982).

Appendix IV

Summary of Clusters

Table IV. Data on Summary of Sentencing Clusters

	DuPage	Peoria	St. Clair	Oakland	Kalamazoo	Saginaw	Montgomery	Dauphin	Erie
Armed Robbery									
Probation Cluster	None	None	Yes	Yes	Yes	Yes	Yes	Yes	Yes
N	—	—	16	3	4	3	3	2	6
Percent of guilty plea cases	—	—	40.0	7.3	19.0	15.0	17.6	13.3	31.5
Low Cluster	Yes	Yes	Yes	Yes	Yes	Yes	Yes	Yes	Yes
Span	0	0	0	0	0	0	0	1	0
Span ratio	—	—	—	—	—	—	—	4	—
Standard deviation								.5	
N	3	3	9	10	4	4	4	4	4
Percent of guilty plea cases	43.0	13.6	22.6	24.4	19.0	20.0	23.6	26.7	21.1
High Cluster	None	None	None	Yes	None	Yes	None	None	Yes
Span	—	—	—	0	—	0	—	—	0
Span ratio	—	—	—	—	—	—	—	—	—
Standard deviation									
N	—	—	—	7	—	4	—	—	3
Percent of guilty plea cases	—	—	—	12.1	—	20.0	—	—	15.8

Table IV. Data on Summary of Sentencing Clusters — contd.

	DuPage	Peoria	St. Clair	Oakland	Kalamazoo	Saginaw	Montgomery	Dauphin	Erie
Robbery									
Probation Cluster	None	Yes	Yes	Yes	None	None	None	None	None
N	—	5	8	3	—	—	—	—	—
Percent of guilty plea cases	—	62.5	57.1	27.3	—	—	—	—	—
Low Cluster									
Span	None	None	Yes	Yes	None	None	None	None	None
Span ratio	—	—	0	0	—	—	—	—	—
Standard deviation	—	—	—	—	—	—	—	—	—
N	—	—	2	2	—	—	—	—	—
Percent of guilty plea cases	—	—	14.3	18.2	—	—	—	—	—
High Cluster									
Span	None	None	None	None	None	None	None	None	None
Span ratio	—	—	—	—	—	—	—	—	—
Standard deviation	—	—	—	—	—	—	—	—	—
N	—	—	—	—	—	—	—	—	—
Percent of guilty plea cases	—	—	—	—	—	—	—	—	—

Table IV. Data on Summary of Sentencing Clusters — contd.

	DuPage	Peoria	St. Clair	Oakland	Kalamazoo	Saginaw	Montgomery	Dauphin	Erie
Aggravated Battery									
Probation Cluster	Yes	Yes	Yes	None	None	None	Yes	None	Yes
N	18	18	19	—	—	—	17	—	4
Percent of guilty plea cases	69.2	58.1	65.5	—	—	—	77.3	—	44.4
Low Cluster	Yes	None	Yes	None	None	None	None	None	Yes
Span	0	—	1	—	—	—	—	—	0
Span ratio	—	—	4	—	—	—	—	—	—
Standard deviation	—	—	.5	—	—	—	—	—	—
N	4	—	4	—	—	—	—	—	3
Percent of guilty plea cases	15.4	—	13.8	—	—	—	—	—	33.3
High Cluster	None	None	None	None	None	None	None	None	None
Span	—	—	—	—	—	—	—	—	—
Span ratio	—	—	—	—	—	—	—	—	—
Standard deviation	—	—	—	—	—	—	—	—	—
N	—	—	—	—	—	—	—	—	—
Percent of guilty plea cases	—	—	—	—	—	—	—	—	—

Table IV. **Data on Summary of Sentencing Clusters — contd.**

	DuPage	Peoria	St. Clair	Oakland	Kalamazoo	Saginaw	Montgomery	Dauphin	Erie
Aggravated Assault									
Probation Cluster	None	None	None	Yes	Yes	Yes	None	Yes	Yes
N	—	—	—	11	7	11	—	15	10
Percent of guilty plea cases	—	—	—	—	—	—	—	—	—
Low Cluster	None	None	None	Yes	Yes	None	None	Yes	Yes
Span	—	—	—	45.8	25.0	73.3	—	62.6	50.0
Span ratio	—	—	—	0	0	None	—	1	0
Standard deviation	—	—	—	—	—	—	—	.45	—
N	—	—	—	4	6	—	—	5	7
Percent of guilty plea cases	—	—	—	—	—	—	—	—	—
High Cluster	None	None	None	None	Yes	None	None	None	None
Span	—	—	—	16.7	21.4	—	—	20.8	35.0
Span ratio	—	—	—	—	0	—	—	—	—
Standard deviation	—	—	—	—	—	—	—	—	—
N	—	—	—	—	6	—	—	—	—
Percent of guilty plea cases	—	—	—	—	21.4	—	—	—	—

Table IV. Data on Summary of Sentencing Clusters — contd.

	DuPage	Peoria	St. Clair	Oakland	Kalamazoo	Saginaw	Montgomery	Dauphin	Erie
Battery									
Probation Cluster	None	None	None	None	None	None	Yes	Yes	Yes
N	—	—	—	—	—	—	15	23	5
Percent of guilty plea cases	—	—	—	—	—	—	78.9	91.9	62.5
Low Cluster	None	None	None	None	None	None	None	None	None
Span	—	—	—	—	—	—	—	—	—
Span ratio	—	—	—	—	—	—	—	—	—
Standard deviation	—	—	—	—	—	—	—	—	—
N	—	—	—	—	—	—	—	—	—
Percent of guilty plea cases	—	—	—	—	—	—	—	—	—
High Cluster	None	None	None	None	None	None	None	None	None
Span	—	—	—	—	—	—	—	—	—
Span ratio	—	—	—	—	—	—	—	—	—
Standard deviation	—	—	—	—	—	—	—	—	—
N	—	—	—	—	—	—	—	—	—
Percent of guilty plea cases	—	—	—	—	—	—	—	—	—

Table IV. **Data on Summary of Sentencing Clusters — contd.**

	DuPage	Peoria	St. Clair	Oakland	Kalamazoo	Saginaw	Montgomery	Dauphin	Erie
Burglary									
Probation Cluster	Yes	Yes	Yes	Yes	Yes	Yes	Yes	Yes	Yes
N	67	91	135	91	47	79	35	44	15
Percent of guilty plea cases	76.1	53.8	76.7	44.8	29.7	55.6	61.4	56.6	39.5
Low Cluster	Yes	Yes	Yes	Yes	Yes	Yes	None	Yes	Yes
Span	3	2	6	3	0	6	—	5	0
Span ratio	4	14.5	3.33	5.67	—	—	—	4	—
Standard deviation	1.4	.76	2.81	1.4	—	—	—	2.47	—
N	12	28	17	32	20	24	—	18	13
Percent of guilty plea cases	13.6	16.6	9.7	15.7	12.6	16.9	—	23.0	34.2
High Cluster	Yes	None	None	Yes	None	Yes	None	None	None
Span	0	—	—	6	—	0	—	—	—
Span ratio	—	—	—	4.1	—	—	—	—	—
Standard deviation	—	—	—	2.8	—	—	—	—	—
N	4	—	—	25	—	11	—	—	—
Percent of guilty plea cases	4.5	—	—	12.3	—	8.0	—	—	—

Table IV. Data on Summary of Sentencing Clusters — contd.

	DuPage	Peoria	St. Clair	Oakland	Kalamazoo	Saginaw	Montgomery	Dauphin	Erie
Theft									
Probation Cluster	Yes	Yes	Yes	Yes	Yes	Yes	Yes	Yes	Yes
N	71	110	177	44	28	15	67	132	29
Percent of guilty plea cases	64.0	72.8	85.1	55.7	33.3	71.4	82.7	77.6	70.7
Low Cluster	Yes	Yes	Yes	Yes	Yes	None	Yes	Yes	Yes
Span	2	0	0	2	2	—	0	3	0
Span ratio	10.5	—	—	5.5	11	—	—	7	—
Standard deviation	.89	—	—	.98	.92	—	—	1.39	—
N	20	9	9	11	22	—	5	20	7
Percent of guilty plea cases	18.0	6.0	4.3	13.9	16.2	—	6.2	11.8	17.1
High Cluster	Yes	None	None	Yes	Yes	None	None	None	None
Span	0	—	—	0	0	—	—	—	—
Span ratio	—	—	—	—	—	—	—	—	—
Standard deviation	—	—	—	—	—	—	—	—	—
N	8	—	—	9	7	—	—	—	—
Percent of guilty plea cases	7.2	—	—	11.4	8.3	—	—	—	—

Table IV. Data on Summary of Sentencing Clusters — contd.

	DuPage	Peoria	St. Clair	Oakland	Kalamazoo	Saginaw	Montgomery	Dauphin	Erie
Fraud									
Probation Cluster	Yes	Yes	Yes	None	Yes	Yes	Yes	None	Yes
N	5	27	52	—	10	8	13	—	7
Percent of guilty plea cases	10.5	79.4	88.1	—	41.7	42.1	65.0	—	70.0
Low Cluster	Yes	None	Yes	None	None	Yes	None	None	Yes
Span	3	—	0	—	—	0	—	—	0
Span ratio	3	—	—	—	—	—	—	—	—
Standard deviation	1.5	—	—	—	—	—	—	—	—
N	9	—	4	—	—	4	—	—	3
Percent of guilty plea cases	18.8	—	6.8	—	—	21.1	—	—	30.0
High Cluster	None	None	None	None	None	None	None	None	None
Span	—	—	—	—	—	—	—	—	—
Span ratio	—	—	—	—	—	—	—	—	—
Standard deviation	—	—	—	—	—	—	—	—	—
N	—	—	—	—	—	—	—	—	—
Percent of guilty plea cases	—	—	—	—	—	—	—	—	—

Table IV. Data on Summary of Sentencing Clusters — contd.

	DuPage	Peoria	St. Clair	Oakland	Kalamazoo	Saginaw	Montgomery	Dauphin	Erie
Vandalism									
Probation Cluster	None	Yes	Yes	Yes	Yes	Yes	None	Yes	None
N	—	7	10	11	4	8	—	7	—
Percent of guilty plea cases	—	63.6	90.9	73.4	33.3	66.7	—	100	—
Low Cluster	Yes	Yes	None	None	Yes	Yes	None	None	None
Span	2	0	—	—	0	0	—	—	—
Span ratio	3	—	—	—	—	—	—	—	—
Standard deviation	1.03	—	—	—	—	—	—	—	—
N	6	3	—	—	3	3	—	—	—
Percent of guilty plea cases	30.0	27.3	—	—	25.0	25.0	—	—	—
High Cluster	None	None	None	None	None	None	None	None	None
Span	—	—	—	—	—	—	—	—	—
Span ratio	—	—	—	—	—	—	—	—	—
Standard deviation	—	—	—	—	—	—	—	—	—
N	—	—	—	—	—	—	—	—	—
Percent of guilty plea cases	—	—	—	—	—	—	—	—	—

Table IV. Data on Summary of Sentencing Clusters — contd.

	DuPage	Peoria	St. Clair	Oakland	Kalamazoo	Saginaw	Montgomery	Dauphin	Erie
Unlawful Use of Weapon									
Probation Cluster	None	Yes	Yes	Yes	Yes	Yes	Yes	Yes	Yes
N	—	2	9	11	7	21	8	7	6
Percent of guilty plea cases	—	12.5	75.0	61.1	38.9	75.0	80.0	70.0	54.5
Low Cluster	None	Yes	None	None	Yes	Yes	None	None	Yes
Span	—	0	—	—	0	0	—	—	0
Span ratio	—	—	—	—	—	—	—	—	—
Standard deviation	—	—	—	—	—	—	—	—	—
N	—	6	—	—	3	3	—	—	4
Percent of guilty plea cases	—	37.5	—	—	16.7	10.7	—	—	36.4
High Cluster	None	None	None	None	None	None	None	None	None
Span	—	—	—	—	—	—	—	—	—
Span ratio	—	—	—	—	—	—	—	—	—
Standard deviation	—	—	—	—	—	—	—	—	—
N	—	—	—	—	—	—	—	—	—
Percent of guilty plea cases	—	—	—	—	—	—	—	—	—

Table IV. Data on Summary of Sentencing Clusters — contd.

	DuPage	Peoria	St. Clair	Oakland	Kalamazoo	Saginaw	Montgomery	Dauphin	Erie
Possession of Hard Drugs									
Probation Cluster	Yes	Yes	Yes	Yes	Yes	Yes	Yes	Yes	Yes
N	93	51	35	19	12	19	31	25	11
Percent of guilty plea cases	85.3	79.7	83.3	38.8	37.5	50.0	77.5	76.6	68.8
Low Cluster	Yes	Yes	None	Yes	Yes	Yes	Yes	None	None
Span	0	0	—	0	2	0	0	—	—
Span ratio	—	—	—	—	3.5	—	—	—	—
Standard deviation	—	—	—	—	1.06	—	—	—	—
N	5	3	—	6	7	5	3	—	—
Percent of guilty plea cases	4.6	4.7	—	12.2	21.9	13.2	7.5	—	—
High Cluster	None	Yes	None	Yes	None	None	None	None	None
Span	—	0	—	0	—	—	—	—	—
Span ratio	—	—	—	—	—	—	—	—	—
Standard deviation	—	—	—	—	—	—	—	—	—
N	—	4	—	7	—	—	—	—	—
Percent of guilty plea cases	—	6.3	—	14.3	—	—	—	—	—

Table IV. Data on Summary of Sentencing Clusters — contd.

	DuPage	Peoria	St. Clair	Oakland	Kalamazoo	Saginaw	Montgomery	Dauphin	Erie
Marijuana Offenses									
Probation Cluster	Yes	Yes	Yes	None	None	None	None	None	None
N	47	43	30	—	—	—	—	—	—
Percent of guilty plea cases	88.6	91.4	90.9	—	—	—	—	—	—
Low Cluster	Yes	None	None	None	None	None	None	None	None
Span	0	—	—	—	—	—	—	—	—
Span ratio	—	—	—	—	—	—	—	—	—
Standard deviation	—	—	—	—	—	—	—	—	—
N	3	—	—	—	—	—	—	—	—
Percent of guilty plea cases	5.6	—	—	—	—	—	—	—	—
High Cluster	None	None	None	None	None	None	None	None	None
Span	—	—	—	—	—	—	—	—	—
Span ratio	—	—	—	—	—	—	—	—	—
Standard deviation	—	—	—	—	—	—	—	—	—
N	—	—	—	—	—	—	—	—	—
Percent of guilty plea cases	—	—	—	—	—	—	—	—	—

Table IV. Data on Summary of Sentencing Clusters — contd.

	DuPage	Peoria	St. Clair	Oakland	Kalamazoo	Saginaw	Montgomery	Dauphin	Erie
Driving While Intoxicated									
Probation Cluster	None	None	None	None	None	None	Yes	Yes	Yes
N	—	—	—	—	—	—	150	236	92
Percent of guilty plea cases	—	—	—	—	—	—	96.8	90.1	86.0
Low Cluster	None	None	None	None	None	None	None	Yes	Yes
Span	—	—	—	—	—	—	—	2	0
Span ratio	—	—	—	—	—	—	—	9	—
Standard deviation	—	—	—	—	—	—	—	.87	—
N	—	—	—	—	—	—	—	18	7
Percent of guilty plea cases	—	—	—	—	—	—	—	6.9	6.5
High Cluster	None	None	None	None	None	None	None	Yes	Yes
Span	—	—	—	—	—	—	—	0	0
Span ratio	—	—	—	—	—	—	—	—	—
Standard deviation	—	—	—	—	—	—	—	—	—
N	—	—	—	—	—	—	—	5	6
Percent of guilty plea cases	—	—	—	—	—	—	—	1.9	5.6

APPENDIX V

GRAPHS OF JUDGE AND PROSECUTOR TRAITS

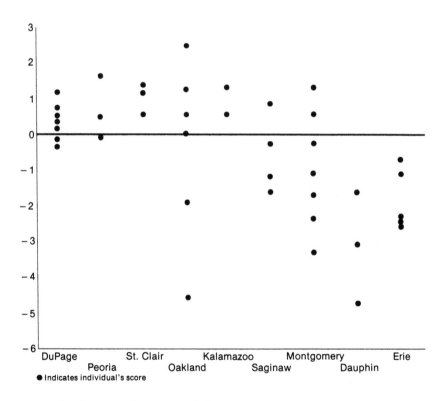

Graph V.1. **Judge's Regard for Due Process Scores by County**

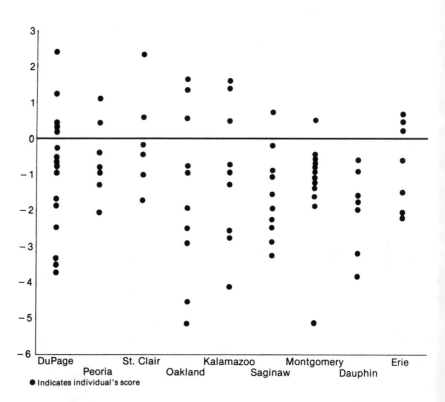

Graph V.2. **Prosecutor's Regard for Due Process Scores by County**

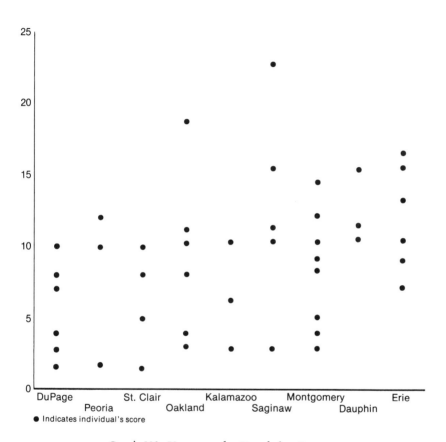

Graph V.3. **Years on the Bench by County**

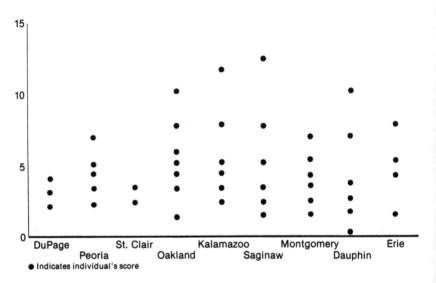

Graph V.4. **Years with Prosecutor's Office by County**

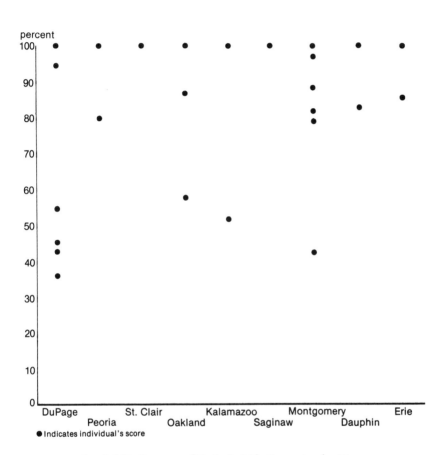

Graph V.5. **Percent of Judge's Life Spent in the County,
Broken Down by County**

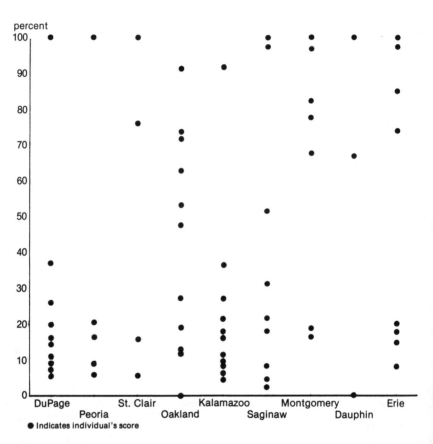

Graph V.6. **Percent of Prosecutor's Life Spent in the County,
Broken Down by County**

APPENDIX VI

RESULTS OF LINEAR ANALYSES OF DUMMY VARIABLES AND ATTITUDINAL AND BACKGROUND MEASURES FOR JUDGES AND PROSECUTORS ON CHARGE AND SENTENCE VARIABLES

The impact of the judge and prosecutor dummy variables upon the various dependent variables is reported in Tables VI.1 through VI.14. In each table we report the adjusted R^2 for the control variable (existence of a multicount indictment, bail status of defendant), the adjusted R^2 after the set of dummy variables is entered, and then the change in the R^2 due to the addition of the dummy variables. We also report the n of cases upon which the analysis is based and the total possible n (the number of guilty plea cases in the county). The discrepancy between these figures is due to missing data on the control variables or the decision-maker variables. The discrepancy here will be especially important in the analyses involving the attitudinal and background measures, because there are few missing cases on the decision-maker dummy variables.

The results of the attitude and background variables for the judges and prosecutors are reported in Tables VI.15 through VI.42. They are organized somewhat differently than the previous tables. After reporting the mean of the dependent variable which is a dummy variable (to determine how skewed they are), and the net contribution of the control variables, we indicate whether a particular variable had a statistically significant impact (0 indicates no significant effect) and, if so, the direction of the impact (+ indicates positive; − indicates negative). One asterisk (*) indicates significance at the .05 level or beyond, two asterisks (**) indicates significance at the .01 level or beyond, and three asterisks (***) indicate statistical significance at or beyond the .001 level. Next, we report the total statistically significant change in the adjusted R^2 and, finally, information on the actual number of cases used in the analysis as well as the possible number of cases.

One point should be noted with respect to the Montgomery analyses. There is a large amount of missing data because of a few decision makers who would not complete a questionnaire. Because we are frequently dealing with only 30-40 percent of the Montgomery cases, we do not feel justified in making any judgments based upon these data, hence they are deleted. Most of the other counties have complete data in 70 to 80 percent of the cases, except Erie. The reason for the relatively low ns in the Erie analyses, however, is that a large number of cases (153 of 466) were handled by pretrial diversion. That meant that a judge and trial prosecutor were not assigned to the case. Thus, the 313 cases available for analysis is a fairly complete set, one that makes it possible for us to feel comfortable in reporting the Erie results.

Table VI.1. **The Impact of Judge Dummy Variables upon _CHRGRED_ in Guilty Plea Cases**

	DuPage (Ring)	Peoria (Autonomous)	St. Clair (Declining)	Oakland (Ring)	Kalamazoo (Autonomous)	Saginaw (Declining)	Montgomery (Ring)	Dauphin (Autonomous)	Erie (Declining)
Adjusted R^2 for control variables	.54	.33	.31	.30	.36	.06	.29	.15	.32
Adjusted R^2 after entering set of judge dummy variables	.54	.33	.31	.33	.37	.05	.30	.17	.32
Net change due to addition of judge dummy variables	0	0	0	.03	.01	-.01	.01	.02	0
N of Cases	500	512	634	670	518	426	572	823	333
Total valid cases	565	689	746	739	565	484	602	875	466

Table VI.2. **The Impact of Judge Dummy Variables upon _CTRED_ in Guilty Plea Cases**

	DuPage (Ring)	Peoria (Autonomous)	St. Clair (Declining)	Oakland (Ring)	Kalamazoo (Autonomous)	Saginaw (Declining)	Montgomery (Ring)	Dauphin (Autonomous)	Erie (Declining)
Adjusted R^2 for control variables	.77	.64	.75	.54	.55	.45	.30	.18	.38
Adjusted R^2 after entering set of judge dummy variables	.77	.64	.75	.54	.55	.46	.31	.19	.38
Net change due to addition of judge dummy variables	0	0	0	0	0	.01	.01	.01	0
N of cases	500	512	634	670	518	426	572	823	335

Table VI.3. **The Impact of Judge Dummy Variables upon *PRIMRED* in Guilty Plea Cases**

	DuPage (Ring)	Peoria (Autonomous)	St. Clair (Declining)	Oakland (Ring)	Kalamazoo (Autonomous)	Saginaw (Declining)	Montgomery (Ring)	Dauphin (Autonomous)	Erie (Declining)
Adjusted R^2 for control variables	.03	.05	.00	.01	.05	.00	.05	.03	.01
Adjusted R^2 after entering set of judge dummy variables	.04	.05	.00	.03	.06	.03	.05	.03	.01
Net change due to addition of judge dummy variables	.01	0	0	.02	.01	.03	0	0	0
N of cases	500	512	634	670	518	426	572	823	329

Table VI.4. **The Impact of Judge Dummy Variables upon *JAILMIN* in Guilty Plea Cases**

	DuPage (Ring)	Peoria (Autonomous)	St. Clair (Declining)	Oakland (Ring)	Kalamazoo (Autonomous)	Saginaw (Declining)	Montgomery (Ring)	Dauphin (Autonomous)	Erie (Declining)
Adjusted R^2 for control variables	.33	.37	.27	.28	.35	.37	.13	.49	.31
Adjusted R^2 after entering set of judge dummy variables	.36	.38	.27	.28	.35	.38	.15	.50	.34
Net change due to addition of judge dummy variables	.03	.01	0	0	0	.01	.02	.01	.03
N of cases	541	641	714	674	553	434	573	842	297
Total valid cases	565	689	746	739	565	484	602	875	466

Table VI.5. **The Impact of Judge Dummy Variables upon** *FRSTJAIL* **in Guilty Plea Cases**

	DuPage (Ring)	Peoria (Autono-mous)	St. Clair (Declin-ing)	Oakland (Ring)	Kalamazoo (Autono-mous)	Saginaw (Declin-ing)	Mont-gomery (Ring)	Dauphin (Autono-mous)	Erie (Declin-ing)
Adjusted R^2 for control variables	.13	.18	.14	.19	.07	.04	.11	.19	.05
Adjusted R^2 after entering set of judge dummy variables	.15	.18	.12	.25	.11	.10	.35	.22	.11
Net change due to addition of judge dummy variables	.02	0	-.02	.06	.04	.06	.24	.03	.06
N of cases	244	246	242	259	140	117	206	133	59

Table VI.6. **The Impact of Judge Dummy Variables upon** *SENTNORM* **in Guilty Plea Cases**

	DuPage (Ring)	Peoria (Autono-mous)	St. Clair (Declin-ing)	Oakland (Ring)	Kalamazoo (Autono-mous)	Saginaw (Declin-ing)	Mont-gomery (Ring)	Dauphin (Autono-mous)	Erie (Declin-ing)
Adjusted R^2 for control variables	.09	.18	.18	.29	.08	.13	.11	.17	.31
Adjusted R^2 after entering set of judge dummy variables	.13	.19	.18	.34	.07	.11	.15	.21	.37
Net change due to addition of judge dummy variables	.04	.01	0	.05	-.01	-.02	.04	.04	.06
N of cases	236	266	347	213	244	177	93	209	129

Table VI.7. **The Impact of Judge Dummy Variables upon *NORMDEV* in Guilty Plea Cases**

	DuPage (Ring)	Peoria (Autonomous)	St. Clair (Declining)	Oakland (Ring)	Kalamazoo (Autonomous)	Saginaw (Declining)	Montgomery (Ring)	Dauphin (Autonomous)	Erie (Declining)
Adjusted R^2 for control variables	.06	.12	.13	.17	.11	.09	.08	.04	.24
Adjusted R^2 after entering set of judge dummy variables	.07	.15	.13	.20	.09	.12	.11	.07	.31
Net change due to addition of judge dummy variables	.01	.03	0	.03	−.02	.03	.03	.03	.07
N of cases	236	266	347	213	244	177	93	209	129

Table VI.8. **The Impact of Prosecutors Dummy Variables upon *CHRGRED* in Guilty Plea Cases**

	DuPage (Ring)	Peoria (Autonomous)	St. Clair (Declining)	Oakland (Ring)	Kalamazoo (Autonomous)	Saginaw (Declining)	Montgomery (Ring)	Dauphin (Autonomous)	Erie (Declining)
Adjusted R^2 for control variables	.54	.33	.31	.30	.37	.06	.29	.15	.32
Adjusted R^2 after entering set of prosecutor dummy variables	.54	.33	.32	.32	.36	.05	.32	.16	.31
Net change due to addition of prosecutor dummy variables	0	0	.01	.02	−.01	−.01	.03	.01	−.01
N of cases	500	512	634	670	518	426	572	823	319
Total valid cases	565	689	746	739	565	484	602	875	466

Table VI.9. **The Impact of Prosecutor Dummy Variables upon *CTRED* in Guilty Plea Cases**

	DuPage (Ring)	Peoria (Autono-mous)	St. Clair (Declin-ing)	Oakland (Ring)	Kalamazoo (Autono-mous)	Saginaw (Declin-ing)	Mont-gomery (Ring)	Dauphin (Autono-mous)	Erie (Declin-ing)
Adjusted R^2 for control variables	.77	.64	.75	.54	.55	.45	.30	.18	.39
Adjusted R^2 after entering set of prosecutor dummy variables	.76	.64	.54	.54	.54	.45	.33	.19	.39
Net change due to addition of prosecutor dummy variables	-.01	0	0	0	-.01	0	.03	.01	0
N of cases	500	512	634	670	518	426	572	823	321

Table VI.10. **The Impact of Prosecutor Dummy Variables upon *PRIMRED* in Guilty Plea Cases**

	DuPage (Ring)	Peoria (Autono-mous)	St. Clair (Declin-ing)	Oakland (Ring)	Kalamazoo (Autono-mous)	Saginaw (Declin-ing)	Mont-gomery (Ring)	Dauphin (Autono-mous)	Erie (Declin-ing)
Adjusted R^2 for control variables	.04	.05	.00	.01	.05	.00	.05	.03	.01
Adjusted R^2 after entering Set of prosecutor dummy variables	.05	.04	.01	.03	.04	.02	.06	.03	.00
Net change due to addition of prosecutor dummy variables	.01	-.01	.01	.02	-.01	.02	.01	0	0
N of cases	500	512	634	670	518	426	572	823	315

Table VI.11. **The Impact of Prosecutor Dummy Variables upon *JAILMIN* in Guilty Plea Cases**

	DuPage (Ring)	Peoria (Autonomous)	St. Clair (Declining)	Oakland (Ring)	Kalamazoo (Autonomous)	Saginaw (Declining)	Montgomery (Ring)	Dauphin (Autonomous)	Erie (Declining)
Adjusted R^2 for control variables	.33	.37	.27	.28	.35	.37	.13	.49	.32
Adjusted R^2 after entering set of prosecutor dummy variables	.32	.39	.27	.28	.35	.36	.15	.49	.31
Net change due to addition of prosecutor dummy variables	-.01	.02	0	0	0	-.01	.02	0	-.01
N of cases	541	641	714	674	553	434	573	842	281
Total valid cases	565	689	746	739	565	484	602	875	466

Table VI.12. **The Impact of Prosecutor Dummy Variables upon *FRSTJAIL* in Guilty Plea Cases**

	DuPage (Ring)	Peoria (Autonomous)	St. Clair (Declining)	Oakland (Ring)	Kalamazoo (Autonomous)	Saginaw (Declining)	Montgomery (Ring)	Dauphin (Autonomous)	Erie (Declining)
Adjusted R^2 for control variables	.13	.18	.14	.19	.07	.04	.11	.23	.04
Adjusted R^2 after entering set of prosecutor dummy variables	.11	.18	.14	.28	.07	.09	.18	.26	.11
Net change due to addition of prosecutor dummy variables	-.02	0	0	.09	0	.05	.07	.03	.07
N of cases	244	246	242	259	140	117	206	488	53
Total valid cases	245	251	242	260	140	120	206	488	194

Table VI.13. **The Impact of Prosecutor Dummy Variables upon *SENTNORM* in Guilty Plea Cases**

	DuPage (Ring)	Peoria (Autonomous)	St. Clair (Declining)	Oakland (Ring)	Kalamazoo (Autonomous)	Saginaw (Declining)	Montgomery (Ring)	Dauphin (Autonomous)	Erie (Declining)
Adjusted R^2 for control variables	.09	.18	.17	.29	.08	.13	.11	.17	.32
Adjusted R^2 after entering set of prosecutor dummy variables	.10	.22	.18	.33	.07	.11	.12	.20	.35
Net change due to addition of prosecutor dummy variables	.01	.04	.01	.04	-.01	-.02	.01	.03	.03
N of cases	236	266	347	213	244	177	93	209	133
Total possible cases	239	315	399	222	252	196	224	224	133

Table VI.14. **The Impact of Prosecutor Dummy Variables upon *NORMDEV* in Guilty Plea Cases**

	DuPage (Ring)	Peoria (Autonomous)	St. Clair (Declining)	Oakland (Ring)	Kalamazoo (Autonomous)	Saginaw (Declining)	Montgomery (Ring)	Dauphin (Autonomous)	Erie (Declining)
Adjusted R^2 for control variables	.06	.12	.13	.17	.11	.09	.08	.04	.25
Adjusted R^2 after entering set of prosecutor dummy variables	.06	.16	.15	.18	.10	.07	.15	.02	.24
Net change due to addition of prosecutor dummy variables	0	.04	.02	.01	-.01	-.02	.07	-.02	-.01
N of cases	236	266	347	213	244	177	93	209	127

Table VI.15. The Linear Impact of Judicial Attitudes upon *CHRGRED* in Guilty Plea Cases

	DuPage (Ring)	Peoria (Autonomous)	St. Clair (Declining)	Oakland (Ring)	Kalamazoo (Autonomous)	Saginaw (Declining)	Montgomery (Ring)	Dauphin (Autonomous)	Erie (Declining)
Mean response (for dichotomous dependent variables only)	.53	.47	.41	.37	.16	.70	—	.11	.08
Adjusted R^2 for control variables (existence of a multicount indictment bail status)	.52	.34	.28	.32	.35	.05	—	.15	.08
Impact of judge's Belief in Punishment	0	0	0	0	0	0	—	0	0
Regard for Due Process	−*	0	0	0	0	0	—	+***	0
Net change in adjusted R^2 due to addition of attitudinal measures	.004	0	0	0	0	0	—	.02	0
N	448	509	601	577	405	375	263	771	282
Total possible N	565	689	746	739	565	484	602	875	466

Table VI.16. **The Linear Impact of Judicial Attitudes upon** *CTRED* **in Guilty Plea Cases**

	DuPage (Ring)	Peoria (Autonomous)	St. Clair (Declining)	Oakland (Ring)	Kalamazoo (Autonomous)	Saginaw (Declining)	Montgomery (Ring)	Dauphin (Autonomous)	Erie (Declining)
Mean response (for dichotomous dependent variables only)	.45	.38	.22	.27	.12	.36	—	.09	.44
Adjusted R^2 for control variables (existence of a multicount indictment bail status)	.77	.67	.72	.57	.53	.45	—	.19	.08
Impact of judge's Belief in Punishment	0	0	0	0	0	0	—	0	0
Regard for Due Process	0	0	0	0	+*	0	—	+***	0
Net change in adjusted R^2 due to addition of attitudinal measures	0	0	0	0	.005	0	—	.01	0
N	453	513	599	585	407	376	263	774	280
Total possible N	565	689	746	739	565	484	602	875	466

Table VI.17. The Linear Impact of Judicial Attitudes upon *PRIMRED* in Guilty Plea Cases

	DuPage (Ring)	Peoria (Autonomous)	St. Clair (Declining)	Oakland (Ring)	Kalamazoo (Autonomous)	Saginaw (Declining)	Montgomery (Ring)	Dauphin (Autonomous)	Erie (Declining)
Mean response (for dichotomous dependent variables only)	.10	.21	.20	.17	.13	.41	—	.05	.12
Adjusted R^2 for control variables (existence of a multicount indictment bail status)	.03	.05	0	.01	.06	0	—	.03	.005
Impact of judge's Belief in Punishment	0	0	0	0	0	0	—	0	0
Regard for Due Process	0	0	0	0	0	+***	—	0	0
Net change in adjusted R^2 due to addition of attitudinal measures	0	0	0	0	0	.026	—	0	0
N	447	534	627	573	398	361	254	785	285
Total possible N	565	689	746	739	565	484	602	875	466

Table VI.18. **The Linear Impact of Judicial Attitudes upon *JAILMIN* in Guilty Plea Cases**

	DuPage (Ring)	Peoria (Autonomous)	St. Clair (Declining)	Oakland (Ring)	Kalamazoo (Autonomous)	Saginaw (Declining)	Montgomery (Ring)	Dauphin (Autonomous)	Erie (Declining)
Adjusted R^2 for control variables (offense seriousness, defendant's criminal record, bail status	.42	.37	.27	.29	.33	.40	—	.50	.27
Impact of judge's Belief in Punishment	0	+**	0	0	0	0	—	0	+*
Regard for Due Process	0	0	0	0	0	0	—	0	0
Net change in adjusted R^2 due to addition of attitudinal measures	0	.01	0	0	0	0	—	0	.01
N	461	607	659	560	420	351	249	782	260
Total possible N	565	689	746	739	565	484	602	875	466

Table VI.19. The Linear Impact of Judicial Attitudes upon *FRSTJAIL* in Guilty Plea Cases

	DuPage (Ring)	Peoria (Autonomous)	St. Clair (Declining)	Oakland (Ring)	Kalamazoo (Autonomous)	Saginaw (Declining)	Montgomery (Ring)	Dauphin (Autonomous)	Erie (Declining)
Mean response (for dichotomous dependent variables only)	.15	.13	.05	.30	.45	.26	—	.22	.38
Adjusted R^2 for control variables (offense seriousness, bail status)	.12	.18	.15	.19	.06	.03	—	—	.07
Impact of judge's Belief in Punishment	0	0	0	0	0	0	—	—	0
Regard for Due Process	0	0	0	0	0	0	—	—	0
Net change in adjusted R^2 due to addition of attitudinal measures	0	0	0	0	0	0	—	—	0
N	210	228	231	212	114	97	62	463	53
Total possible N	245	251	242	260	140	120	206	488	194

Table VI.20. The Linear Impact of Judicial Attitudes upon *SENTNORM* in Guilty Plea Cases

	DuPage (Ring)	Peoria (Autonomous)	St. Clair (Declining)	Oakland (Ring)	Kalamazoo (Autonomous)	Saginaw (Declining)	Montgomery (Ring)	Dauphin (Autonomous)	Erie (Declining)
Adjusted R^2 for control variables (offense seriousness, defendant's criminal record, bail status)	.11	.22	.23	.30	.05	.17	—	.21	.33
Impact of judge's Belief in Punishment	0	+*	0	0	0	0	—	0	0
Regard for Due Process	0	0	+*	0	0	0	—	0	0
Net change in adjusted R^2 due to addition of attitudinal measures	0	.01	.01	0	0	0	—	0	0
N	197	302	359	182	183	154	107	207	121
Total possible N	239	315	399	222	252	196	224	224	133

Table VI.21. The Linear Impact of Judicial Attitudes upon *NORMDEV* in Guilty Plea Cases

	DuPage (Ring)	Peoria (Autonomous)	St. Clair (Declining)	Oakland (Ring)	Kalamazoo (Autonomous)	Saginaw (Declining)	Montgomery (Ring)	Dauphin (Autonomous)	Erie (Declining)
Adjusted R^2 for control variables (offense seriousness, defendant's criminal record, bail status)	.13	.12	.13	.18	.13	.12	—	.16	.23
Impact of judge's Belief in Punishment	0	+**	0	0	0	0	—	0	+*
Regard for Due Process	0	0	+**	0	0	0	—	0	0
Net change in adjusted R^2 due to addition of attitudinal measures	0	.03	.02	0	0	0	—	0	.03
N	196	253	314	175	178	138	50	193	118
Total possible N	239	315	399	222	252	196	224	224	133

Table VI.22. The Linear Impact of Judicial Background Measures upon *CHRGRED* in Guilty Plea Cases

	DuPage (Ring)	Peoria (Autonomous)	St. Clair (Declining)	Oakland (Ring)	Kalamazoo (Autonomous)	Saginaw (Declining)	Montgomery (Ring)	Dauphin (Autonomous)	Erie (Declining)
Mean response	.52	.47	.41	.39	.16	.70	—	.11	.45
Adjusted R^2 (for control variables)	.50	.33	.28	.32	.35	.05	—	.15	.36
Impact of judge's political affiliation	0	0	0	0	0	0	—	0	0
Length of time on bench	0	0	0	0	0	0	—	0	0
Extent of community ties	0	0	0	0	+*	0	—	0	0
Percent of life in county	0	0	0	0	0	0	—	0	0
Status as a former prosecutor	0	0	0	0	0	0	—	+***	0
Net change in adjusted R^2 due to addition of background measures	0	0	0	0	.002	0	—	.02	0
N	385	499	598	479	405	375	263	771	296
Total possible N	565	689	746	739	565	484	602	875	466

Table VI.23. The Linear Impact of Judicial Background Measures upon *CTRED* in Guilty Plea Cases

	DuPage (Ring)	Peoria (Autonomous)	St. Clair (Declining)	Oakland (Ring)	Kalamazoo (Autonomous)	Saginaw (Declining)	Montgomery (Ring)	Dauphin (Autonomous)	Erie (Declining)
Mean response (for dichotomous dependent variables only)	.44	.38	.22	.29	.12	.36	—	.09	.43
Adjusted R^2 (for control variables)	.75	.66	.73	.58	.53	.45	—	.19	.41
Impact of judge's political affiliation	0	0	0	0	0	0	—	0	0
Length of time on bench	0	0	0	0	0	0	—	0	0
Extent of community ties	0	0	0	−*	0	0	—	0	0
Percent of life in county	0	0	0	0	+*	0	—	+***	0
Status as a former prosecutor	0	0	0	0	0	0	—	0	0
Net change in adjusted R^2 due to addition of background measures	0	0	0	.002	.01	0	—	.01	0
N	390	503	596	487	407	376	263	774	298
Total possible N	565	689	746	739	565	484	602	875	466

Table VI.24. The Linear Impact of Judicial Background Measures upon *PRIMRED* Guilty Plea Cases

	DuPage (Ring)	Peoria (Autonomous)	St. Clair (Declining)	Oakland (Ring)	Kalamazoo (Autonomous)	Saginaw (Declining)	Montgomery (Ring)	Dauphin (Autonomous)	Erie (Declining)
Mean response (for dichotomous dependent variables only)	.10	.21	.20	.18	.13	.41	—	.05	.11
Adjusted R^2 (for control variables)	.02	.05	0	.01	.05	0	—	.03	.01
Impact of judge's political affiliation	0	0	0	0	0	0	—	0	0
Length of time on bench	0	0	0	0	+*	+**	—	0	0
Extent of community ties	+*	0	0	0	0	0	—	0	0
Percent of life in county	0	0	0	0	0	0	—	0	0
Status as a former prosecutor	0	0	0	0	0	0	—	0	-**
Net change in adjusted R^2 due to addition of background measures	.01	0	0	0	.01	.02	—	0	0
N	386	524	624	478	398	361	254	785	294
Total possible N	565	689	746	739	565	484	602	875	466

Table VI.25. The Linear Impact of Judicial Background Measures upon *JAILMIN* in Guilty Plea Cases

	DuPage (Ring)	Peoria (Autonomous)	St. Clair (Declining)	Oakland (Ring)	Kalamazoo (Autonomous)	Saginaw (Declining)	Montgomery (Ring)	Dauphin (Autonomous)	Erie (Declining)
Adjusted R^2 (for control variables)	.42	.37	.27	.38	.33	.40	—	.50	.27
Impact of judge's political affiliation	0	+**	0	0	0	0	—	0	0
Length of time in office	0	0	0	0	0	0	—	0	+*
Extent of community ties	0	0	0	0	0	0	—	-**	0
Percent of life in county	0	0	0	0	0	0	—	0	0
Status as a former prosecutor	-**	0	0	0	0	0	—	0	0
Net change in adjusted R^2 due to addition of background measures	.01	.01	0	0	0	0	—	.005	.02
N	398	597	656	475	420	351	249	782	260
Total possible N	565	689	756	739	565	484	602	875	466

Table VI.26. The Linear Impact of Judicial Background Measures upon *FRSTJAIL* Guilty Plea Cases

	DuPage (Ring)	Peoria (Autonomous)	St. Clair (Declining)	Oakland (Ring)	Kalamazoo (Autonomous)	Saginaw (Declining)	Montgomery (Ring)	Dauphin (Autonomous)	Erie (Declining)
Mean response (for dichotomous dependent variables only)	.16	.13	.05	.30	.46	.26	—	.11	.38
Adjusted R^2 (for control variables)	.10	.18	.15	.17	.05	.03	—	.26	.09
Impact of judge's political affiliation	0	0	0	0	0	0	—	+***	0
Length of time in office	+**	0	0	0	0	0	—	0	0
Extent of community ties	0	0	0	0	0	0	—	0	0
Percent of life in county	0	0	0	0	0	0	—	0	0
Status as a former prosecutor	0	0	0	0	0	0	—	-**	0
Net change in adjusted R^2 due to addition of background measures	.04	0	0	0	0	0	—	.10	0
N	180	226	229	191	114	97	62	463	53
Total possible N	245	251	242	260	140	120	206	488	194

Table VI.27. The Linear Impact of Judicial Background Measures upon *SENTNORM* in Guilty Plea Cases

	DuPage (Ring)	Peoria (Autonomous)	St. Clair (Declining)	Oakland (Ring)	Kalamazoo (Autonomous)	Saginaw (Declining)	Montgomery (Ring)	Dauphin (Autonomous)	Erie (Declining)
Adjusted R^2 (for control variables)	.17	.22	.23	.29	.05	.17	—	.21	.33
Impact of judge's political affiliation	0	0	0	0	0	0	—	0	0
Length of time in office	0	0	0	0	0	0	—	0	0
Extent of community ties	0	0	+*	0	0	0	—	0	0
Percent of life in county	0	0	0	-**	0	0	—	0	0
Status as a former prosecutor	-**	0	0	0	0	0	—	0	0
Net change in adjusted R^2 due to addition of background measures	.03	0	.01	.03	0	0	—	0	0
N	173	296	358	142	183	154	107	207	121
Total possible N	239	315	399	222	252	196	224	224	133

Table VI.28. The Linear Impact of Judicial Background Measures upon *NORMDEV* in Guilty Plea Cases

	DuPage (Ring)	Peoria (Autonomous)	St. Clair (Declining)	Oakland (Ring)	Kalamazoo (Autonomous)	Saginaw (Declining)	Montgomery (Ring)	Dauphin (Autonomous)	Erie (Declining)
Adjusted R^2 (for control variables)	.37	.12	.14	.18	.13	.12	—	.16	.23
Impact of judge's political affiliation	+*	+***	0	0	0	0	—	0	0
Length of time in office	0	0	0	0	0	0	—	0	+*
Extent of community ties	0	0	+**	0	0	0	—	0	0
Percent of life in county	0	0	0	0	0	0	—	0	0
Status as a former prosecutor	0	0	0	0	0	0	—	0	0
Net change in adjusted R^2 due to addition of background measures	.02	.02	.01	0	0	0	—	0	.03
N	172	247	313	136	178	138	50	193	118
Total possible N	239	315	399	222	252	196	224	224	133

Table VI.29. The Linear Impact of Prosecutorial Attitudes upon *CHRGRED* in Guilty Plea Cases

	DuPage (Ring)	Peoria (Autonomous)	St. Clair (Declining)	Oakland (Ring)	Kalamazoo (Autonomous)	Saginaw (Declining)	Montgomery (Ring)	Dauphin (Autonomous)	Erie (Declining)
Mean response (for dichotomous dependent variables only)	.53	.48	.41	.38	.18	.70	—	.10	.46
Adjusted R^2 for control variables (existence of a multicount indictment bail status)	.53	.32	.28	.27	.34	.07	—	.14	.10
Impact of prosecutor's Belief in Punishment	0	0	0	0	0	0	—	0	0
Regard for Due Process	0	0	0	0	0	0	—	0	0
Net change in adjusted R^2 due to addition of attitudinal measures	0	0	0	0	0	0	—	0	0
N	313	503	514	519	398	350	217	674	269
Total possible N	565	689	746	739	565	484	602	875	466

Table VI.30. **The Linear Impact of Prosecutorial Attitudes upon _CTRED_ in Guilty Plea Cases**

	DuPage (Ring)	Peoria (Autonomous)	St. Clair (Declining)	Oakland (Ring)	Kalamazoo (Autonomous)	Saginaw (Declining)	Montgomery (Ring)	Dauphin (Autonomous)	Erie (Declining)
Mean response (for dichotomous dependent variables only)	.45	.39	.22	.29	.13	.37	—	.08	.44
Adjusted R^2 for control variables (existence of a multicount indictment bail status)	.77	.65	.76	.52	.54	.49	—	.20	.09
Impact of prosecutor's Belief in Punishment	0	0	0	0	0	0	—	0	0
Regard for Due Process	0	0	0	0	0	0	—	0	0
Net change in adjusted R^2 due to addition of attitudinal measures	0	0	0	0	0	0	—	0	0
N	315	509	511	528	399	353	220	676	267
Total possible N	565	689	746	739	565	484	602	875	466

Table VI.31. The Linear Impact of Prosecutorial Attitudes upon *PRIMRED* in Guilty Plea Cases

	DuPage (Ring)	Peoria (Autono-mous)	St. Clair (Declin-ing)	Oakland (Ring)	Kalamazoo (Autono-mous)	Saginaw (Declin-ing)	Mont-gomery (Ring)	Dauphin (Autono-mous)	Erie (Declin-ing)
Mean response (for dichotomous dependent variables only)	.09	.22	.20	.16	.14	.44	—	.05	.12
Adjusted R^2 for control variables (existence of a multicount indictment bail status)	.03	.05	0	0	.04	0	—	.03	.01
Impact of prosecutor's Belief in Punishment	0	0	0	0	0	+**	—	0	0
Regard for Due Process	0	0	0	0	0	0	—	0	0
Net change in adjusted R^2 due to addition of attitudinal measures	0	0	0	0	0	.02	—	0	0
N	312	525	537	513	388	342	211	690	273
Total possible N	565	689	746	739	565	484	602	875	466

Table VI.32. **The Linear Impact of Prosecutorial Attitudes upon** *JAILMIN* **in Guilty Plea Cases**

	DuPage (Ring)	Peoria (Autonomous)	St. Clair (Declining)	Oakland (Ring)	Kalamazoo (Autonomous)	Saginaw (Declining)	Montgomery (Ring)	Dauphin (Autonomous)	Erie (Declining)
Adjusted R^2 (for control variables)	.38	.37	.27	.24	.30	.42	—	.50	.28
Impact of prosecutor's Belief in Punishment	0	0	0	0	0	0	—	0	0
Regard for Due Process	0	0	0	0	0	0	—	0	0
Net change in adjusted R^2 due to addition of attitudinal measures	0	0	0	0	0	0	—	0	0
N	322	600	565	506	407	331	213	682	246
Total possible N	565	689	746	739	565	484	602	875	466

Table VI.33. The Linear Impact of Prosecutorial Attitudes upon *FRSTJAIL* in Guilty Plea Cases

	DuPage (Ring)	Peoria (Autonomous)	St. Clair (Declining)	Oakland (Ring)	Kalamazoo (Autonomous)	Saginaw (Declining)	Montgomery (Ring)	Dauphin (Autonomous)	Erie (Declining)
Mean response (for dichotomous dependent variables only)	.17	.13	.06	.36	.46	.20	—	.11	.42
Adjusted R^2 (for control variables)	.12	.23	.16	.16	.05	.05	—	.26	.04
Impact of prosecutor's									
Belief in Punishment	0	0	0	+**	0	0	—	+*	0
Regard for Due Process	0	0	0	0	0	0	—	−**	0
Net change in adjusted R^2 due to addition of attitudinal measures	0	0	0	.04	0	0	—	.01	0
N	146	216	178	182	97	87	60	426	48
Total possible N	245	251	242	260	140	120	206	488	194

Table VI.34. **The Linear Impact of Prosecutorial Attitudes upon** *SENTNORM* **in Guilty Plea Cases**

	DuPage (Ring)	Peoria (Autonomous)	St. Clair (Declining)	Oakland (Ring)	Kalamazoo (Autonomous)	Saginaw (Declining)	Montgomery (Ring)	Dauphin (Autonomous)	Erie (Declining)
Adjusted R^2 (for control variables)	.06	.22	.19	.32	.06	.15	—	.23	.35
Impact of prosecutor's Belief in Punishment	0	0	0	0	0	0	—	0	0
Regard for Due Process	0	0	0	+**	0	0	—	0	0
Net change in adjusted R^2 due to addition of attitudinal measures	0	0	0	.04	0	0	—	0	0
N	146	305	326	178	194	157	76	170	119
Total possible N	239	315	399	222	252	196	224	224	133

Table VI.35. The Linear Impact of Prosecutorial Attitudes upon *NORMDEV* in Guilty Plea Cases

	DuPage (Ring)	Peoria (Autonomous)	St. Clair (Declining)	Oakland (Ring)	Kalamazoo (Autonomous)	Saginaw (Declining)	Montgomery (Ring)	Dauphin (Autonomous)	Erie (Declining)
Adjusted R^2 (for control variables)	.15	.12	.10	.15	.15	.12	—	.16	.23
Impact of prosecutor's Belief in Punishment	0	0	0	0	0	0	—	0	0
Regard for Due Process	0	+*	0	+*	0	0	—	0	0
Net change in adjusted R^2 due to addition of attitudinal measures	0	0	0	.03	0	0	—	0	0
N	145	257	280	172	188	143	39	159	116
Total possible N	239	315	399	222	252	196	224	224	133

Table VI.36. **The Linear Impact of Prosecutorial Background Measures upon** *CHRGRED* **Guilty Plea Cases**

	DuPage (Ring)	Peoria (Autonomous)	St. Clair (Declining)	Oakland (Ring)	Kalamazoo (Autonomous)	Saginaw (Declining)	Montgomery (Ring)	Dauphin (Autonomous)	Erie (Declining)
Mean response (for dichotomous dependent variables only)	.56	.48	.41	.37	.15	.70	—	.10	.46
Adjusted R^2 (for control variables)	.53	.32	.28	.32	.36	.08	—	.14	.37
Impact of prosecutor's									
Political affiliation	0	0	0	0	0	0	—	0	0
Length of time in office	0	0	0	0	0	0	—	0	0
Extent of community ties	0	0	0	+**	0	0	—	0	0
Percent of life in county	0	0	0	0	0	0	—	0	0
Net change in adjusted R^2 due to addition of background measures	0	0	0	.003	0	0	—	0	0
N	361	511	512	538	398	346	225	672	270
Total possible N	565	689	746	739	565	484	602	875	466

Table VI.37. **The Linear Impact of Prosecutorial Background Measures upon** *CTRED* **Guilty Plea Cases**

	DuPage (Ring)	Peoria (Autono-mous)	St. Clair (Declin-ing)	Oakland (Ring)	Kalamazoo (Autono-mous)	Saginaw (Declin-ing)	Mont-gomery (Ring)	Dauphin (Autono-mous)	Erie (Declin-ing)
Mean response (for dichotomous dependent variables only)	.48	.39	.22	.28	.11	.38	—	.08	.43
Adjusted R^2 (for control variables)	.78	.66	.76	.57	.57	.50	—	.20	.40
Impact of prosecutor's									
Political affiliation	0	0	0	0	0	0	—	0	0
Length of time in office	0	0	0	0	0	0	—	0	0
Extent of community ties	0	0	—*	0	0	0	—	0	0
Percent of life in county	0	0	0	0	0	0	—	0	0
Net change in adjusted R^2 due to addition of background measures	0	0	.008	0	0	0	—	0	.05
N	368	516	509	545	401	348	227	673	272
Total possible N	565	689	746	739	565	484	602	875	466

Table VI.38. **The Linear Impact of Prosecutorial Background Measures upon** *PRIMRED* **Guilty Plea Cases**

	DuPage (Ring)	Peoria (Autono-mous)	St. Clair (Declin-ing)	Oakland (Ring)	Kalamazoo (Autono-mous)	Saginaw (Declin-ing)	Mont-gomery (Ring)	Dauphin (Autono-mous)	Erie (Declin-ing)
Mean response (for dichotomous dependent variables only)	.11	.22	.20	.16	.13	.46	—	.05	.12
Adjusted R^2 (for control variables)	.03	.05	0	0	.06	0	—	.03	.03
Impact of prosecutor's									
Political affiliation	0	0	0	0	0	0	—	0	0
Length of time in office	0	0	0	0	0	0	—	0	0
Extent of community ties	0	0	0	0	0	0	—	0	0
Percent of life in county	0	0	0	0	0	0	—	0	0
Net change in adjusted R^2 due to addition of background measures	0	0	0	0	0	0	—	0	0
N	362	533	535	533	391	337	218	687	268
Total possible N	565	689	746	739	565	484	602	875	466

Table VI.39. The Linear Impact of Prosecutorial Background Measures upon *JAILMIN* in Guilty Plea Cases

	DuPage (Ring)	Peoria (Autonomous)	St. Clair (Declining)	Oakland (Ring)	Kalamazoo (Autonomous)	Saginaw (Declining)	Montgomery (Ring)	Dauphin (Autonomous)	Erie (Declining)
Adjusted R^2 (for control variables)	.39	.37	.26	.24	.28	.41	—	.35	.29
Impact of prosecutor's political affiliation	0	0	0	0	0	0	—	0	0
Length of time in office	0	0	+***	0	0	0	—	0	0
Extent of community ties	0	0	0	0	0	0	—	0	0
Percent of life in county	0	0	0	0	0	0	—	0	0
Net change in adjusted R^2 due to addition of background measures	0	0	.02	0	0	0	—	0	0
N	373	608	563	522	407	330	221	679	233
Total possible N	565	689	746	739	565	484	602	875	466

Table VI.40. The Linear Impact of Prosecutorial Background Measures upon *FRSTJAIL* in Guilty Plea Cases

	DuPage (Ring)	Peoria (Autonomous)	St. Clair (Declining)	Oakland (Ring)	Kalamazoo (Autonomous)	Saginaw (Declining)	Montgomery (Ring)	Dauphin (Autonomous)	Erie (Declining)
Mean response (for dichotomous dependent variables only)	.17	.13	.05	.32	.44	.20	—	.11	.42
Adjusted R^2 (for control variables)	.18	.22	.11	.20	.05	.04	—	.26	.06
Impact of prosecutor's political affiliation	0	0	0	0	0	0	—	0	0
Length of time in office	0	0	0	0	0	0	—		0
Extent of community ties	0	0	0	0	0	0	—	−**	0
Percent of life in county	0	0	0	0	0	0	—	0	0
Net change in adjusted R^2 due to addition of background measures	0	0	0	0	0	0	—	.01	0
N	167	223	177	197	100	93	60	426	45
Total possible N	245	251	242	260	140	120	206	488	194

Table VI.41. The Linear Impact of Prosecutorial Background Measures upon *SENTNORM* in Guilty Plea Cases

	DuPage (Ring)	Peoria (Autonomous)	St. Clair (Declining)	Oakland (Ring)	Kalamazoo (Autonomous)	Saginaw (Declining)	Montgomery (Ring)	Dauphin (Autonomous)	Erie (Declining)
Adjusted R^2 (for control variables)	.06	.22	.19	.33	.11	.12	—	.35	.35
Impact of prosecutor's political affiliation	0	0	0	+*	0	0	—	0	0
Length of time in office	0	-**	+***	0	0	0	—	0	0
Extent of community ties	0	0	0	0	0	0	—	0	+*
Percent of life in county	0	0	0	0	0	0	—	0	0
Net change in adjusted R^2 due to addition of background measures	0	.02	.03	.02	0	0	—	0	.03
N	165	306	325	173	193	152	80	168	113
Total possible N	239	315	399	222	252	196	224	224	133

Table VI.42. **The Linear Impact of Prosecutorial Background Measures upon *NORMDEV* in Guilty Plea Cases**

	DuPage (Ring)	Peoria (Autono-mous)	St. Clair (Declin-ing)	Oakland (Ring)	Kalamazoo (Autono-mous)	Saginaw (Declin-ing)	Mont-gomery (Ring)	Dauphin (Autono-mous)	Erie (Declin-ing)
Adjusted R^2 (for control variables)	.13	.12	.10	.16	.12	.10	—	.18	.22
Impact of prosecutor's political affiliation	0	0	0	+*	+*	0	—	0	0
Length of time in office	0	−***	+***	+*	+*	0	—	0	0
Extent of community ties	0	0	0	0	0	0	—	0	0
Percent of life in county	0	0	0	0	0	0	—	0	0
Net change in adjusted R^2 due to addition of background measures	0	.05	.04	.015	.02	0	—	0	0
N	164	258	279	168	186	136	41	157	110
Total possible N	239	315	399	222	252	196	224	224	133

APPENDIX VII

RESULTS OF THE DEFENSE ATTORNEY VARIABLES FOR OTHER CHARGE AND SENTENCE VARIABLES

Table VII.1. **The Impact of Defense Attorney Variables upon *CTRED***

	DuPage (Ring)	Peoria (Autonomous)	St. Clair (Declining)	Oakland (Ring)	Kalamazoo (Autonomous)	Saginaw (Declining)	Montgomery (Ring)	Dauphin (Autonomous)	Erie (Declining)
Mean response (for dichotomous dependent variables only)	.46	.39	.22	.28	.12	.37	.39	.09	.58
Adjusted R^2 (for control variables)	.75	.66	.73	.55	.57	.49	.28	.18	.15
PRIVDC	0	0	+**	0	0	0	0	0	0
REGULAR	0	0	0	0	0	0	0	0	0
NN, NG (Not Nice, Not Good)	0	0	0	0	0	0	0	0	0
N, NG (Nice, Not Good)	+*	0	0	0	0	0	0	0	0
NN, BG (Not Nice, But Good)	0	0	0	0	0	+*	0	0	0
NAG (Nice and Good)	0	0	0	0	0	0	0	0	0
Net change in adjusted R^2 due to addition of defense attorney variables	.003	0	.002	0	0	.01	0	0	0
N	433	451	531	554	523	414	408	780	395

Table VII.2. **The Impact of Defense Attorney Variables upon** *PRIMRED*

	DuPage (Ring)	Peoria (Autonomous)	St. Clair (Declining)	Oakland (Ring)	Kalamazoo (Autonomous)	Saginaw (Declining)	Montgomery (Ring)	Dauphin (Autonomous)	Erie (Declining)
Mean response (for dichotomous dependent variables only)	.11	.21	.20	.16	.12	.41	.09	.05	.08
Adjusted R^2 (for control variables)	.04	.04	.0002	0	.05	0	.04	.03	.04
PRIVDC	0	0	0	0	+*	0	0	0	0
REGULAR	0	0	0	0	0	0	0	0	0
NN, NG (Not Nice, Not Good)	0	0	+***	0	0	0	0	0	0
N, NG (Nice, Not Good)	0	0	0	0	0	0	0	0	0
NN, BG (Not Nice, But Good)	0	0	0	0	+***	0	0	0	0
NAG (Nice and Good)	0	0	0	0	0	0	0	0	0
Net change in adjusted R^2 due to addition of defense attorney variables	0	0	.01	0	.02	0	0	0	0
N	425	463	554	542	511	400	397	795	391

Table VII.3. The Impact of Defense Attorney Variables upon *FRSTJAIL*

	DuPage (Ring)	Peoria (Autonomous)	St. Clair (Declining)	Oakland (Ring)	Kalamazoo (Autonomous)	Saginaw (Declining)	Montgomery (Ring)	Dauphin (Autonomous)	Erie (Declining)
Mean response (for dichotomous dependent variables only)	.15	.11	.05	.30	.43	.21	.04	.12	.12
Adjusted R^2 (for control variables)	.08	.21	.12	.24	.06	.01	.02	.27	.13
PRIVDC	0	0	0	0	0	0	+***	+**	0
REGULAR	0	0	0	0	+*	0	0	0	0
NN, NG (Not Nice, Not Good)	0	0	0	0	0	0	0	0	+**
N, NG (Nice, Not Good)	0	0	0	0	0	0	+*	0	0
NN, BG (Not Nice, But Good)	0	0	0	0	0	0	0	0	0
NAG (Nice and Good)	0	0	0	0	0	0	0	0	0
Net change in adjusted R^2 due to addition of defense attorney variables	0	0	0	0	.03	0	.08	.01	.03
N	203	196	199	208	135	108	157	451	176

Table VII.4. The Impact of Defense Attorney Variables upon *SENTNORM*

	DuPage (Ring)	Peoria (Autonomous)	St. Clair (Declining)	Oakland (Ring)	Kalamazoo (Autonomous)	Saginaw (Declining)	Montgomery (Ring)	Dauphin (Autonomous)	Erie (Declining)
Adjusted R^2 (for control variables)	.16	.27	.20	.35	.10	.28	.19	.24	.48
PRIVDC	0	0	0	0	0	0	0	0	0
REGULAR	0	0	0	0	0	0	0	0	0
NN, NG (Not Nice, Not Good)	0	0	0	−*	0	0	0	0	0
N, NG (Nice, Not Good)	0	0	0	0	0	0	0	0	0
NN, BG (Not Nice, But Good)	0	0	0	0	0	0	0	0	0
NAG (Nice and Good)	0	−*	0	0	0	0	0	0	0
Net change in adjusted R^2 due to addition of defense attorney variables	0	.05	0	.04	0	0	0	0	0
N	155	218	217	80	218	102	93	151	80

Table VII.5. The Impact of Defense Attorney Variables upon NORMDEV

	DuPage (Ring)	Peoria (Autonomous)	St. Clair (Declining)	Oakland (Ring)	Kalamazoo (Autonomous)	Saginaw (Declining)	Montgomery (Ring)	Dauphin (Autonomous)	Erie (Declining)
Adjusted R^2 (for control variables)	.09	.13	.22	.21	.16	.16	0	.18	.25
PRIVDC	0	-*	0	0	0	+*	0	0	0
REGULAR	0	0	-*	0	0	+	0	0	0
NN, NG (Not Nice, Not Good)	0	0	0	0	0	0	0	0	0
N, NG (Nice, Not Good)	0	0	0	0	0	0	+***	0	0
NN, BG (Not Nice, But Good)	0	0	0	+*	0	0	0	0	0
NAG (Nice and Good)	0	-*	0	0	0	0	0	0	0
Net change in adjusted R^2 due to addition of defense attorney variables	0	.04	.01	.03	0	.02	.02	0	0
N	199	237	303	170	253	170	66	212	119

INDEX

ABOUT THE AUTHORS

PETER F. NARDULLI, professor in the political science department and at the Institute of Government and Public Affairs at the University of Illinois at Urbana-Champaign, is the author of *The Courtroom Elite: An Organizational Perspective on Criminal Justice.*

JAMES EISENSTEIN is a professor of political science at Pennsylvania State University and co-author of *Felony Justice: An Organizational Analysis of Criminal Courts.*

ROY B. FLEMMING, associate professor of political science at Wayne State University, is the author of *Punishment Before Trial: An Organizational Perspective of Felony Bail Processes.*